Di

/

Here, in one volume, learn everything you need to know to become an excellent director, not merely a good one. Covering everything through prep, shoot, and post, the authors offer practical instruction on how to craft a creative vision, translate a script into a visual story, establish and maintain the look and feel of a television show or film, lead the cast and crew, keep a complex operation running on time and on budget, and effectively oversee editing and postproduction.

This newly updated edition features:

- All-new "From the Experts" sections with insider info known only to working professionals;
- Additional "How I Got My First Job" stories from directors currently in the trenches;
- A companion website (www.routledge.com/cw/rooney) featuring video interviews with the authors.

Bethany Rooney has directed over two hundred episodes of primetime network shows, including *NCIS*, *The Originals*, *Nashville*, *NCIS New Orleans*, and *Criminal Minds*. She teaches the Warner Brothers Directors' Workshop and serves on numerous committees at the Directors Guild of America.

Mary Lou Belli is a two-time Emmy Award-winning producer, writer, and director as well as the author of two books. She has directed episodes of *NCIS New Orleans*, *Monk*, *Hart of Dixie*, *The Game*, *Girlfriends*, and *The Wizards of Waverly Place*. She teaches directing at USC's School of Cinematic Arts.

"The success of the directors coming out of the Warner Bros. Directors' Workshop has been undeniable. A huge reason for that is because we use this book as its main teaching tool. In my opinion, if you are serious about being a television director, buying this book should be the first thing you do."

—Christopher Mack, Vice President, Warner Bros.

"The information, tips and advice these two fine directors have collected in their books are invaluable and presented in a way that allows the reader to not only understand what is offered, but to use it effectively."

—Michael Zinberg, Director

"This is one of the most specific and detailed books about directing television I've ever read. As experts in directing both comedy and drama, and hundreds of television shows between them, the authors have deftly translated their years of practical knowledge and acquired skills to the page, giving insightful instructions that will benefit a television director on any level."

—Jennifer Warren, Associate Professor of Practice and Chair of Directing Track, School of Cinematic Arts, USC, Chair of Board of Alliance of Women Directors

"As a new director, you are constantly feeling like you want a refresher course on things you've previously learned. The thing I love about Bethany and Mary Lou's book is that it's so accessible. It's packed with so many jewels that you employ throughout every stage of the director's process. From an actor's perspective, chapter 10 is invaluable. I wish it was mandatory for every director to read that chapter before their first day on the set."

—Regina King, Actress, Director

Directors Tell the Story
Master the Craft of Television and Film Directing

Second Edition

Bethany Rooney and Mary Lou Belli

Routledge
Taylor & Francis Group

NEW YORK AND LONDON

Second edition published 2016 by Routledge
711 Third Avenue, New York, NY 10017

and by Routledge
2 Park Square, Milton Park, Abingdon, Oxon, OX14 4RN

Routledge is an imprint of the Taylor & Francis Group, an informa business

First edition published by Focal Press in 2011

Library of Congress Cataloging in Publication Data
A catalog record for this book has been requested

ISBN: 978-1-138-95210-2 (hbk)
ISBN: 978-1-138-94847-1 (pbk)
ISBN: 978-1-315-66781-2 (ebk)

Typeset in Times and Optima
by Florence Production Ltd, Stoodleigh, Devon

Praise for the First Edition

This is a precise and smart book about directing in general and directing television specifically.
Sally Field

Rooney and Belli, by dint of their considerable and varied directing experiences, have compiled a bible about the technical and emotional aspects of being a director. I wish I would have had this book when I started my directing career!
Mark Tinker
Executive Producer/Director
Private Practice, Deadwood, NYPD Blue

I've had the pleasure of being directed by both Mary Lou and Bethany on multiple occasions. As clear and precise as they are as directors, I'm pleased to say they are even more so as writers describing the craft of directing. Their step-by-step approach includes even the smallest detail and yet is still interesting—and informative—to those of us who've been on sets for years. Even better, they manage to convey the subtleties of how a director can alter the mental and emotional state of a set to create the best environment for a cast and crew to create art.
Jason George
Actor
Off the Map, Grey's Anatomy, What About Brian, Eve

It assembles information in a way I have never seen before and has a level of subtlety concerning the process of directing that I haven't read in any other book. It is great about describing the challenges, the thinking, and ultimately the practice of directing for television. There is nothing quite like it—it is the best, most grounded explanation for the complex art of directing I have read.
Michael Niederman
Chair, Television Department
Columbia College Chicago

There are quite literally no other books like this one. **Most of the other "Directing" books out there are either "interview" books or "Indie Filmmaker" books . . . but there are very few "How-To" and/or "Tell it Like it Is" books by** *working professional directors.* **The authors have very successfully presented both the fundamental concepts of Hollywood Directing, and then walk you through a very robust process by which to succeed at it!**

Dave A. Anselmi
Director, Producer, Instructor
PracticalMysticProductions

The writers make you, the reader, feel as if they are simply having a conversation with you. A conversation full of good advice, useful exercises, and instructive concepts. I'm gratified to see the words "respect for actors" as a priority because without them, we have nothing. Mary Lou and Bethany emphasize the truth that it's our job, as directors, to tell the story and it's the actors' job to tell the truth.

Anne Drecktrah
Professor
Virterbo University

In memory of Bruce Paltrow, who got me started;
For Christopher, who inspires me to keep going;
And for Matthew, who tucks me in at night.

Bethany Rooney

For Charlie, who reminds me that
it doesn't get better than this!

Mary Lou Belli

Contents

Section Three
Post   **235**

Section Four
Being a Director   **269**

Acknowledgments

Everyone at ABC Studios, *Brothers & Sisters*, and *Castle*:

Barry Jossen, Howard Davine, Michelle Kamme, David Marshall Grant, Ken Olin, Sarah Caplan, Michael Cinquemani, Linda "Sparky" Hawes, Oliver Coke, Allison Weintraub, Margery Kimbrough, Sally Sue Lander, Brian O'Kelley, Chandler Hayes, Jason Hoffman, Arlene Getman, John Smith, Ben Spek, Nick Infield, Cranston Gobbo, Shauna Duggins, Andrew Marlowe, Rob Bowman, Howard Grigsby, Joe Mason, Brooke Eisenhart, Imelda Betiong, and Noreen O'Toole.

And especially the actors pictured: Matthew Rhys, Luke McFarlane, Dave Annable, Mark Harmon, and Joe Spano. As always, we send our love and thanks to Sally Field.

And of course, the dedicated Elinor Actipis, Michele Cronin, and Melinda Rankin at Focal Press, as well as Peter Linsley and Simon Jacobs at Taylor and Francis, and Megan Symons and Quentin Scott.

For this second edition, we are grateful for the contributions of Gary Glasberg, Mark Horowitz, and Paul Snider at *NCIS*, Jeffrey Lieber and Christopher Silber at *NCIS New Orleans*, Julie Plec, Matt Hastings, and Eva McKenna at *The Originals*, and Marlene King, Oliver Goldstick, Lisa Cochran-Neilan, Jacquelyn Ryan, and Fred Andrews at *Pretty Little Liars*.

We thank our families: for Mary Lou, children Maggie and Tim Dougherty, and for Bethany, parents Connie and Jim Rooney.

Our other contributors: Anita J. Lee, Devon DeLapp, Matthew Bohrer, Mark West, Edgar Bennett, Suzanne Welke, Stephen Welke, Regina Render, Marcia Gould, Mark Tinker, Katie Enright, Jason Tomarik, Matthew Collins, Jason George, Anne Drecktrah, and Stephan Smith Collins.

We thank the following reviewers who generously helped us add the finishing touches: Michael Niederman (Columbia College Chicago), Dave A. Anselmi (UC Berkeley Extension), and Warren Bass (Temple University).

And last, but so very important to our book: the generous professionals who contributed to our *Insider Info* features, as well as *How I Got My First Directing Job* stories, and *From the Experts*.

Bethany Rooney began her directing career on the 1980s iconic television show *St. Elsewhere*, where she served as Associate Producer. She has directed more than 200 episodes of primetime network shows, including *NCIS*, *NCIS New Orleans*, *Criminal Minds*, *Nashville*, and *The Originals*.

Bethany has also directed eight television movies, including three Danielle Steel adaptations for NBC. She has directed Oscar winners and contenders Denzel Washington, Hilary Swank, Mary Tyler Moore, Angela Bassett, George Clooney, Alfre Woodard, Felicity Huffman, Sally Field, and Robert Downey, Jr., among many others.

Bethany graduated from Bowling Green State University in Ohio, earning a masters' degree.

She teaches the Warner Brothers Directors' Workshop and serves on multiple committees at the DGA.

Mary Lou Belli is an Emmy Award-winning producer, writer, and director with more than 150 episodes to her credit. She directed *NCIS New Orleans*, *Monk*, *Hart of Dixie*, and *The Wizards of Waverly Place*. On the CW, Mary Lou directed the hit show *Girlfriends* for seven consecutive seasons as well as its spinoff, *The Game*, and on Lifetime, *Devious Minds*.

Mary Lou directed *Living with Fran* starring Fran Drescher, *Eve* starring hip-hop artist Eve, as well as *The Hughleys*, *Charles in Charge*, *Major Dad*, and *Sister, Sister*. Mary Lou received BET nominations for directing *Girlfriends* and *One on One* as well as a Prism Award for *Girlfriends*.

Mary Lou earned her BA in theatre from Penn State and lectures frequently at film schools and universities such as the American Film Institute (AFI), NYU, Northwestern, the University of Connecticut, and many more. She serves on multiple committees at the DGA and is coauthor of two additional books: *The NEW Sitcom Career Book* and *Acting for Young Actors*.

This is the second edition of a guide for anyone who wants to do what we do: direct television and film. It is a clear, concise approach to the craft that fulfills us artistically and pays us handsomely for our expertise. We put in things we forgot, things we've learned, and more of what readers told us they loved about the book.

We direct narrative (nonreality) primetime network episode and television movies. That is, we direct dramas and single-camera comedies using the same process that Steven Spielberg (or any other movie director) uses. We are filmmakers. We tell stories. We just have less time and less money than a feature director. We direct shows seen by perhaps ten million people at one time.

When either of us directs a network television show, we are the fulcrum upon which balances the efforts of roughly 200 people and a budget that can be as much as 3 million to 5 million dollars. It's a powerful, creative, and complicated job. We want to examine the requirements of this job and tell you how to do it well. We don't want you to be just a good director; we want you to be a great one!

So what makes one director better than another? Being a director can absolutely be done with no experience and no training, but like anything else, the more knowledge and practice you have, the better you'll be at it.

But it's more than that. There is an intangible quality, an almost indescribable way of *being* that often distinguishes the excellent director from the merely good one. And what is even more astonishing about this "x" factor is that the job of the director is a multitasking one that requires many different skill sets, from knowing how to communicate with actors, to understanding the physical requirements for accomplishing a shot, to editing the final product perfectly.

So what is this "something" a true director has? It is an ability to both have a vision and lead others to help you create it. That is, a director is first and foremost a leader—a Moses, if you will, that leads a motley group toward the promised land of a successful project: one that creatively expresses the ideas of the script in the fullest way possible. It's a big job, challenging and exciting, different every day, requiring someone who deals easily with stress and pressure, someone who is physically robust and healthy, and most important, someone who can *see* how the written word can be interpreted on film.

1

So there it is. The short list of what a great director is:

- A leader
- with creative vision
- who understands and can execute the craft, and
- who can physically and mentally handle the demands of the job.

Most of *Directors Tell the Story: Master the Craft of Television and Film Directing* deals with creative vision and executing the craft to fulfill that vision. What first separates the good director from the great director is the creative vision, because without that, you're just a technician.

Before you can direct, you must have a story that you want to tell. In our case, as TV directors, we are given a script—a written story that we translate into the visual medium. The artistry of the director begins with interpreting the script. We are storytellers, inheritors of the tradition of telling tales around a campfire. We have to figure out what each scene really means, how each scene contributes to telling the whole story, and then design how to communicate that visually.

So how does a director fulfill creative vision? A great director:

- Interprets the script
- Chooses every element within the frame
- Shapes the actors' performances
- Tells the story with the camera.

Did you notice, as we described each aspect, that they all begin with a verb? We interpret, we choose, we shape, we tell. It's an active job. It requires decision-making. It requires action. We'll talk much more about this in the book, but for now, we want you to realize that to be a director with creative vision, you must act on that vision.

To give you an idea of how we do that, we'll break the process down to the three stages that every single director goes through in order to produce an episode of television or a movie:

- Prep
- Shoot
- Post.

These stages are our first three sections of the book. In the preparation stage, you'll learn how to make choices that will appear in the film, from casting to production design and shot listing. In the section on produc= tion, we show you how the director guides a huge number of people toward the realization of his or her creative vision. (But that's the last time we say it that way. From here on, those pronouns will be used interchangeably.)

In postproduction, you'll see how those efforts are put together into one cohesive story told in the director's unique way.

After you understand the demands and complexities of this job, we discuss in the final section what is required for leadership and what kind of shape, both physical and mental, that you have to be in to actually do the job.

We use our experience teaching master classes in directing and acting to explain what we want you to learn in small instructional units. We'll give you *directing exercises* to assist you in mastering your skills. Because we both write as well as direct, we have included *original scenes* with which you can practice.

In addition, we'll **boldface** lingo we think you should have at your fingertips and list these *vocabulary words* at the end of each chapter. We even ask our colleagues who are in the trenches with us to share their wealth of information in our bonus Insider Info and From the Experts boxes.

For a final piece of inspiration, we tell you how we got our first jobs and suggest ways you might get yours. And as an added bonus, we ask a number of our generous colleagues to share their *How I Got My First Directing Job* stories as well.

So let's dive into *Directors Tell the Story: Master the Craft of Television and Film Directing*.

Prep

Overview

What is prep? Prep (preparation) is the critical time period of a week to ten days before principal photography begins, which is when a director prepares for the upcoming shoot. It happens during the film or television show's preproduction period.

What does a director do during prep? The director interprets the script and selects every element that will appear in the frame. It is a time to gather the troops and share the vision as the leader of the upcoming episode. The director reads the script and breaks it down for story, character, style, and color. The director casts, or chooses, the actors who will appear in this episode along with the series' regulars. It is a time to discuss tone with the episode writer and have countless meetings with department heads to answer their questions so that they (and their crews) can have everything ready. The director scouts and chooses locations during prep.

Finally—and probably most important—the director plans how to shoot the episode and generates shot lists or storyboards (or both) that will be his roadmap during the shoot.

Chapter 1

Breaking Down the Script for Story

The late great director Sydney Pollack said, "The director is the teller of the film, the director tells the movie, like you would tell a story, except in this case you're telling a movie."[1] So how do you become a good teller? One of the most important skills a director needs is to be able to read *well*! The director's first task is to interpret the script, so it is critical that you develop the ability to read and understand the material. You have to be able to break down the story into its parts and map out how those parts add up to the whole.

The good news is that people have been telling stories forever: Homer writing about Odysseus, troubadours singing epic tales, cowboys spinning yarns around campfires. Storytellers intuitively knew what the writers of television scripts try to achieve with every episode they create: that a story is a journey.

As the director, you must read the script and be able to see how to take the viewer along on the trip as you tell the story. You want to inspire your audience to feel as you did when you first read the script—to experience the highs and the lows, the tears or the laughter that the screenwriter inspired in you—while they are watching the pictures you created in our visual medium. Ideally, you will not only recreate the script in picture form but also elevate it by making the words come to life.

The first step in accomplishing this goal is reading and interpreting the script.

READING WELL: YOUR SECRET WEAPON

So how do you, the director, acquire this basic tool in your arsenal of needed skills? You read . . . a lot. In fact, you read everything you can. You go along for a ride with each and every book, story, and script you read. Then you look at the ride that you took and figure out how you got there. By analyzing every story you've read, you'll start to see the similarities and differences between them. You'll notice that some engage you and others don't. You'll see why our brethren in the Writers' Guild are to be respected and admired for their skill at constructing a script that has an interesting plot and enough pathos to engage us for an hour (including six commercial breaks).

You know that basic dramatic structure has three parts: the **rising action**, the **climax**, and the **dénouement**. An **inciting action** can kick off the story and **complications** keep your attention. Once you are engaged and along for the ride, there will be more complications and turning points to keep you interested, and it will all build to one big moment: the climax of the story. The resolution, or dénouement, brings you home or completes the story. The basic concept is to make sure that the story points follow each other logically. You should ask yourself whether each event leads to the next and provides both the information and the emotional arc that you need.

You might ask why a director has to know about screenwriting and dramatic structure. The simple answer is that an architect cannot design a beautiful building without first having the knowledge of how to build that structure. Otherwise, he will design a building that will fall down. A director similarly needs to know how a story is structured in order to tell it beautifully.

> *An architect cannot design a beautiful building without first having the knowledge of how to build that structure. Otherwise, he will design a building that will fall down. A director similarly needs to know how a story is structured in order to tell it beautifully.*

Without the building blocks of structure, a story will collapse. If you are lucky enough to direct a script that is already in great shape, you can move on to your other directing tasks, explanations of which constitute the rest of this book. But if the script needs work, your efforts will be more complex. Either way, the director's first job is to break down the script for story.

READING FOR FUN AND TO GET THE BIG PICTURE

How do you begin? You read it. Your first read should be just for fun because this is the only read when every element of the story is a surprise. You will hopefully have an emotional response to the story. Notice where that happens:

it will be key to your directing the episode and the choices you make. You want your audience to experience those feelings at the same places in your completed film. Next, summarize the story for yourself in one sentence. Writers call this the **logline**. You've seen these one-line summaries countless times in *TV Guide*s or on your TiVo summary: So and so does so and so and it results in so and so.

Also ask yourself: what the idea is behind the episode. Sidney Pollack gave a great example of this when describing one of his critically and

> Writers call this the logline: So and so does so and so and it results in so and so.

financially successful hits in which Dustin Hoffman, in a brilliant comic turn, portrayed an unhappy, out-of-work actor who impersonates a woman in order to get a job. Pollack often said, "The idea in *Tootsie* is that a man becomes a better man for having been a woman."[2]

In the television shows like *Grey's Anatomy* and *Sex and the City*, it is simple to identify the idea behind the episode: the voiceover at the beginning of the episode tells you. What the show is about, or its central **theme**, is important to keep in mind while you're directing, so every scene helps illuminate that concept. But it's also important to keep in mind that the theme is not the plot; the theme is illustrated by the plot. Pollack gives you an example in the "better man for having been a woman" phrase. You should be able to describe the theme simply: for example, an underdog classic, a faith-versus-science struggle, a tale of redemption, a fish-out-of-water story. We are using the same themes today that the ancient Greeks and Romans employed; a TV director today is a modern-day Homer. The plots are most definitely different, but the themes are universal.

There are other things that you should also note during the first read, beginning with the basic structure of the story. If it's a **procedural** drama, there might be a tried-and-true formula that is the spine of every story. Let's take the popular and well-crafted *Law & Order* and its many spinoffs. It starts with a crime that is investigated by the officers (the *Law* part) who find the culprit who has perpetrated the crime. Then the lawyers (the *Order* part) prosecute the suspect; it ends in the climax, when we find out whether the culprit is going to jail for the crime. The episode concludes with a quick wrap-up based on the verdict of the trial.

While you are doing that initial read of a procedural or law-based drama, you should be curious about who did the crime. *Law & Order* purposely leads you down a circuitous path before the story reveals who actually did it. It makes the viewer feel clever for following along, and it gives them insight into the way the police officers' minds and jobs work. Once you know who did it, the viewer should be rooting for the culprit to be taken down and then either rejoice in the satisfaction of justice being served or empathize with the prosecutors and detectives who got ripped off if the culprit goes free. After the first read, you should know the emotional arc on which you want to take your audience because you've just experienced it yourself. Regardless of the genre, take care to note your emotional reactions at each point of the script, because from this point on, the director is the stand-in for the audience. You are creating a story and orchestrating every single element so that the audience will have the same emotional responses you had when reading the script. Everything you do as a director is intended to duplicate for the audience what you first felt when you read the script.

> *You are creating a story and orchestrating every single element so that the audience will have the same emotional responses you had when reading the script.*
> *Everything you do as a director is intended to duplicate for the audience what you first felt when you read the script.*

From the Experts

Peter Jankowski, the President and Chief Operating Officer of Wolf Films Inc., the company responsible for the popular *Law & Order* series, its spinoffs, as well as *Chicago PD*, *Chicago Fire*, and *Chicago Med*, shared some insights with us:

Dick Wolf has a sign on his desk that reads, "It's the WRITING stupid." I've always felt that the success of the *Law & Order* brand was based on extremely complex writing. The template for the shows was always story driven. The A story leads to the B story, which leads to C. What it comes down to in television, which is a machine that eats scripts, if you don't have great scripts, you don't have great shows.

Law & Order is a vastly different kind of storytelling, a different pace, than an *ER* or our other shows, *Chicago PD* and *Chicago Fire*, in which the characters drive the stories. It's a different kind of cutting than an action driven drama. And the cities also make a difference. NY is more vertical, high stress, intellectual while Chicago is more Midwestern . . . and as a result, more affable. The cities have vastly different energies and so do their respective shows.[3]

IDENTIFYING THE VARIOUS STORIES

Next, you need to identify the basic plot or **"A" story**. In a *Law & Order* script, it might look something like this:

- Someone is found murdered.
- The police investigate witnesses. (This plot point may have several subdivisions.)

- The police make an arrest.
- The prosecuting attorneys introduce their witnesses; the defense attorneys pick them apart.
- The defense attorneys introduce their witnesses; the prosecuting attorneys pick them apart.
- The attorneys make their closing arguments.
- The jury gives the verdict.
- The murderer goes to prison or is set free.

After figuring out the **"A" story**, see if there is a **"B" story** or a **"C" story** or subplot(s).

These often have something to do with a character's personal life. Sometimes they echo, replicate, or complement the "A" story. Other times, they stand completely on their own. Let's take a "B" story from *Cold Case*. The actor Danny Pino plays Scotty Valens, a detective whose mother has been raped, but she has not told anyone. He learns about the rape through another case he is investigating. Over several episodes, the detective uses his influence and accesses enough information to figure out who committed the crime and sees the rapist suffer for the pain he inflicted on all the rape victims, especially the detective's mother. In another "B" story from *NCIS New Orleans*, the actress Shalita Grant plays Sonja Percy, a federal undercover agent who has infiltrated a gang that deals drugs and arms. She helps several NCIS investigations over a four-episode arc, hoping to make herself valuable enough to be hired by NCIS and stop her undercover federal gig. In this case, it is a **serial** "B" story because it plays out over many episodes. There are also characters who come in for several episodes as part of a season story arc. Tony Shalhoub did one as the terminally ill Dr. Bernard Prince, on the seventh season of *Nurse Jackie*. It is the director's job to make sure that the plot points are clear for both the main plot and the subplots. The director should also ask to read the episodes in which a serial subplot is introduced to track its progress over many episodes. For example, as in the case of the aforementioned *Nurse Jackie*, it was not revealed for many episodes that Shalhoub's character had a brain tumor and the way he played the episodes before the reveal needed to foreshadow that information.

When Mary Lou was deciding to morph her career from acting into directing, she went to the **AFI** library many times a week. She was not a student there, but the library was (and still is) open and free to the public. Mary Lou created a do-it-yourself "film school" for herself. She either read a book in their collection (often recommended by the librarian) or listened to prerecorded lectures of visiting speakers that AFI had available from their archives. One of those speakers was Mary Lou's favorite director, Sydney

Pollack, who was quoted earlier in this chapter. Pollack started as an actor, became a dialogue/acting coach, and then became a director. Mary Lou emulated his path and hoped it would be her own.

In one of Pollack's lectures, she recalls him saying that he "named his scenes." That is, he gave each scene a short name that reminded him how each scene moved the main plot forward. It was just a thumbnail sketch but also a critical reminder to him of the underlying importance of every scene to the whole, not just what the conflict was between the characters in each individual scene (something we will explore in the next chapter).

BUILDING YOUR STORY ONE SCENE AT A TIME

Once you have a handle on the big picture, the main plot, and subplot, it's time for you to dissect the subtleties. Read the script again. Get out your pencil. Jot down your ideas in the margin.

Notice all the individual plot points and how they logically and sequentially build on the previous point. Bethany usually lists the named scenes on a separate sheet of paper, breaking it down into columns for each storyline, which essentially provides an outline of the script. It also serves as a "cheat sheet" during the shooting when you need to ask yourself, "What is this scene really about?" And "What is its importance to the plot as a whole?" It is also a useful tool when an actor asks, "Where was I before this scene?" because you can quickly find the answer rather than taking time to page through the script.

This Director's Diagram (Figure 1.1) is really a critical tool in breaking down story, and it allows you to discover what the writer had in mind when he had just the glimmer of an idea that developed into a complex screenplay. This is a way of simplifying and telescoping from the external layers of dialogue and description back down to the nub of it all: the theme. What is this story really about? And how does each scene contribute and advance the plot to serve that theme?

A television script typically has six acts, though the trend seems to be a five-act structure. (Until about 1990, television shows had four acts. Many movies and plays are in three acts.) These are separated by commercial breaks, so each act must be a unit that can stand on its own. (You'll learn in Chapter 9 that you should design a beginning and ending for each act.) These acts are the building blocks of the episode. Act 1 typically introduces the subject and main characters and jump-starts the audience's interest. Identify for yourself who is the **protagonist** and who is the **antagonist** of the "A" story. The protagonist is the central character, the hero, the leading role. It is nearly always a **series regular**, that is, a person who appears in

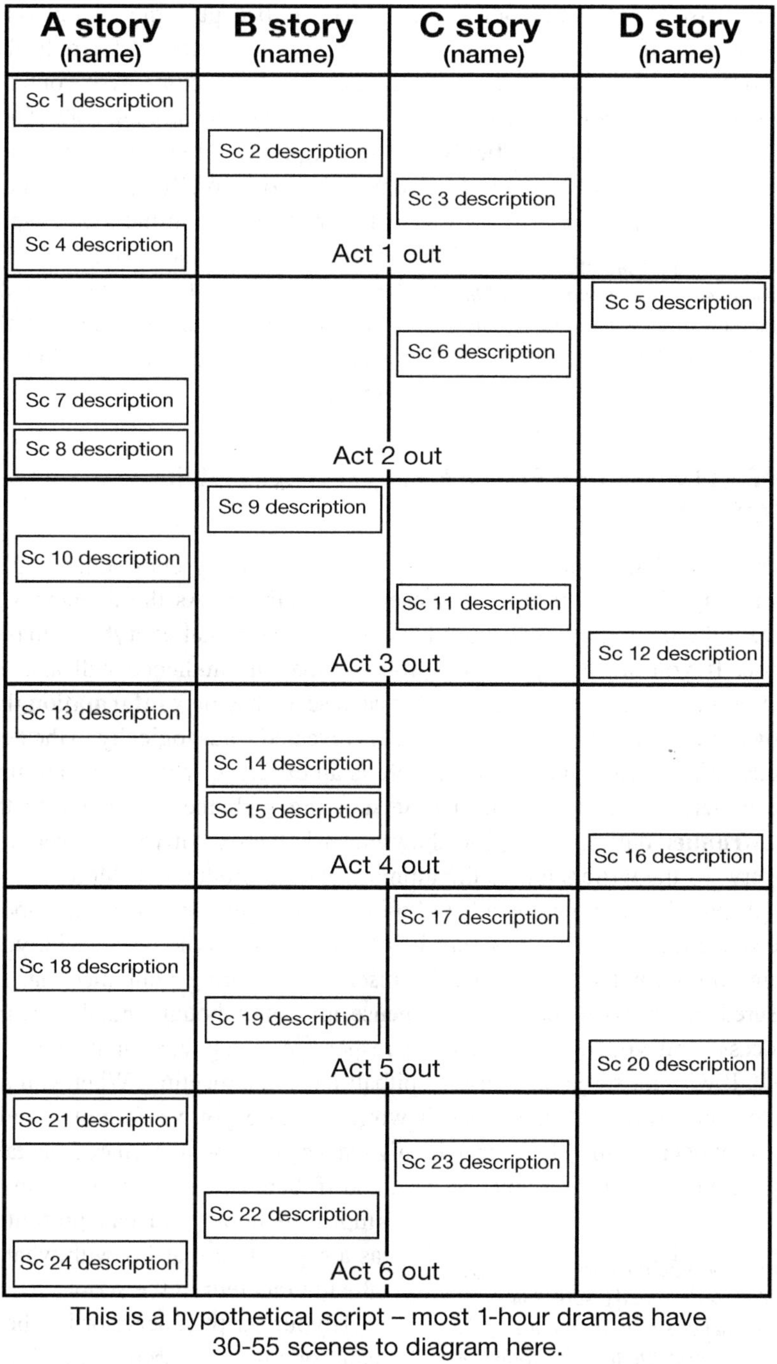

A story (name)	B story (name)	C story (name)	D story (name)
Sc 1 description			
	Sc 2 description		
		Sc 3 description	
Sc 4 description	Act 1 out		
			Sc 5 description
		Sc 6 description	
Sc 7 description			
Sc 8 description	Act 2 out		
	Sc 9 description		
Sc 10 description			
		Sc 11 description	
	Act 3 out		Sc 12 description
Sc 13 description			
	Sc 14 description		
	Sc 15 description		
	Act 4 out		Sc 16 description
		Sc 17 description	
Sc 18 description			
	Sc 19 description		
	Act 5 out		Sc 20 description
Sc 21 description			
		Sc 23 description	
	Sc 22 description		
Sc 24 description	Act 6 out		

This is a hypothetical script – most 1-hour dramas have
30-55 scenes to diagram here.

FIGURE 1.1 The **Director's Diagram** helps you to really understand the story you're telling.

every episode. The antagonist is the rival, the bad guy, the enemy. This character is often played by a **guest star** who is contracted for only that episode or the number of episodes it takes to tell his story. Ask yourself, "What is the antagonist doing or what has he done to the protagonist?" Their journey together is the **conflict** within the script; they are at cross-purposes, and the stronger the conflict, the stronger the story. We'll talk more about their relationship in the next chapter when we break the script down for character. Just note how the act ends. Ask yourself what will compel the audience to come back and find out more.

> *The journey of the protagonist and antagonist together is the conflict within the script; they are at cross-purposes, and the stronger the conflict, the stronger the story.*

THE CLIMAX: THE PAYOFF TO TELLING YOUR STORY WELL

It is more of the same in Acts 2 through 5: somebody does something to somebody else, which leads us closer to the climax. As the director, you have to be the logic police. You have to make sure that everything makes sense. If you are confused, it's probable that the audience will also be confused. You need to make sure that each scene has **new information** that moves the story forward, and that what is revealed leads logically to the next scene. When that is not the case, there is an expert to whom you can turn: the writer. You'll be having a **tone meeting** with the writer and/or the **showrunner** during prep. (The showrunner is the executive producer who supervises the writers and is the ultimate boss in production. More on that in Chapter 7.) Start making a list of things you might want to ask him about the sequence of events. It is very helpful if you go to the writer with your suggestions for fixes, so you can present them during your meeting. Be assured that the writer has put an immense amount of thought into the writing process, and you owe him/her the respect of doing your homework as well. It will not serve the story to spitball fixes in a meeting. When you are called out on a "fix" that doesn't work (because you've forgotten some relevant background plot point), it only makes you look unprepared. So take the time to outline the named scenes, and if there is something that can be improved upon, you can present it as a suggestion that fits with what is already inherent in the script.

> *As the director, you have to be the logic police. You have to make sure that everything makes sense. If you are confused, it's probable that the audience will also be confused.*

If your script supervisor has been paid for a week of prep, she will read and time the episode.

The script supervisor might also point out any **continuity** problems because this is one of the fields of her expertise. Continuity requires both consistency and logic. For example, Character A shouldn't talk about how much he cherishes the memory of his mother throwing him a great fifth birthday party if the script said earlier that the poor woman died giving birth to Character A. So just note the progression of events in Acts 2 through 5 and how they all lead up to the climax at the end of Act 5. See how the writer begins each act with some propelling information that moves the plot forward, and notice how the writer ends each act with a **cliffhanger**, a moment that will compel the audience to come back after the commercial break to see how that moment turned out.

If the story that you will be telling unfolds out of chronological order in the script, for example in flashbacks or flash-forwards, take the time to organize the story in chronological order for yourself. Then go back and look at the intended complicated structure of the script and it will be more relevant to you for having done the analysis.

The climax is the big payoff. It must be the most important moment of the show, and it is never too soon to start thinking about how you will make it so. When breaking down the script for story, make sure that all the necessary plot points add up and logically lead to this moment. Notice if there is any **foreshadowing**, or deliberate clues that must be created earlier in order to earn or reach the climax of the show. Make sure these clues have been introduced in the right sequence, and you understand why the writer has ordered them in that way. This process of breaking down the script for story is all about analysis, noting each building block and its place in the story. It should all add up to a solid structure that allows the audience to go on the emotional ride without getting hung up by deviating facts.

> When breaking down the script for story, make sure that all the necessary plot points add up and logically lead to the climax.

THE DÉNOUEMENT: WRAPPING UP THE LOOSE ENDS

Finally, you should look at the falling action or dénouement in Act 6. Figure out the tone that the writer is trying to achieve. In a *Monk* episode that Mary Lou directed, Monk gets his day in court after being decimated on the stand. His testimony allows a murderer to go free. But Monk rights the wrong when the same murderer is rightly convicted of a second crime due to Monk's clever investigative process. The final scene begins with the foreman of the jury delivering the guilty verdict and Monk and the investigative team leaving the courtroom triumphantly . . . or so we think. If *Monk* were a courtroom procedural show, that would be a fine ending. But that is not how writers Josh Siegal and Dylan Morgan end their script. In a typically quirky Monk moment, the protagonist reenters the empty courtroom and adjusts the microphone on the witness stand where he was earlier decimated then leaves the courtroom, compulsively straightening some papers on the prosecution table as he leaves. The tone is funny, quirky, and triumphant . . . *Monk* style.

The actions of Mr. Monk in the dénouement of that episode illuminate character, as well as the "story under the story," which is known as **subtext**. Subtext is essentially what is really going on in a scene. It is not necessarily revealed in plot or dialogue. Subtext is about the characters' inner feelings and about their relationships to each other. So the subtext of that *Monk* scene is "I'm back!" It was Mary Lou's job, as director of that episode, to make sure that the subtext of that scene and every other was clear to the audience without **hanging a lamp on it** (being too obvious). We could say that each script could be diagrammed twice: once for plot and once for subtext (which would illustrate theme). A good writer adds dimension to the scene by having the plot and subtext differ. In other words, the plot point of the Monk scene is one thing; the subtext is another. And it should be the same for every script and every well-written scene. If a character has dialogue that is **on the nose**— too obviously referring to the scene's subtext—then that is an issue that you should take up with the writer when you have your tone meeting.

You must know and understand the script as well as the writer does. He has been living with it a long time. It's catch-up time for you. Get on top of your game! Read the script and all the revisions to the script, the moment you get them. And then read them again!

Dissecting the Plot

Read any screenplay or teleplay. Identify what the movie is about—the idea or theme. Next, identify the A, B, and C stories. Finally, outline each act by listing the named scenes in columns under the headings of "A story," "B story," and "C story." Note the propelling action that begins each act, subsequent key plot points, and finally the cliffhanger, by using different-colored highlighters. Note subtext when it is an important story point.

When you have completed the plot dissection exercise, you will have a template for all your future work at breaking down your directing assignments for story. By going through this process, you come to know the story intimately, so that when you are facing decisions during the shooting of that script, you will know exactly what to do. The story will live in your heart and mind; it will inhabit your subconscious in your sleep and your every waking moment. Directing is an involving and complex task but one that is ultimately exhilarating when you realize that you have elevated the story in bringing the script to the screen, no matter whether it's in a theater multiplex, a living room TV, or a teenager's smart phone. Breaking down the script for story is your first step on a wonderful journey for both you and your audience.

From the Experts

**Excerpt from *Dan O'Bannon's Guide to Screenplay Structure*
by Dan O'Bannon with Matt R. Lohr (ISBN 978-1-61593-130-9,
www.mwp.com) (Michael Wise Productions)**

Story structure is a set of predefined relationships between story elements that give shape to the finished story.

As an architectural term, "structure" refers to the beams and walls that hold a building together. The structure of a house performs two functions: (1) it defines the shape of the house, and (2) it holds the pieces of the house together. The analogy to story structure is an exact one; however, the structure of a house is a manifest physical object that you can see with the naked eye. If you knock a hole in the wall, you can see the beams and cross-braces that make up the house's structure. Some parts of the structure of a house are not even hidden; certain beams and supports are exposed. In the graphic arts, structure usually takes the form of an under-sketch. There are, of course, all kinds of art, but in many traditional forms, such as Italian Renaissance painting, the under-sketch is hidden. The artist starts out with a pencil drawing on the canvas; that is the picture's structure, although artists don't use that terminology (they speak instead of "composition"). By the time the artist gets through putting down the paint, the under-sketch is no longer readily visible. But it's not absolutely unseeable; you could view it by X-raying the canvas, the way art conservators do.

But in a story, an X-ray would reveal nothing because the structure is not physical. It is conceptual—an abstraction. Story structure is made of words, but those words are not in the script. They are floating in the writer's head, or spoken by collaborators or studio executives, or written in a story outline or treatment. The only way to detect a story's structure is for a knowledgeable person to examine the story and infer that structure from the story's visible parts, those little marks of ink that describe places and characters and dialogue and events.

If you omit the structure from the house, it will collapse. It won't even stand up in the first place. So nobody ever leaves out the structure when building a house. But if you leave out the structure when writing a screenplay, nothing that obvious will happen. Superficially, it looks the same as a structured script; the pages won't go flying apart or anything. Not until later, when you start inflicting that screenplay on other people, will you realize your story has collapsed.

Story structure is an invisible construct that describes the relationships between parts of the story. It is a dressmaking pattern that shows you where your story's arms and legs go, a stencil that points out the locations of the little (or big) windows inside which you can be creative. It was invented in order to get the audience to sit though a movie all the way to the end.

More elegantly, story structure is a way to make certain your story's themes are realized and fulfilled. If something is missing, structure will show you exactly what's missing and where. It is formal and restricting, yes, but empowering as well.[4]

Insider Info

How Do You Interact with the Director (in your Executive Producer/Showrunner capacity)?
Bringing the writer's vision from page to screen is a complicated process. What starts out as a set of ideas in the mind of one writer gets translated into script and interpreted by many. The showrunner is ultimately responsible for ensuring the writer's vision and the look and feel of the show, which comes alive on the screen with the help of the director. Making the show come alive requires a close working relationship and excellent communication between the parties.

The director should feel welcome to give notes and feedback on the script in an effort to bring a unique vision to the final product.

What Do You Want Directors to Know About Breaking a Script Down for Story?
Directors should understand the process from the point of view of the writer. By the time a script reaches the final production draft, the writer has taken "notes" from the studio, network, showrunner, production staff, and the actors. Script changes are often made in favor of a production concern (budget, scheduling, advertiser demands) and not because they serve the story.

What is Your Advice to Young Directors?
The writer is your friend. The two of you want the same thing: to make a great episode of television. Understand what forces are pushing and pulling the writer. Ask questions. Challenge inconsistencies with respect, and know when it's time to let it go.

Steve Blackman
Fargo, Private Practice

Vocabulary

	conflict	procedural
	continuity	protagonist
"A" story	dénouement	rising action
AFI (American Film	foreshadowing	serial
Institute)	guest star	series regular
antagonist	hanging a lamp on it	showrunner
"B" or "C" stories	inciting action	subtext
cliffhanger	logline	theme
climax	new information	tone meeting
complications	on-the-nose	

NOTES

1 "A Conversation with Sydney Pollack with Host Ben Wattenberg," *Think Tank*, May 27, 2000. Transcript. Available at www.pbs.org/thinktank/transcript896.html.
2 "A Conversation with Sydney Pollack with Host Ben Wattenberg," *Think Tank*, May 27, 2000. Transcript. Available at www.pbs.org/thinktank/transcript896.html.
3 Peter Jankowski, phone interview with author. March 13, 2015.
4 Dan O'Bannon with Matt R. Lohr. *Dan O'Bannon's Guide to Screenplay Structure*. Studio City: Michael Wiese Productions, 2012, pp. 21–23.

Chapter 2

Breaking Down the Script for Character

Once you have identified the story and its structure, you have more analysis to do, this time involving the characters of your story. Though the plot is the structure of every movie or television episode, it is the characters in that story that create the conflict. First, you need to find out who these characters are.

Making a COW Chart

 You should start with a "COW chart" for each character. What is a COW chart? Mary Lou wants to give credit where it is due. The term was so named by the Innercity Filmmakers group of students she co-taught with actress Yvette Nicole Brown (*Community*, *The Odd Couple*) at the University of Southern California some summers ago. After Mary Lou and Yvette taught their master class about the relationship between the director and actor, they received thank-you notes from every single student. Nearly all of the notes mentioned how helpful it was to learn how to do a COW chart. Mary Lou and Yvette were truly bewildered until they received a photograph of themselves with the students some weeks later. Behind all of them was a blackboard on which Mary Lou had written three columns. The columns were labeled: C, O, and W. She had posed these questions:

What does the **C**haracter say about himself?
What do **O**thers say about the character?
What does the **W**riter say about the character?

C	O	W
Character says about himself	Others say about character	Writer says about character

FIGURE 2.1 Mary Lou sets up her COW chart like this.

A very easy way to break down each character is to examine the script line by line and outline the information in these categories. You'll find the information for the first two questions in the **dialogue** (scripted lines) and the last question in the **stage directions**, in which the writer describes the action or describes the state of the character physically and emotionally. The interesting thing you'll notice is that the first two questions may not always lead to the truth because characters often lie about themselves, and others always have opinions that will color their truth about a character. The last question, on the other hand, nearly always leads to the truth—unless the writer has written a physical description of the character as merely a guide. For example, when Michael Hirst described Henry VIII in the stage directions of his recent Showtime miniseries, he may have said "The king is portly, as Holbein painted him long ago." The physical attributes serve as only a guide because the talented Jonathan Rhys-Meyer was cast in the role; he is anything but portly and remained svelte for most of the series. Or Christopher Silber in the "More Now" episode of *NCIS New Orleans* describes the character Sonja we spoke about in the last chapter: "a Young Woman in street clothes, eyeing LaSalle" [played by Lucas Black]. She is at an "urgent care facility in one of the city's worst neighborhoods." This description is simple until

Silber adds what happens: "As Brody [played by Zoe McLellan] keeps showing the Doctor's photo around, LaSalle cuts the Young Woman off as she heads for the door." And later,

You will surmise things about the character based on what they say and actions they take.

"The Young Woman holds LaSalle's gaze." Notice the descriptions are very simple . . . but it is the interpretation that will lead the director to a deeper understanding of the character.

After you have the basic COW information written down, you must interpret the data.

Remember what we said about reading well? That skill will again be vital. Now you are going to read *between* the lines. You will surmise things about the character based on what they say and actions they take. In her last scene of the aforementioned episode Silber tells us at the end of a contentious scene between LaSalle and Sonja: "Sonja cracks the subtlest of smiles." This action describes so much more than a facial expression. It is the clue to an ongoing flirtatious relationship between Sonja and the series regular LaSalle.

You are going to take each piece of data and form a picture in your mind about the character the writer has created. What makes this character different from all the others in the story? Is there a particular line that is quintessentially his and his alone? Why would no one else in the script ever utter those words or deliver that line that particular way at that particular time in that particular place?

EXPLORING ARCHETYPES, ESSENCE, AND IMAGERY

Sometimes it helps to conceive of a character as an **archetype**. This is a quick **label** to place on character that would define their inherent characteristics. For example, in an *L.A. Times* article about Clint Eastwood and Morgan Freeman, the following paragraph used several archetypes to describe their previous career choices:

They've played geriatric astronauts and battle-scarred Secret Service agents, no-name cowboys and a San Francisco cop nicknamed "Dirty" . . . as well as ruthless pimps, kick-butt high school principals, a cool-under-fire president . . . and the almighty himself.[1]

You might use any label as a shorthand device to help you grasp the essence of a character.

Entertainment Weekly described Robert Pattinson's character in *Eclipse* as "like James Dean."[2] Perfect and precise. There is also the famous story about John Huston providing Kate Hepburn with the perfect label for her character in *The African Queen* by referring to Rose Sayer as "an Eleanor Roosevelt." But both Huston and Hepburn had to dig deeper to determine what that meant. What myriad qualities did "an Eleanor Roosevelt" entail? The danger, of course, is in focusing on the label almost as a nickname for the character while ignoring the character's subtleties. But as a good director, you won't let that happen!

Another shorthand device to help you pin down your characters is to start thinking of their **imagery**. When you picture a character in your imagination, what do you see? See that image as a **title card**, or poster, for a movie. If you were the advertising and marketing director for this character, what physicalities would you focus on? Is the character alone or in a crowd? Is it a silhouette or a color close-up? What expression is on her face? What accessories does she have?

Think of Robert Downey, Jr.'s walking stick as Sherlock Holmes, or the cane that Hugh Laurie uses as Dr. House. How does costuming help? Think of Johnny Depp's pirate attire or Meryl Streep's Julia in a 1950s suit and pearls. Actors will say that when they put on the costume and pick up the prop, they become the character. At the "Hollywood Costume" exhibit, presented by the Academy of Motion Picture Arts and Sciences, there was an entire section of the exhibit devoted to Meryl Streep, who we learned was a costume design major in college. The curator of that exhibit, Deborah Landis, in a TV interview with Gayle Anderson of KTLA described "how she [Streep] uses costume to transform into character."[3] Working from the exterior (costumes and props) to interior (feelings) is a literal way to approach a character, and the first costume fitting is an important part of an actor's process. But actors generally are hired late in the schedule, just before production begins. Previous to that, during the prep period, the director has communicated her vision to the appropriate department heads, giving guidance about her character discovery prior to the actor's arrival.

THINKING IN PICTURES

Your costume designer and prop master bring experience and creativity to the table; together, you will come up with proposals and gradually hone them into a concept as one idea leads to the next. One of the things you can do to spur your imagination is to create a **vision board** for each character. You can cut out pictures and words from magazines or other sources that illustrate an aspect of the character and provide a reference point for discussion. This board can be as simple as taped pictures on a file folder or as complex as a PowerPoint presentation. You will talk about color and style, as well as cultural and historical accuracy. You will refine your choices as you work with the material and gain deeper understanding. As always, it is the director's overall vision that leads the way.

You will talk about color and style, as well as cultural and historical accuracy. You will refine your choices as you work with the material and gain deeper understanding. As always, it is the director's overall vision that leads the way.

When you start thinking in pictures for your characters, this can have the effect of clarifying your thinking regarding the story. Bethany had that experience on a TV movie called *Remembrance*, which originated as a Danielle Steel novel. She described what she had in mind to the prop master, and—after a massive search through antique shops and flea markets—the perfect piece was found. The faux diamond pin that the main character wore was an example of the level of sophistication for the character, but more important, its image became the focal point and title card for the entire movie. It became the **iconic image** that communicated the essence of the story. Another show that can serve as an example is *Mad Men*. If you think of Don Draper without his cigarette and cocktail in hand, a whole dimension is lost. And those specific character props, and the need that the character has to have them in his hand, will be key when you begin to pre-visualize how a scene might be blocked . . . but we'll talk more about that in a future chapter.

FINDING THE CHARACTER INTENTION

You will inevitably have some casting ideas at this point. Jot them down. Before you cement that image though, you need to really look at how the character behaves. We spoke of the story being a journey in Chapter 1: The character's needs are the fuel for that trip. You know who the protagonist and antagonist are in the overall story. Now you have to figure out the purpose they serve in every scene. And you have to do this not only for the main characters, but also for every character, no matter how many lines of dialogue he has. Every actor knows the phrase, "There are no small parts, only small players." The director must embrace the truth of this statement.

You must ask yourself the question: "What does each character want to accomplish in the scene?" The best way to figure out the answer to this question is to ask another one: "What does a character need from another character?" You should be able to express the answer to this question in active terms: Character A needs Character B to leave. Character A needs Character B to tell her he loves her. Character A needs Character B to give him the treasure. And ideally, if the scene is well written, the characters will have diametrically opposed needs. Character B needs Character A to tell him to stay. Character B needs Character A to stop needing his love. Character B

When you know what each character needs, then you will understand the conflict in the scene. And the basic truth of storytelling is this: more conflict, better scene.

needs Character A to get out of his life without the treasure.

If it's difficult to determine what Character A's needs are, go to Character B. That might be clearer. Then, when you have an idea of Character B's needs, see if you can phrase Character A's needs in an opposing way.

When you know what each character needs, then you will understand the conflict in the scene. And the basic truth of storytelling is this: more conflict, better scene. It's a simple equation. The more conflict you show—while keeping the performances grounded in reality— the better the scene will be.

Another word for need is **intention**. This is an important word in an actor's vocabulary; we talk more about it in Chapter 10 when we talk about directing the actor's performance. You should be able to rate the need of each character. A simple way to do this is to ask yourself: "What will happen if the character does not achieve their intention? How big are the consequences?" A good example of those consequences is in an action movie: If the character cannot shoot his way out of a bank, he will die! Clearly, if the conflict is more important, it will be a more interesting scene than the one in which very little is at stake. We suggest rating the conflict in every scene on a scale of 1–10. If you get an important 10 scene as a director, you're lucky. If you get a 1 scene, it will be your job as a director to make it seem more important. But we'll get to that in a little bit.

What the Characters Need

Select a two-character scene from the appendix. Read it and determine three things:
• What does Character A need?
• What does Character B need?
• What is the conflict of the scene and how important is it?
Remember to try to phrase each character's needs as diametrically opposed to each other, if possible. Rate the conflict on a scale of 1–10. (A score of 10 might be a scene in which the character dies if he does not get what he needs. A score of 1 might be a scene in which the character will be mildly annoyed if she does not get what she wants.)

EXPLORING THE CHARACTER OBSTACLES

You should also notice any obstacles to the characters getting what they want, other than the opposing character not wanting them to get it. Be assured that a good actor will come to the set having asked the same questions you asked:

what does my character need to accomplish? They will have asked themselves a second question, to which you must know the answer also: "What is the **obstacle** to that intention?" Let's take the example of the action movie. Our hero needs to shoot his way out of a bank. What's the obstacle? The police are outside with guns drawn. Or perhaps, at this moment, the character is guilt-ridden, remembering that his grandma told him never to hurt anyone. A good writer makes sure that each character has two things: an intention and an obstacle to achieving that intention. Could that obstacle merely be the other character in the scene? Yes, but a more layered scene gives a character an obstacle that is separate from the other character and their intention, one that is an internal emotional conflict. For example, in a love story, a character might have the intention of making a woman fall in love with him, but the obstacle might be that in his heart, he doesn't feel like he's good enough for her.

There is one more area that is directly related to knowing the conflict of each scene. As you break down the script, note where there is a lot of **pipe** or **exposition**—an area where the writer has had to share a lot of information (lay the pipe) in a short amount of time so that the viewer will understand the story. This is often background information that doesn't move the plot forward and is therefore not dynamic.

The director can help hide or mask exposition by distracting the viewer with conflict. Or the director can even give the character who lays the pipe an inner obstacle while saying the line. It's a trick, but a handy one, and you can get a double bang for your buck: the obstacle or conflict will say something specific about the character and you've made the writer look better by hiding the exposition. Mary Lou directed a short film called *Straight Eye for the Gay Guy*, written by Jonathan Dorf. Jonathan told her "Information doesn't have to be static; it can be used to hurt or attack other characters, and released at just the right moment can be just as deadly as a gun. I call it weaponizing the exposition. Instead of your script feeling contrived and bogging down in exposition, it'll feel dynamic and organic—and we'll be so busy watching the proverbial bullets fly that we won't even notice all of the information you're feeding us."[4] His website is full of helpful info for writers and directors who want to know about writing.

Another trick is to give the actor a physical task to complete while giving the exposition. During an episode of *Weeds*, Bethany had to cover some exposition about the backstory of a character's father, which led to a physical fight between the characters played by Kevin Nealon and Hunter Parrish. In the lead-up to that fight, the two characters were engaged in painting the walls of their new marijuana dispensary. That activity disguised the exposition and added a literal texture to the scene. In an episode of *Hart of Dixie* that Mary Lou directed, writers April Blair and Leila Gerstein (the latter created the show) hide all the updated information about Zoe's (played by Rachel Bilson) pregnancy and finding out the sex of the child in a very funny scene where Wade (played by Wilson Bethel) mistakes an arm for a penis while viewing an ultra sound during a doctor's visit. The exposition was hidden in the activity and the jokes!

What Is the Character's Obstacle?

Use the same two-character scene from the appendix. Examine it and determine answers to the following questions:
- What is Character A's obstacle?
- What is Character B's obstacle?

As in the exercise on intention, the obstacles of the two characters should be opposing or different. In the first season of *Glee*, all of the characters in the vocal group had the intention of being successful. But each character's obstacle to that goal was very different. Rachel didn't think she was good enough, Finn feared his football team would disapprove, and Kurt knew that being really good would also mean being truly authentic, which was difficult for a gay person in the process of coming out.

A scene might be short but critical in either plot or character development, so you might spend more time shooting it than a longer scene that accomplishes little. It's the director's job to prioritize the scenes in order to most effectively tell the story.

The more you direct, the easier it will be to find your own way of quickly rating the conflict and identifying the obstacle. It is vital that you do this task so that you know the level of importance that each scene has in the overall story, which in turn will affect how much time you dedicate to shooting the scene.

A scene might be short but critical in either plot or character development, so you might spend more time shooting it than a longer scene that accomplishes little. It's the director's job to prioritize the scenes in order to most effectively tell the story. This preliminary work of breaking down the scene for character will be the foundation of your shooting decisions.

From the Experts

Excerpt from *The Eight Characters of Comedy* by Scott Sedita[5]
A character without conflict is boring. In every storyline, characters must either *face* conflict as they pursue their Want, or *be* the conflict for another character's Want. If there are two characters in a scene, each of them will have a Want, and each of their Wants will be the other character's external obstacle [. . .].

You can also find conflict *within* your character, what I call *Internal Obstacles*. Internal obstacles are defined as those conflicting thoughts and emotions such as doubt, insecurity, embarrassment and fear, which try to self-sabotage the character from getting their Want. As an actor or writer, infusing this source of conflict within your character will make that character funnier and more complex [. . .].

Also, at one point or another, every character will be the source of conflict for another character, thus becoming the "voice of reason." . . . Desperation is the adrenaline that fuels the character as they pursue their Want. That desperation is derived from various places, such as the character's history and temperament . . . When a character incorporates this *desperation*, it is then complemented by other more positive characteristics such as *endearing, hopeful,* and *vulnerable.* It is what keeps the desperation funny, thus keeping a comedy from turning into a drama.

Insider Info

How Do You Interact with the Director?
As an actor, I am always hopeful and eager to work with a good director. When you have a creative partner to collaborate with and give you feedback, it not only enhances the work, but it can also save time and money! I am looking for someone to bounce ideas off of, help me get to the best choices, shape the scenes and the other actors work in a cohesive manner, offer suggestions, and push me to do better work! I try to figure out quickly what each director's strengths are and then look for ways to work to highlight those strengths. Each director has a particular style and unique vision and you want to take advantage of that. I love it when a director comes in with a plan but is also willing to improvise and explore and discover on the spot. It feels spontaneous and creative and keeps everyone on his or her toes!

What Do You Wish Directors Knew About Acting or Your Process?
I wish more directors weren't afraid to bring the actors into their process. We can do more than recite lines and hit marks! If a director can be open to suggestions and/or quick conversations about the goals of a scene or a character's intentions, that's a plus! I want you to make your day and get your shots, and if you take a moment to bring me into the loop about what you're hoping for, we can work through the day together. It helps me when a director can be clear and specific with notes, and when there's time, it's always nice for the actors to get a free take, such as, "We've got the scene, try one however you want." If you are coming onto a long-running show, be advised that the actors can be possessive of "their"

characters. No one has spent more time thinking about their characters than us. Tread lightly in terms of radical suggestions. You are trying to catch up to a speeding train and jump onto it while it's still going!

What Advice Would You Give a Director Who is Just Starting Out?
Being a guest director in hour television is a difficult and often thankless job! You want to show up and impress the producers, the cast, and the crew with your talent, creativity, and insight, but I strongly suggest that you check your ego at the door. Try to observe before you direct on a show. Get the vibe of the set. Have a plan, but be flexible. You're not going to get every shot or set up you want. Keep your eyes and ears open—you can learn from every person on the set, but not if your head is buried in your iPhone or laptop! *The director of photography (DP) is your best friend or your worst enemy!*

Scott Bakula
Actor NCIS New Orleans, Men of a Certain Age,
Star Trek, Enterprise, Quantum Leap

Vocabulary	iconic image	pipe (laying the pipe)
	imagery	stage directions
archetype	intention	title card
dialogue	label	vision board
exposition	obstacle	

NOTES

1 Reed Johnson. "The Unconquered Lions of 'Invictus.'" *Los Angeles Times*, December 6, 2009, sec. D.

2 Owen Gleiberman, "The Twilight Saga: Eclipse," *Entertainment Weekly*, September 16, 2010.

3 Deborah Landis. Hollywood Costume Exhibit, retrieved from http://ktla.com/2014/10/14/hollywood-costume-exhibit/KTLA. Posted 8:03 AM, October 14, 2014, video interview with Gayle Anderson and Nancy Cruz. Updated at 10:48AM, October 14, 2014, http://ktla.com/2014/10/14/hollywood-costume-exhibit/.

4 Jonathan Dorf. Email, June 15, 2015. Website last modified May 15, 2015, www.jonathandorf.com/freeplaywritingtips.

5 Scott Sedita. *The Eight Characters of Comedy, 2nd Edition*, Los Angeles: Atides Publishing, 2014, pp. 16–21.

Chapter 3

Casting

Any director will tell you that casting is a huge part of the job. John Frankenheimer, director of *The Manchurian Candidate* and *Birdman of Alcatraz*, went so far as to put a number on it. He said, "Casting is 65 percent of directing."[1] Why would he say that casting is more than half the job? It goes back to what we already talked about in the first two chapters: breaking down the script for story and character. You can't cast unless you know what you need. Once you do, you need the additional skill of being able to recognize talent and suitability.

If you can do all these things, you will have the right faces on the screen to help you tell the story in the best way possible. To continue our metaphor of the story being the journey and the characters' needs being the fuel for the trip, the cast members are the people who take the journey, and they have to serve your needs in two ways: as hired employees who can do the job and as artists who can bring their characters to life. Why mention both parts of the actor's job? It's the practical part of this book. For the same reason that we said a director has to be a leader with creative vision who understands and can execute the craft and who can physically and mentally handle the demands of the job, an actor must also be gifted in his craft *and* physically and mentally be able to handle the demands of the job.

> You can't cast unless you know what you need. Once you do, you need the additional skill of being able to recognize talent and suitability.

We've all heard stories about "difficult" actors. Director John Badham even entitled one of his excellent books *I'll Be In My Trailer*.[2] Mary Lou has a scale that she uses to decide whether she wants to work with an actor. The two things weighed are talent and degree of difficulty. The thing about her scale is that the degree-of-difficulty side must never outweigh the talent side. That being said, the degree of difficulty can be pretty darn high if the level of talent is too. Weighing the importance of getting our job done on time and on budget, it's important to take into consideration when casting how well you'll work with an actor. As the saying goes, "Fool me once, shame on you, fool me twice, shame on me."

Don't get the wrong idea, Bethany and Mary Lou *love* actors. Mary Lou is married to one, has a son who acts, and Mary Lou used to be an actress herself. Both Bethany and Mary Lou have the reputation of being an **actor's director**—a director who doesn't merely move the camera but also fine-tunes the performances because she understands the actor's process. In fact, for both directors, working with actors is the favorite part of their job.

As a television director, you will cast the series regulars (the actors that appear in each episode) only if you direct the **pilot**, or first episode, of a series. The exception to this is if a new character is added once the series has begun. A good example of this is Erica Durance, who played Lois Lane on the CW series *Smallville*, a series that began in 2001. She didn't join the cast until 2004. This series, which has enjoyed success for over a decade, began with iconic Clark Kent in high school. The show didn't add the *Daily Planet* characters until he got older. Greg L. Beeman, who directed the first episode (and was also a producer on the show) in which Lois appeared, was part of the casting process. Because Durance was going to be a new series regular, the network undoubtedly took a special interest in casting this role too.

CASTING ROLES OTHER THAN THE SERIES REGULARS

You may get to cast a character that will **recur**—appear in multiple episodes—usually for a specific story arc. Mary Lou did this many times over the course of the seven years she directed the show *Girlfriends*. More often than not, it was a new love interest: British actor Adrian Lester (*Primary Colors*, *Redband Society*, *Hustle*) recurred eight times over two seasons. Other actors stayed longer when their characters evolved from love interest to spouse: Jason Pace (*My Trip to the Dark Side*, *Friends with Better Lives*) played Dr. Todd Garrett for 30 episodes and married the Toni character played by Jill Marie Jones; Keesha Sharp (*Everybody Hates Chris*, *Are We There Yet?*) played Monica for 40 episodes and wed the William Dent character played by Reginald C. Hayes (*Hart of Dixie*).

The most common kind of role that you'll be casting as an episodic director is a guest star or **costar**. A guest star part is larger, works more days, and earns more money. The biggest guest stars are sometimes referred to as **top of show** because that is where their screen credit appears when the show airs, as opposed to the smaller roles that are listed in the end credits. Top of show also refers to the basic salary cap, as negotiated by the **Screen Actors Guild/American Federation of Television and Radio Artists (SAG/AFTRA)**. Salaries of well-known actors can break that top of show ceiling if the production company or network is willing to pay for it. The size of the role, and how much the actor is paid for it, often have to do with an actor's fame or **TVQ**, that is, TV quotient, or how well known they are. What an actor was paid for his last appearance is known as his **quote**. Obviously, an actor would prefer to meet or improve his quote, rather than negotiate something lower. In addition to negotiating salary, there is also the negotiable issue of **billing**, or credit. The top of show guest usually gets a **single card credit**, which is his name on the screen alone, again depending on the guest's TVQ. Other guest stars and costars get a **shared card**, that is, their name on the screen with others. Why do you need to know this?

All these things matter to an actor who is plotting the strategy by which he will advance his career. An established actor may love the role in a show, but if the part isn't big enough, or if he will not get the billing wanted, the actor may not take the part or even audition for it. Another option is for the actor to take the part, but remain uncredited.

Negotiations are the responsibility of the **casting director**, under the supervision of the producers. The casting director is the department head who uses her creative judgment in seeking out the pool of actors who will audition for the parts indicated in the script. You will have a **casting concept** meeting at the beginning of prep, along with the writer and/or the showrunner, to communicate initial thoughts about the characters: what type of physicality you might be looking for, including age range and ethnicity, and what type of "feel" is needed. The writer may indicate who she had in mind while writing the part, and at this point, it matters not if that actor is available— he will serve as an archetype, creating a focus for discussion between you and the casting director. It's sort of like doing the casting version of the vision board that we discussed in the last chapter.

> An established actor may love the role in a show, but if the part isn't big enough, or if he will not get the billing wanted, the actor may not take the part or even audition for it.

There are also other types of casting called **stunt casting**, which has nothing to do with stunts, and **crossover casting**, which has nothing to do with casting. The website *Celebuzz* defines stunt casting as, "Hiring a huge celebrity for a small part on your TV series in hopes that the guest appearance will jump start both your fortunes."[3] This definition is a rather jaded way of looking at it, even though commerce is always a consideration: the network is always looking for a guest star that is promotable. More often than not, though, the celeb is doing a favor for the lead on the series or the network and is happy to appear because they like the show or want a chance to work with the series lead. This was often the case when Tony Shalhoub would ask such fine actors as David Strathairn, Stanley Tucci, Tim Curry, and Gena Rowlands to appear on *Monk*. Because Tony is such a splendidly fine actor himself, he attracted other distinguished talent. On the first season finale of *black-ish*, the club owner/ruthless gangster was played by rapper/record producer Sean "Diddy" Combs. Mary Lou has also had the pleasure of working with basketball players Kareem Abdul Jabbar, Denis Rodman, attorney Johnny Cochran, and prima ballerina Gelsey Kirkland and rappers Common and Missy Elliot when they were stunt-cast. In every case, the networks took advantage of the celebrity's popularity to promote the show.

Crossover casting doesn't require any casting because it is a part given to an actor who is doing another show for that same network. Often the actor is playing the same character, but on the other show. *Grey's Anatomy* and *Private Practice* did this often: a doctor from the Seattle show would come down to L.A. in the story line or vice versa. It cross-promotes both shows and makes both episodes "event" television, which will hopefully draw a bigger audience.

Here is the reality of television: You are not the only person who is making this casting decision, because the ultimate bosses (those who provide the money) get the final vote. The **Directors Guild of America (DGA)** negotiates creative rights to guarantee that you are part of the casting process, so you should participate to the furthest extent possible, which helps preserve the right for every future director while claiming it for yourself.

The Director's Guild of America (DGA) negotiates creative rights to guarantee that you are part of the casting process, so you should participate to the furthest extent possible, which helps preserve the right for every future director while claiming it for yourself.

As a freelance director, you will be blending with the production team, which probably already has a way of working. Don't wait for the casting director to call your assistant director (AD) to tell you when the first casting session is scheduled. Call the casting director and introduce yourself. You can chat about previous guest stars cast on the show. The casting director will be flattered that you bothered to notice and will know you value the casting director's work. Because the casting department gets the script sooner than other departments (sometimes even before the director), you can tell them how you see a part and, conversely, pick their brains to find out if the writer or producers have suggested to them any information about how they see the roles to be cast.

THE PROCESS OF CASTING AND MAKING THE ACTORS' DEALS

Your job of casting will start on paper, especially with the top of the show guest stars or stunt casting. The casting director will do a substantial amount of work to generate lists of actors whom you might want to consider for the role. These lists often include the name of the actor's talent agent, availability, and whether the actor is willing to audition or will consider an **offer only**. Generating such a list is a huge amount of work. Always be appreciative and acknowledge the work and creativity that went into generating the casting availability lists.

If you want the casting department to bring in specific actors you know, give them a list with adequate time to set up an audition. If the casting department is not familiar with an actor's work, they might set up a **preread**, or preliminary audition, at which only the casting director, not the director or the producers, is present. Because cameras are so readily available to actors, casting directors will often watch **self-taped auditions** sent to them from actors who don't have agents or couldn't make it to a casting session.

Casting is the first time you come into contact with the actor. The casting session you attend, scheduled by the casting director or one of her assistants, may be the first, second, or third time that the actor has come to audition for this role. More established actors come straight to the **producer session**, the audition that you first attend, so called because in addition to you, there will also be a producer present—often the writer of the episode—or a writing producer who oversees casting. The executive producer or showrunner, often the show's creator, might also be present at casting. The star of the show— especially if he is an executive producer—may also come to casting and choose to read with the actors if the shooting schedule permits.

Actors are scheduled in timed intervals. They come into the room and are introduced by the casting director. As you greet them, you are handed their picture and resume. There may be time for small talk, but more often than not, it is straight to the job of auditioning. Sometimes the audition will be taped, but not always. The audition is almost always one actor reading the role for which they are auditioning and the casting director reading all the other characters in the scene.

Always be appreciative and acknowledge the work and creativity that went into generating the casting availability lists.

After the actor finishes reading, he thanks you and leaves, unless you want to see him read the scene(s) again with an acting **adjustment** that you give. You should do this only when you are seriously interested in an actor. There simply isn't enough time to do it for every actor. For example, you may think the actor looks perfect for the part, but did not agree with his performance choices. Tell him what you want instead, and see if he can deliver that. The best way to communicate this change (adjustment) to the actor is to refer to either their intention or their obstacle: "I'd like to see you play the obstacle [like being afraid to speak up to an authority figure, let's say] more strongly." You don't have to get into a big discussion or give the whole **backstory**. Give the actor something specific to do, and then ask if you've made yourself clear. If not, the actor will ask a question, and you can clarify your request. And then the actor takes a deep breath, makes the internal calibration, and reads the scene again. Thank him, compliment him if you can do it honestly ("Good adjustment!"), and smile at him with the empathy you hold for his courage in putting himself before you for judgment.

After the actor has left the room, you will either discuss the audition or wait until you've seen every actor that has come in for that role being auditioned that day. In deference to his responsibility for telling the story, the director states his preferences first, and then the discussion begins. More often than not, there is a consensus among those attending the session about who should get the part. Or if there isn't, the folks in the room may review the taped auditions together to reach consensus. You may see a detail in an actor's audition while reviewing a taped audition that you did not see while you were in the room watching the actor live. After reviewing the tape, there may be an embarrassment of riches and there are too many actors who will do the part ably. Or, more problematic, you haven't seen anyone who is right for the part and the casting director has to schedule another session. If another session is necessary, specifically talk about why the people you saw were not right. It may be that there is a specific moment that none of the actors filled or fleshed out. It may be something as simple as that you conceived the role as younger or older than the actors you've already seen. The casting director can also serve as a coach to the next batch of actors who come in to audition and guide them to the performance you want. At the very least, the casting director can give feedback to the actor's agent about his client's audition.

A personal session is always better than a recorded one for you to pick exactly the right actor for the part.

For smaller roles, especially **under 5s** (roles with five lines or fewer), you may receive a DVD of a casting session that you did not attend or a link to a casting website where the taped auditions are uploaded. This type of review is done to avoid wasting your time during prep. (But if you are not overloaded in prep, you should express your preference for holding a casting session, during which you can give adjustments if needed. A personal session is always better than a recorded one for you to pick exactly the right actor for the part.) You should look at the link as soon as time allows and inform the casting director of your choices. Also tell her if you have a second or even third choice based on what you've seen. If you don't have a strong feeling and all the actors who read were equally qualified for the job, remember that the casting director is part of your team and defer to her opinion about who should be cast. There may be an extenuating circumstance that might influence whom she suggests casting in a role. Casting directors are people who have friends or may want to help out an actor who is struggling to earn the last few hundred dollars that qualify the actor for health insurance for his family.

If a casting director asks you to see an actor again whom you've already seen (or don't particularly visualize in the role), by all means, do so. The casting director is probably more familiar with that actor's work, just because it's her job to know the talent pool. Acting is hard. It takes talent, craft, intelligence, and vulnerability. The skill set it takes to audition is not necessarily the same skill set it takes to do the job.

Trust that your casting director understands the actors' craft as well as the business side of her job. If the casting director sees potential in an actor whom you didn't think performed well in the casting session, be open to looking at that actor with the additional information the casting director has to offer. That actor may be the perfect person for the role and it may be something as simple as the actor was having a bad day or something as big as that actor is out of rehab and is trying to resurrect his career and was just nervous. It has happened. We all know those stories.

> *Acting is hard. It takes talent, craft, intelligence, and vulnerability. The skill set it takes to audition is not necessarily the same skill set it takes to do the job.*

FIGHTING FOR YOUR CASTING CHOICES

You may not like an actor whom the executive producer or the network really wants in a role. How do you deal with this issue, which may be the first of many political situations that you will have to navigate? We talk more about this is in Section Four of this book. If you think you can sway their thinking at all, we suggest that you use your position as director to openly discuss their idea—not because it is a bad choice, but because you have a better one. Do it carefully.

Compliment the other's idea, but be more enthusiastic about somebody else on the list. For example, you may reference a particular story point or moment because of your familiarity with the script and then suggest how you see another actor (or type of actor, usually referring to age or ethnicity), making that moment work better. Remember that disagreement probably has nothing to do with whether their choice of actor is talented. It's about appropriateness and you telling the story. Sometimes your passion may sell it, sometimes not. If you can enlist the help of the showrunner and have a united front, you might say, "We just don't see the audience believing him/her doing this." Sometimes time and money will be your friend, when the casting department isn't able to **make a deal** and agree on dates or terms with someone you don't want in the role.

LEARNING BY WATCHING

If you don't have much experience in casting, there are a couple things that you can do. First, try to sit in on a casting session for something you are not directing. If you get this opportunity, it is important to not share your opinion unless asked. Just be a fly on the wall. You will learn a lot by just watching. What you can do, though, is ask whether you can read the script. Then you will have the benefit of knowing the story and exploring how you would have cast it. But don't be offended if you are not allowed to see the script because many shows guard the written word or sharing information about upcoming storylines like a Brink's truck full of cash . . . and to a network, their product is that valuable. On *The Sopranos*, even recurring characters did not get the whole script—only the pages for the scenes they were in. If you don't read the script, you can often piece together information about the story from the different scenes you see in the audition, especially if a lot of characters are being cast.

LEARNING BY FANTASY CASTING

The second thing you can do is practice casting for a fantasy project. We're not talking about fantasy as a genre, just any project that isn't really going to happen. Here's an exercise you can do over and over again.

Casting a Novel

Use any novel that you have recently read. Even better, read a novel that you know is going to be made into a movie but hasn't been cast yet. Cast the main characters by listing an actor's name next to the character's name. Because this is a fantasy project, you can use actors who are alive or dead. You can even cast actors at any age in their career. For example, cast Robert Redford from *Three Days of the Condor* or Dakota Fanning from Steven Spielberg's sci-fi masterpiece *Taken*. You can do this exercise with one or two results in mind: familiarity or suitability. If familiarity is your goal, you will get practice casting and learn the names of actors whom you haven't known before. If suitability is your goal, you will get the experience of selecting the perfect talent to tell the story that so far you've only read on paper. Either are great skills to practice and important to your development as a director.

TRAPS TO AVOID

One thing we want to caution about casting: don't fall into the trap of going for a "look," rather than casting a better actor. In our experience, it is always safer to cast a better actor in a role than someone who simply looks right for the part.

There are a couple reasons for this. First, with a good actor, you always have credibility: your audience will believe him in the role because that is what good acting is all about—"acting as if." If your actor becomes the character and breathes life into the role he is playing, the audience will accept him, too. The added benefit is that you have the chance to break a stereotype in the process.

> In our experience, it is always safer to cast a better actor in a role than someone who simply looks right for the part.

For example, not all bullies are big; not all dumb girls are blond. Bethany directed an episode of *The Cleaner* in which the main guest star part was a young man, in the process of becoming a woman, who had a drug addiction and worked as a cheap prostitute. The producers wanted a smaller-boned actor so that the transgender aspect would be more believable. The best actor for the part, however, was over six feet tall and well-muscled. But Bethany felt that he was the only actor who auditioned that could bring the severe internal conflicts of the character to life. So she fought for Reiley McClendon and assured the producers that she'd make it work. While casting the extras who were portraying prostitutes on the street corner in physical proximity to Reiley, she cast women who were exceptionally tall and added to that height by putting them in four-inch heels. So the tall actor whose character was masquerading as a woman did not look out of place. And he was brilliant.

You might also enter a casting session with no preconceived ideas about a role and find an actor who brings that character to life for you. The prolific Steven Bochco, who created *NYPD Blue, LA Law, and Hill Street Blues*, said "Casting is sort of like looking at paintings. You don't know what you'll like, but you recognize it when you see it."[4] Bethany was casting a TV movie years ago, looking for the antagonist in a women's prison story called *Locked Up: A Mother's Rage*. Multiple actresses had read for the part over many days, and no one seemed right, until a young and unknown Angela Bassett (*What's Love Got to Do with It, How Stella Got Her Groove Back*) came in and just nailed it. As the door closed behind Angela, Bethany jumped up and said, "That's it! She's it! Now I can make this movie!"

THE MAGIC OF CASTING

There is so much about casting that is intuitive: that feeling in the gut, the hairs that stand up on your arms, the prickle on the back of your neck. You know it when you see it. The actor makes you believe that he inhabits the part: that he *is* the character.

But sometimes there is an actor who is close to being perfect in the audition. Where your skill comes into play is knowing whether you can take the raw material that the actor presents and form it into the character you're looking for. Can you speak the simple, perfect words that provide the key to making a good actor great? You'll find out more about how to do that in Chapter 10. But never forget where the magic starts, as we've discussed in these first three chapters. As director Peter Weir (*Dead Poets Society, Master and Commander*) said, "If you've cast the picture right and you don't have script problems—those are the two essentials—then on the day you have this little piece of life in the story you're telling and anything can happen."[5]

There is a wonderful secondary benefit to casting. You find out who the best actor is for the part, but you also find out more about the story by watching gifted actors bring their interpretations of the role to the casting session. The actors' readings help the director discover the strengths and weaknesses of material (after you've listened to it twenty times, you can usually put your finger on the problem) and clarify hazy notions of

> There is so much about casting that is intuitive: that feeling in the gut, the hairs that stand up on your arms, the prickle on the back of your neck. You know it when you see it. The actor makes you believe that he inhabits the part: that he is the character.

intention and obstacle. Plus, it's fun. It's a place to play, to experiment, to hone in on your interpretation of the script as you give adjustments to actors. You see what works and what doesn't. It's a crucial part of prep, and an amazing gift to the director!

From the Experts

Excerpt from *The Audition Bible* by Holly Powell
Authors' note: Holly Powell wrote this book for actors, but we think her advice to them is helpful for directors to know.
There are two circumstances in which you will have a camera in the audition room:

- You will be going "on tape for producers," so the casting director will record your audition on-camera and send it to the director and producers for viewing.
- The producers will be "live" in the room, with the camera there as a fly on the wall. Your recorded audition will be watched only if they liked you enough to see how you look on-camera.

More and more casting directors are recording actors' auditions on-camera and sending them off to the director and producers. Many productions are shooting away from Los Angeles now, and technology has advanced to the point where your audition can be viewed within moments wherever in the world the production happens to be shooting.

Having a camera in the room during a producer/callback session is almost a given in today's audition world, but in this case the camera functions more like a fly on the wall, recording the entire day of auditions so producers can review them at the end of the day to jog their memory. If there is a camera in the room, it will be a digital camera with the microphone embedded in the camera. This is not the same thing as a film camera, which is used during actual filming. If your volume is too low, the microphone in the camera may fail to adequately pick up the sound of your voice and instead by overwhelmed by the voice of the reader, who'll be sitting closer to the camera.

Understand that you need to project enough so that the microphone in the camera will pick up your voice. It comes down simply to energy. Don't worry; you won't be overacting . . . unless, of course, you forget the tone of the piece and start playing to the room as if you were in a theater. It's all about getting the right balance.

Self-taping for projects is more common in today's audition world. The casting director may ask an actor to self-tape if they aren't familiar with the actor's work or if the actor lives far from where the project is casting.

All you need is a decent camera (or even a smartphone), a tripod, a few good lights, and a solid colored wall as a background. Recruit a good reader and make sure you frame yourself close, just below the shoulders. When you state your name, it's a good idea to get a long shot of yourself so they can see your full body.

Being prepared, knowledgeable, and comfortable when there is a camera in the room is the most important audition skill the professional actor must perfect.[6]

From the Experts

Excerpt from *Gardner's Guide to Writing and Producing Television* by Dee LaDuke and Mark Alton Brown. [7]

Authors' note: Dee and Mark wrote this book for writers, but we think their advice to them is helpful for directors to know.

Pitfalls of Casting

Casting sessions are long and arduous. You will cast lead roles before you cast recurring roles, so you may be hearing the same character's lines over and over for hours day after day. Eventually, you stop hearing. This is good in an odd way. You will bolt up and take notice of the extraordinary actor who makes the material sound fresh again. But you may miss a perfectly good actor who was passed over because you could not bear to hear your own writing one more time. Create a checklist for each actor you see. If they have some sparkle or look, if they have an easy way with patter or if they are engaging, even if they aren't getting the character, they may deserve a call back. You are free to give them notes and send them out of the room to think about the role in a new way. You are within your rights to make performance requests and see how actors respond to adjustments. Because the material is fresh the first few auditions will have an advantage and may not seem as strong in the callback after you've heard a hundred actors say the lines.

Another pitfall of casting is being locked into an image of a character. Height, weight, race, gender, coloring, and looks are, or can be, surface features. In television be open to a character being a different "look" or of a race or even opposite gender beyond your first imagining.

Beware of actors who paraphrase and speak their subtext. You want disciplined actors who can use words to build their characters. We have always been open to actors who throw in a new joke and have sometimes used them. But actors who constantly rewrite the dialogue you have written should raise a red flag. First, they don't have the sense to grasp they are insulting the author and executive producer. Second, they think their ideas are better than yours and are not, because of that, team players.

Once an actor takes on a role it becomes collaboration between you as the character writer and the actor who now embodies and takes ownership of the character. You must listen to their concerns and honor their input. You should know in advance if the vision you have in mind for a character is one an actor is going to be willing to undertake. Most actors are so eager to have a role they will say yes to everything at first, so it behooves you to be very clear about your vision and the character's development. There are conservative actors who will not want to spout liberal politics or actors who will not want their character to appear "unrefined." And there are actors who feel that because they would not do something irrational, their character would not either.

The long and short of casting is this, if you cast well, chances are good you will have a great pilot. It pays to spend as much time as you have becoming familiar with the actors you cast.

Insider Info

How Do You Interact with the Director?

If we're able to be in touch with our director before our first casting session, we like to have a meeting or a phone call to discuss specific qualities or characteristics we should be looking for in that episode's cast beyond the obvious. But sometimes we're interacting with the director for the first time at that episode's casting session. By the time we have the director in our room, we've narrowed down all of the submissions and all of our ideas for each role, and are presenting him or her with a select few actors. We've done a lot of leg work, so at this point we hand the reins over to that episode's director, and let them more or less run the session; directing actors, choosing which scenes to hear and so on. After the session, we work with them to make a final decision as to who should be our choice for each role.

What Do You Want Directors to Know about Casting?

The casting process is interactive. My favorite directors are those who know how to communicate with actors. If you don't give an actor an opportunity to adjust their performance, you may never know if they are right for the role.

What is Your Advice to Young Directors Who Are Just Starting Out?

If I were a young director who was just starting out, I would jump in and take an acting class. I think having just a glimpse at the actors' perspective can help the director understand what an actor requires to give their best performance.

Liz Martinez-Nelson
Casting Director,
Hart of Dixie, 90210, Vampire Diaries

Insider Info

How Do You Interact with the Director?

Television is the writer/producer's medium when it comes to casting. Depending on the project and the director, I find most of the input I receive is from the showrunner (producer/writer of the show) rather than the director, whether I'm casting a half-hour show, one-hour show, or a pilot.

The director is always invited to the casting sessions, but it is usually at the producer's availability. I have had directors call or email with ideas for casting, which I will incorporate into a discussion with the showrunner or into the casting session.

What Do You Wish Directors Knew About Casting?

When a director is at a casting session, I find that the more prepared they are with the script, the more their voice is heard as far as their ideas for the casting. It is my job as the casting director to bring in actors that fit the role and to think outside the box of a casting choice that the writer may not have thought of. The more knowledge the director has of the script, the more understanding he or she has as to where the character should go. The producer will ask your opinion. Usually, you are of like minds, but if you're not, you need to be prepared to explain why you think it should go one way and be prepared if they choose to go another.

What Advice Would You Give a Director Who is Just Starting Out?
I have noticed that there are usually two kinds of directors. One kind is the director that is prepared with the shots, editing, and making the episode look great—all technique. The other kind is the director that does all of the first kind, but also knows how to speak to the actor about what the scene may need from his or her character. When a director knows how to speak to the actor, it makes all the difference in the world to the project. Directors should take acting classes, directing classes with actors—anything that will help them understand how to help an actor get what you are looking for within a scene and the best words to help them get there.

Suzanne Goddard-Smythe
Casting Director
K.C. Undercover, School of Rock, Warehouse 13, The Game

Vocabulary

actor's director
adjustment
American Federation of Television and Radio Artists (AFTRA)
backstory
billing
casting concept

casting director
costar
crossover casting
Directors Guild of America (DGA)
make a deal
offer only
pilot
preread
producer session
quote

recur
Screen Actors Guild (SAG)
self-taped auditions
shared card credit
single card credit
stunt casting
top of show
TV quotient (TVQ)
under 5s

NOTES

1　Jerry Roberts. "John Frankenheimer and the Playing of *Reindeer Games*," *DGA Monthly*, 24, March 2000.
2　John Badham. *I'll Be in My Trailer*. Studio City: Michael Wiese Productions, 2006.
3　The Top Ten Television Stunt Casting Stints, *Celebuzz*, July 26, 2008.
4　Steven Bochco Quotes, Brainy Quotes, retrieved May 1, 2011, from www.brainyquote.com/quotes/authors/s/steven_bochco.html.
5　Terrence Rafferty. "Uncommon Man," *DGA Quarterly*, Summer 2010, pp. 30–37.
6　Holly Powell. *The Audition Bible*. Los Angeles: Tavin Press, 2014, pp. 166–168.
7　Dee LaDuke and Mark Alton Brown. *Gardner's Guide to Writing and Producing Television*. New York: GCC Publishing, 2007, pp. 137–139.

Chapter 4

Production Design

Back when most productions were shot on film, we knew that a camera recorded what was transpiring in front of it at a rate of 24 frames per second. And we could imagine that each of those frames was a literal picture: a moment in time that was frozen in a little box. And everything in that box— except the actors—was an element of the production design. Although now most "films" are shot digitally (and are thus are sadly lacking in frames), the concept remains the same. Everything within the "frame" that is not human is part of the **production design**.

The production design helps tell the story. The color of the walls, the style of the furniture, the specificity of the props, the cut of the costumes—each choice helps the director clearly communicate the story that he is trying to tell. Although there are many, many people to assist the director in making those choices, ultimately it is the director's responsibility alone. Just as President Harry Truman said, "The buck stops here," so it does with the director, who is the president of the production. Therefore, in order to be best prepared to make such major (and minor) decisions, it is helpful to have gained some background in art history, to have traveled and navigated different cultures, and to have read widely. Having done so gives the director a platform of learning that inspires self-confidence and perspective. It's simplistic but true: if you've walked the streets of Barcelona (or Beijing, or Boston, or wherever your story takes place), you'll have a different point of view from someone who has merely

> The job of the director is to have a point of view—a creative vision that pulls every department together to create a cohesive story.

read about it. The job of the director is to have a point of view—a creative vision that pulls every department together to create a cohesive story. So the director ideally comes to the project with both a varied personal background and specific research regarding the script.

COLLABORATING CREATIVELY WITH DEPARTMENT HEADS

If the project is an episode of a television show, all the **department heads** (leaders of each division) will have already been hired and will remain consistent through the season of production. However, if you are making a movie (feature or TV) or pilot, it is the job of the director (with the producer) to interview and hire the department heads, who will supervise their particular area of expertise and help the director bring a script to life. The critical factors in hiring people are finding someone who:

- Shares the director's sensibilities.
- Brings inspiration and enthusiasm, contributing new and original ideas.
- Can communicate those new ideas clearly.
- Knows they are part of a team, not an independent voice.
- Can work within the budget allowed.

The production designer is a particularly eminent hire because that person supervises several departments and is a pivotal link between the ideas in the director's head and their realization on film, tape, or digital recording.

Making a film is a very creative and therefore emotional experience. People give: they give their ideas, their loyalty, their time, and their effort. They do so in the interest of making the best project. And there will be differences of opinion that may lead to interpersonal disasters. It is crucial for the director and producer to find department heads who "fit": who can work together with this staff and crew for an extended period of time in an environment, which—due to budget and deadline pressures—can be stressful.

The **production designer** is a particularly eminent hire because that person supervises several departments and is a pivotal link between the ideas in the director's head and their realization on film, tape, or digital recording.

COMMUNICATING WELL IN CONCEPT MEETING

Once everyone has been hired, there is a **concept meeting**. All of the department heads—along with the producer, the writer, and the director— gather to discuss the script and receive preliminary information from the director about the approach that will be taken. Let's say that you are directing a family drama that takes place in London during the Blitz in 1940. At that first concept meeting, your staff and crew will want answers—direction—from you. What does the set look like? How much money and status does the family have? Is the environment one of positive energy or negative? What kind of transportation do they use? How do they dress? What set pieces or props are needed to help tell the story? How do you want the actors to look in costume, makeup, and hair? What is the overall color palette? In order to provide some answers, the director will have done some research.

As we all know, people in Paris live differently from people in Pittsburgh. And people in 1940 (or 1440, or 2140) live in a different environment from the one we live in today. So you will have investigated by looking at source material from the time and place. Thank goodness for the Internet! But don't forget, in addition to those resources, to take advantage of what exists not only in virtual reality but in reality itself. Visit relevant places. Go to museums. Interview experts. Start to forge pictures in your head of what your film or TV show will look like.

Accumulate **visual aids** so that you can illustrate your points. This activity is necessary because it's all **subjective**. One person's idea of "red" is different from another's. The director's vision of "poor" might be very different from the prop master's. So the director will show pictures and say, "This is the kind of [chair, sheep, car, house] that I am thinking about." And keep in mind that your department heads will have done their research, too. They will come with files, with pictures, with layout boards covered in fabric swatches and drawings. Everyone wants to contribute creatively by providing the most specific and wonderful fulfillment of the director's requests. So it's incumbent upon the director to have put some thought and work into the script before bringing the department heads on board.

On day one of your prep of this hypothetical WWII film, you'll be asked: red lipstick or coral? Car, bicycle, subway, or walking? Homemade pine furniture or antique Chippendale? Chicken on the dinner table or beef stew? Down and dirty brawl or stylized fight? A thousand extras or isolation? Moody lighting or sunlight? At that first concept meeting, you may not yet have all the answers, and it's okay to say that. You can say, "I'll have more specific information about that later, but for now, the general direction we're heading in is . . ." Nevertheless, at the very beginning of prep, the director provides literal direction; that is, in which direction in the universe of choices do you want your department heads to go?

At the very beginning of prep, the director provides literal direction; that is, in which direction in the universe of choices do you want your department heads to go?

For most productions, the primary departments relating to production design are: art, props, costumes, **makeup/hair**, and **transportation**. Other departments that may be a part of a production, depending on the script, are visual effects, special effects, choreography, and stunts. (Animals generally fall into the props department.) All of these departments execute the director's requests to the best of their ability, and their work takes place primarily in the preproduction stage, unlike the production stage, in which departments like **camera**, electric, and grips come to the forefront. But it all begins and ends with the director, who initiates and/or approves every single choice that appears in every frame of the production. From hairstyle to architecture, choreography, and colors, it's your choice. Whether you have a multimillion-dollar budget or you're making a short film on your smart phone on the weekend, it's all your choice. And here we're talking about production choices. In postproduction, you will continue to make choices in sound and music that also help you tell the story.

Scripts very seldom offer details of production design; nor should they. Writers use their vivid imaginations to create the story and the characters and no doubt "see" the film in their heads, but if a writer were to dictate the myriad details of production design, they would be closer to writing a book than a script. It is up to the director, with the production designer's input and effort, to visualize the film's environments and make them become the stage upon which the characters come to life.

The director's choices illuminate the characters' exterior lives and, more important, their interior lives. The production design lends a feeling that the audience picks up. Are the characters rich or poor? Happy or sad? Sick or well? Determined or depleted? Loving or hateful? Determining the answers to these kinds of questions tells the director (and by extension, the production design team) how to proceed. You did this work already when you broke down the script for story and character. Now you just need to share that information with your production designer.

So let's go back to the hypothetical London Blitz story. We know that architecturally, it's necessary to be accurate to the period. But the housing of the characters could be relatively new, or (as was the case in much of London then) the building(s) could be hundreds of years old.

Which choice tells more about the mental and physical state of the characters? The director tells the production designer what his concept is, and together they flesh out the basic idea. Generally, after a lot of discussion ("I like this, but I'm not sure about this; could you give me more of this?"), a set design is decided upon.

> The director's choices illuminate the characters' exterior lives and, more important, their interior lives.

Both the director and the production designer speak the same language when discussing the concepts that are fundamental to this process.

THREE KEY ELEMENTS TO PRODUCTION DESIGN

Let's go over the three elements of choice in production design that are relevant to all departments. They are:

- Style
- Color
- Impact.

When we talk about "style," we're referring to incorporating time or period specificity with artistic design choices. Style can be as big as creating a whole world (*Avatar*) or as small as two chairs and a table in a stark police interrogation room.

Basically, a film or television show creates an environment in which the characters interact, and that environment helps to inform the story. So the job of the production design in terms of style is to effectively "set the stage" for the story.

The production designer is the director's right hand in creating the environment of the story. The production designer has an art and architecture background, enabling him to take ideas and artistic concepts and shape them into a concrete reality.

The director discusses her ideas, and the production designer incorporates those ideas into set design, as well as offering his own artistic contributions. The designer then presents drawings, computer or physical models, and blueprints (also called a **floor plan**) as the preproduction process continues in order to hone in on the specific style that the director is proposing.

The production designer is the director's right hand in creating the environment of the story. The production designer has an art and architecture background, enabling him to take ideas and artistic concepts and shape them into a concrete reality.

So the first element of production design is style. The second is color. And this choice has an amazing impact on the storytelling. Color elicits an emotional response, universally interpreted. You could be watching a foreign language film, but if a sexy young woman enters the story wearing a bright red dress, you instinctively know that she's trouble. Conversely, a young woman entering the story in a demure white dress is likely to be an innocent (or the director wants the audience to perceive her that way). Almost any scene has more energy when the environment's color is heightened, and when

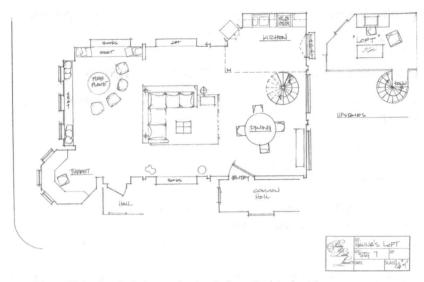

FIGURE 4.1 Floor plan depicting production designer Fred Andrews' new permanent set on the Warner Brothers/ABC Family show *Pretty Little Liars*, with input from producers and the director.

FIGURE 4.2 The final version, with set decoration by William DeBiasio.

a director wants to tell a story of deprivation, the lack of color is important. Think of the movies *The Devil Wears Prada* and *Out of Africa*. In the first film, the rich saturation of color is essential to illustrate the vibrant, busy, intense world of high fashion in New York and Paris. Conversely, the muted savannah-like palette of Africa gives an open, airy, languid feel to illustrate the wide extent of this beautiful and inviting—yet not widely explored—continent.

Part of the director's storytelling includes color-coding the story. This element filters throughout the production, including the lighting design, which you will discuss with your **director of photography** (**DP**). As a generalization, blue light is moody and cool, warm light (orange-red) is happy and sensuous. Blue light is for night; warm light for day. Blue light is for danger and emotionally constricted characters. Warm light is for love and laughter. And of course there are many settings between these opposite ends of the lighting scale. We discuss many more specific lighting aspects in Chapter 12, but for now, we're talking about how color influences story.

Color influences the environment of the story, too. Bethany learned this in Toronto when she was directing a Danielle Steel book adaptation as a TV movie. The story was about the emotional turbulence of an upscale family. The homeowner of a practical location had made specific decorating choices that served the script perfectly. The foyer floor was covered in a dramatic checkerboard pattern of black and white. Immediately to the right was the living room, where the walls were a vibrant yellow. Just to the left was the dining room, painted a deep and inviting red. The scenes that took place in that house were much better with those color choices than if the walls had been drab. If the story had been about turbulence between characters in a mental institution, then the walls would probably be white to signal to the audience that the environment was lacking emotion. Just a coat of paint can contribute immensely to the feeling of a scene.

According to the book *Signs and Symbols*, these are some of the attributes of colors:

red: fire, war, love, passion, blood
orange: renunciation, splendor, fidelity
yellow: sun, treachery, homecoming
green: nature, youth, fertility, jealousy
blue: divinity, naivety, calm
purple: imperial or priestly power, wealth
pink: femininity, gay pride
black: evil, mourning, age, death
white: surrender, innocence, cowardice, holiness.[1]

Everything within the "frame" has color or lack of it. There is immense opportunity here for a director to subtly or grandly influence audience perception by choosing colors that elicit emotional response. And everything within that frame is chosen: there is nothing that magically appears without thought and effort, although it may seem that way when watching a movie or a TV show. In fact, if the choices fit seamlessly into the story, enabling the audience to go on the journey with the characters without having anything pierce the veil of believability, then the director has done the job well.

That brings us to the third element of production design: impact. And this is a tricky one, because sometimes you want to have everything blend in, and sometimes you want an element to stand out. That is part of the storytelling. We said at the beginning of this chapter that the essential part of production design is to remain true to the period and environment of the story.

> *There is nothing that magically appears without thought and effort, although it may seem that way when watching a movie or a TV show. In fact, if the choices fit seamlessly into the story, enabling the audience to go on the journey with the characters without having anything pierce the veil of believability, then the director has done the job well.*

That is true 99 percent of the time. From the architecture to the interior design, from the hairstyles to the cars—everything is doing its part to help tell the story. But it's a continuum of choices—from a one to a ten, the yin and the yang, the bold and the whisper. And everything in between.

Think of Tim Burton's *Alice in Wonderland*. There is absolutely no choice in that movie that is timid. The environment of the story *is* the story, because Alice fell down a hole into a subjective reality. The production designer of that movie (Robert Stromberg) couldn't just go to IKEA and pick up a few things for the set. Following Burton's lead, he had to design and model and form and create every single element, from the dishes on the table at the Mad Hatter's Tea Party to the watch that the White Rabbit carried. Each of the choices was all high-impact, meant to be observed, meant to create an atmosphere of wonder, meant to exaggerate the realistic world.

On a quieter note, consider the television comedy *Modern Family*. There are three (related) families as characters, and each family has a distinct environment. The richest (patriarch) has a modern home of glass and steel. The gay couple has a cozy Spanish bungalow. And the typical American family (a couple with three children) has a traditional home. Within each of these environments, there are thousands of elements that have been chosen to depict the life of those characters, with varying degrees of impact. Which kind of sofa does each family have? Beds? Decorating touches? Here the impact of the production design is subtle, with nothing standing out but everything fitting in.

The look of a television series is usually established in the pilot and then it evolves as the story and characters evolve during the course of the episodes. So Jason Winer (director) and Richard Berg (production designer) of the pilot of *Modern Family* created the template with input from the producers, the studio, and the network. And all of those voices must be considered, especially the ones who are paying for it (the network.) Money talks, and paychecks are at stake. The executives at a network (broadcast, cable, or web) are buying a property that has been pitched to them as having certain qualities. It is therefore the responsibility of the director to see that those qualities are present in the finished product.

> *Money talks, and paychecks are at stake. The executives at a network (broadcast, cable, or web) are buying a property that has been pitched to them as having certain qualities. It is therefore the responsibility of the director to see that those qualities are present in the finished product.*

So if a network bought "a stylistic family drama set against the high-stakes world of Las Vegas," then all of those elements should be there: style, family, drama, high stakes, Vegas. And everything the director chooses as part of the production design should complement that concept. Often, the first choice the director will confront is, "Where exactly will we shoot this story?"

SHOOTING ON A SOUNDSTAGE OR GOING ON LOCATION?

The initial two choices that a director has regarding the set(s) are to build a **set** or shoot on a practical **location**. We talk more about locations in Chapter 5, but the basic factors as to which way a production goes include the following:

- How much of the script takes place in a specific set? If it's a lot (more than ten pages), it's likely that building a set would provide the director with the most options and keep a crew located in one place, which is less expensive generally than going to a location for a long period.
- What is the budget for the production? It requires a decent budget to rent stage space, hire a construction crew, and create a set from scratch. It might be cheaper to shoot on a practical location (but see the following factor).
- Can you shoot what you need in a practical location, where the walls don't move, the windows might not open, it might be a noisy environment, and there is limited access? Does the practical location provide everything you need to tell the story, or is compromise required? (Compromise is not always a bad thing, especially in television. It sometimes forces a director to think more creatively.)

- How much stage space and time does the art department have to build and then **strike** the set? If the company is shooting on the same stage where you want to build the set, that would be disruptive (pounding hammers and recording dialogue don't mix) and therefore unlikely to happen. Similarly, when it's time to take down the set, the company has to be shooting somewhere else.

This decision will be made in concert with the producing team because ultimately, this choice balances creative needs against financial ones. This is otherwise known wryly as **art vs. commerce**. It is the daily internal dilemma of every director: you always want more, in every possible way, to tell your story. But more of anything will undoubtedly mean that it costs more, too.

Do you have a budget that will support steak choices, or are we talking tuna in a can? And there is also the balancing aspect of meeting the needs of all the scenes in the script. If the script has 20 different places in which the story takes place, it's likely that some of those places will be sets and some will be practical locations. (The exception in television is for pilots or television movies, which are **one-offs**, that is, the producing team will not want to spend money to build sets for a show that stands alone without further installments. For a pilot or TV movie, a director will probably be required to shoot the entire script in practical locations.) For a feature film or a television series, sets will be built. And the director and the production designer, together with the producer, will decide which scenes require building sets and which will be shot on location. Whichever is chosen, further work must be done.

> It is the daily internal dilemma of every director: you always want more, in every possible way, to tell your story. But more of anything will undoubtedly mean that it costs more, too.

DECORATING THE SET AND SELECTING THE PROPS

Rarely does a director pick a location and deem it perfect as it is. There may be things that need to be added or subtracted, requiring construction and/or painting. A location might be almost perfect, except for (let's say) the handicap ramp that needs to be added or the wall that needs to be torn down. Under the supervision of the production designer and the **art director**, those things would be addressed. (The art director assists the production designer primarily with creating the blueprints and administrating the department.) And then there will be work for the **set decorator** to do, whether it's a location or a set. The decorator and her team turn a set from bare walls to finished room. Whether a show is a period piece (requiring perhaps a throne) or a contemporary one (requiring an up-to-the-minute media room), the job of the set decorator is often that of an elite scavenger hunter, finding just the right piece. What does the furniture look like? The window dressing? What kinds of dishes are in the kitchen? What kinds of toiletries are in the bathroom? Each choice needs to be in line with the production design and the intention to illuminate each character, and the director approves each significant choice.

The set decorator provides the surroundings of the set or location that the production designer has dictated, but the person who provides the things that actors physically touch or use in a scene is the **prop master**. Again, choosing props provides an opportunity for the director (through the prop master) to be specific about story and character. Even something basic and simple—a dishtowel, a screwdriver, a purse, a pair of eyeglasses—can speak volumes about a character.

So in the concept meetings, a director can provide direction to the prop master about what to look for. Then, during the prep period, the prop master brings items to the director for approval. By the time the production moves from prep to shooting, all of those elements have been chosen, and each reflects the period, the story, and the character.

> *Choosing props provides an opportunity for the director to be specific about story and character. Even something basic and simple—a dish towel, a screwdriver, a purse, a pair of eyeglasses—can speak volumes.*

DRESSING THE ACTORS

Another department involved in production design is Costumes, sometimes called Wardrobe. This department head (the **costume designer**) has autonomy and does not (usually) report to the production designer, but they work together to create a cohesive look. Here again, it is the director's inspiration that provides the basis for all of the choices. And, once more, it is important for the costume designer's work to remain consistent with the overall look of the production, respecting its basis in time period and environment. During the concept meetings, visual aids are especially important in this department because a picture is worth a thousand words, and it's difficult to describe a suit or a dress or a set of chain mail, but when the director and costume designer look at photographs or art work that illustrate the possibilities, they can be sure that they are dealing with the same reference point.

Depending on the budget and the script requirements, the costumes may be bought, rented, or built (made). As with the production designer,

A picture is worth a thousand words, and it's difficult to describe a suit or a dress or a set of chain mail, but when the director and costume designer look at photographs or art work that illustrate the possibilities, they can be sure that they are dealing with the same reference point.

the position of the costume designer requires someone who can create from scratch or find the perfect piece at a flea market, depending on budget and time—someone who is both brilliant and flexible.

OTHER PRODUCTION DESIGN DEPARTMENTS

Other department heads with the same type of capabilities are the **makeup** and **hair designers**, who—in addition to making the actors look good—also need to be practical psychologists. These are people who deal with actors who have fragile egos and who see them first every day. A good makeup artist does her best to help the actors face the day with confidence. Doing so is difficult if an actor does not feel positive about his "look."

An actor's look is especially important in period pieces, whether it's the past or the future. The actors' looks contribute to the overall production design by cementing the characters' place in time and designated space. Contemporary scripts can lead to less specific styles, unless there is an event in the script (a prom, a banquet, a race, or a competition of some kind) for

A good makeup artist does her best to help the actors face the day with confidence. Doing so is difficult if an actor does not feel positive about his "look."

which the characters would change their everyday look. Referencing pictures or movies helps to make sure that the director and the makeup and hair designers are communicating clearly.

The last general department head with which the director works during prep is the **transportation coordinator**, who is responsible for "picture cars," in addition to transporting the company and its equipment during the process of production. Picture cars are those that will appear as part of the production design, whether in the background or for use by principal characters. Just as costumes and hair and makeup illuminate characters, so do the cars they drive. Like everything else, this is a choice the director makes that will help tell the story. Does the character drive a big black Mercedes or a broken-down Ford Fiesta?

Although all department heads contribute their creativity and effort in each specific area, the director is the ultimate arbiter of the choices that are right for the script.

If the script requires it, the director may also work with department heads in special effects, visual effects, stunts, and choreography. That is covered more in Chapter 12, but suffice it to say here that choices will be made that help tell the story and adhere to the overall production design.

This process of creating the production design for a story can exhilarating, frustrating, and exceedingly creative. Choosing the style of each possible choice—whether it's a set design, a piece of set decoration, a prop, a costume, a car, or an actor's look—brings the director closer to telling the part of the story that is surrounding the actors. Although all department heads contribute their creativity and effort in each specific area, the director is the ultimate arbiter of the choices that are right for the script.

Creating a Scrapbook

 Choose a scene from the appendix. Create a scrapbook from magazines or images from the Internet that illustrate your visual concept of style, color, and impact for the costumes and set dressings.

The process of creating the finished product must be one of collaboration because it takes roughly 200 people to put out one episode of a network television show. But it is the director who is hired to provide the creative vision and the leadership required to get everyone on the same team, telling the same story. And when talking about production design, that means that among other qualities required for this multilevel job, it would behoove the director to have a good education in art history, architecture, popular culture, design, and aesthetics. If you're lacking any of that, you can make up for it by doing your research; seeing what others have done in art, print, and film; and then making choices based on your story and your preferences. Just remember that the first rule is *always* to tell the story.

Insider Info

How Do You Interact with the Director?
Working as a designer in television, with a new script and new director every eight days, I need to move quickly to get a handle on how a director sees the material. To that end, my work with a director always starts with the script—learning from the script what the world of the particular story needs to be. Then we begin to define and shape the physical, emotional, and photographic requirements of that world. We make decisions about what we'll seek as a location vs. what we'll build on stage.

We look through a collection of location photos, which I've already edited. I present a variety of flavors and directions, stylistically and spatially. Listening to a director's thoughts on and reactions to location photos allows me to see their vision for the specifics of a scene, as well as how they deal with space and shots more generally.

As we scout, we discuss how each location could work for the scene, in terms of blocking and shooting, and where it falls short. I offer physical amendments to a location that will make it conform to a director's requirements.

Once we choose a location, I design a groundplan (floorplan) that lays out the specifics of furniture and lighting. Concurrently, I design groundplans for the sets we're building, discuss these plans with the director, and work to accommodate their ideas about blocking and shooting. I continue to share designs of key props, set dec, and graphics and solicit director input throughout production.

What Would You Like Directors to Know about Production Design?

In television, one job of the designer is to weave new elements from an episodic script into the fabric of the existing world that's been created for the show. The designer is also there to help a director get as close to their vision of how they want to shoot that world as possible.

What moves me forward in that process is hearing big key word ideas from a director, discussing how the characters in this world are behaving, which leads to how who's coming and who's going, who's still and who's moving. And discussing the shots the director wants to best tell that story.

Once a designer knows that, a fruitful collaboration about how close we can get to a director's wish-list is possible, given the ever present limitations of time and money. A designer is there to make the director's ideas physically real, to give shape to the space so it can accommodate the shots the director wants. The more information I have, the better the product I can deliver.

What is Your Best Advice to Young Directors?

Do share your ideas on the emotional tone of the piece; don't micromanage how to get there:

I find it incredibly helpful when directors share how they want the piece to feel: "It should be as if it's all happening underground"—A director said this about a piece on coal miners, with much of it happening above ground. This gave me a rich jumping off point—I scouted for a windowless bar, kept windows shuttered, used practicals that were bare bulb rather than soft glowing shades. When we did have natural daylight, it was a purposeful contrast.

"It should feel like New York in the 70's"—A director said this about a contemporary procedural. It immediately gave me a visual vocabulary in terms of color & texture, from thinking about films like *Serpico* & *Dog Day Afternoon*. I knew where I was headed in palette, and in layering the sets for set dec.

Use what you ask for:

My entire physical production team is there to service the story and help make the show the director wants to make. But we all have only so much time and so much money. Asking for a lot of (whatever—fill in the blank here) will cause us to do many things shoddily, rather than allowing us to do fewer things really well.

If many elements are wanted, be specific about how much will be seen, so we can build, paint and dress what will be shot, and not waste our time and money on what will never be shot.

What we build should correlate to what can be shot on the day—and time is limited there as well.

The best thing a director can do is be very realistic about what they can shoot in a day, which allows us to use our resources where they can be seen and not waste them.

Victoria Paul
Production Designer
NCIS New Orleans, Mistresses, Lie to Me

Insider Info

How Do You Work with Directors?

Communication and collaboration are the most important tools I use when working with a director. As the production designer for a television series, I am frequently caught in the middle. I must be fiscally responsible to the production and remain true to the established style, all the while trying to make the director's vision a reality. It can be a slippery slope.

I maintain open communications as much as possible and try to help the director find design solutions that will please them within the parameters of our show. I try to ask thoughtful questions to help us establish a shared vision that I can translate to paper. I share research, ideas, and color theory and try to keep the director dialed in during all of the design process.

What Would You Like Directors to Know About Production Design?

I would like them to know the established look of our show and how we shoot. I especially like it when directors ask questions; it helps me understand where I need to be clearer in my communications with them. Our collaboration seems to work best when a director trusts me and I try very hard to instill that trust. It is always very helpful if they understand a basic floor plan and how color is used on set to create contrast and mood. I can learn so much about a director and her style when we share our personal favorite films and architecture that we find inspires us for the episode at hand.

What is Your Best Advice to Young Directors?

Don't be afraid to *ask questions*. A good production designer should be a confidante to a young director, helping her create a shared vision. Making shot lists will help a young director communicate better with their designer. Also, watch the previous episodes, read the previous scripts, and walk through the standing sets for a show. There is a gold mine of information there just waiting to be tapped.

Denny Dugally
Production Designer
Brothers & Sisters, Without a Trace, Arrested Development (pilot)

Vocabulary

art vs. commerce
art director
camera
concept meeting
costume designer
department heads

director of photography
floor plan
location
makeup and hair
designers
one-off
production design
production designer

prop master
set
set decorator
strike
subjective
transportation
coordinator
visual aids

NOTE

1 Nicola Hodgson and Neil Lockley (Eds.). (2008). *Signs and Symbols*. New York: DK Publishing, pp. 280–283.

Chapter 5

Scouting Locations

Part of the director's prep process is scouting for locations: looking for practical places to shoot that meet the needs of the script. It could be a stadium, a church, a street, a house, a skyscraper, or whatever suits the story. It could be for exterior scenes or interior scenes. It could be for night or day scenes. Sometimes it feels like looking for a needle in a haystack. But the director is aided by the capable assistance of a specific department that focuses on finding that needle.

One of the department heads you will be working with is the **location manager**. His job is to find potential locations and—once you have chosen them—to negotiate the deal, then to oversee the interaction between the shooting crew and the site. Whether the dog is barking next door, the gardener down the street has a loud leaf blower, or the homeowner's wall paint got nicked while furniture was being moved, the location manager has to deal with it. But first, he has to show you some options.

BEFORE THE SCOUT

On day one of your prep, as you know, there will be a concept meeting, in which department heads gather to discuss the script and get the director's input. One of the things that will be discussed is whether sets will be built or **practical** (the real thing), which is generally the producer's call, based on the budget. If the script calls for something big and complicated (a street, a stadium), it will probably be a practical location. If it's a location that isn't already a **standing set** (previously constructed and used) but it's conceivable

61

financially and logistically to build it (a living room, a jail cell), the choice
might be to create that set on stage. If so, the production designer, with input
from the director, will design a **swing set** that is specifically built for the
needs of that individual script.

If the decision is to find a practical location, the first step is to discuss
exactly what you will be looking for with the location manager. You will
talk about size, style, and concept. Let's say you're looking for an exterior
of a house. What is the architecture? Is it mid-century modern, craftsman
bungalow, brick Tudor? Is it small and cozy or big and expensive? Is it on
a busy street or a quiet street? What does the **reverse** (across the street) need
to look like? What script specifics are needed—a porch, a walkway, a
garage? What overall feeling does the location need to impart—is this a happy
place, a sad place, a haunted place? Most important, what does the location
tell us about the characters?

The location manager sends a team of assistants out to look for sites that
meet the criteria.

Then pictures of potential opportunities are presented to the director and
producer, and if any of them look like they might work, then a trip (or **scout**)
will be organized to see the place(s) in person. In the scout van will be the
director, the production designer, the line producer, the 1st AD, and
the location manager. You all ride together driven by a **Teamster** (union
driver) who knows how to get there.
The director generally sits in the front
passenger seat next to the driver.
(Bethany doesn't because she gets
carsick when she continually turns
around to talk to those behind her.)

> If the decision is to find a practical location, the first step is to discuss exactly what you will be looking for with the location manager. You will talk about size, style, and concept.

CHOOSING THE LOCATION (A.K.A. THE SMALL VAN)

The first thing to determine is whether a location has the right "feeling." A
location is a character, in the same way that an actor is a character. What
does this location "say" about the script? Second, does this location provide
everything the script dictates? Once those questions have been answered,
then there are many nuts-and-bolts questions to answer as to whether this
location is feasible financially and
logistically.

Here is a list of questions to ask
yourself about a location in order to
determine whether it is right for you
and your script:

> The first thing to determine is whether a location has the right "feeling." A location is a character, in the same way that an actor is a character.

- Does this place have the right feeling?
- Does it physically provide what I need?
- Does it have the right style, colors, and impact?
- Is the surrounding environment conducive to shooting? Or is the neighborhood unfriendly—too much traffic to control, an airport or railroad track nearby, or any other factors that make it difficult to shoot?
- If it's a day exterior, does the situation of the site allow for shooting the actors in **backlight**? (That is, is the sun behind them rather than in front of them?) We talk more about this in Chapter 11 because it is a critical factor in lighting well and quickly.
- If it's a night exterior, is the site conducive to bringing in large **condors** (electric high-rise platforms) in order to put brilliant lights up high to illuminate the surroundings?

Is there enough parking nearby for **base camp** (location hub; Figure 5.1) and crew and extra parking? Ten-ton ("forty-footer") trucks carry the equipment of the crew, and there are usually at least four of those: camera, grip/electric, prop, wardrobe. Then there are actor **trailers** (portable dressing rooms), makeup/hair trailer, and **honeywagons** (bathrooms). Plus, you need parking for the cars of the cast and crew. Even if you are directing a smaller production, there will still be base camp requirements.

FIGURE 5.1 A base camp requires many trucks to hold all the departments' equipment. Photo by Paul Snider, *NCIS*

- For commercial locations, like a restaurant or a store, can you disrupt their business hours in a way that works for production and for the site owner?
- For public locations, like streets or stadiums, does the city allow filming there? Will you be able to get a **permit** and governmental/police support?

And here are some questions to ask yourself regarding interior locations:

- Is it big enough? Remember that you need double the space because a camera and lights take up a lot of room. You can always make a room look smaller by photographing only a section of it. But you cannot make a small practical space larger than it is.
- Is it air-conditioned? (Lights get hot.) If it is not, the production will have to bring temporary air conditioners, unless you're shooting somewhere like Minnesota in the winter, in which case they'll have to bring heaters!
- Is there space for **video village** (where the monitors are) and is there an additional space (a **green room**) for actors to wait? Is there a place for equipment (a **staging area**) to be kept while waiting to be used? Is there an additional space that can serve as a **holding area** for background artists?
- Is there a way to run electrical cable to the generator so that it will not be seen on camera?
- Are there enough entrances? With cast and crew coming and going from base camp and equipment trucks, you need extra access. If there's only one door in and out of the place, it will be extremely frustrating.

Keep in mind that you can always make a room look smaller by photographing only a section of it. But you cannot make a small practical space larger than it is.

Often, a practical location will provide good **bones** (the basic requirements) but will need augmenting by the art department. Such a case is to be expected, because after all, the location wasn't built with your script in mind. You may need to remove furniture and replace it with pieces that will suit your story better, or paint some walls, or repurpose a room. So when you are scouting, it's best to keep an open mind and see the potential that might be hiding under the current owner's choices. And speaking of owners, be careful how you talk about a place, especially if they are graciously showing you their house. Be kind. It can only help if you ingratiate yourself with the owners rather than alienating them. The location may be logistically "almost" perfect, and you will need to find a creative way to make up for deficiencies. For example, if you are shooting in a house that doesn't have extra space for a green room and video village, you could put tents up in the driveway and provide space that way.

The location may be logistically "almost" perfect, and you will need to find a creative way to make up for deficiencies.

The location manager will not show you pictures of a location you cannot choose. In other words, the basics have been done. The owner has been approached, has given tentative approval, and the preliminary requirements (getting a permit, parking, and neighborhood viability) have been deemed possible. Once the director has chosen a location, the work begins in earnest.

Sometimes that means getting the permission of every property owner in the vicinity and sometimes that kind of saturation approval is impossible. It always means getting a permit from the local government and pre-posting in the neighborhood to make sure parking is available. If it's a residential neighborhood, it means ascertaining that you can complete the work and exit the area by 11:00 p.m., which is often the local government requirement. And most important, it means negotiating with the location owner on the site rental. Sometimes a deal cannot be made.

So there is a decent chance that the location you picked for artistic reasons will be denied to you for practical reasons. In that case, you go back to the drawing board, have a backup plan, and continue on with your prep. In our experience, you always end up with the right place anyway. It may take more creativity, but it always ends up with you shooting *somewhere*, and it turns out to be the exact perfect place.

If necessary, go back to the drawing board, have a backup plan, and continue on with your prep. In our experience, you always end up with the right place anyway.

THE TECHNICAL SCOUT (A.K.A. THE BIG VAN)

At the end of your prep, you will go back to your chosen location(s) for a **technical scout** (tech scout). This time, in addition to those who previously scouted the location, you will take the following crewmembers:

director of photography (DP)
transportation coordinator
art director
set decorator (set dec)
leadman (set dec's second-in-command)
electric best boy (reports to the gaffer)
grip best boy (reports to the key grip)
rigging gaffer
2nd assistant director (AD).

Each of those people is responsible for duties that need to be done at this location, and each of them will have questions. Once the group has assembled at the location, the first order of business is for you, the director, to explain how you plan to shoot the scenes. It is critical to be specific and thorough, so your crew can prepare themselves to do their best work. So you will talk them through each of your angles, especially for exterior locations. Everyone needs to know what will be seen and what will not be seen on camera so they can plan ahead.

> *You will talk them through each of your angles, especially for exterior locations. Everyone needs to know what will be seen and what will not be seen on camera so they can plan ahead.*

The transportation (often shortened to "transpo") coordinator will want to know where to park the trucks and the generator. The DP will want to know exactly where you plan to put the camera and what the scope is of each shot. If you plan to use a **crane**, you will discuss where to put its base and how you plan to use the arm's sweeping motion. Figure 5.2 gives you an idea of the size of a crane; this one is a technocrane, which means the camera is operated remotely and the arm can telescope in and out.

FIGURE 5.2 With its telescoping arm and remote-controlled camera, a technocrane can achieve many different angles for visual filmmaking.

The DP will also discuss with the best boys and the rigging gaffer how to pre-rig with lights and their cables ahead of time so that there is more time for actual shooting. The art department will be interested in what needs to be taken out of the location and what needs to be provided in the way of production design. The assistant directors will discuss where to put the people: actors, extras, and caterer. Everyone will base their decisions on what the director has specified, so it is vitally important that the blocking and shot listing has been completed. If you need to return to the location after the initial scout but before the tech scout to walk through the set and finalize your shot list, that can absolutely be arranged.

If you don't arrange for this interim scout, the skills of remembering a location become very important. The production designer will make sure that you receive a floor plan and photos of this location, and you can plan your shots based on that. However, many directors feel more confident about their blocking when they have planned it while revisiting the space without a lot of crewmembers in tow.

Improve Your Visual Memory

Go to a mall. Visit a small store, a restroom, and a restaurant. Leave. From memory, draw a basic floor plan for each location. Note doors, windows, and larger pieces of furniture and/or appliances. Place a compass next to each drawing to indicate geographical direction.

SHOOTING AT YOUR LOCATION (A.K.A. PUTTING THE MONEY ON THE SCREEN)

Once the shooting day arrives, remember to actually shoot the location in a way that shows why you picked it. If it's a grand location, show it. Shoot a wide shot that encompasses all the location's qualities. If you picked it for its texture and history, show that too. Make sure that the location's storytelling contribution is actually on film, because it's easy to forget that when you are in the midst of a hectic day. We repeat: your location is a character in the story too!

Going on location is the filming equivalent of the circus coming to town. There are a lot of people, a lot of equipment, and the production company is going to pitch their tent and do a show for a day or two (or more, especially if it's a feature). And then they're going to pack up again and move somewhere else—ideally, leaving the location intact, without damage or destruction. It will be noisy and chaotic and will interrupt the usual everyday pattern of the site. But if it's done well, with adequate preparation and with respect for those whose lives are disrupted, it can be fun, productive, and bring a sense of verisimilitude that only a real place can bring to storytelling.

Insider Info

How Do You Interact with the Director?

First off, at the beginning of each new project or episode, I try to find a common visual approach to the story with the director. This common approach can come from sharing a passion for favorite directors, genres, or specific films. I'm a student of cinema, so if I can understand right off where a director is coming from in terms of their approach to the narrative, I find that very helpful before I begin pulling location files. If need be, I try to suggest film references, like the seedy quality of the inner city from *The French Connection* or *Mean Streets* or "Are you thinking it's like that 1980s Spielberg neighborhood from *E.T.*?" I find it helpful to agree on a starting point on which to base the search.

To that end, I try to ask as many qualifying questions as possible prior to assembling a location concept meeting based on an initial creative and concept discussion with the director. If possible, I use a website to post a variety of location ideas to try and engage the director so that we are in agreement on a look before spending valuable scouting resources.

Second, I work very hard at listening to what the director and production designer are trying to communicate because finding the right location is often about more than just the exterior look. Interiors need to work as well, especially in budget-conscious shows on which additional set decoration or logistics issues (filming on the third floor of an office tower, for instance) could create additional production costs and unwelcome logistics.

What Would You Like Directors to Know About Location Managing?

Be patient! Seriously, one of the hardest jobs in film is working directly with the public in the locations department. The public's sense of time and urgency is often very much at odds with the filmmaking process. Also, certain looks may not exist in the area that your production is based in, so understand that a specific look may not be available or exist exactly how you might have originally envisioned.

Be curious. Seek to understand the processes of the location manager you are working with.

Find a common language. Ask questions about how they present location files: do they show their best choice first or last? Do they hold back files that are not completely qualified? Are they actually scouting locations personally or are they managing a team of location scouts? How many days are required to permit a specific location? What kind of information do they need from you to make the search easier?

Be prepared. Any "tone boards" or location concept examples that you can provide for a location manager at the beginning can be very helpful in creating a pathway to success.

What is Your Best Advice for Young Directors?

Location scouting is a process, so make sure you understand your own process and communicate clearly how you work best with the production designer, AD, and location manager so that they can adjust to your style.

Don't get yourself hung up on whether it may be the perfect location based on the location reference photos; sometimes it's best to get into the van and begin walking through several choices in person. The reality is that "being" in the real location and "looking" at the reference photos are often very different experiences. More often than not, the process of eliminating locations with your production team will jump-start the creative process, allowing you to discover what may actually be the best set of elements necessary to create the right look or what type of practical location may be best suited for the story (which is part of the fun of making a film!).

Be aware of how the sun is going to interact, either positively or not, with your location choice. If you have an iPhone, invest in Sun Seeker, a $4 app. It really helps pinpoint the exact path of the sun on your scheduled date. Communicate with your DP what kind of lighting choices are going to be most effective for your story and make sure that these conversations influence the kinds of location options you consider as a team.

Michael Gazetas
Location Manager
Hector and the Search for Happiness, If I Stay, Warrior's Gate

Vocabulary

backlight	holding area	staging area
base camp	honeywagon	standing set
bones	location manager	swing set
condor	permit	Teamster
crane	practical	technical scout
green room	reverse	trailers
	scout	video village

Chapter 6

Organizing the Shoot with the First Assistant Director

In an average one-hour single-camera production, you have about 52 pages of script that must be shot in 7, 8, or 9 days, depending on the budget. With a half-hour single camera show, you have about 38 pages that usually must be shot in 5 days. How do you decide what to shoot on what day? How do you fit it all in?

Those decisions are made during prep. There are many factors to juggle, and you—the director—are mostly focused on the creative aspect of blocking and shot listing, so you need someone to focus instead on the logistics. That person is the **first assistant director**, or **1st AD**. (There is also a 2nd assistant director, and a 2nd 2nd assistant director, and there are production assistants on staff, too. But more on that later.) He is your right hand, the person who has your back, the one to whom you tell every thought and plan you have, the one who disseminates the information and gets everything you need in place so that you can actually do your job. The 1st AD is the conduit between production and the director who makes sure that every department head knows what you require ahead of time. You can and will have those kinds of conversations directly with the department heads, but the AD will follow up and make sure that the crane or the car or whatever you need is there for you on the shooting day.

THE SERVANT OF TWO MASTERS

Your AD will also serve as your sounding board, your sympathetic shoulder (though hopefully you will do no crying on it), and will ideally be your friend—in the sense that he will tell you the truth. Because there are so many personalities at play in the course of prep and production, there is sure to be some interpersonal drama. The AD is usually tuned in to those undercurrents and can help you navigate them. You need someone to be your eyes and ears, someone who tells you what's really going on because everyone else will defer to your position as director. The AD is the one in the middle, the one who is considered part of the crew, yet is close to you, too. The AD has to be many different things to different people, as AD Jim Hensz of *Modern Family* said in a charming self-deprecating interview for the *DGA Quarterly*: "I have no skills, I just know the people who do know how to do something. My job is part camp counselor, part cheerleader, part disciplinarian, part coach. The director is the captain, and my job is to make sure the boat goes."[1] Everyone knows that the AD is the gateway to accessing the director, so— in addition to logistics—the most important function of the AD is to keep the communication flowing in both directions, that is, to the director and from the director.

The AD also communicates with the producer, basically reporting what is happening with you and your decisions. Be aware that the AD is hired by the producer and therefore is loyal first and foremost to that boss. (Again, the entity with the money is the ultimate boss.) And in episodic television, the AD is hired for the whole season; a director comes in for just one episode at a time. So the AD may find himself between a rock and a hard place: between the needs of production and the needs of the director, if they are not in sync. (In a feature or a long-term one-off, like a TV movie or pilot, the synergy between the director and AD is more pronounced. The AD will truly be the right hand of the director. In episodic television, however, the AD's loyalties may be more divided.) Basically, the AD is hired to be helpful to you, but he is also hired to keep an eye on you.

> Everyone knows that the AD is the gateway to accessing the director, so—in addition to logistics—the most important function of the AD is to keep the communication flowing in both directions, that is, to the director and from the director.

The strength of your relationship with your 1st AD is dependent on your personalities and whether you have a symbiosis of philosophy. Essentially, do you get along? Do you see eye to eye?

If you are hired to be a director on a new project, you will have the final say in hiring the 1st AD. You can then look for an assistant with whom you feel comfortable in representing your interests, as that is essentially what an AD does. If, however, you are one of many directors to work with an AD

> Basically, the AD is hired to be helpful to you, but he is also hired to keep an eye on you.

within the schedule of a season, you will be meeting a stranger and hoping to quickly create a respectful working relationship that functions with clear communication. If you work to make an ally of the AD, you will be glad you did so during production. If, on the other hand, you two are at odds, it will be detrimental to you, because the crew perceives the AD as one of them, and relationships can quickly deteriorate into an "us vs. them" confrontational paradigm. There are many of "them" (the crew) and one of you. So regardless of whether you hired the AD, it is in your best interest to create a good partnership with that person.

If you are a freelance director, you will be introduced to your AD on the first day of prep. Together, you will proceed to the concept meeting, hopefully having had an opportunity to discuss your thoughts on that script. The 1st AD runs all of the meetings; that is, he is the moderator. The 1st AD will say, "Welcome to the concept meeting for (name of show) episode #, written by, directed by (you). Let's begin with scene one." And you and all the department heads, along with the producer, start at the beginning. You proceed, with the 1st AD leading the meeting, to work your way through the script, discussing potential solutions to the script requirements. You can interject information as the 1st AD leads the meeting if it is needed. The department heads will also have questions that only you can answer. The 1st AD will defer to you when these kinds of inquiries come up.

GENERATING AND JUGGLING THE SHOOTING SCHEDULE

After that first concept meeting, the next job of the 1st AD is to create a **shooting schedule**, which tells everyone involved in the production what is to be shot each day, and what elements are necessary. Which set will you be on? What props are needed? What actors are working? Of course, the shooting schedule can be created only if the script exists because that is the template from which everyone works. Very often, in episodic TV, the script is not yet written on the first day of prep. Obviously, the more time that everyone has to prepare, the better the shoot will go. If the writers are late in delivering the script, the preparation time will be condensed. Of course this shouldn't happen, and in fact the DGA has guidelines specifically to avoid this kind of situation in order to protect the director when he works. The reality is that scripts are often delivered late. But once the script is delivered, the first order of business is to determine what will be shot and when.

The 1st AD breaks down each page of the script into eighths, so a scene might be listed as being "one and three-eighths of a page," or 2⅝, or whatever it is. He then "names" each scene by number and a one-phrase description (Larry and Jane meet, Larry and Jane kiss, Larry and Jane break up). He chronicles what specifics are called for in sets and locations, props, wardrobe, special effects, stunts, transportation, and so on.

The 1st AD then uses a software program such as Movie Magic to create a schedule by putting groups of scenes together to shoot over the course of each day, which is called **boarding** the script (because it used to be done by hand, using cardboard strips mounted on a folding board). Once the 1st AD has a tentative board, he will bring it to you for discussion and approval. There are usually many editions of a board as factors emerge during the prep time, which force a reordering of the shooting days. But by the last day of prep, there will be a board and its offshoot, a shooting schedule, released to staff, cast, and crew that tells everyone what will be shot and when. You will see an example of one in Chapter 9.

The ideal shooting day would be 12 hours or less (excluding lunch), and everything would be organized to create flow and the least amount of disruption.

The ideal shooting day would be 12 hours or less (excluding lunch), and everything would be organized to create flow and the least amount of disruption. There are many factors for the 1st AD to take into consideration when putting a board together, such as:.

Actor Availability

Cast regulars are committed for the duration of the shoot, though they may request time off for personal or publicity reasons. If the producers grant a request, then the actor cannot be scheduled to work during that time. Guest actors are booked according to the shooting schedule, so it is incumbent upon the 1st AD to group a guest actor's work together so that they are paid for the fewest days.

Set or Location Availability

If you want to shoot at Staples Center, but in the week that you want to shoot, they already have a Lakers game, a concert, and a Kings game, you'll have to fit in when they have an open time. Or if you want to shoot in a restaurant that is busier as it gets closer to the weekend, you'll probably have to shoot there on Mondays when they're closed. If the production designer is building a set, you can't shoot in it until it's constructed and decorated. The more locations and swing sets (sets that are new and specifically for this script), the more complicated this juggling act becomes.

Actor Turnaround

By SAG/AFTRA agreements, actors are given 12 hours off between completing work on one day and beginning work on the next day. This is called **turnaround**. So if you finish one day at 7:00 p.m. with Actress A, you can give her a **call time** of 7:00 a.m. the following day. But if she needs two hours at the beginning of the day in hair and makeup, then the **crew call** (time of day when the work begins) would have to be when that **precall** (preliminary) work in the hair and makeup trailer is finished, at 9:00 a.m. If that happened every day of the week, you would be starting your day on Friday at 5:00 p.m. and working through the night. So the 1st AD will try not to end on Monday and begin on Tuesday with the same actress. This sort of thing is a particular challenge on a show with one main lead who is in most of the scenes. Multiply this conundrum by the number of actors in the cast, and you can see that it's quite a jigsaw puzzle. Appreciate the organizational skills that your AD must have to juggle all this.

Company Move

Every time a crew has to pack up their equipment and move from one place to another, it takes time. And time is money. A **company move** from one stage to another generally requires a half hour. If you have to load everything onto the trucks and move across town, that could take two hours or more. And that is two hours you are not shooting, when you're trying to complete your scheduled scenes for the day. Two hours of overtime could cost a production company anywhere from $15,000 to $75,000 (or more), depending on many factors. So when putting a shooting schedule together, the 1st AD will try to consolidate company moves by putting all of one location together, then all of the next location together, and so on. If there are individual scenes in multiple locations, the best thing would be to try to find them all in one basic area, so that base camp (where the trucks park) doesn't have to move. The equipment could be loaded onto **stakebeds** (smaller trucks) or the crew could **roll the carts** to each location. (Equipment is always stored on handcarts that can be wheeled short distances.) On the ABC show *Brothers & Sisters*, Bethany had one location day in South Pasadena that was a good example. The scenes in the script were located in a baby products store, a coffee house, an interior college president's office, and an exterior (night) Alcoholics Anonymous meeting. All were shot within two blocks of each other, and the work was completed in under 12 hours. The baby products store and the coffee house already existed in proximity, and the company created the interior set of the office inside the lobby of the nearby public library, whose steps also served for the night exterior scene. A company move would have rendered that day unshootable.

Amount of Work

The 1st AD will divide the shooting days into groups of scenes he thinks can be accomplished in a 12-hour day. The factors taken into account include the speed at which the crew works, the stamina of the actors, the physical demands of the space, and the number of shots planned by the director. If it all adds up to more than can be done in one day, then there are two choices. You can either take more than one day to shoot at a location (perhaps it will be scheduled for numerous days) or you can go to the writers and suggest moving the location of a scene. What you cannot do, as a responsible director, is think that somehow it will just turn out all right. You have to plan during your preparation time how you will **make the day**, that is, complete the scheduled work on time and on budget. For example, if a script has 11 pages in a restaurant over 5 scenes, that does not seem like a doable day (within the 12 hours). So you might suggest to the writer that one two-and-a-half-page scene be relocated to somewhere else. That would make it four scenes, eight-and-a-half pages. That's still a lot.

How many characters are in each scene? If it's only two, that might be possible. But if it's more than that, the complications increase. More characters require more shots, which require more lighting, which requires more time.

On a TV schedule, you can usually shoot a maximum of eight pages, though the salient factor is really the number of scenes (and therefore, the number of **setups**, or individual shots, for each scene) and not page count. If you have more than 25 setups planned, then the day is probably overloaded. When you go to a writer to say, "This day is unmakeable," the most constructive thing is to propose a solution. Look at your other shooting days. Is there one that's lighter to which this orphan scene might be moved? Could the scene be moved to a **standing** (already existing) **set**? Or could it become a different type of scene and still accomplish the scene's objectives? For example, could the characters have left the restaurant and finish their conversation walking up to the front door of their house? As long as the intent of the scene remains the same, it is often possible to move locations. Doing so sometimes forces the writer and director to think more creatively about this particular area of production problem solving, which makes for a better show in the end.

Day or Night

The top of every **call sheet** (the day's schedule and its requirements) lists the exact time for sunrise and sunset because, though film people think they're in charge of everything, we have not yet figured out how to control the sun. If you have three scenes of exterior day work and one of night work scheduled, you'd better make sure to complete the day scenes before the sun goes down. (You can, however, shoot interior night scenes during the day by blacking out the windows.) The 1st AD will estimate how long each scene might take to shoot and schedule it accordingly. But if there's a miscalculation, or it takes longer to shoot than you anticipated, you'll be in a mad race to light a scene with the sinking sun, counting down the moments until you're forced to concede to a greater authority.

The Intuitive

When putting a schedule together, the 1st AD has to take into account this final aspect, which generally has to do with the effort and impression a scene will make. Often, you'll want to start with the **meat of the day** (the biggest and hardest scene). As the saying goes, "You'll be shooting *Gone with the Wind* in the morning and *Dukes of Hazzard* in the afternoon." You'll take a lot of time shooting an important scene, and the less important one is done at the end of the day in a single, uncomplicated shot as you're running out of time. The director and the 1st AD will discuss which scenes hold special meaning and which may be more complex than they seem. Although the 1st AD can take into account what is on the page, he can't read your mind. If you plan a particularly difficult shot or you think it will take longer to achieve the performance you're looking for, you need to let the 1st AD know so that the appropriate amount of time is scheduled.

Peter Weir shared a story about this in an interview in the *DGA Quarterly*.[2] Talking about his movie *Fearless*, he recalled a moment that stood out for him as he read the screenplay. "There are two men flying on a plane that's in trouble, that's going to go down, and one of them, the Jeff Bridges character, says to his partner, 'I'm going to go forward and sit with that kid up there.' And then the script says, 'He moves down the aisle and sits beside the boy.' It's maybe an eighth of a page. That was the line that struck me ... When we came to schedule it, I told the AD I wanted half a day to shoot it, which I think was a bit of a surprise. It's always hard to speak about what interested you in a piece, because it's often something unknowable. It's the nonintellectual, the unconscious that's most important to me."

The other intuitive part of scheduling has to do with making a good impression. When the producers (and studio, and network) see the **dailies** (the raw, unedited footage) of your first day of directing, you want them to see scenes that are dynamic with good performances. But you know that on the first day, you won't yet have a strong working relationship with the actors because you'll just be figuring each other out, not quite yet committed to trusting each other. You also won't yet have the kind of working relationship with the crew that allows for shorthand communication and a shared vision of the way you shoot. So those first scenes need to be ones that have strong energy but are not overly ambitious or overly interpretative. They need to be fairly straightforward yet creative. And of course those first scenes need to fit all the other requirements, too, like having available actors and sets!

The shooting schedule lists all the elements needed for each day of shooting. But it is also broken down into more succinct documents that characterize particular needs. The **one-liner** is a short version of the shooting schedule that lists the scene numbers, the page count, the scene description, the actors needed, and what **script day** it is in the continuity of the story. (A story may take place in a short time span such as one day, or it may take place over many years. All department heads need to have the same understanding of when the **daybreaks** are, to plan accordingly. If it's script day 3 in scene 22, the lead actress should not be wearing the wardrobe from script day 2, scene 21, if the daybreak was at the end of that scene.) The **day-out-of-days** (**DOOD**) is a chart that specifies which days of the schedule each actor will work. The AD may also generate a **special needs chart**, which shows what special equipment or personnel must be ordered for each day (that the company does not normally carry, like a technocrane or a choreographer).

Creating a One-Liner

Even though this is a 1st AD's job, try creating a one-liner for a movie you know. Using the script, describe each scene in one short line. Group together scenes that are in the same location or set and have the same actors. Look at the page count for each day. Could that day be made? If not, divide those groups of scenes into the number of days required for shooting. Don't forget to be aware whether it's a day scene or a night scene. How many days of shooting do you think the movie required? In what order would those scenes be shot, according to your one-liner?

While you, the director, are spending your non-meeting times of the prep period blocking and shot-listing, your 1st AD is spending that same time creating the shooting schedule and arranging for the logistics of making that schedule come to pass. But the rest of the prep time is spent together, as you go on location scouts, walk the sets, and attend meetings. (However, the 1st AD is not present for casting sessions.) You will have conducted dry runs of any big **set pieces**, that is, a large event in the script that requires special advance planning. For example, if you have a scene with a big car crash, you might ask the art department for a scale model of the location and use toy cars to plan your blocking and shot placement. (Don't laugh! That works really well, as it's a physical/tactile way of "seeing" the set piece before you have to shoot it.) The 1st AD will **gaffe** (arrange) anything you need— whether it's assembling people or toy cars—to make your prep the most thorough it can be.

You and your 1st AD will get to know each other well during prep and develop a relationship that fosters a strong connection during the shooting and production periods.

YOUR RIGHT ARM WHILE SHOOTING

For a one-hour episode, you have seven days of prep. For a TV movie or small feature, you will have three or four weeks of prep. But the day eventually comes when it's time to begin shooting. You and the 1st AD have made everyone aware of your intentions, and everyone and everything has been scheduled and arranged. If you have done your prep well, you are ready for any foreseeable difficulties. You know how you intend to shoot the script; you have broken down the script for story and character; you know the whole thing inside and out. You are ready, and your 1st AD is there to help you begin.

Just as the 1st AD runs the meetings in preproduction, the AD also runs the set during shooting. That means the 1st AD will call out what's to be done and the crew and cast will react accordingly. So the first thing that happens on your first day is for the AD to call out (both loudly and on the walkie-talkie radio), "First-team rehearsal." The **first team** is the actors, and the **second team** is their stand-ins, the people who stand on the actors' **marks** (or locations) while the set is being lit. We talk about this more in Chapter 13. What is important to know now is that the AD is in command of the set, by virtue of being the one to give instructions. We could use a military metaphor here and say that you, the director, are the captain, and the 1st AD is your lieutenant, the one who communicates your desires.

What is important to know now is that the 1st AD is in command of the set, by virtue of being the one to give instructions. We could use a military metaphor here and say that you, the director, are the captain, and the 1st AD is your lieutenant, the one who communicates your desires.

So when you are ready for rehearsal, or you want to speak to someone specifically, or you want to begin shooting, you communicate that to the 1st AD, who then in turn communicates it to the relevant parties. Although it may seem dubiously roundabout—why not just call it out yourself?—it's actually more streamlined. The AD has the radio and can tell the entire crew with one command what you want, and it's important for the AD to know what's happening as you think of it, because everyone else will ask him. It's the way the power structure is set up, and it's effective.

The 1st AD is the troubleshooter, to whom all departments report regarding ongoing work flow and the obstacles to it. This includes you, the director. If you are facing any difficulties, it warrants discussion with the 1st AD, so he may act as your sounding board and/or your "bad cop" to make things happen. This strategy allows you to continue to be the "good cop" and function as the nurturing leader you are.

During the shooting day, the 1st AD is always on set, right by the camera. The 1st AD is aware of everything that is going on and is the point man for all communications, including that from the producers. The 1st AD will make the producers aware of shooting progress or lack thereof and be included in discussions about how to make the day. The 1st AD is the troubleshooter, to whom all departments report regarding ongoing work flow and the obstacles to it. This includes you, the director. If you are facing any difficulties, it warrants discussion with the 1st AD, so he may act as your sounding board and/or your "bad cop" to make things happen. This strategy allows you to continue to be the "good cop" and function as the nurturing leader you are.

The 1st AD is your assistant. And just as you have people above you (the ones with the money; the showrunner/studio/network) and below you (those whom you direct), within the power structure, so does the 1st AD. He reports to the **unit production manager** (**UPM**), who is responsible for the day-to-day operations of the crew, with direct supervision of those **below the line**. On a production budget, there is a literal dividing line. **Above the line** people (and therefore, costs in a budget) are the producer, writer, director, and actors. Everyone else and their equipment are below the line. The UPM is in charge of maintaining operating costs per the budget below the line. The UPM is a DGA member, as are you and the rest of the directing staff. Although productions are shot without being a DGA signatory, it is not recommended for any professional production. The DGA provides a framework for your protection, with legal agreements binding the producing company to abide by negotiated rules. These rules keep you and the rest of the DGA members (and consequently, the rest of the crew) safe from physical risks and poor working conditions. The DGA also negotiates salary minimums and provides health insurance and pension benefits. When you are working with a DGA staff, you know they are well trained in all aspects of production and will capably assist you in every way to achieve a creative final product done in a professional manner.

> *The 2nd AD needs to be someone with strong attention to detail and a facility for communication. And she is rarely on set, due to the intensity of pulling tomorrow's call sheet together.*

The 1st AD is, in turn, assisted by the 2nd AD, the 2nd 2nd, and production assistants (PAs). The 2nd AD is always looking toward the next day's shoot, preparing the call sheet, which lists the call (beginning of the day) time, the scenes to be shot, and the personnel and equipment required.

This means a lot of time on the phone (in all its incarnations, especially texting) and communicating with the production office. The 2nd AD's initial preparation is taken from the 1st AD's shooting schedule and then augmented by whatever daily changes are made due to shifting circumstances (somebody got sick, the director dropped a scene from yesterday, ordering a third camera, etc.). The 2nd AD needs to be someone with strong attention to detail and a facility for communication. And she is rarely on set, due to the intensity of pulling tomorrow's call sheet together. At the end of the day, she also completes the **production report**, which is an accounting of what took place: which scenes were actually shot, who worked, what equipment was used, how much film/tape/digital memory was expended.

The 2nd 2nd AD is in training to move up the ladder; this job takes place primarily on set. The 2nd 2nd helps the 1st AD **set background**, which means placing the daily hires of "extras" or "background artists," who populate the frame to create the human environment of the film.

They are the people in the theatre seats surrounding the principal actors or the office people rushing by as the leading lady walks with her leading man. The ADs tell them where to start, where to go, and what "job" they're doing. For example, a background artist in a lawyer's office set will be instructed to walk from point A to point B carrying files and a coffee cup and to play the part of a harried underling who is late for a meeting. In short, walk fast, look like you belong there, and arrange to be on camera consistently from take to take when the principal actor is saying a specific line. The 1st AD is in charge, but the 2nd 2nd does the first pass at setting background, training to do it well by the time they are promoted through the ranks to become a 1st AD.

The AD staff also facilitates production in any way necessary: by calling for quiet when the camera is going to roll, by communicating with other departments who need to know how the day is going, like transportation or catering, and by mediating interdepartmental misunderstandings. The PAs also assist in these tasks, and any others—like making a run to Starbucks—

TITLE:

CALL SHEET

CALL SHEET FOR:

SHOOT DAY: OF
CREW CALL:
SHOOT CALL:
LUNCH:

SUNRISE:
SUNSET:
WEATHER:

REPORT TO CREW PARKING

PROD. OFFICE:

PH: FAX:

DIRECTOR:

SCENE NO., SET, & SCENE DESCRIPTION	D/N	CAST	PGS.	LOCATION

TOTAL SCENES: TOTAL PAGES:

#	CAST/STATUS	CHARACTER	RPT/PU	M/U-HAIR	READY AT	SPECIAL INSTRUCTIONS, MISC.

ALL CALLS SUBJECT TO CHANGE AT WRAP BY UPM OR AD'S. NO FORCED CALLS OR MPV'S WITHOUT PRIOR APPROVAL BY UPM. SAFETY MEETINGS CONDUCTED BY
FIRST AD ON FIRST DAY OF EPISODE, ON FIRST DAY AT NEW LOCATION, WHENEVER STUNTS, SPECIAL EFFECTS, OR UNUSUAL ACTIVITY IS SCHEDULED.

ATMOSPHERE	RPT @	DEPARTMENTAL NOTES

TOTAL EXTRAS COUNT: 0

STAND-INS	RPT @	

ADVANCE SHOOTING SCHEDULE

SCENE NO., SET & SCENE DESCRIPTION	D/N	CAST	PGS.	LOCATION

UPM: V.P. OF PRODUCTION:
1ST AD: KEY 2ND AD:

FIGURE 6.1 The front side of a blank call sheet.

that are required. There is also one PA (or sometimes an additional 2nd AD) who mans the base camp. That is, he informs the actors when it's time to come to set and communicates with wardrobe, makeup, and hair as to what is needed and when. This is a job that requires extremely well-developed people skills and is a great training ground for the vicissitudes of working with 100 highly creative, passionate crew and cast over long hours in condensed spaces. The PAs and the 2nd ADs report to the 1st AD, who is ideally aware of everything happening during the production day.

Though there may be a large AD staff, depending on the show's budget and size of cast and crew, the director's primary interaction is with the 1st AD, in part because the AD assists the director during prep as well as production. For the length of time it takes to go from script to completed production, the director and the 1st AD are a team. It is a partnership that is built to serve the director well on a practical level, and a superb AD will be indispensable by backing you up creatively and personally as well.

Insider Info

How Do You Interact with the Director?

My interaction with directors varies from director to director ... whatever their personality is I try and match that, from high energy (directors) to directors that need to take everything in, to impulse directors. No matter which type of director I am working with there will be a lot of communication back and forth, that is key to get their vision of how they want a scene to be or a certain shot. You have to be on the same page with them or the day's work will not be accomplished or done the way they wanted.

What Would You Like Directors to Know about Your Job?

This is a very good question ... I feel most directors know what it takes to do my job because we work so closely together. If there was one thing maybe it would be that breaking down a script is time-consuming. Most directors get a script and feel a oneliner should come out 30 minutes later.

What Is Your Advice for a Director Starting Out?

When you get a take you like, move on!

Eric Hays
1st AD
The Best of Me, Captain Phillips, Two Guns, NCIS New Orleans

Insider Info

How Do You Interact with the Director?

The relationship will differ with each project and each director. A director who wrote the script and managed to get the project greenlighted will not have exactly the same needs as a director fulfilling an episodic TV assignment. But in either case, the moment we start working together, my actions and general attitude must be all about figuring out what those needs might be. I do that simply by asking them but also by observing and listening to them very carefully, feeling out who they are and how they like to work. Some directors love the rehearsal process, for example, and some shun it all together, looking for spontaneity instead. Some love the preparation process, spending hours making shot lists and storyboards and taking meetings with department heads; others prefer to keep all that to a minimum, and expect me to handle everything they don't absolutely have to be there for.

It didn't take long for me to embrace the idea there are many ways to skin a cat, and I should not judge directors by their methods. Even though directors differ, my job stays the same—with the script as a guiding light, and the budget and schedule as parameters: (1) learn how the director envisions turning that script into sounds and images, (2) communicate that to the cast and crew, (3) monitor as everyone proceeds to facilitate this vision, and (4) rebound whenever an obstacle surfaces, be it the weather, losing a location, or unexpected script rewrites.

Personality very much comes into play as well. None of us can really change who we are, so I warn prospective directors about my relaxed and friendly nature. Some prefer to hire an AD that operates more like a Marine sergeant, but I run the set using humor and empathy, which I find far more productive than shouting orders. When interviewing with a director, I make sure they see the real me, hoping a kindred spirit will recognize and hire me, but I also assess who they are, gauging whether I want to work for them, because in the end, the relationship will be a two-way street, very much like a temporary marriage, and will produce the best results when it works for both of us. As in a marriage, trust and respect are the key elements. Regardless of the specific dynamic at play with each director, I make sure to show them the utmost respect and always try my best to tell the truth. It's admittedly difficult in certain cases, but it's the only road I know that leads to a good working relationship. When it works, it can be immensely rewarding for both of us and for the project. When it doesn't, at least you know you gave it your best shot.

What Things Do You Wish Directors Knew About the AD's Job?

That the best results can be achieved only if they trust us. Most ADs—certainly the good ones—don't have an individual agenda. We're here to serve the big picture. We don't have a line-item budget to spend or outside vendors to please, overtime means little to us, and we don't get meal penalties. Our only beacons are the script, the budget, and the schedule—in that order, the order they were created. Yes, we came up with the schedule and are keen to defend it, but are also ready to change it in a heartbeat if we see an opportunity to better serve the script. Although others in the crew are responsible for only a specific aspect of the project, the 1st AD is responsible for overseeing everything—just like the director and the producers. It's something we have in common; it's what makes us a team, the fact that we're the only ones focused not on any one aspect of the project but on the entire picture.

But although directors can focus on their vision, we ADs have to actually get on the ground and make it happen, and we can do that well only when the director trusts us to handle it how we see best. When I go to a crewmember to implement something that the director wants, I may not put it to them the same way the director put it to me. The same is true the other way: when I bring a concern to the director, I may not say it the same way it was told to me. I call it English-to-English translation. ADs may act as the set's nervous system, collecting and sending information up and down, keeping everyone informed of what's going on at any given moment. But that doesn't mean we should parrot everything exactly as it was told to us. Good ADs use experience and discretion to relay information in the manner that will most likely lead to the best results. Good directors recognize that and let us go about our business the way we know best. It's very hard to make a movie—even harder to make a good one—and maintaining a solid trust between the director and AD can only tilt the odds your way.

What Advice Might You Give a Director Who has not Worked in Television Before?

I've often heard that film is a director's medium, and TV belongs to the writer. But I disagree with that perception. There are three storytellers involved in making a movie: writers, directors, and editors, and all three are equally important. The writers are the source: they come up with the story in the first place—without them, you have nothing. The editors are the end user and give the film its final shape: they decide what goes on screen and what is left out. Both are determining steps, the beginning and the end, but it is the director who connects them and who in doing so may have the most important job: to dissect the writer's words into short individual pieces and then oversee their creation as sounds and images in a way that allows the editor to put the story together in the best way possible. In television, a lot of the groundwork is done by a writer/showrunner, but that's only because of schedule and financial constraints. Yes, the director's role is somewhat limited: the lead actors have been cast, the main locations picked, and the permanent sets built. But it's still left to the director to turn that script into great footage, into what Peter Bogdanovich called "pieces of time."

The role of the AD is also different in episodic television. Because we are present from beginning to end, guest directors depend on us to get them up to speed and keep them true to the course that the showrunner has set. Trust becomes doubly important during prep days, which are preciously few and during which there is no time to waste. The process may appear to be more challenging than in a movie because here, the director cannot choose who the AD is, but I actually find it liberating—we're stuck with each other, so why not make the most of it. Veteran TV directors know this and are easier to work with. As in a movie, it's still my job to quickly assess who they are and what they want, and the director is still very much in command. But in episodic TV, I will often know things about the cast, the crew and the script that they don't, and by putting their trust in me, they only stand to benefit. It's still the same basic relationship, but the balance of information is different, and the AD's role is by default a stronger one.

Ricardo Mendez Matta
First Assistant Director
Astronauts' Wives, Hart of Dixie

Vocabulary

	(DOOD)	script day
	first assistant director	second team
above the line	(1st AD)	set background
below the line	first team	set piece
boarding	gaffe	setups
call sheet	make the day	shooting schedule
call time	marks	special needs chart
company move	meat of the day	stakebeds
crew call	one-liner	standing set
dailies	precall	turnaround
daybreaks	production report	unit production
day-out-of-days	roll the carts	manager (UPM)

NOTES

1 David Kronke. "Family Planning," *DGA Quarterly*, Spring 2012, p. 77.
2 Terrence Rafferty. "Uncommon Man," *DGA Quarterly*, Summer 2010, pp. 35–36.

Chapter 7

Sharing the Vision

Let's say you are a freelance director, coming in to direct an episode of a show. You've never worked there, you don't know the people, and you have a limited understanding of the show itself: its tone, storytelling requirements, logistics. Yet in just seven days, you are supposed to be the leader on set. You are supposed to know everything there is to know about the show, including its history and internal power dynamics, and you are expected to be successful in creating an above-average episode—hopefully, a great one. How do you do that?

First, you will have done your homework before you even arrived. If there are episodes available, you will have viewed them, taking note of the show's style and content. You will have looked up the producer's credits on **IMDB.com** (Internet Movie Data Base), a website that lists all television and film credits. You will have talked to anyone who may be able to give you some advance press on the working conditions and personalities. You will have called the production office and procured and read any scripts available. You will have done an advance scouting trip to the office to introduce yourself, find out where you'll park, get a crew list if it is available, and get your security badge. It's just a bad first impression if you've done none of that and you bumble into the office late on the first day because you got held up by security, couldn't find your parking space, and don't know what anyone is talking about as you commence the first concept meeting. You can do better than that, and you need to make a strong first impression, because within ten minutes of your arrival, the phone tree is working, with everyone asking, "What's the new director like?"

So you get there early. You know where you're going, and you walk in with head held high, a smile on your face, a firm handshake for everyone you meet. Your 1st AD will introduce you around, and you should make eye contact and mentally register names and job descriptions as quickly as possible. Pay special attention to those with whom you will have a close working relationship in prep: the line producer, the UPM, the production designer, the costume designer, the prop master, the location manager. You will be spending a lot of time together over the next seven days in group meetings, location scouts, and one-on-one department-head meetings. You don't have to be instant friends, but respectful, positive energy should inform your dealings with them.

Within ten minutes of your arrival, the phone tree is working, with everyone asking, "What's the new director like?"

THE SHOWRUNNER (YOUR BOSS)

The advice we've given you goes double for the most important person you will meet: the showrunner. This person is usually the writer who conceived the show's idea, sold it to the buyer or network, wrote the pilot, and who now oversees the writing and production of subsequent episodes. Sometimes, if the creator of the show is a relatively new writer, a more experienced showrunner will be paired with him. Or if the show has been in production for several seasons, the original showrunner may have departed and a new one hired by the network. The network is always the ultimate authority because it is the buyer, but the person at the apex of the production pyramid is the showrunner: in short, the boss.

The showrunner may be in your day 1 concept meeting but is not usually there. He is probably in the **writers' room**, **breaking stories** for upcoming episodes with the staff of writers who create the scripts. Every show is run differently, but the basic concept is one of brainstorming, in which the plot lines are discovered in a group environment: "Hey, I got an idea. What about this?" And then the next writer breaks in with, "That's great! But what if we take that and twist it a little, with this complication I just came up with?" The showrunner is the ringmaster for the writers' room—the final authority.

The network is always the ultimate authority because it is the buyer, but the person at the apex of the production pyramid is the showrunner: in short, the boss.

There is some version of a whiteboard on the walls of the room, where the plots for future episodes are outlined. After a particular script has been broken, and each plot point summarized in outline form, the showrunner will assign it to a particular writer, who will go off and create the dialogue for each scene. After the **first draft** is written, the showrunner will **take a pass** at the script, sharpening the story points and making sure the dialogue is true to each character's voice and as smart and funny (if applicable) as it can possibly be. You may receive this **writers' draft** before your first day of prep, depending on the showrunner's comfort level with letting the story ideas be available outside the writers' room.

Whichever version of the script you receive, the contents of any script are not for public knowledge. Some shows guard the storylines more closely than others, but regardless of whether the new plot line is treated as a state secret, you are part of the creative team and confidentiality must be maintained.

At this point, the script is sent to the studio and network for approval. The executives assigned to the show will usually call the showrunner with their **notes**, or comments, and after discussion the showrunner will incorporate the notes that were agreed upon. Then the **script coordinator** will issue a **production draft**, which is the script that (hopefully and ideally) is distributed the day before your prep starts, so that all departments can read it and process it mentally prior to the first day's concept meeting. As we said, the showrunner will probably skip the concept meeting because it is a preliminary discussion and his time is better spent dealing with the fires that need to be put out that day in the writers' room, in production, dealing with the network, or in postproduction. The showrunner has a crazy, intense job that requires him to work 12 hours or more a day. He is expected to be the father/mother figure, the sales person (to the network), the taskmaster, and the point at which all roads meet. He is expected to be everything to everybody.

THE LINE PRODUCER (THE MONEY GUY)

Because of the demands on his time, the showrunner delegates to a couple of right-hand people who support him. In production, that's the **line producer**. Though she may have an executive producer credit, which is often the domain of writers, the line producer's background and experience will be in production. That person probably got started in the business as an AD, then moved up to UPM and then on to producing. Her expertise is in knowing how to "put the money on the screen," or getting the most **production value** for the least cost, which means getting the most bang for the buck visually. That's often a process of bartering, in a sense: "We'll do this scene in our own parking lot so that we can save the money and pay for the big expensive location." The line producer will also make sure

So be bold. Say what you think (on first reading) that you'll need to bring this script to life. At the end of your prep, when you have reached the various compromises required by the budget, you will hopefully retain the minimal necessities that will allow you to achieve your creative vision.

that the show looks consistent, even though many directors are coming in to do the episodes. Line producers oversee a budget of between $3 and $5 million per episode, the money for which is provided by the **license fee** given to the production company by the network. (Cable networks provide a lower license fee; therefore, their shows have an extremely tight budget.) The concept meeting—and all future production meetings—are overseen by the line producer (even though the 1st AD does most of the talking and keeps the meeting on track), and the main order of business will be to discuss how to meet the requirements of the script that are beyond the **pattern budget**, which is the cost of a typical episode.

The pattern will dictate what the usual demands are; for example, does the pattern provide for any camera toys, like a technocrane or a Steadicam? How many background artists are expected to be employed over your eight days of production? What is the pattern for the location department? The art department? The costume department? If the writers have delivered a script with a set piece outside the pattern—that is, some scene that requires additional manpower or equipment—then the line producer and the UPM will be looking to cut costs in one department in order to provide the extra money that a different department needs.

FIGURE 7.1 A Steadicam is sometimes part of a show's camera package or it may require specific ordering and additional cost, depending on the show's visual style and budget. Photo by Paul Snider, *NCIS*

You will be expected in the concept meeting to share your preliminary ideas about your visual approach to the script. The line producer will let you know whether your thinking corresponds to the pattern budget. We encourage you to start big because every budget request gets whittled down gradually— and it almost never goes the other way. It's similar to the process of buying a car, in which the first announced cost is the largest and is negotiated downward from there. So be bold. Say what you think (on first reading) that you'll need to bring this script to life. At the end of your prep, when you have reached the various compromises required by the budget, you will hopefully retain the minimal necessities that will allow you to achieve your creative vision.

Sometimes there will be an additional producer, a **producer/director**, who will be present during all the meetings in preproduction with the express intention of helping you to achieve your vision while maintaining the show's consistency in tone and visual representation. He generally directs the first and last episodes, and maybe one in the middle of the season. In between, he supports your decisions while guiding you to best fit in with the series' established look.

The first day of prep consists of the concept meeting and free time. Sit down with the line producer (and the producer/director if there is one) and find out if you have similar sensibilities because you'll be working together closely. You will have the opportunity to **walk the sets** with the production designer and begin to think about how the scenes in your script might play out. If you've had the time, you may choose to come in before your first prep day like Julie Anne Robinson, who "always arrives a day or two early to explore the sets on her own, examining their nooks and crannies and viewing them from different angles for creative ways to block the scenes."[1] You'll probably meet with the location manager to look at pictures of possible locations, so arrangements may be made for you to scout them on day 2. Talk with the 1st AD about the scheduling for the week and how you prefer to approach the demands of prep. If the previous episode is shooting on stage, you can watch for a while and be introduced to cast and crew. And hopefully, you'll get to meet the showrunner.

ASKING FOR SCRIPT FIXES

Your first meeting with the showrunner will probably be a quick meet and greet, a chance for you to connect personally. He'll ask what you think of the show and of the script you are assigned to direct. Both answers should be energetically positive. Remember, you need to make a good first impression, and this is how you play the game. If you can be authentic while you're being enthusiastic, great. That means you got a good script. And we all know a director can make a good script great. But you can't make a bad script good.

The showrunner has put a lot of time and energy into creating this show and your script, and it will not make a good impression if you waltz in and blithely criticize his work. Instead, say something specific and positive. So that you don't sound like an inane cheerleader, you can mention that you "might have a couple of script notes, but they're no big deal and we can get to them later." Then it's up to the showrunner. If he says, "Great, let's hear them now," you'd better be prepared. If he says, "Great, it was nice to meet you," then smile, shake hands, and depart.

> As we all know, a director can make a good script great. But you can't make a bad script good.

> So if you have questions about things that don't make sense, articulate that. If you have a suggestion that is easily implemented, mention it. If you think the intent of a scene can be achieved in a way that is more production-friendly, say so. Other than that, say what you did like, say you're grateful for the job, and get out of his office.

Remember that you are dealing with the production draft. This script has already been through many incarnations, and a lot of careful thought went into it. Moreover, it's already been approved by the network. So at this point, you are no knight in shining armor, riding in to rescue the day. You are here to shoot this script in the best way possible. So if you have questions about things that don't make sense, articulate that. If you have a suggestion that is easily implemented, mention it. If you think the intent of a scene can be achieved in a way that is more production-friendly, say so. Other than that, say what you did like, say you're grateful for the job, and get out of his office.

If the showrunner dismissed you without hearing your notes, take them to the writer who is credited on the script. (If the showrunner wrote the script, mention your concerns to the line producer, and she will schedule a meeting if it's needed.) Sit down with the writer, compliment him specifically on the well-written script, and then go over your notes. Propose your **pitch**, which is a potential solution for every criticism you have. These may not be accepted, but you've shown that you put thought into it and that you're not a complainer, you are a constructive thinker.

Remember that the script is basically in its final phase, and it's not possible at this point (six days away from shooting) to overhaul story structure. We're talking **band-aid fixes** here.

This writer, or one assigned by the showrunner, will probably be present on set during the production of your episode. The writer is charged with making sure that the intent of each scene is met and performances are what the showrunner expects. Because this is a totally subjective call, and because you are traditionally supposed to be "the buck stops here" creative voice on set, it is in your best interest

When the time comes, propose your pitch, which is a potential solution for every criticism you have. These may not be accepted, but you've shown that you put thought into it and that you're not a complainer, you are a constructive thinker.

to forge a cordial relationship of mutual respect with the writer, who will be basically hanging over your shoulder for 12 hours a day. If your point of view is that this writer is a valuable resource, a partner in achieving your vision (as is every member of the crew and cast), then you'll avoid ego clashes that detract from your focus.

Sometimes the role of the director requires not only leadership and confidence, but humility as well. You will be required not only to accept other opinions but also to embrace them. During production, the writer may say, "The actor's performance isn't there yet," but you think it is.

Look at the note, see whether there's truth in it, and if so, go back to the actor and pull that performance out of him. If there isn't truth in the writer's statement, then it's your choice whether to **print and move on** or go for another take. It's a judgment call, taking into account factors such as your respect for the writer's point of view and your desire to fit in (or not) with the culture of the show's permanent staff (the writer/producers). As an episodic director, you have to live with this tradition of having a writer on set. Make that work for you, rather than against you. But we are definitely not advising subservience here. Stand up for yourself and your creative vision. Sometimes you may feel the need to justify your choices, sometimes you may feel that is unnecessary. Regardless, do not look for the writer's approval before you announce that you are checking the gate and moving on. To do so is to accede the director's authority to the writer, and that is not acceptable. Remember, you are hired as the director to be the one voice that determines how this script will be shot. On the other hand, you want to have a good working relationship with the writer so sometimes you have to give a little. This is one of those tough subjective/relationship arenas that require advanced people skills. The thing that takes precedence is telling the story in the best way possible.

Clearly, the role of an episodic TV director is different from that of a feature director, pilot director, or TV movie director. With those kinds of

Sometimes the role of the director requires not only leadership and confidence, but humility as well.

scripts, the director is more involved at an earlier stage than as a guest director of an episode. A feature director usually feels that he is the originator, or the *auteur*, as the French say: the person whose imprint is all over the film. In television, it is the writer/showrunner's medium. (We talk more about that in Section Four.) Accept these limitations and work within them to create the best episode you can make. After all, you are still the one and only director for that episode. See the problems as challenges that propel you to creative solutions while staying within the style of the show. You were hired to deliver to the showrunner and the network the show that they have created. It is not your job to reinvent their creation. It is your job to meld completely with the tone and style you have inherited and to bring your individual creativity to support the structure, not tear it down. If you feel that this role is too constraining for you, then this is not your arena.

MEETINGS AND MAKING CRITICAL DECISIONS

Beginning on day 2 of prep are the scheduled events as proposed by your 1st AD and discussed in Chapter 6. In between those events (meetings, location scouts, and casting), you will be breaking down the script for story and character (see Chapters 1 and 2) and beginning to block and shot-list (see Chapters 8 and 9). All of this work is intended to get you ready to begin shooting your episode. But in every script, there will probably be an unusual challenge to meet—a set piece that requires extra thought, planning, and additional meetings. This challenge could be anything for any department. Following are just a few from Bethany and Mary Lou's experiences.

For production design: On *Touched by an Angel*, which had no standing sets, every week was a challenge. But one of the biggest was creating a hotel in Jerusalem, the desert landscape surrounding it, including a cave and the chamber where the Holy of Holies was discovered. The solutions: the hotel was a location (a Masonic lodge in Salt Lake City stood in for a Jerusalem hotel!) and the chamber was a set. Bethany and her crew shot in an actual desert cave in the mountains on the border of Utah and Nevada to get the landscape vistas needed.

> In every script, there will probably be an unusual challenge to meet—a set piece that requires extra thought, planning, and additional meetings.

For costumes: On a TV movie of a Danielle Steel book adaptation called *Mixed Blessings*, there were three weddings in the first ten minutes of the movie that established the characters and their stories. That meant designing and planning three different weddings, each evoking a unique style. The solutions: Bethany and the production team designed three complete weddings as if they were actually going to happen, including locations, colors, flowers, and additional wardrobe for bridesmaids, grooms, and families. The three wedding dresses were designed and handmade for each actress.

For props: On *Grey's Anatomy*, the script called for a man to saw off his leg with a power saw. There were four elements for props and special effects to pull off: a fake leg, a gurney that would accommodate the actor's real leg, the method of blood splatter, and a rubber chainsaw. The solutions: several rehearsals/trial runs were done during prep to help figure out the requirements and determine what looked real and what didn't. When it was shot, though, it was all up to the actor to make his agony believable.

For art/set decoration: The murderer on an episode of *Monk* was a sculptor. His alibi was based on how long it would have taken him to carve a large nude out of a giant piece of marble. This nude, partially sculpted, appears in the artist's studio when he is first interrogated and again later, completed, in a courtroom sequence. The solutions: Mary Lou worked closely with the production designer to assure that the foam versions of the marble sculpture were beautiful enough to make this sculptor credible as a successful artist, light enough to transport, and bold enough to make Monk uncomfortable in its nude presence. She also had the set decorator find gravel that matched the faux marble finish on the piece of art because the murderer "hid" the evidence (chopped up marble) in plain view on his rock driveway. This department also had to come up with enough sculptures to fill a gallery.

Any show that is a period piece will have many preproduction challenges to meet. On *The Pacific*, all of the weapons, wardrobe, cars, ships, and props of every kind had to look faithful to the period. And then there were American versions and Japanese versions. On *Boardwalk Empire*, there were an amazing number of vintage and operating 1920s cars, not to mention the same verisimilitude of the period necessary in every department. All department heads will be hired based on their experience and expertise in creating the make-believe world of the past. But you, as the director, will make the final decisions, and you need to do your own research.

> During prep, there will be many meetings to assess the progress of each department and to approve each step, leading everyone closer to the shoot. Your efficient and effective communication skills will be critical in every meeting.

During prep, there will be many meetings to assess the progress of each department and to approve each step, leading everyone closer to the shoot. Your efficient and effective communication skills will be critical in every meeting.

Here is an exercise to help you practice your ability to sequence and explain that sequence to someone else.

> ### How to Do Something Brand New
>
> With a partner, figure out something you know how to do that your partner doesn't. It can be cooking something, building something, or solving a math or chemistry problem. Almost anything will work as long as it has a lot of steps. Teach your partner how to do something new. Figure out how your partner learns. Is your partner more visual, kinetic, or auditory? Teach her in the shortest amount of time possible. Try to utilize words like first, last, next, then, finally, and after. Then see if your partner can turn around and teach someone else what she has learned.

DISCUSSING TONE AND ANYTHING ELSE YOU WANT TO BRING UP

The final aspect to completing your preparation is the tone meeting with the showrunner. This is the showrunner's opportunity to acquaint you with his point of view about the show and give you the insider scoop on the internal workings of this production. As such, the "tone" of the tone meeting is based on that person's personality. Bethany's tone meetings have run the gamut, from a showrunner who said, "I hate tone meetings—let's not have one" to a five-hour extravaganza that consisted mainly of the showrunner reading the script aloud. Somewhere in between is where most of these meetings fall. (The writer who is assigned to be on set during production may be present for this meeting as well, in order to also understand what the showrunner is looking for tonally. It is also helpful to invite the episode's editor to this meeting so that she can hear the notes and sculpt the editor's cut accordingly.) Generally, the two of you go through the script, scene by scene, and if you have a question about the intent of a scene, now is the time to ask. The showrunner will fill you in on actors' personalities and caution you against things ("Actor X pulls on his eyebrow when he's bored with a scene, don't let him do that,") and for things ("Actress X has really been going deeper lately, see if you can even bring more out of her,") of which he is aware. The showrunner will also communicate to you any studio or network notes he deems important for you to keep in mind. But all of your communication will be to and through the showrunner regarding those notes. Aside from the occasional social set visit, there is never any direct interaction between the director and the studio or network

It is your leadership and creative vision that will cause the actors to be better, the production design to be strong and specific, and the filmmaking to be more inspired than the showrunner ever could have imagined.

executives during the shoot of an episode. If, however, you are directing a pilot or TV movie, you will be included in all of the script and production communications from those buyers.

There will be others besides the showrunner who will whisper in your ear and give you their "take" on the culture of the show. They do it with the intention of being helpful, of pointing out the pitfalls that they, themselves, have encountered. The line producer, the AD, the DP—each of them, and many more, may take you aside for their tutorial. It's all valuable, but take it with a grain of salt. As Ralph Waldo Emerson wrote, "Do not require a description of the countries towards which you sail. The description does not describe them to you, and tomorrow you arrive there and know them by inhabiting them."[2] In many ways, every film production feels like you're on the Atlantic in a canoe as you are buffeted at every side by waves you can't foresee.

Nevertheless, you will take up your oar and navigate it well, using your intuition and intelligence, as well as drawing upon any past experience you may have.

Ultimately, your success or failure is determined by the showrunner's perception of the episode, which he is entrusting to you. As you finish prep and embark on the shoot, the showrunner wants to feel like you can read his mind and will direct the show exactly as he would have done, only better. It is your leadership and creative vision that will cause the actors to be better, the production design to be strong and specific, and the filmmaking to be more inspired than he ever could have imagined.

Insider Info

Authors' note: Entertainment Life Coach Barbara Deutsch wrote a fascinating anecdotal book about the business called Open Up or Shut Up. *This excerpt comes from a chapter about actors meeting casting directors, but we think it could apply completely to directors meeting showrunners.*

It's fascinating how a person with a full, rich life can be face to face with another human being, get asked one question and then completely sell out on who they are. I've come to believe that in situations like this, the selling out part happens way before the question. It begins as soon as the call comes in to set up the meeting. You fade into the "I am nothing, they are everything" place. Even the mere title of their position is enough to flatten you.

Then when you walk in to meet them, a glaze comes over your eyes and the first thing you say is, "Thank you for taking the time to see me." That opener, in my opinion, is pathetic. Come on. Are you so nothing that your presence doesn't warrant another person's time? Especially since this meeting was agreed upon by both of you. You didn't beg to come in. You were invited and yet the first thing you say sounds like an apology. You've lost your power in the first breath. You know it and they know it. It's all downhill from there unless you have tools to intervene and turn things around.

. . . It's one person meeting another person and just liking each other. It's all up to you and how you begin. It's always up to you how any meeting goes. Even if the elements or the obstacles aren't in your favor—the other person keeps checking his Blackberry, for example—you want to walk away feeling like you didn't sell out on yourself.[3]

Insider Info

How Do You Interact with the Director?

As executive producer, I meet with the director and discuss the script. I welcome the director's notes and we discuss her concerns. During the rewrite process, the director is welcome to continue noting the script. Once the script is approved by the network, the draft shouldn't change except for location issues and little things that come up on the set.

The writer of the episode attends all prep meetings with the director and communicates any issues to me. The director is always welcome to discuss concerns with me.

I attend the tone meeting before shooting begins to talk the director through the episode and point out any particular moments I want to be sure that we get. I'll also discuss anything we've learned about the actors and their ways of working to prepare the director for what she may face.

I try to visit the set while the director is working, to make sure she is getting all necessary support and that the shooting is going well.

What Things Do You Wish Directors Knew About the Executive Producer's Job?

Our biggest pressure is studio and network approval. As EP, I have a vision of what I want the episode to be and how I want the audience to feel. Often, the notes we are getting on a daily basis from the studio and network run counter to that vision and can blow us off course. I need the director to be my partner—to listen to my notes and also keep a watch on the story with me so we don't lose our way in the process.

My favorite directors are the ones who love actors and engage them. Actors feel well taken care of when they think a director has a strong hand and is paying attention to the acting. It's a strange thing to say, but in television, a lot of directors are shooters who leave the performances to the actors and don't engage on that level. I need someone on that set to work with the actors, and if the director doesn't do that, I'll get those calls from the actors, which means leaving what I'm doing to come to the set. Most actors won't be thrilled to see that director back for another episode.

What Advice Might You Give a Director Who is Just Starting Out?
Have a vision and passion for the story you've been asked to tell. You are the new blood, the fresh energy on a set that may have been going for a while. Having you come in with energy and enthusiasm gets everyone focused and excited.

Don't try to rewrite the script. Respect the writers—you work for them and they will determine whether you're asked back.

Make your days. Don't obsess about small things or special shots you've been dying to do. The day goes by quickly. *Tell the story.* The more you do it, the faster you'll become, and *then* you can get in all those cool shots and flourishes, but please *tell the story first.*

Don't yell at the crew. Stay calm and communicate clearly.

Shoot inserts when you can. Takes a little longer, but it's better than us having to redress sets and bring actors back during another episode. Sure, you'll be long gone, but we'll remember who left all that work undone.

I have such respect for what television directors do. You come into a party that's already in progress—full of personalities and dramas—and you take charge. You become the leader for a week or two. People look to you for answers and for confidence in their own work. At the same time, you have to collaborate with a team of people you may have never met and didn't choose. Be decisive. Communicate clearly. Come to the EP if you have concerns. We want you to do well. We want a kickass episode. We want you to love working on our show. We want to want you back.

Carol Barbee
Executive Producer
Girlfriends' Guide to Divorce, Dig, Touch, Three Rivers, Judging Amy

Vocabulary	line producer	production value
	notes	script coordinator
band-aid fixes	pattern budget	single shot
breaking stories	pitch	take a pass
first draft	print and move on	walk the sets
IMDB.com	producer/director	writers' draft
license fee	production draft	writer's room

NOTES

1 Ann Farmer, "Life (and Lots of It) Behind Bars," *DGA Quarterly*, Fall 2014, p. 34.

2 Emerson's Essays, "The Over-Soul." New York: Harper & Row, originally published by Thomas Y. Crowell Company, 1926, p. 200.

3 Barbara Deutsch, *Open Up or Shut Up*. Bloomington: Author House, 2006, pp. 111–112.

Chapter 8

Blocking and Shot Listing, Part One

You tell an actor while rehearsing a scene, "Why don't you walk over to the desk and sit down?" The actor replies in front of the crew and the rest of the cast, "Why would I do that?" Right at that moment in this hypothetical rehearsal (let's say the script is a cop drama), his character wants to get a direct answer from another character. So he'd rather walk over and get in that person's face. But you're telling him to shy away, put something (like the desk) between him and the person he's questioning. Your direction doesn't make any sense to him, so he questions you. It's embarrassing for you. It looks like you haven't understood what his character is trying to do (intention), and now that actor doesn't trust you. He thinks you haven't done your homework—or worse, he thinks you have, but you don't understand anything. In the actor's mind, you—the director—are now suspected of being a sham: someone whom he cannot trust.

> Actors are made to look stupid if they do or say something that's not believable, and the actor has to trust the director will make sure everything has integrity and purpose. So if you ask that actor, in that moment when his character needs to get a straight answer, to do something evasive, he will look stupid. And then the trust is ruptured, and very difficult to recapture.

All of this may sound a bit dramatic in response to a simple directing suggestion, but it's not. The quality of the actor/director relationship depends on the actor believing that the director will not let him look stupid.

Actors are made to look stupid if they do or say something that's not believable, and the actor has to trust that the director will make sure everything has integrity and purpose. So if you ask that actor—in that moment when his character needs to get a straight answer—to do something evasive, he will look stupid. And then the trust is ruptured and is very difficult to recapture.

Because filmmaking is a creative venture of a highly collaborative nature, it's imperative (at least if you want to run a happy set) that the director's relationship with everyone is respectful and communicative. This rule is especially true between the director and his actors. If you don't have that kind of relationship, then every request could be met with indifference—or worse, defiance. Some people prefer this mode of combative drama, thinking it makes for heightened performance from the actors and more power for the director. (Director John Ford was famous for chastising his actors and sometimes hitting them. He even did that to John Wayne.) But creative people are sensitive by nature, and criticism closes them down emotionally, which is not conducive to letting inspiration flow. We all work better when our work is praised, providing a base to allow even more inspiration to follow.

So, going back to our example, you thought you made a simple suggestion: "Why don't you walk over to the desk and sit down?" But that could be the blow that knocks the foundation out from underneath your relationship with your actor.

How can you, the director, prevent such a catastrophe? First, never come to the set unprepared. Always read the script, understand it, and work with the writer to make it the best it can be; then—and this is the most crucial part of a director's job—prepare your work. Come to set on your first shooting day having decided in advance two things about each scene:

- How the actors will move
- How you will use the camera.

The first task is called **blocking**. Imagine how each scene will play out, and picture in your mind the physicality of the scene. Then second, imagine where you need the cameras to be in order to photograph the action. Make either a **shot list** or a **storyboard** that indicates how you intend to break down the scene into individual shots. Though both processes require your imagination, they are two very separate skills. For a director to block a scene, he must intuit the scene, understanding each character's intention and translating that into physical movement, intonation, and communication— that is, performance. For a director to shot list or storyboard a scene requires more of a logical mind because it's like solving a Sudoku puzzle, determining where each missing piece fulfills a need in the overall design. Blocking is right-brain work; shot listing is left-brain work.

We all work better when our work is praised, providing a base to allow even more inspiration to follow.

WHERE, WHEN, AND WHY THE CHARACTERS SHOULD MOVE

The more important skill is blocking because you can have a magnificent shot, but if the intention of the scene is unrealized because of poor performance, your film suffers. You want your audience to empathize with your characters, to be touched by them in some way—you want them to laugh, cry, gasp. This emotion is not achieved by camera work, no matter how sophisticated it is. Director Arthur Allan Seidelman recently reminded us that the sure way to get an audience to like a character is to let them see the character's vulnerability.[1]

Touching the emotions of the audience is achieved by their identification with the story and with the actors' performances. We have already talked about approaching the story from the actors' points of view in Chapter 2. What we're talking about here is how the physical action of the actors illustrates their intentions. Does Character A want to be close to Character B or far away? Does a particular moment in the script require stillness or movement? If it's movement, is the movement needed to cover the character's emotions or to illustrate them? (More on this in Chapter 10.) Are props required, and if so, how are they used? Is there an entrance or an exit? What is the energy level of the scene, and how does that play into character movement?

> You want your audience to empathize with your characters, to be touched by them in some way—you want them to laugh, cry, gasp. This emotion is not achieved by camera work, no matter how sophisticated it is.

An average TV drama script has anywhere from 30 to 60 scenes, and each one must be blocked and shot listed (or storyboarded) before you begin your first day of shooting. In a desperate pinch, you can break the script down by shooting schedule and use your weekends to prepare for the week ahead. But doing so is not recommended because you get too much information during the process of blocking during prep to share with other department heads. For example, you might get the idea to have two characters prepare dinner during a scene. It's much better for the prop master to know that ahead of time. Also, if you block the whole script out sequentially, you can better plan your **transitions** (how the frame looks from the end of one scene to the beginning of the next). If you block by shooting schedule, you will probably do something like shoot scene 30 in week one and scene 29 in week two; therefore, you might miss planning a beautiful transition shot between them.

You have already analyzed each scene for story and character. But how do you get the scenes on their feet? Begin with the obvious: is there an entrance? If so, where is that within the set or location? Where do the other character(s) begin in relation to the character who is making an entrance? This gives you the **starting point** for each character. If there is not an entrance, there might be something else scripted that gives you the starting point for each character. If there is no indication in the script, you are free to imagine the actors anywhere you want within the space.

Now what? You look to the script for clues. Very often, the writer will tell you in stage directions what she had in mind. If so, you may choose to follow that suggestion, or you may not. It is your choice, but it's good to remember that the writer has put a lot of thought into this and is "seeing" the scene in her mind. The writer might give you some good ideas! But regardless of whether you accept the script suggestion, or if there isn't one, you now begin to imagine each character, how they feel, what they do. What is it they're trying to achieve in the scene (there's that intention again) and how does their movement in the scene facilitate that goal? Play each part in your mind, or out loud within the empty set if you need to. As you see it in your mind's eye, be sure that it feels **organic** (natural) and that everything you ask your actors to do is **motivated** movement. (You're asking them to **make a cross**, or move across the room, for a specific reason.) What you definitely should not do is ask an actor to make a cross because "it will make a better shot." A justification like that tells the actor that you are not on his side, that you care mostly about the visuals rather than performance. Plus, the actor needs a specific reason from the character's point of view to move, and camera has nothing to do with character.

You can use theatre terms, such as **upstage** (farther from the audience/ camera) and **downstage** (closer to the audience/camera), as a shortcut term both for yourself and for your actors when you're explaining your plan to them. The one directional term that is different between theatre and film is caused by the fact that, in order to shoot a scene, everyone must relate to the camera, which is opposite the actor. So when you ask actors to move to their right, that is actually **camera left**. And their left is **camera right**. It's not confusing for you because you stand behind the camera, but for the actor facing it, some practice with this terminology is usually needed.

Double-check your script: Is there an exit? Is there something that needs to be accomplished by a character, such as picking up a shovel, closing a window, setting the table? If so, the character must be physically proximate to those items. If nothing is scripted but you have an idea for framing the scene in some physical action (like the task of preparing dinner, as previously mentioned), make sure those elements are ordered during prep via conversations with your 1st AD and the relevant department heads.

Because Mary Lou has directed so much comedy, she always examines the scene to see if an actor's specific placement next to another actor will help the "funny." Two actors who are good with comedy standing next to each other can be gold! Conversely, you can make a comedy-challenged actor look better by placing him farther away from the actor to whom he is speaking to force an edit so that you can be in charge of the comic timing in postproduction. You also want to be sure to **frame the joke**: don't plan to have your actors walking or moving (and don't move the camera either) as they say the all-important punch line. If it's a drama scene that contains information or exposition that the audience needs to hear, frame that as well. Don't bury important information in distracting physical movement by the actors.

After meeting the physical requirements of the scene, turn to the psychological ones. Do the characters hate each other? Do they love each other? What is the power balance between them? Does the power shift in the scene? Unless it's a setup scene or a dénouement scene, there will be conflict between the characters. How is that conflict best illustrated in blocking? Is it hot conflict (a physical fight) or cold conflict (icy distance between them)? What is the outward picture of the characters' inner emotions?

Translating the Script to Movement

Take one of the scenes in the appendix and copy it. Imagine that it takes place in a familiar environment: your own home. Imagine how the characters would interact in this space. Write each character movement down next to the dialogue line on which this movement would happen. If possible, ask two people to run the scene with you, being the actors and doing the blocking you've planned. Pay close attention: is the blocking you planned organic and motivated by character intention?

Once you've met the basic questions in translating the script to (imagined) actor movement—Is it justified? Does it make sense?—begin to think about how you will place the cameras to best record this blocking that

After meeting the physical requirements of the scene, turn to the psychological ones. What is the outward picture of the characters' inner emotions?

you have worked out. But before we talk about types of shots, there are some structural requirements of which to be aware.

STORYTELLING AROUND THOSE ALL-IMPORTANT TV COMMERCIALS

In broadcast television programming, the story is interrupted by commercials. (And that's a good thing, because that's what pays for the show.) After a commercial, you will have an **act-in**, or beginning of the next segment, and when the story is about to go to commercial, the last shot is the **act-out**. Most hour-long dramas today (which actually span about 42 minutes without commercials) have six **acts** or segments between commercials. So it's essentially like having six beginnings and six endings. The director needs to plan special shots for these act-ins and act-outs, for they have additional meaning and importance. Act-in shots should be visually interesting and entice the viewer to return to the story. Act-out shots should provide resolution and gravity, letting the viewer know they've come to an ending.

When you break down the acts into scenes, you also have the opening shot and the ending shot for each scene. They fulfill the same purpose as the act-ins and act-outs, just on a smaller scale. Plan an opening shot for each scene that is a visual way into the scene, and plan an ending shot that telegraphs to the audience the scene is completed. You also need to know what the **first cut** (edit) is out of your opening shot. This cut is really the key to shot listing because when you know what your first shot is, and you know the place or line of dialogue during which you will make the first cut, then the pattern and rhythm of the editing begins to be established. So you will have your opening visual shot, and you will know exactly where you plan to cut out of it and into the second shot. Once that happens, it should be clear to you where you need to go. For example, let's go back to the exercise you just did. What would be the opening visual shot? Imagine it, watching the scene unfold in your mind's eye. Where do you need to shift your attention and when? That is the first cut. Now you are in the second shot, which would tell you the next part of the story. When do you need to shift your attention again? Is it back to the first shot, or something else? Now the scene is starting to take you on a journey: giving you (and the audience, because the director is standing in for the audience) some information and making you feel something. As you build the scene by putting together sequential shots, you are telling the story.

> *Act-in shots should be visually interesting and entice the viewer to return to the story. Act-out shots should provide resolution and gravity, letting the viewer know they've come to an ending.*

VARIATIONS ON A HOMECOMING

Let's say you're working a scene about a soldier coming home to his wife from Afghanistan. Perhaps you decide that the **story point** (the crux of the matter; why you are telling this story) is the surprise that his wife (let's call her Wife) will feel upon seeing him and how much he's changed. So to build to that moment, you might shoot a mini-**montage** of **inserts** of the Soldier. (A montage is a storytelling device of putting non-dialogue shots together, usually accompanied by music scoring; inserts are tight shots on objects.) So you might begin with a shot of his worn boot stepping out of the cab. And as he walks up the path, there's a shot of his backpack, his name badge, and his tense hand pulling at his straps in anticipation. Then there's the back of his head, poised at the front door, and his finger on the doorbell. The doorknob turns, the door opens, and you tilt up to see the Wife, whose expression changes from curiosity (Who's at the door?) to surprise, joy, and then consternation. Your first cut out of that montage is to the face of the Soldier, who is happy to see his Wife, but also tentative, because he has a terrible scar on one side of his face and is missing an ear. Now the scene falls into place. You know you will cut back to her, then back to him. Now they have some dialogue. They embrace. He steps over the threshold and the door closes. Because you have two shots there (one of him, one of her), the story is told. Of course, you could do many variations: you could add multiple shots; you could choose to **push in** (the shot becomes tighter as the camera goes toward the actor) or **pull out** as the door closes to lend a sense of completeness. Or maybe you want to keep it simple, either for time constraints or because you just think that's the best way to tell that part of the story. It's up to you—and only you. It's not the producer's responsibility, or the script supervisor's, or the DP's. It is the director's sole responsibility to shoot the script so that the story is told.

Take the same scene, a Soldier coming home. But now you decide that the story point is his yearning for the safety and innocence of the life he left behind. Perhaps you begin the same way, with the boot coming out of the cab, but then you might continue that shot and tilt up to his face as he steps out. The expression on his face changes. But why? And your first cut is to what he's seeing: his beautiful house, with flowers growing in front of the porch, it all looks so peaceful.

You cut back to him: how is he feeling? And then the door opens, and his Wife stands there. You're still in his **point of view** (also called **POV**; the camera sees what the character sees) so it's a **wide shot** toward the house and the front door. But then you'll want to see how his Wife feels as she stands there, so you have a **close-up** (**CU**) shot of the Wife. You cut back to him. In Figure 8.1, you can see the camera placement for this scenario.

There's a long sidewalk in front of him; the house seems very far away. What is he going to do? What is she going to do? He starts up the walk toward her, slowly at first, and the camera will **dolly back** to hold his face in the shot as he walks. You cut to his Wife, who also begins to approach him. You let both of them **exit frame** (leave the shot) so you can cut to a **50/50**, a shot in which the two characters **break** (enter) **frame** to face each other.

The Soldier and his Wife meet in the middle of the sidewalk and exultantly embrace (Figure 8.2).

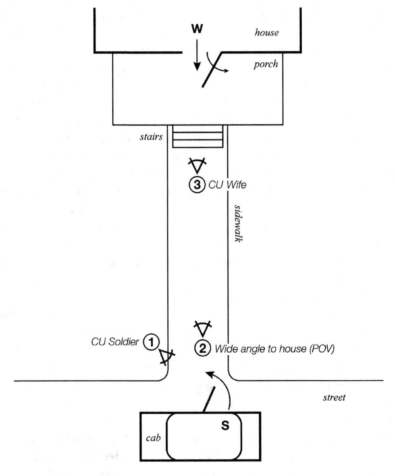

FIGURE 8.1 The characters' and camera placement for the wide POV shot as well as the Soldier and Wife close-ups.

Okay, let's take the same scene again. A Soldier is coming home from Afghanistan, his Wife greets him. But this time, the story point is that they have grown apart while he's been gone.

Perhaps your opening shot is an **establishing shot**, one that shows the environment from a wide point of view. The cab pulls up in front of the house, the passenger door opens, and your camera is across the street on a **wide lens**, and sees all of that. Where do you think the first cut out of that shot will be? You have to ask yourself the following questions: What is the story? What do I (as the director, standing in for the audience perception) want to see? Well, if we see a cab pull up in front of a house, we want to know who is in that cab. So that would be the first cut. And because the camera is across the street, we know the cab is going from right to left in the frame so that the passenger can get out on the correct side. So to show "Who is getting out of the cab?" the **camera angle** would be opposite from

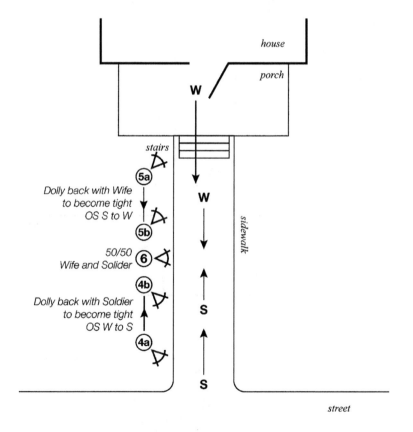

FIGURE 8.2 The blocking and camera placement for the second Soldier/Wife scene.

where it was in the establishing shot: on the other side of the street in front of the **hero** house, pointing 180 degrees away from the angle of the first shot, toward the passenger door. This time, we won't start on the boot but rather **overlap** the car door opening (do it again), and the Soldier steps out.

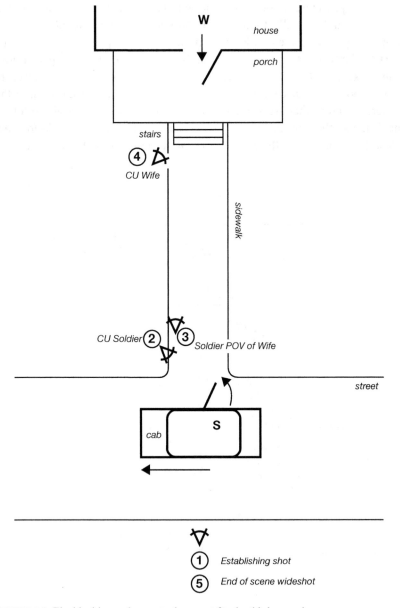

FIGURE 8.3 The blocking and camera placement for the third scenario.

We see his face, and we want to know what he's thinking. We cut to his point of view. The front door opens, and the Wife stands there. We cut back to the Soldier. Back to the Wife. Neither of them move. The cab driver pulls away. The two people are stranded there, far apart and not moving. The story is told (Figure 8.3).

So there we have three examples of the same plot point: the Soldier comes home to his Wife. But the story is different, even though it's the same plot. The blocking is different in each one, and so are the shots. It helps to ask yourself, as you're reading a scene and deciding how to block it, "Yes, but what is the real story?" In other words, "I see the plot point(s), but what is underneath that? What are the characters feeling? What is the real story?" As you know (from Chapter 1 on breaking the script down for story), this is subtext. That is always the job of the director: to know the subtext of each scene. Then you have to know how to illustrate that subtext by blocking and shots. That is the essence of the visual aspect of director's job, and there are many directors who are known as a "**shooter**," that is, someone who uses the camera in very specific and sometimes elaborate ways. But think back to a director like Frank Capra, and his iconic movies like *Mr. Smith Goes to Washington* or *It's a Wonderful Life*. His camera use was simplistic but the performances in his movies continue to echo in our hearts and minds. Remember that the director's job of telling the story is constructed through two elements: actors and camera. It's our responsibility to use them both well.

YOUR PALETTE OF SHOTS

Let's go over the names for each type of shot, going from wide to tight:

- Establishing shot: A wide shot that shows the environment.
- **Master**: A shot that holds all the actors in the frame; usually shot first, it creates a template for the scene because in every shot after the master, all the actors will **match** (repeat) their movement and actions.
- **Mini-master**: A smaller grouping of actors within the same scene from the same camera position as the master; a **reverse** mini-master is shot from the opposite side of the set.
- 50/50: Two actors face each other in the scene; this can be wide to show **full figures**, or tighter to cut them (hold the frame) at the waist.
- **Two-shot**: Two people are in the frame.
- Over-the-shoulders (OS; Figure 8.4): The camera looks over the shoulder of one actor toward the other actor; when the camera looks in the opposite direction, it is a reverse angle. In your shot list, indicate

FIGURE 8.4 Camera operator Ben Spek shooting an OS shot of Luke McFarlane (facing camera) and Matthew Rhys from *Brothers & Sisters*.
Brothers & Sisters trademarks and copyrighted material have been used with the permission of ABC Studios.

specific placement by using OLS (over left shoulder) or ORS (over right shoulder).

- Close-up (CU): A tight shot of the actor, **clean**, that is, with no one else in the frame; this can be in varying sizes, from a **cowboy** (bottom of frame is where the bottom of the holster would be, mid-thigh) to **waist**, to **two-t** ("two tits" at the bottom of the frame) to a **choker** (bottom of frame is the neck) to **extreme** (the frame can hold only a part of the face). A close-up can also be called a **single**; if the camera **pans** (goes sideways) from one character in close-up to the next character, it's called a **swingle.** In Figure 8.5, we have diagrammed where the camera frames these shots. Figure 8.6 shows how a director might ask for a waist shot.
- Inserts: Extremely tight shots of objects or movement to illustrate a story point. For example, if a character reads something, an insert may be necessary of that paper so that the audience can see it also. If you do an **integrated insert** by including the object within another shot, it's called a **tag**.
- **Rake** (raker, raking): The camera is not directly in front of its object, but off to the side. It's a nice way to **stack the frame** by, for example, lining up several people in more of a **profile** shot rather than looking at them straight on and creating a flat effect (Figure 8.6).

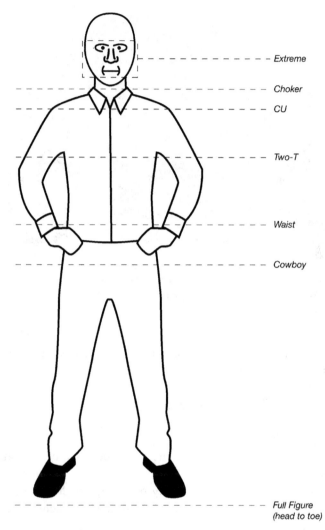

- - - - - - - - - - - Extreme

- - - - - - - - - - - Choker

- - - - - - - - - - - CU

- - - - - - - - - - - Two-T

- - - - - - - - - - Waist

- - - - - - - - - - Cowboy

- - - - - - - - - - - - - - - - - - - Full Figure
(head to toe)

FIGURE 8.5 The camera frames the actor in various sizes.

In our story about the Soldier and his Wife, a shot list of the first scenario might look like this:

Opening montage:
1 a) boot steps out of cab
   b) name badge: dolly back
   c) hands on straps
   d) reverse angle: backpack
   e) back of head waiting at door

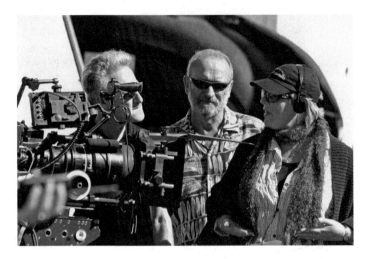

FIGURE 8.6 Bethany describes a waist shot on *Brothers & Sisters* to 1st assistant cameraman Nick Infield and dolly grip Cranston Gobbo.
Brothers & Sisters trademarks and copyrighted material have been used with the permission of ABC Studios.

2 door knob turns: tilt up to reveal Wife, becomes close-up of Wife (she looks camera right to Soldier), at end, he steps toward her and door closes in **fg** (**foreground**, close to camera)
3 tighter on Wife (choker)
4 reverse: CU Soldier (he looks camera left to Wife), he steps out of frame at end
5 choker Soldier
6 pull-back to **high and wide**, camera in street, possibly a **crane shot** (camera is on an arm that allows it to swing up, down, and sideways; used for fluid movement generally requiring a higher angle than the camera dolly can provide). Figure 8.7 illustrates the height a crane can achieve.

Notice that the shot list indicated **screen direction**, that is, which side of the frame the actors were looking to in order to achieve the illusion that they were talking to each other. The Wife looked right, the Soldier looked left. If the director made a mistake and didn't set the shots up in that way, it would be **crossing the line**. It's a big topic that we will cover in the next chapter.

In order to complete this shot list, you must have physically been in the space as part of your prep. You will imagine the scene and possibly act it out yourself or have an early rehearsal with your actors (and no crew) so that you can all work it out together. You will be provided with a blueprint,

FIGURE 8.7 A traditional crane; the operator and dolly grip sit on the arm of the crane. Photo by Paul Snider, *NCIS*

or floor plan, by the art department, or you can draw a small diagram for yourself on the same page as your shot list. (The diagrams for this chapter showing the house, the porch, and the sidewalk would be the floor plan.) You can do this on the computer or by hand. Our preference is to have a separate shot list for each scene, on the *backside* of a piece of paper, which is then inserted into your script, facing the relevant scene. This method is very helpful when a script gets revised—you can reinsert your shot list on its separate page, rather than having to do the work over.

Let's go back to where we started in this chapter, with the actor asking you, "Why would I do that? Why would I walk over to the desk and sit down?" Because you will have thought everything through, broken down the scene for story and character, and know how the physical blocking of the scene is a visual representation of each character's point of view, you can say, "Because there's a power struggle in this scene, and if you ask for the information straight out, he knows you're in the weak spot. If you walk around the desk and sit down, you're covering, you're bluffing, you're making him sweat, and you'll realize the intention of forcing him to concede to your power and give you the information." The actor will look at you with a little smile. "Okay," he'll say, and then he'll walk over to the desk and sit down, knowing he's in good hands.

Have a separate shot list for each scene, on the backside of a piece of paper, which is then inserted into your script, facing the relevant scene. This method is very helpful when a script gets revised—you can reinsert your shot list on its separate page, rather than having to do the work over.

Subjective POV

Authors' note: *This is just one of many explanations we will share with you from the wonderful book* Cinematography Theory and Practice *by Blain Brown.*

When we show someone tilt his head up and his eyes turn toward something off-screen, then cut to a clock tower or an airplane, the audience will always make the connection that our character is looking at that tower or plane.

This demonstrates not only the usefulness of subjective POVs for storytelling and emotional subtext, but also hints at the importance of the off-screen space as part of our narrative. It also reminds us that we are almost never doing shots that will be used in isolation: ultimately shots are used in combination with other shots. This is really the essence of filmmaking: doing shots that are good on their own is important but in the end what really counts is how the shots work when they are put together in editing.[2]

Insider Info

How Do You Interact with the Director?
I always want to make sure that I'm visually telling the story: the camera, the lighting, the lensing have to contribute support and enhance the story, whether it's a comedy or drama. As a DP in episodic TV, I am hired by the producer, so my first responsibility is to the continuity of the show. I need to protect whatever the signature of that show is. At the same time, I feel an obligation to be the director's compatriot, to be his eyes, to execute his vision. If a director, for example, is going off in another direction, I won't say, "No, we can't do that." I try to cloak it and say, "On this show, we don't generally stage something like that, or we don't generally use a wide lens." I want to give the director the parameters of how we're working. Then if the director still wants to go with that route, I will work with him, supporting and respecting his wishes, but I will try to massage it, blending the signature and style of the show I was hired for while still trying to execute his vision.

What Do You Wish Directors Knew About the DP's Process?
Cinematography is an element of storytelling and lighting is an element of cinematography, so indirectly, lighting is very much an element of storytelling. Often, directors don't understand that when a DP wants to add another light, it will make a difference. It will illuminate the scene both literally and—more importantly—figuratively. People will forget the extra 10 or 15 minutes of overtime when the film is great, but they don't ever forget when the film is mediocre. Just as the director may need extra takes to embellish a performance, a cinematographer may also need several takes to tweak the lighting and camera from his point of view as a visual storyteller.

Also, when I am willing to compromise the look of the show to make the shoot work and accommodate a director's wishes, the director needs to meet me halfway.

For example, if I'm lighting opposing angles simultaneously (as they often want to do on a sitcom) but I'm still trying to give the show a "cinematic look" and we're still rolling and we have zoom lenses on, and the director says "go tighter," I may want to change the lighting minimally when we go from a wide shot to a tight shot. It may take only 30 seconds, but I wish I didn't feel like the director was resenting the time it would take to make a 30-second change. I want them to let me do my thing, safeguarding the style and look of the show. For instance, they need to trust me to know whether this actress needs more front light or whether I need to do this with a long lens instead of a wide lens. Or if we're staging something, it's better sometimes to not go from the beginning of the scene all the way to the end of the scene, because at a certain point, I just run out of places to put lights. Finally, having now worked with directors who were formerly cinematographers, like Michael Watkins, I appreciate the respect they pay me by asking me after rehearsal and before releasing the first team, "Are you going to be okay with this?"

What Advice Would You Give a Director Who is Starting Out?

See as many films and watch as much television as you can. Understand the medium you are going to work in. I think it is important to spend time on sets and observe directors at work. Shadowing a director is a great way to understand what is going on. And do this on all kinds of shows. Every situation has a different rhythm, a different beat, a different lingo, a different style.

Joe Pennella
Director of Photography
Mistresses, Red Band Society, The Neighbors

Vocabulary

50/50	downstage	organic
act	establishing shot	overlap
act-in	exit frame	over-the-shoulders
act-out	extreme shot	(OS)
blocking	first cut	pan
break frame	foreground (fg)	point of view (POV)
camera angle	frame the joke	profile
camera left	full figure	pull out
camera right	hero	push in
choker shot	high and wide shot	rake
clean	inserts	reverse
close-up (CU)	integrated insert	screen direction
cowboy shot	make a cross	shooter
crane shot	master	shot list
cross the line	match	single
dolly back	mini-master	shot
	montage	stack the frame
	motivated	starting point

storyboard	transitions	waist shot
story point	two-shot	wide lens
swingle	two-t shot	wide shot
tag	upstage	zoom lens

NOTES

1 Arthur Allan Seidelman. Email, June 26, 2015.
2 Blain Brown, *Cinematography Theory and Practice*. New York: Focal Press, 2015, p. 36.

Blocking and Shot Listing, Part Two

Now that you've imagined how the actors will move in the scene (blocking), it's time to imagine how you will shoot the scene (shot listing). Come to the set with your plan and enlist the services of the DP. If it's an exterior location (where the light is less controllable because no one has figured out yet how to manage the sun), the DP will definitely have an opinion about in which direction he would like to shoot first. If it's a night exterior or an interior set, the DP will give you more options.

Your DP will generally prefer to light the widest shot first and condense the scope of the lighting as you go on. So in your shot list, go from wide to tight. The DP will also want to light **directionally**, that is, to shoot everything in one direction, using the same group of lights, before you **turn around** to have the camera look in the opposite direction. If you have multiple scenes in the same area (like a courtroom), you may want to **block shoot** those scenes, that is, to shoot every scene with the witnesses on the stand before you turn around to shoot the attorneys. You begin your shot list by indicating where you want to put the camera to establish the scene; then you ask yourself, "What would be the next shot while lighting in this same direction?" After you have continued that process and listed all shots, finishing with your tightest/last shot in your first direction, you note on your shot list that you are going to turn around/reverse, and you begin again with the widest shot and work your way down to the tightest shot. When you have completed the shot list, **double-check** the work by indicating next to the dialogue or scene description on the script page which shot you anticipate using—this method helps make sure that you haven't forgotten anything. It is important to note that your shot list is created in the order in which you plan to *shoot* it, not the order in which it will be *edited*. For example, you may be putting an insert shot or montage first (like in our first scene with the Soldier) when you *cut* it together, but you would *shoot* the widest shot first, (in that case, that is probably the dolly shot that leads the Soldier to the porch). So your shot list will be in shooting order, but when you double-check your work and put a shot number in your script next to each piece of dialogue or stage direction, that will illustrate your editing order.

Once you have all your shots, you can edit it in multiple ways (more to come on this in Chapter 14). Your job as a director on the shooting day is to make sure that you have all the coverage you need. The best way to ensure this is to plan it out ahead of time (block and shot list) so you're able to focus on understanding the subtext and providing all the shots required to illustrate the story.

You could also storyboard this scene, which would be a literal depiction of the blocking and the shots, shown in a succession of boxes (frames). This step can be done by skilled artists who listen to the director describe the scene and then translate it by drawing a picture of each shot onto storyboards. (Or if you can draw, you can do it for yourself.) Since Bethany can draw nothing but stick figures, a talented artist named Joe Mason drew the storyboard for the opening sequence of an episode of *Castle* she directed (Figures 9.1 and 9.2).

The storyboards essentially show in still frames what the finished product will look like. A storyboard is a visual representation, rather than the logical/literal method of shot listing. You then shoot it so the shots resemble the storyboard.

You will probably want to storyboard when the scene calls for major stunt work or substantial visual effects, because it's a way of determining exactly what you need in production. In Figure 9.3 you can see part of a storyboard for a scene in *The Originals*.

Whether you shot list or storyboard, the point is to "see" the movie in your head before shooting a single shot.

This depiction helped the department heads understand the sequence (a picture is worth a thousand words sometimes) and allowed accurate budgeting for the VFX. (After all the work that went into the scene both in prep and in production, it was cut in post because the episode was too long.) If you choose storyboarding, there are several computer programs for this, including Google Sketchup and Adobe Photoshop. There is even a Hitchcock storyboarding application for the smartphone or tablet.

The reason Mary Lou and Bethany prefer shot lists is that they better illustrate how shots are reused during scenes. In the example from Chapter 8,

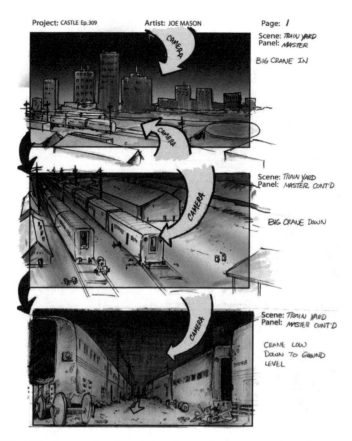

FIGURE 9.1 The first storyboard panel from the opening sequence of an episode of *Castle* that Bethany directed.
Castle copyrighted material is used with the permission of ABC Studios

FIGURE 9.2 This frame from the episode matches the third frame on the storyboard panel.
Castle copyrighted material is used with the permission of ABC Studios

SC. 30 CONT.

(9) INSERT
TIGHT ON THIRD TAROT
READER TURNING OVER
DEATH CARD

DEATH

(8A) DAHLIA WALKS INTO
SCREAMER WITH A
SMILE. THEN EXITS
LEFT

TILT UP TO:

(8B) STEEPLE BELLS
RINGING

FIGURE 9.3 A storyboard artist's skill (in this case, John Lund) helps a director to "see" what elements are to be done in production and which are postproduction visual effects (VFX; the last shot of the steeple was planned to be a visual effect).

you would cut back and forth between shots #2 and #4, between the Wife and the Soldier, and as you wanted to go tighter, you would cut back and forth between shots #3 and #5. But storyboards might help you "see" the finished film better because with computer programs, you get a better three-dimensional sense of the set in which the actors are moving. Whether you shot list or storyboard, the point is to "see" the movie in your head before shooting a single shot.

Just as blocking and shot listing utilize two separate abilities of a director (feeling and logic), shots deliver two kinds of impression: **objective** or **subjective**. Objective means the camera is merely recording the scene as an unseen and non-participatory observer. The audience should not be aware of what the camera is doing; that is, the camera movement is organic to the action and does not call attention to itself. Subjective camera is used when the lens of the camera is the eye of a character; that is, the camera is a character. This impression is prevalent in action or horror sequences and in cases in which the director wants the audience to feel as if they are "in" the scene with the actors. So when planning the shot list, the director should take into consideration the kind of feeling the script requires and know how to integrate the camera with the actors in front of it to provide either an objective or subjective point of view.

The most subjective type of shot is when the camera is photographing a character's point of view. It is extremely personal and subjective. The audience members feel as if they are in the story—almost as if the camera is not only the character, but also the audience's perspective. The next most subjective shot is when the actor looks directly into the lens, making each member of the audience feel as if the character is speaking personally to him. The shot starts to become more objective when characters talk to each other and the camera records that interaction, showing the audience the story but not making them feel inside of it. This sense of objectivity or subjectivity is achieved not only with the camera, but with the object of the actors' focus— where they are looking during the scene. When two characters are talking to each other and there's a sense of intimacy, you'll want a tight **eyeline**, meaning that when Character A looks to Character B, she is looking very close to the camera lens. The wider the eyeline, the more objective the feel.

Let's go back to one of our scenarios with the Soldier and his Wife, the one that ended on the 50/50 shot of them embracing. If you want to see what each of them is thinking after they embrace, you have the choice of where to place your camera to get these reactions. The closer the camera is to the Soldier's or the Wife's eyeline, the more subjective the shot will be and the more the audience will be placed inside the feelings of the character. The farther you move the camera from the eyeline, the more objectively observant the shot will be (Figure 9.4).

To summarize, the farther away the camera is placed from the action, the more objective the feel. (The exception would be a close-up on a long lens, which—because it throws the background out of focus—can make the storytelling intimate, even though the camera is far away from the actor. More on that to come.) Conversely, the closer the camera is to being inside the character(s), the more subjective an impression it gives.

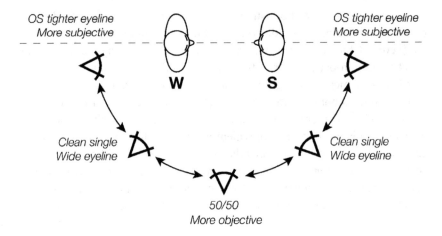

FIGURE 9.4 Camera placement for subjective and objective shots.

THE CAMERA AND OTHER EQUIPMENT

The director needs to know not only how the actors will move and what shots are planned, but also what equipment is used to achieve those shots. (We'll go over this subject next, but understand that only a general knowledge is needed.) The director has an entire crew behind him that specializes in different areas of equipment, and they do not need to be told how to use that equipment. They need to be told only what shot the director is looking to achieve; they know how to best utilize their resources.

- Camera: The device for recording pictures. These used to be primarily film cameras (35 mm or 16 mm) but now are generally **digital**, using a hard drive or memory cards as the recording element. For a better quality of recording, cameras are now usually **high-definition (HD)**.
- **Dolly**: The platform or wagon on wheels to which the camera is attached.

> The director has an entire crew behind him that specializes in different areas of equipment, and they do not need to be told how to use that equipment. They need to be told only what shot the director is looking to achieve; they know how to best utilize their resources.

- **Steadicam**: A handheld product for moving the camera; the operator wears a harness and the camera is attached to a floating head. This approach is used for **tracking shots** that move with the actor, particularly over unsteady terrain.
- **Dolly track**: Looks like a railroad track. It comes in sections and is

FIGURE 9.5 The camera waits at the end of the dolly track.
Photo by Paul Snider, *NCIS*

laid by the grip department. (We talk about crewmembers and their jobs in Chapter 11.) The wheels of the dolly move on the track, enabling the camera to move in a straight line backward or forward in a smooth way (Figure 9.5). It collapses together on an angle for easy storage and portability.

- **Dance floor**: Used when the camera movement is not in a straight line. The grips lay a floor of plywood or plastic over the existing floor to create a smooth surface.

You can also choose to use the camera **handheld**, which tends to create a bit of a bumpy frame. The camera operator simply holds the camera and moves to create the best shot as the actors move, for a very subjective feel that is an increasingly popular method of shooting.

Bethany and Mary Lou favor it only when the story truly warrants it, as it tends to call attention to the method of shooting. The audience becomes aware of the shot, rather than the story. It's essential that the audience loses any thought that interferes with their immersion in the story; they should not think about *how* it was done. As director Mike Nichols said about his classic movie *The Graduate*, "We did a lot of fancy camera shit, but nobody has ever mentioned it in 40 years because if you have events that are compelling you're completely unaware of what the camera is doing, which is the idea."

A shot is the sum of two things: (1) what is in the frame, the actors, the set, and every production design element, and (2) how those things are recorded by the camera. The camera isn't simply a box with a recording element inside of it. It is a box with lenses on it that change the size and feel of the shot. So the director also needs to know what lenses can do and what perceptions they create. (Even though most shows today are shot digitally, the lenses used are adaptations of 35 mm film lenses, and are therefore referred to in those terms.)

Lenses are the curved glass circles set into a tube and attached to the front of the camera that bend and refract light and "see" the scene, just as the lenses in your eyes do for you. The difference is that if you are standing and looking at the front of the house as if you were the Soldier in our story, your vision dictates that you will see with roughly a 35 mm lens. You can't zoom your eyes in to suddenly see an up-close version of the house. But a camera lens can. Wide lenses (9–50 mm) are short and squat. They show a picture that opens up peripherally (on the sides) but can't look deep (long). Long lenses (75–250 mm) show the up-close version. So if you are shooting from the point of view of the Soldier standing on the sidewalk, 50 feet away from the front door, a wide lens will show you the whole house. A 75 mm lens (which is a long lens because the number refers to the length of the lens, i.e. a bigger number is a longer lens) would show you the full figure of the Wife as she opens the door. A 250 mm lens from the same camera position would photograph her close up.

Why would a director choose to shoot the Wife's close-up with a long lens from far away, rather than moving the camera closer to her and shooting her with a wider lens? Both are valid choices, but lenses have properties that lend different feelings to their shots; they provide different-looking shots. A wide lens can hold focus for the foreground, middle ground, and background of a shot. In our Soldier's house example, both the flowers in front of the porch (35 feet away from the camera) and the door (50 feet away from the camera) would be in focus.

Wide lenses are used for establishing shots and masters whenever you want to see the "big picture." Conversely, long lenses have a shallow depth of field. The longer the lens you use, the more shallow the focus. (This is an oversimplification in that depth of field is determined by f-stop, focusing distance, and format size. But the director need only say, "I'm looking for a close-up on a long lens," and the DP will set up the shot. The director can then assess whether that shot is really what he's looking for and continue the discussion with the DP, refining the shot until it corresponds to what the director sees in his mind's eye.) So on a 250 mm lens, the Wife's eyes might be in focus, but her nose will not be. But the feeling that a long lens gives is more filmic because the background is out of focus, bringing the viewer's attention precisely to the point that is in focus. Figures 9.6 and 9.7 show the different feelings that two lenses can give you when the framing is identical.

FIGURE 9.6 A close-up shot with a wide lens.
Actress Katie Enright, photo by Matthew Collins

FIGURE 9.7 A close-up shot with a long lens.
Actress Katie Enright, photo by Matthew Collins

There are extremes at both ends of the lens continuum. At the wide end is the **fish-eye lens**, which distorts what is in front of it. It is often used when a character is looking through a peephole in a door. At the long end, you can use an **extender**, which doubles or quadruples the capability of the lens so that a 250 mm lens becomes a 500 mm lens. The best use for this type of lens is when you want to give the impression that the subject in front of the lens is being watched from a distance, as by a paparazzo.

A shot is the sum of two things: (1) what is in the frame, the actors, the set, and every production design element, and (2) how those things are recorded by the camera.

There are two types of lenses: **fixed** (**prime**) and **zoom**. A fixed lens gives you only one focal length (25 mm, 35 mm, 50 mm, 75mm, 100 mm, and so on). A zoom lens is a continuum of sizes. Most often used is a 5:1 (five to one), which provides any focal length between 20 mm and 100 mm. The other favorite lens is the 10:1, which runs from 25 mm to 250 mm. The advantage to a zoom lens is that you have every shot possibility at the first assistant camera's fingertips. The disadvantage is that the lens may not be quite as **crisp** as a fixed lens because of the optical compromises required by the necessity of light passing through three times as many glass elements, making it difficult for a zoom lens to match the optical quality of a prime lens.

Therefore, your DP is more likely to used fixed lenses in a low-light situation such as a night exterior. However, the quality distinction between these two types of lenses is decreasing as the zoom lenses are improved, and whether you use one or the other is primarily a matter of the DP's preference.

Let's say you're shooting something like *The Bourne Identity*, in which your main character is hunting for another character in the environment of New York's Grand Central Station. You want to show the audience where you are. So you'll shoot an establishing shot, probably from a high angle, on a wide lens, which shows the space and the people in the space and gives the feeling of the crowds and urgency. You then might shoot both a master (full figure plus some of the environment) and a mini-master (the main character who is being hunted plus whomever he interacts with) so that the audience understands the action but still has a sense of the environment. Then you might shoot the close-ups in various sizes to show the hunted's physicality and expression so that the audience can see how that character is feeling, and if you want to show how frantic or disoriented the character is, you might **dutch** (tilt) the angle. If the director wants to show that the hunted one is being watched from a distance, he will use a long lens. If, instead, the director wants to depict immediacy and have the audience feel as if they are in the same space as the character, he will use wider lenses and be closer to the actor. You might even go handheld and get right up in the actor's face. All of this would be intercut with the other character who is watching: the hunter. You would choose lenses, shot size, and shot movement in order to tell his side of the story.

MOVING THE SHOT

What is shot movement? We have already briefly mentioned push-ins and pull-outs, which means that the camera goes closer to the actor or withdraws from the actor. These are **dolly shots** because the camera is mounted on the dolly. These shots are storytelling devices in that they help give a feeling to the audience. A push-in says, "This is important, let's get closer." A pull-out says, "All's well that end's well." (Or it could say, "This character is all alone in this space.") Another kind of dolly shot is the **lateral dolly**, in which the camera moves sideways across the plane in front of the actor(s). This shot is used when characters are in one place for a long time, like sitting on a park bench side by side and you want to be graceful and lyrical in movement, not static. A type of lateral dolly is the **counter**, in which the camera moves in the opposite direction from a walking actor. All of these shots can be done on a dolly, Steadicam, handheld, or crane.

There are various types of crane available, ranging from the kind that was used in *Gone With the Wind* in 1939 to the technocrane of today, which has a hydraulic arm and is operated remotely.

Your crew can usually figure out a way to achieve any shot that you can imagine. And they want to do so because helping the director achieve her vision engages their own creativity and ingenuity. They will use their knowledge and skills so that the director will say *what* she wants to see, but not *how* to achieve that look. The DP and his crew will give you your shot, often in ways you didn't know about or hadn't foreseen.

There are ways to move the camera that don't involve moving the dolly; that is, the camera stays in one place, but it "looks around." The camera operator steers it, using control wheels.

One wheel is for up-and-down movement or **tilt**. The other wheel controls side-to-side movement or **pan**. You can imagine how this works if you picture an actor walking into a room and the camera is placed in the middle of the room. The actor enters left-to-right and the camera pans with him as he walks. When he sits down, the camera would tilt down to continue to hold him in the shot. If you wanted an

> *Your crew can usually figure out a way to achieve any shot that you can imagine. And they want to do so, because helping the director achieve her vision engages their own creativity and ingenuity.*

extremely low or high angle, you could take the camera off the dolly and attach it to a flat mounting device called a **high-hat**. The high-hat can sit on the floor, or it can be attached to the top of a ladder.

If the camera doesn't move, but the lens does, that is a zoom: the physical act of rotating the lens so the frame of the picture squeezes in or pulls out. If it's done quickly, that's a **snap-zoom**, a storytelling device that tells the audience, "Quick! Pay attention! Look at this!" Generally, zooms are for effect: a way of saying, "I want you to be aware of what the camera is doing so that you will see what I want you to see." A dolly move is less visible, and if done correctly, the audience will never be aware that in one shot, they have seen a two-shot become a close-up because they are so involved in watching the story. This move is a coordinated effort by the camera operator, the dolly grip (who physically manipulates the dolly), and the 1st camera assistant (focus puller). We talk more about this in Chapter 11.

After you have blocked the entire script, go back through it to check all your ins and outs (for both acts and scenes) and look at all your transitions, or how you get from one scene to the next. Unless it's a specific story point, you don't want to end a scene on a close-up of a character and then start the next scene in the same way or same shot. To determine the visual, look at the feeling of the scene. If it's fast and funny, you might want to have a character make a sudden entrance or even actually pop into the frame. If there's a story point you want to make, you might want to begin with that. For example, if a young woman just received some money, you could start on her (new and fancy) shoes as she enters. If the scene is somber, you would talk to your DP about the lighting, and perhaps plan a shot that showed the isolation of the character. And then check all the endings of the scenes to make sure that you have a compelling visual and have told the story and that the ending works with the beginning of the next scene.

During prep for a one-hour drama (which is usually seven days), there is much to be done. One of your most critical tasks is blocking the scenes and shot listing or storyboarding. The entire script should ideally be prepared in this way before beginning to shoot. But before you begin, you have to understand the concept of screen direction.

Because each shot is done separately (often not even in the same space and time) but ultimately must fit seamlessly into the edited end product, the director needs to adhere to the proper screen direction. That is, each character seems to be in the right place looking in the right direction in order for the audience to believe that the characters haven't crossed the line. The "line" is a figurative one that ensures that when your footage is cut together, it will appear that Character A and Character B are actually looking at one another. Picture two people facing each other, and in the rectangle of your frame, Character A (let's call her Alice) is looking left-to-right to Character B (Bob) who is looking right-to-left (Figures 9.8–9.11).

The "line" would run through the center of their figures, best seen if you imagine that you are looking at them from overhead.

In its most basic form, the important thing to understand is when you are cutting between the close-ups of Alice and Bob, they need to look at opposite sides of the frame to create the illusion they are talking to each other. So Alice looks right, and Bob looks left, and the audience believes they are facing each other and talking. When you shoot the close-up of Alice, put Bob on

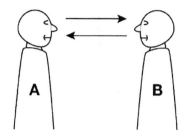 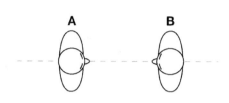

FIGURE 9.8 Character A (Alice) looking left-to-right to Character B (Bob), who is looking right-to-left.

FIGURE 9.9 An aerial view of Alice looking at Bob, with an imaginary line running through their bodies.

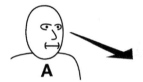 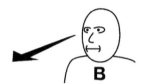

FIGURE 9.10 Alice looks left-to-right.

FIGURE 9.11 Bob looks right-to-left.

the right side of camera ("camera right") and vice versa. Seems simple enough, until Alice and Bob move around the set, and leave their cozy face-to-face position. Then how do you know where the line is?

What you have to do is cut the scene together in your head while you are shooting it, so you know which shot you will be cutting *from* and which shot you will be cutting *to*. If a character looks camera right to the other character, you would set up the reverse shot in the opposite direction. (Character A looks right, Character B looks left.) For example, in our ongoing story of the Soldier and Wife from Chapter 8, we know the line was set up in the master so the Wife looked right to the Soldier, and the Soldier looked left to the Wife (Figure 9.12).

The camera angles on the diagram show that although the first shot is next to (or over the shoulder [OLS]) of the Soldier, the lens is seeing the Wife, who looks camera right, and the camera next to/ORS the Wife depicts the Soldier looking camera left (Figure 9.13).

So it would be incorrect to place a camera on the other side of the line, because then the Wife would look left and the Soldier would look right. (Stick with us here; we know it's confusing, but once you get this, it's easy.) In your shot list, you might write: OLS Soldier to Wife, ORS Wife to Soldier. However, it's best to pay attention not to the "shoulder" aspect but to their looks: the Wife looks right, the Soldier looks left. That is how the footage will appear in the edited version in your head as well as the finished film.

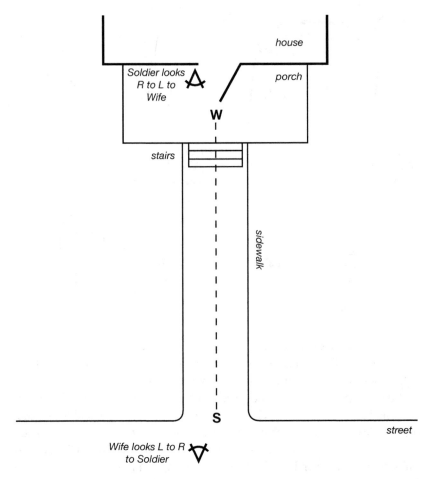

FIGURE 9.12 The "line" runs through the characters and the cameras are placed to the left of the line.

But what if the story took a turn, and the Soldier decided he wasn't ready to reunite with his Wife, and he wanted to walk away? He could turn 180 degrees and exit, and because he's on the same plane/trajectory, nothing would change. The Wife would still look camera right to him. He could choose to walk off down the sidewalk in a straight line towards camera from where he was standing at the door. Again, because the Wife would still look right to him, that is acceptable blocking. But if the Soldier reached the end of the path and turned camera left on the sidewalk and **crossed camera** (Figure 9.14), the Wife would no longer be looking camera right. She'd be looking camera left, and that is crossing the line because it has been established that she looks camera right to him.

Line

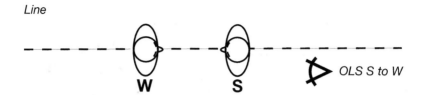

OLS S to W

The camera placement for the over the shoulder (OS) shot.

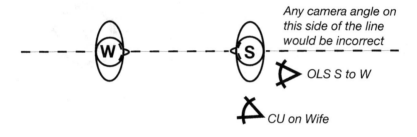

Any camera angle on this side of the line would be incorrect

OLS S to W

CU on Wife

50/50

FIGURE 9.13 What the camera sees.

At that point, the director has three options. The first is to let it be incorrect. We advise against this option, because it's jarring for the audience when the scene is cut together. The audience registers subconsciously that the Wife always looked camera right to the Soldier, so to have her suddenly look left makes it seem wrong. The second option is to move the camera (dolly) left with the Soldier, always keeping him on camera right. So the **looks** stay in the same direction, even though the actors have moved. The third option is to show the Soldier crossing the lens, and then shoot another shot of the Wife's close up and have her look camera left. That way, when it's cut together, and the audience sees the Soldier **cross the lens,** and then the next shot is of her looking left, it still **cuts together,** and everyone follows the flow and the story.

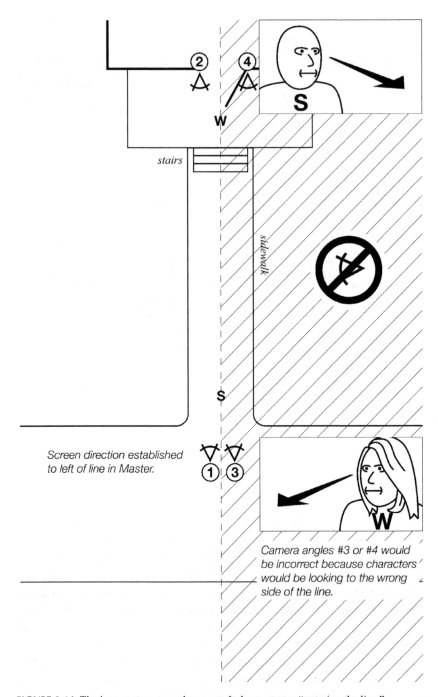

FIGURE 9.14 The incorrect camera placement. It demonstrates "crossing the line."

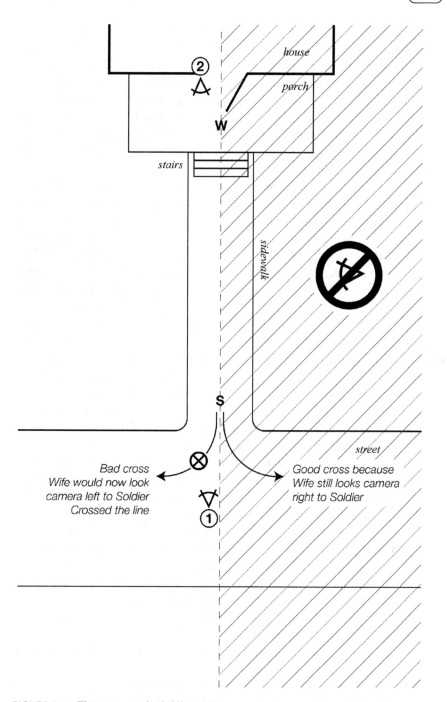

FIGURE 9.15 The two ways the Soldier might cross and why one cross maintains the correct screen direction and the other does not.

Most directors will choose option 2 when shooting a scene, in which the actors move so as to maintain the established screen direction. Remember, as long as the characters are looking in the same directions (Wife looks right, Soldier looks left) throughout the scene, it will cut together seamlessly. It doesn't matter so much exactly where they are but rather that the looks are consistent. So while you are shooting, keep in mind how the scene will cut together—which shot you are cutting *from*, which shot you are cutting *to*, and know that as long as your characters are consistent—or you show the change in screen direction—all will be well.

It sounds complicated, and it can be—especially when you are shooting a party scene, or a Thanksgiving dinner scene, or any scene with multiple characters who move around within the set. One of Mary Lou's mentors, Michael Lembeck, told her, "You're not a director until you've shot a poker game." But you will have done your blocking and shot listing in prep, and you'll feel confident that you have a handle on it because you have indicated in your script which shot you anticipate using on every line. And your script supervisor will help you keep track of this line, or screen direction, especially if the blocking deviates from the way you have planned.

Your script supervisor will help you keep track of this line, or screen direction, especially if the blocking deviates from the way you have planned.

The other person who can assist you in this is the DP, who is very aware of screen direction. If you question whether you've crossed the line, it warrants discussion with your script supervisor and DP. The DP will also help you place the cameras and the actors to get the shot with the correct screen direction. For example, if you need a character to look camera right (as the Wife does), then you would put the actor playing the Soldier to the right side of the camera, which means the camera is on the actor's left. Or if it's an OS shot, the camera would again be on the actor's left side, looking over his left shoulder and incorporating his body in foreground (fg), but most of the frame would be filled by and focused on the Wife. This is written in your shot list as OLS Soldier to Wife. If, however, you make a mistake, and put the camera on the right side of the actor, that would make the Wife look left to the Soldier, which would be crossing the line. Generally, the script supervisor or the DP will catch the mistake. But as always, the final responsibility rests with the director. So while you are shooting the scene, it's best to continually be double-checking yourself by cutting and recutting the scene in your head. Where are you cutting *from*, and where are you cutting *to*?

No matter how long a person has been directing, these questions of crossing the line continue to come up, especially in a scene in which the blocking is complex. When that happens, imagine cutting the scene together and what the previous shot screen direction is. The difficulty happens when you haven't yet shot the previous shot because in the shooting order, lighting takes precedence. As you may remember from Chapter 8, you ask your DP to light the widest shot (probably the master) in one direction and then continue lighting in that same direction. After you and the crew have lit and shot everything in one direction, you'll turn around to shoot in another direction. If, however, you are not on one axis, but looking in all four directions, the screen direction becomes complicated. Just know that you can discuss it with your script supervisor and DP and agree on the correct looks. But sometimes you end up shooting a close-up "both ways," meaning that you do it twice, once with the actor looking right, and once with the actor looking left. Then you know that in the editing room, you are protected and the film will cut together.

COVERING A TRIANGLE

When two people are talking in a scene, they are often facing each other, and we call that a 50/50 or a two-shot. But when three people are in a scene, they usually get into one of two configurations. Either one person faces the other two, or they get into a triangle (Figure 9.16). This formation can seem difficult to shoot, but there is a way to cover a triangle in just three set-ups (with two cameras).

A director will plan to put the **pivot** character, the one with the weight of the scene and/or the most dialogue, at the top point of the triangle. That character is usually talking to both of the other characters equally (often trying to convince them of something). In this case, Alice is making her case to Bob and Carl. So then your shot list would look like this:

1a: med. wide three shot with the pivot character furthest from camera
1b: clean single pivot person in center (with **split looks**, that is, to both sides of the camera; Alice looks camera left to Bob and camera right to Carl)
2a: OLS Carl to Bob (Bob looks right to all)
2b: OLS Alice to Bob
3a: ORS Bob to Carl (Carl looks left to all)
3b: ORS Alice to Carl.

This is a very efficient and clear way to cover a triangle. (It is also easy for the DP, because each setup is looking in one direction, not divergent ones.) The main reason for doing a clean single on the pivot person is that when cutting the scene together, you will want to have special emphasis on that character, and you'll have the added benefit of having one angle that

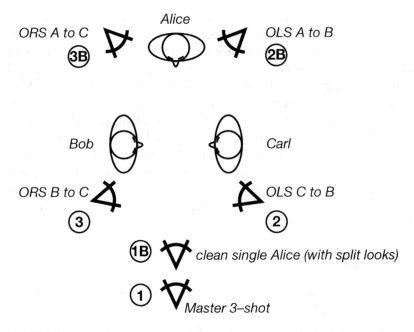

FIGURE 9.16 Illustrating camera positions when shooting a triangle formation.

doesn't have a shoulder in it. It's a little like the story about covering a conversation at a table that has a lit candle in the middle. You don't want that candle in every shot, because it would be jumping around: in one frame it would be on the left, in the opposite coverage it would be on the right, and soon the audience is just looking at the jumping candle, and not the characters talking in its background. Similarly, when watching a scene with three characters which was shot only in overs, it becomes a scene about a lot of foreground shoulders. It's helpful to have the three shot and the single to intercut with the overs to make it a more dynamic scene.

There is so much to think about when doing your shot listing, isn't there? Complicating your already arduous thought process as you shoot is another consideration: How much time do you have to shoot?

MAKING THE DAY

In an average 12-hour single-camera production day (7:00 a.m. to 8:00 p.m.), most television shows average about 25 setups (individual shots) per day. It takes that long because each scene must be rehearsed, blocked, and shot. There is also time allotted for things like hair and makeup touchups. Uncomplicated shots take a minimum of 30 minutes. Depending on the lighting, and what kind of shot it is, it could take far longer than that—up to 2 hours. (Feature films usually top out at 10 setups a day.)

In an average 12-hour single-camera production day (7:00 a.m. to 8:00 p.m.), most television shows average about 25 setups (individual shots) per day.

But then there are complicated shots, plus things can go wrong, which is statistically likely because of the sheer number of people involved. If there are 50 crewmembers, plus let's say 5 actors, that's 55 opportunities for obstacles, not to mention the equipment snafus. So let's say that almost every TV production can accomplish 25 setups within the usual 12-hour day. If two cameras are used, obviously you could double the amount of setups. You are normally expected to shoot 4 to 7 scenes in a day.

What if, in your prep, you planned to shoot 12 setups in each scene? Well, 4 (scenes) times 12 (setups) is already 48 setups, which is generally not possible. If you have two cameras, you might make it. But what if you have 6 scenes, not 4? Logistically, you have to look at your day and know that only a certain amount of sausage will fit in the casing. You have to add up the shots you planned in all the scenes scheduled for the day and determine whether what you have planned is feasible. You also have to restrict the number of **takes**, or tries, of each shot. Three good takes require much less time than ten takes, especially if you know what you're looking for in terms of performance or shot execution. If you have overloaded your day, then you have to make adjustments to your plans. If you stubbornly don't adjust your shot planning and think, "I'll just make it somehow," you run the danger of having the producers **pull the plug**. That's a pretty literal description: suddenly, it's all over, and you may have to **drop a scene** and not finish your planned work.

So now you are over budget and you didn't make the day (complete the scheduled work while staying on time and on budget). Not a good place for a responsible director to be in. So let's go back: How could you have figured out what to do in order to tell the story in the time allotted? Perhaps you get less **coverage**, which refers to the number of shots it takes to do a good job of telling the story. You might choose to shoot a scene as a **oner**, with only one shot. This is generally effective if it's a **walk 'n' talk**, when two characters stroll in a straight line while talking. You could either have the camera at the end point on a long lens, or dolly alongside the actors, or you could do both at the same time if you have two cameras, and that would be a very effective and efficient way of covering the scene.

A director going for less coverage as a means to save time (and therefore, money) might play a moment of a scene in a two-shot (one shot, thirty minutes) rather than getting the two-shot plus two singles (three shots, ninety minutes). But less coverage is potentially dicey because you'll want as much film as possible in the editing room—more choices could mean better storytelling. We say "could," because there is also a case to be made for spare, decisive directing, like that of Clint Eastwood. It's a little like that old game show *Name that Tune*, in which a contestant would say, "I can name that tune in four notes." Well, a director like Eastwood might tell the story in only four shots, but they are magnificently perfect ones. And he might **print** only two **circled takes** of each shot (which means that only two completed shots are forwarded to the editor), but he is confident that the performance is the best it can be and that no more takes are needed. As actor Matt Damon said of Eastwood, "He's so prepared and expects everyone else to be, and so there's nothing wasted, ever. It's a real lesson in how to run a super-efficient set."[1]

The other method of condensing your shot list so that you can make the day is to block the scene more efficiently. The way to do that is to try to make sure all of the movement by the actors in a scene is on the same **axis**, which allows you to shoot in two directions instead of four. And that means less lighting and fewer setups. In other words, in a two-person scene, both actors may move north and south, but not east and west. Another way to say it is that the actors can come closer to the camera or go farther away from the camera, but cannot go side-to-side in front of the camera. There is nothing to be gained by shooting all four directions because, as we know, every time the DP and his crew have to light in a different direction, it takes more of the director's precious time. But sometimes it is necessary, given the scripted action or if there are multiple characters, to shoot in all four directions. All we're saying here is that if you can block it on the same axis, it will serve you well. Playing all the action on the same axis will not dumb down the energy of the scene because it will still register with the audience as movement. The audience is not counting how many directions or shots it takes to tell the story. The audience is just caught up in performance, going along with the story.

Bethany directed a scene in *Brothers & Sisters* that is a good model for the work process in prep, both on the director's part and the 1st AD's part. The script called for a happy occasion (a charity event) to turn bad when one of the main characters punched someone—the wrong someone. Figures 9.17 and 9.18 show a script page from this scene. The undulating marks on the left side of the page are made by the script supervisor during production to indicate which lines of dialogue were covered in which shot.

The script supervisor kept all the data about the coverage, including the slate, the shot description, and how many takes, as a facing page at the beginning of both scenes.

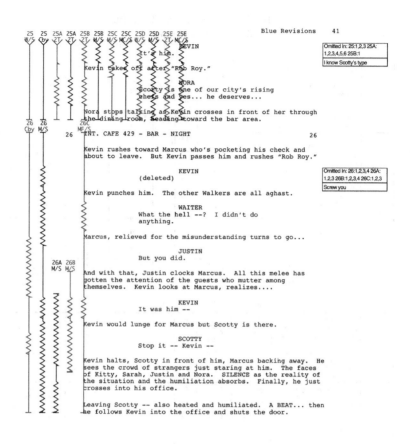

FIGURE 9.17 The marked script supervisor's page 41 of the *Brothers & Sisters* script entitled "An Ideal Husband."

Brothers & Sisters trademarks and copyrighted material have been used with the permission of ABC Studios

SCRIPT FACING PAGE (REVISED) Page: 41 (1 of 1)
506 An Ideal Husband 11/15/2010

ScriptE

Slate	Description	CR	SR	Take #	Time	Lens	Ft	T	LH	Dist	Comments
26	H/H, Cby Kevin to Rob Roy OTLS {Kevin} to Kevin OTLS Scotty to Scotty P/I to MC/S, XTDSR H/H, Cby Kevin XDS past Marcus, pan L as he turn XL into Rob Roy OTLS {Kevin}, turn DS into Kevin XDS as Scotty ent CR into Cby Kevin OTLS Scotty, XTDSR, Iv Cby Scotty P/I to MC/S Scotty XTDSR	A168 A168 A168 A168	85 85 85 85	1 2 3 4 PU	0:41 0:41 0:36 0:29						- (Take 2) -Kevin punch good (Take 4 PU) NG-NO ROLL
26	H/H, M/S H/H, M/S Marcus to M/S Justin OTRS {Marcus} to Justin FG, Walkers BG (2) H/H, M/S Marcus to M/S Justin OTRS {Marcus} to Justin FG, Walkers BG (4 PU) H/H, M/S Marcus to M/S Justin OTRS {Marcus} to Justin FG, Walkers BG	B160 B160 B160 B160	85 85 85 85	1 2 3 4 PU	0:41 0:41 0:36 0:29						- (Take 3) -P/I to M2/S Sarah, Kitty at end (Take 4 PU) BEST-BEST PUNCH FOR JUSTIN
26A	H/H, 2T Sarah, Kitty to 2T Nora (3) H/H, 2T Sarah, Kitty to 2T Nora	B160 B160 B161	85 85 85	1 2 3	0:35 0:18 0:29						-wider, also a mess (Take 2) -
26B	H/H, M/S Marcus OTLS {Justin} fall, XTUSC through door H/H, M/S Marcus OTLS {Justin), fall, XTUSC through door	A168 A168 A168 A168	85 85 85 85	1 2 3 4	0:13 0:26 0:16 0:11						- (Take 3) -good hit, but soft on push in (Take 4) BEST-
26C	HH, MF/S Kevin to Kevin OTRS {Rob Roy} to Marcus on floor to Scotty OTRS {Kevin} to Walkers OTRS {Scotty} HH, MF/S Kevin to Kevin OTRS {Rob Roy} to Justin punch Marcus to Scotty OTRS {Kevin} to Walkers OTRS {Scotty}	A168 A168 A168	85 85 85	1 2 3	0:45 0:42 0:40						- (Take 3) -good punch
26C	H/H, M/S Marcus to Justin DS, Walkers US H/H, M/S Marcus, KevinX frame USL-DSR, Justin ent USL as Marcus XR into M2/S Justin, Marcus, Marcus fall out of frame. Scotty Xinto FG, turn XTUSR, Pan L to Walkers watching in BG (3) H/H M/S Marcus to Justin DS, Walkers US	B161 B161 B161	85 85 85	1 2 3	0:45 0:42 0:40						- (Take 2) -tighter (Take 3) -good punch

FIGURE 9.18 The facing page of page 41.

With the script and floor plan in hand, Bethany sketched a small version of the floor plan on her shot list page and gave each of her characters a starting point, then imagined where each of them would go during the scene (Figure 9.19).

She then began shot listing the scene. By the time she was finished, she had 12 shots planned, which was extremely economical because several shots evolved to become multiple-use coverage (Figures 9.20 and 9.21).

Meanwhile, after the appropriate concept, department head, and production meetings, the 1st AD (Sally Sue Lander) initiated a shooting schedule and later the call sheet (Figures 9.22 and 9.23).

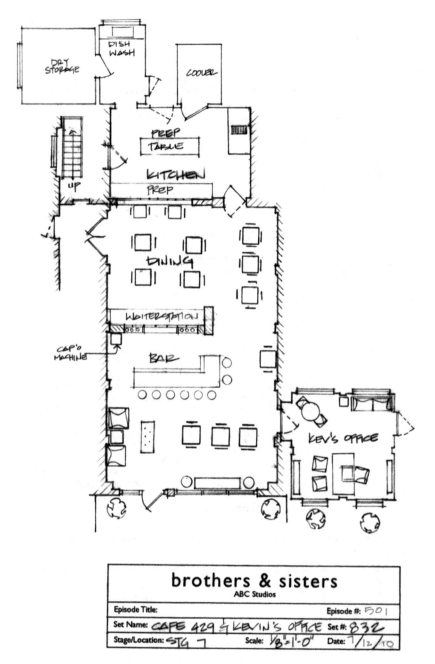

FIGURE 9.19 The floor plan for Café 429 and Kevin's office of the *Brothers & Sisters* script entitled "An Ideal Husband."

Brothers & Sisters trademarks and copyrighted material have been used with the permission of ABC Studios

SHOT LIST, B&S #506, Sc. 25-26

1)   MASTER — wide and high from left, see party, Sarah (S) and Kitty (K) foreground (fg), to end to incl. all, see Scotty (Sc) ent. right from kitchen

1B)   50/50 S&K, pull back to incl. Justin (J) when he lands for wide ORS J to S&K, pull back to incl. Kevin (Ke), see Nora (N) deep background (bg), all exit left

2)   OLS K to S (x2 sizes)

3)   ORS S to K (x2)

4)   ORS J to Ke

5)   Over crowd to N

5B)   single N

—   REVERSE   —

6)   ORS N to crowd, Woman #1 & Woman #2 fg, see Sc enter from bg kitchen, Sc exits right

6B)   clean group, rack to Sc on Woman's head turn

7)   waiter thru crowd (Is that him?)

8)   OLS Ke to J

8B)   OLS K to J

Sc. 26 (hand-held)

9)   overlap Ke exit from fg table, pan him left past Marcus (M) and cam drops in behind him, follow to become ORS Ke to M for punch, (M falls onto chair,) then Ke turns to fg ("That's him?"), then Sc steps into fg to stop Ke, becomes OLS Sc to Ke. Let Ke cross out frame right, Sc pivots onto Ke's mark, looks off cam right to others. Pan Sc out right (to office doorway) drop off onto crowd (J fg, N, S, K bg plus party crowd) (x2 – tighter)

9B)   ORS M to J for hit, crowd bg, see Ke & Sc cross thru frame. On 2nd take, push past J to tight 2 S&K, pan to N

10)   50/50 Ke and Sc after punch tie them fg to crowd bg

11)   OLS Waiter to Ke for punch, cam pushes behind Ke on turn to become ORS Ke to Sc, watch them walk away to doorway, door slams (poss. Last visual)

12)   OLS J to M for punch, pan M to front door for escape

FIGURE 9.20 Bethany's shot list for scenes 25 and 26 of the *Brothers & Sisters* script entitled "An Ideal Husband."

Brothers & Sisters trademarks and copyrighted material have been used with the permission of ABC Studios

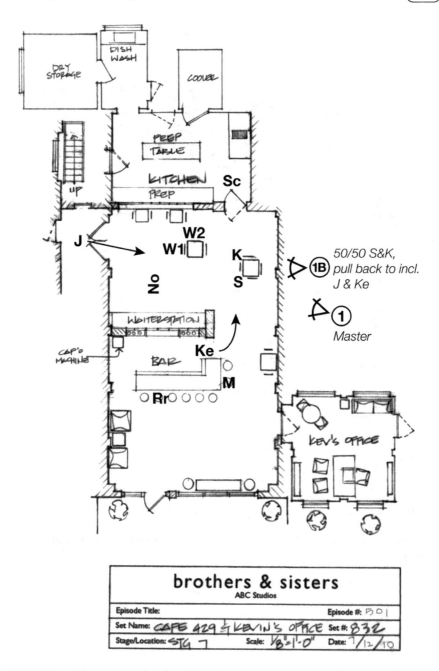

FIGURE 9.21 The starting points for all the principals in scene 25 of the *Brothers & Sisters* script entitled "An Ideal Husband."
Brothers & Sisters trademarks and copyrighted material have been used with the permission of ABC Studios

episode #506 - "an ideal husband"

Nov 19, 2010 — Shooting Schedule — Page #: 1

episode #506 - brothers + sisters - "an ideal husband"
"PINK" stripboard - dated 9/8/10
based on "PRODUCTION DRAFT" - dated 9/3/10

#7, 8, 31, 32 & 100 in @ call time to rehearse while lighting
scenes 25 & 26 will be rehearsed as one scene
Shoot Day # 1 Wednesday, September 15, 2010

Scene #	39PT, 40	INT	CAFE 429 - KEVIN'S OFFICE	Day	5/8
		SCOTTY & KEVIN TALK			D2

Cast Members
17. Scotty Wandell
Background Actors
STAND-IN FOR O.C. LINES

Props
SCOTTY'S CELL PHONE
SEE PHONE RING

Set Dressing
BEDDING ON SOFA

Wardrobe
SCOTTY IN LAST NIGHT'S CLOTHES

Scene #	25	INT	CAFE 429 - DINING ROOM	Night	3 3/8
		KEVIN FINDS OUT THE GUY IS HERE...			N1

Cast Members
1. Kitty Walker
2. Sarah Walker
3. Nora Walker
7. Justin Walker
8. Kevin Walker
17. Scotty Wandell
29. Older Woman #1
30. Older Woman #2
32. Waiter
Background Actors
3 KITCHEN STAFF
3 WAITERS
40 PARTY GUESTS

Props
BENEFIT PAMPHLETS
CENTERPIECE & PLATTER
DRINKS & APPETIZERS
KITTY'S DRINK
NO RING ON SARAH
NORA'S BENEFIT STUFF
SARAH'S DRINK

Makeup/Hair
BENEFIT LOOKS

Set Dressing
NORA STANDS ON CHAIR
NORA'S BENEFIT STUFF

Wardrobe
BENEFIT LOOKS
SCOTTY IN CHEFS' JACKET

Notes
*#7, 8, 31, 32 & 100 IN AT CALL
JACK IS NOT THERE
SAUL IS NOT THERE

FIGURE 9.22 An excerpt from the shooting schedule for that day's work on *Brothers & Sisters*.
Brothers & Sisters trademarks and copyrighted material have been used with the permission of ABC Studios

episode #506 - "an ideal husband"

Nov 19, 2010

Shooting Schedule

Page #:   2

Scene #	26	INT	CAFE 429 - BAR	Night	4/8

THE BOYS START PUNCHING

N1

Cast Members
1. Kitty Walker
2. Sarah Walker
3. Nora Walker
7. Justin Walker
8. Kevin Walker
17. Scotty Wandell
31. Marcus
32. Waiter
100. Stunt Coordinator

Background Actors
3 KITCHEN STAFF
3 WAITERS
40 PARTY GUESTS

Stunts
STUNT PADS, ETC
KEVIN PUNCHES WAITER
JUSTIN PUNCHES MARCUS

Notes
JACK IS NOT THERE
SAUL IS NOT THERE

Props
BENEFIT PAMPHLETS
CHECK
NORA'S BENEFIT STUFF
Makeup/Hair
BENEFIT LOOKS

Set Dressing
NORA'S BENEFIT STUFF
Wardrobe
BENEFIT LOOKS
SCOTTY IN CHEFS' JACKET

Scene #   27   INT   CAFE 429 - KEVIN'S OFFICE   Night   1 5/8

SCOTTY SAYS HE'S NOT PERFECT

N1

Cast Members
8. Kevin Walker
17. Scotty Wandell
Background Actors
REPEAT FEW SC. 25 & 26 BG

Props
BENEFIT PAMPHLETS
FOOD & DRINK REMINENTS

Wardrobe
SCOTTY IN CHEFS' JACKET

Notes
SEE INTO BAR

End Day # 1 Wednesday, September 15, 2010 -- Total Pages: 6 1/8

FIGURE 9.22 *continued*

TITLE: "An Ideal Husband" #E506

EXECUTIVE PRODUCER
EXECUTIVE PRODUCER
EXECUTIVE PRODUCER
EXECUTIVE PRODUCER
EXECUTIVE PRODUCER
EXECUTIVE PRODUCER
CO-EXECUTIVE PRODUCER
CO-EXECUTIVE PRODUCER
CONSULTING PRODUCER
PRODUCER
CO-PRODUCER
CO-PRODUCER
CO-PRODUCER
CO-PRODUCER
DIRECTOR: BETHANY ROONEY

abc studios

SINGLE-CAMERA FILM CALL SHEET

brothers & sisters

REPORT TO STUDIO:

800A

CALL SHEET FOR:

Wednesday, Sept. 15, 2010

SHOOT DAY:	5 of 8
CREW CALL:	800A
SHOOT CALL:	815A
LUNCH:	200P	1 HOUR WALKAWAY LUNCH
SUNRISE:	636A	
SUNSET:	700P	
WEATHER:	90°/56°	
	Sunny	

PROD. OFFICE: 500 S. BUENA VISTA ST., STAGES 6 & 7, 5TH FL., BURBANK, CA 91521

SCENE NO., SET, & SCENE DESCRIPTION		D/N	CAST	PGS.	LOCATION
-- CAST #7, 8, 31, 32, & 100 WILL REHEARSE SC. 26 AT CREW CALL --					
Sc. 39pt, 40: INT. CAFÉ 429- KEVIN'S OFFICE Scotty & Kevin talk.		D1 715A	17	5/8	STAGE 7
Sc. 25: INT. CAFÉ 429- DINING ROOM Kevin finds out the guy is here.	Scs. 25 & 26 will be rehearsed as one scene.	N1 830P	1, 2, 3, 7, 8, 17, 29, 30, 32, Atmos.	3 3/8	
Sc. 26: INT. CAFÉ 429- BAR The boys start punching.		N1 832P	1, 2, 3, 7, 8, 17, 31, 32, 100, Atmos.	6/8	
Sc. 27: INT. CAFÉ 429- KEVIN'S OFFICE Scotty says he's not perfect.		N1 834P	8, 17, Atmos.	1 5/8	
TOTAL SCENES: 4			TOTAL PAGES:	6 3/8	

#	CAST/STATUS		CHARACTER	RPT/PU	M/U-HAIR	READY AT	SPECIAL INSTRUCTIONS, MISC.
1.		W	KITTY WALKER	RPT	745A	900A	REPORT TO STUDIO
2.		W	SARAH WALKER	RPT	800A	900A	REPORT TO STUDIO
3.		W	NORA WALKER	RPT	800A	900A	REPORT TO STUDIO
7.		W	JUSTIN WALKER	RPT	800A	900A	RPT TO STUDIO, Reh. Sc. 26 at Call, Ftg. during day
8.		W	KEVIN WALKER	RPT	745A	900A	REPORT TO STUDIO, Rehearse Sc. 26 at Crew Call
17.		W	SCOTTY WANDELL	RPT	730A	815A	REPORT TO STUDIO
26.		H	LUC LAURENT	--	--	--	HOLD
29.		SW	OLDER WOMAN #1	RPT	715A	900A	REPORT TO STUDIO
30.		SW	OLDER WOMAN #2	RPT	715A	900A	REPORT TO STUDIO
31.		W	MARCUS	RPT	730A	900A	REPORT TO STUDIO, Rehearse Sc. 26 at Crew Call
32.		SW	WAITER	RPT	730A	900A	REPORT TO STUDIO, Rehearse Sc. 26 at Crew Call
100.		SWF	STUNT COORDINATOR	RPT	--	800A	REPORT TO STUDIO, Rehearse Sc. 26 at Crew Call

ALL CALLS SUBJECT TO CHANGE AT WRAP BY UPM OR AD'S. NO FORCED CALLS OR MPV'S WITHOUT PRIOR APPROVAL BY UPM. SAFETY MEETINGS CONDUCTED BY FIRST AD ON FIRST DAY OF EPISODE, ON FIRST DAY AT NEW LOCATION, WHENEVER STUNTS, SPECIAL EFFECTS, OR UNUSUAL ACTIVITY IS SCHEDULED.

ATMOSPHERE	RPT ©		DEPARTMENTAL NOTES
14 Party Guests (f)		700A	PROPERTY Benefit pamphlets. Sc. 40: Scotty's cellphone (rings on camera). Sc. 25: Centerpiece &
14 Party Guests (f)	BG ready at 900A	730A	platter, Drinks & appetizers, Kitty's drink, Nora's benefit stuff, Sarah's drink. Sc. 26: Check,
12 Party Guests (m)		800A	Nora's benefit stuff. Sc. 27: Food & drink remnants.
3 Waiters		800A	
3 Kitchen Staff		800A	WARDROBE Sc. 40: Scotty in last night's clothes. Scs. 25, 26, 27: Benefit looks, Scotty in chef's jacket.
TOTAL EXTRAS COUNT:	46		SET DRESSING Sc. 40: Bedding on sofa. Scs. 25, 26: Nora's benefit stuff. Sc. 25: Nora's stands on chair.
STAND-INS	RPT ©		
Scotty Stand-in (Johnny W.)		800A	STUNTS Sc. 26: Justin punches Marcus, Kevin punches waiter, Stunt pads, etc.
Kitty Stand-in (An)		830A	
Sarah Stand-in (Karen)	Male SI's dress for camera	830A	
Nora Stand-in (Candy)		830A	MAKE-UP/HAIR Scs. 25, 26, 27: Benefit looks.
Justin Stand-in (Ed)		830A	
Kevin Stand-in (Danny)		830A	
Marcus Stand-in (Travis)		830A	
Older Woman #1 Stand-in (TBD)		Out of BG	
Older Woman #2 Stand-in (TBD)		Out of BG	
Waiter Stand-in (TBD)		Out of BG	

ADVANCE SHOOTING SCHEDULE					
SCENE NO., SET & SCENE DESCRIPTION		D/N	CAST	PGS.	LOCATION

FIGURE 9.23 An excerpt from the 1st AD's call sheet of the *Brothers & Sisters* script. *Brothers & Sisters* trademarks and copyrighted material have been used with the permission of ABC Studios

Shot Listing

Using the scene you blocked in Chapter 8, shot list the scene, making sure (for purposes of practice) that you have planned at least six shots. List your shots by type (master, two shot, and so on) and in shooting (lighting) order, giving each shot a number. Finally, double-check your work by indicating on your script which shot (by its number) you anticipate using next to each line of dialogue or stage direction to show editing order.

It requires a fair amount of effort to stay focused and creative while deciding how to block and shot list every scene in a script. Some people might refer to it as the drudgery of the job, compared to the excitement of being on set, saying "action" and "cut," being the boss, and making movies. But by blocking and shot listing ahead of time, during your prep period, you free yourself to live in the moment on set and allow the magic to happen. You will understand the script and the story you're telling so thoroughly that you can adapt to whatever may come up on your shooting day and embrace the difficulties, knowing that in this collaborative effort, it probably won't go exactly as you planned it. But if you haven't done blocking and shot listing in prep, you'll be all knotted up in anxiety on set, wondering how to shoot a scene, unsure whether you've really told the story. It's hard to be a leader when you're not sure where you're going.

Insider Info

How Do You Interact with the Director?

To me the director is my leader, the one that knows the story and how they want to tell it, and that gives me the direction to know how to shoot and light it.

Before meeting with a director I want to have read the script and know the story and characters well. I try not to form too many opinions or form too many ideas on lenses or angles, lighting style and colors used on the lights. I may have some ideas in my head but I really don't want to settle on anything. Then as I sit down with my director, I want to listen to their ideas and thoughts, I want to know how they feel about the characters and locations, what kind of feel they want. Then ideally we would go through the script from beginning to end, that's where I ask questions, listen and give ideas. Listening is a big key, that's where we'll talk about look, hand held, steady, constant movement, stationary camera, or a combination. What lenses we will use, height of camera, style of lighting, color on lights. I think it's important to just talk about everything, not worry about budget yet, let's kind of just let the ideas flow. Some of the ideas will fit the location and budget, some will not, but maybe we can make things work by thinking hard about how to accomplish our goals.

What Should Directors Know about the Job of the DP?

I like to think of our relationship as a partnership, we are working together towards a common goal. The director of photography is a resource and the more experience they have the more solutions they will have to obstacles that will come up during the shoot. From my own experience: I was directing an episode of a TV series, on one particular day everything seemed to be going wrong and we were behind. All the scenes were daylight contingent and there we were just rehearsing our last scene of the day, I called cut on the rehearsal and turned to see the sun just go below the horizon. A moment of doom came over me. My director of photography looked at me and said I have an idea; we'll shoot the whole scene against the sky. I trusted him, I knew what I needed to tell the story and turned over the angles to him. We finished shooting the scene and as we walked to our cars the last light faded in the sky.

There come times in a director's day they must direct their full attention to getting performances, comforting actors and answering a million questions about what's happening today, tomorrow and next week. It is good to know they can trust their director of photography to carry out their vision, while they take care of business. I love it when I set up a shot and the director tells me that is exactly how they saw it. I want to be in my director's head and hopefully preparing ahead so they get all the setups and angles they need to tell the story.

What Advice Would You Give to Directors Just Starting Out?

The person you choose for your director of photography can make a huge difference. It's important to meet them, to interview carefully, to check references, more than one. Know who you are partnering up with and know what you want. There are times you can be with a director of photography that does beautiful work and has many great references, but if you don't get along, the true joy of filmmaking will be lost in poor communications, expectations not being met and visions not realized. When you find the right director of photography you become one entity, working together to reach common goals. Things are done without you having to ask, and problems are overcome. When this happens you reap the reward of seeing your work as you envisioned it on the screen.

Gordon Lonsdale
NCIS New Orleans, Bones

How Do the Director and the DP Interact During Prep?

For me, the best part of prep is the set walk with the director. Some already have detailed shot lists; others bring nothing more than note-taking materials. Either way, it provides me with the most productive time during prep.

Because there is no crew present, we are free to explore the scenes and their blocking without 40 pairs of eyes waiting for our directions.

We are free to mull over as many variations as we wish and not worry about the ever-present time considerations of a production crew. I find the resulting notes and diagrams crucial in coordinating all the departments during a shoot and pre-rigging sets correctly for the scene, making my lighting setups better and more efficient.

Tones and themes also get discussed, and those conversations tend to percolate through my mind after the walkthrough, leading to further lighting and blocking ideas.

Another benefit of set walks—less tangible than notes—is establishing a rapport with the director. Both the director and I get to communicate and collaborate on what is eventually a shared enterprise. We are able to walk onto the working set and quickly lead the crew because of our shared understanding of what we are trying to accomplish.

John Smith
Director of Photography
Brothers & Sisters, Revenge, Containment

Vocabulary

axis	dolly shot	oner
block shoot	dolly track	pan
circled takes	double-check	pivot
counter	drop a scene	print
coverage	dutch	pull the plug
crisp	extender	snap-zoom
cross camera	eyeline	split looks
cross the lens	fish-eye lens	Steadicam
cross the line	fixed (prime) lens	subjective
cut together	handheld	take
dance floor	high-definition (HD)	tilt
digital	high-hat	tracking shot
directionally	lateral dolly shot	turn around
dolly	looks	walk 'n' talk
	objective	zoom

NOTES

1   Iain Blair, "Matt Damon: 'Good Will Blessings,'" *Daily Variety*, March 26, 2010.

Prep

During the week to ten days of prep, the director does critical work to prepare for the upcoming shoot. You intensely dissect the script, you discuss the tone of the show with the writer or showrunner, and you make creative decisions about how the story you're telling should be translated to the screen, selecting every element that will appear in the frame. You also interact and share your vision with the team that you are now leading.

Before you can do anything else, you break down the script for story and character. This is where your good reading skills come into play so that you can understand the structure, beginning with the inciting action and following the plot complications that propel you to the climax and wrap up in the dénouement. You identify the plot and subplots as well as the protagonist and antagonist of the story. You figure out how all these things fit together.

You break down each character based on what the writer tells you, what the characters say about themselves, and what other characters say about the character. Then you examine what each character wants in each scene and what are the obstacles to that character achieving his intention. By the time you've done this, you are ready to cast the guest actors for your episode.

Casting goes on throughout your prep or even until the very day an actor works. Not only does the actor have to be right for the role, but the casting director must also be able to close the deal. It is a time for you to select and sometimes fight for whom you want in the part. You get the opportunity in a casting session to evaluate talent and expand your knowledge of the character by critically watching the choices that every actor makes.

Prep is when you work with the three key elements of the production design: style, color, and impact. You meet with your department heads for a concept meeting, which allows them to get the ball rolling in their individual areas of expertise. Most important, you interact with the production designer to create the overall look for the show. You give the costume designer an idea of how the characters are to be dressed, and the prop master starts finding or creating the things those characters will handle. You also discuss with the transportation coordinator any vehicles that you need for an episode, so he can find them. Prep is a time of answering questions and making decisions.

It is also a time for creating a bond with your assistant director (AD) because this relationship is key when you are shooting. During prep, your 1st AD will walk you through the sets, board the script, and create a shooting schedule. He will also arrange all your meetings, including your location and technical scout (at which you will be determining what will happen when you come back to shoot, which you later communicate to the crew).

The single most important thing you do during prep is block and shot list or storyboard. You visualize each scene and create motivated movement for the actors. Then you decide how you will shoot the script, paying specific attention to the beginning and ending of scenes and acts.

This preparation work is fundamental to the next part of your directing job: the shoot.

Shoot

Overview

What is the shoot? The shoot is the critical length of time it takes to complete principal photography. A primetime network episode usually shoots for somewhere between seven to ten days. It is also known as the production period.

What does a director do during the shoot? The director shapes the actors' performances and runs the set while those performances are being recorded on tape, film, or some other digital medium.

Specifically, during the shoot, the director works closely with the actors in an atmosphere of trust and respect so that the actors' performances tell the story as interpreted by the director. In addition, the director oversees all aspects of telling the story with the camera and sound recording equipment on the sets or within the locations selected so that the filming of the script is done in an orderly and efficient way in order to stay on time and within budget.

It is a critical time for the director to lead. It is a magic time when everyone works together to create the director's vision.

Chapter 10

Directing the Actor

Volumes have been written about acting. Mary Lou coauthored one of them with actress and author Dinah Lenney, *Acting for Young Actors* (Back Stage Books). Bethany and Mary Lou believe that the more you know about the actor's process, the better director you'll be. So where do we start when talking about directing actors? Let's begin with the 5 Ws: who, what, where, when, and why. These are the same words a journalist explores when writing the lead to a story to ensure that all the essential information is addressed in the first paragraph of a news article.

An actor begins with those same words when finding out all the information about a character he is beginning to explore.

THE ACTOR'S HOMEWORK: THE 5 WS

In acting, each word is the beginning of a question actors ask themselves about the characters they are playing, in order to provide the character with a **point of view**, or a way of being, within the world created by the script. Those questions are:

Who am I? What do I want? Where am I? When is it? Why do I want what I want?

Remember the COW chart from Chapter 2 when we talked about breaking down the script for character? This is the same work an actor hopefully does when approaching a character and asking him the first question: "Who am I?" (What does the **C**haracter say about herself, what do **O**thers say about the character, and what does the **W**riter say?) The difference between the actor and director is what they do with the raw data. The information helps directors interpret the script. For the actor, the information is the first of many clues in a complex quest toward building a character. (By the way, those last three words are the title of another acting volume *Building a Character* by the famous Russian director and actor, Konstantin Stanislavski. In one of its American inceptions, the book is the jumping-off point for the Method style of acting as explored by director Elia Kazan and members of the Group Theatre. We could go on and on about the history of modern acting, but suffice it to say that the more you know, the better director you'll be.) The actor takes the information from the script or COW chart and will, at the very least, learn the lines of dialogue written for his character. Going from the basic to the sublime, at the point of artistry, he will embody or become that character to its fullest.

The heart of playing the character is in the art of answering the next question: "What do I want?" It is essentially what the character needs and is what you explored when you looked at the character's intention in Chapter 2. The actor looks at this question in a way similar to that of the director. The actor, as the character, has to know what he wants or needs from another character. The actor can phrase this in the form of an action verb: to beg, to seduce, to demolish. And not only does the actor want to "do" something, but he also needs the other character to "do" something, too. "My character intends to seduce the other character, so the other character will do what? Leave, give me money, fall in love with me, hate me?" Intention is always a verb that provokes another action. An actor's preparation should always include the answer to the question: "What do I need to do in this scene that will cause the other character to do something in return?" When the actor plays his intention, he becomes active and doesn't play a mood. The actor's work is specific. The character gets a spine.

> *The actor takes the information from the script or COW chart and will, at the very least, learn the lines of dialogue written for his character. Going from the basic to the sublime, at the point of artistry, he will embody or become that character to its fullest.*

Moving from the actor's process to the director's for a moment: when a scene is not working well, the first thing to look at from the director's viewpoint is whether each character's intention is being pursued with full commitment. Most of the time you will make a scene better simply by addressing that question and pushing your actors to achieve their character's intention.

In exploring the third question—"Why do I want what I want?"—the character gets passion. This is where the actor takes the character from being the archetype we mentioned in Chapter 2 (which is a helpful tool to label and find the essence of a character for a director) and develops that character into the living, breathing person with specific subtleties and aspects of the personality of the actor who creates the character. Or if the character is distinctly different from the actor, the specific subtleties come from the imagination of the actor who creates the character. Either way, when actors find in themselves *why* the character needs what they need and does what they do, they explore the raw motivation of the character. And with every actor, those motivations will be unique. As Meryl Streep said, "All an actor has, I think, is their heart, really . . . that's the place you go for your inspiration."[1]

> An actor's preparation should always include the answer to the question: "What do I need to do in this scene that will cause the other character to do something in return?" When the actor plays his intention, he becomes active and doesn't play a mood. The actor's work is specific. The character gets a spine.

The last two questions are simple but crucial information for the actor to ask. The answers to "When is it?" and "Where am I?" affect an actor's sense of urgency and grounds the actor in a sense of place. There is a brilliant scene between a couple in love played by Keira Knightley and James McAvoy in Christopher Hampton's faithful screen adaptation of Ian McEwan's novel *Atonement*. It takes place in a crowded restaurant, where the two have tea. This is their first time meeting since McAvoy's character has served jail time due to a lie told by the Knightley character's sister. McAvoy has also faced brutal combat conditions in the interim. Knightley has been estranged from her family, living on her own, and working at a hospital during the war. The "when" of the scene is informed by these timely past events. Even more pressing is the limited amount of time for this reunion because Knightley's character needs to return to the hospital in half an hour. The "where" of this scene is influenced by the lack of privacy available with so many nearby restaurant patrons, especially as both characters have such intimate things they want to say.

Exploring these five questions will hopefully be the thorough kind of work an actor will do before he ever auditions for you or even meets you on a set. Hopefully, the actor—like you—has also analyzed what obstacles the characters encounter to getting what they want in each scene. But that might not be the case.

> When a scene is not working well, the first thing to look at from the director's viewpoint is whether each character's intention is being pursued with full commitment.

There are so many different ways in which an actor prepares (another three words that are the title of a Stanislavski volume: *An Actor Prepares*).

Some actors have a distinct way of working based on studying their craft; others purposely choose not to study formally. Meryl Streep went through an intense graduate program at Yale; Johnny Depp has been quoted saying, "If you catch me saying 'I am a serious actor,' I beg you to slap me."[2] The director must be prepared for either of these scenarios—and everything in between.

The most important thing to have is respect for acting. (Those last three words are the title of yet another book: *Respect for Acting* by Uta Hagen.) You need empathy for what actors do and how they put themselves on the line. If you haven't already, take an acting class. Once you've walked a mile in an actor's shoes, you'll have a firsthand understanding of what they do and how hard it is to do it because they figuratively get naked by putting their heart out there for everyone to see. You will understand why actors need a safe place to work. Figure 10.1 shows Bethany on the set of *Brothers & Sisters* giving a direction to Dave Annable, who played Justin Walker.

FIGURE 10.1 Actor Dave Annable ("Justin Walker") with director Bethany Rooney on the set of ABC's *Brothers & Sisters*.
Brothers & Sisters trademarks and copyrighted material have been used with the permission of ABC Studios

Notice the connection between actor and director. We can't stress how important it is for an actor to feel safe in his working environment, and we will talk about it more later in this chapter.

If you haven't already, take an acting class. Once you've walked a mile in an actor's shoes, you'll have a firsthand understanding of what they do and how hard it is to do it.

SHAPING A PERFORMANCE ON SET

The practical part of directing actors happens on set during rehearsal. This time is when you shape an actor's performance. It should be a **closed rehearsal**, that is, no crew members other than the script supervisor, the director of photography, and your 1st AD invited. Your actors will have done their homework, hopefully, and they will know their 5 Ws and obstacles. You don't need to discuss the scene unless they want to. Rather, begin the rehearsal by letting the actors act. You watch.

You must make sure that you and the actors are telling the same story. Here is the crucial difference between the director and the actors: the actors have asked themselves these questions about just the scene(s) they are about to do. The director has asked herself these questions about the entire script and carries the arc of the story in her head. Actors are not expected to calibrate the performance based on the overall arc of the script; that is, they may cry in the scene, when holding back tears is what is called for. Only you—the director—are responsible for knowing that each scene is a puzzle piece and where that piece fits.

This is a very subtle thing, as your actors will have read the whole script; they know the story, and they know the arc. But in that moment, when rehearsing an individual scene out of

Only you, the director, are responsible for knowing that each scene is a puzzle piece and where that piece fits.

sequence, the director is responsible for the tone of the performance.

If you are not on the same page, then discussion is warranted. Ideally, this discussion takes place during rehearsal and the actors trust you to guide them. In large-budget productions, you will get rehearsal time before you begin production. You can work through every scene and figure each one out together before camera ever rolls. But in episodic television, the only rehearsal you have is the one before you shoot the scene. Mary Lou likes to streamline this process by addressing the **subtext**, or the meaning under the line. She finds it an efficient and specific way to make sure that you're on the same page.

Here is an exercise to illustrate how subtext works.

Changing the Subtext

This exercise works great with a group. Sometimes you are the actor; sometimes you are an observer. Both are valuable ways to benefit from this exercise. Sit in a circle. The first "actor" turns to the next "actor" in the circle, makes eye contact, then delivers the line, thinking the first subtext. The line is, "I want to see you." The first subtext is, "Can't you give me a second?" Go around the entire circle. Let every person take a turn delivering the line. If it is not your turn to speak, observe whether the actor is specifically using the subtext given. As soon as everyone has said the line, change the subtext and go around the circle again. The second subtext can be, "I love you." Third, "You will stop what you are doing and pay attention to me." Fourth, "I can't stand being here."

So how does Mary Lou use the exercise on set? First, she addresses what she observed. "When you said this . . ." and here she paraphrases, being careful not to give a **line reading**, or saying the exact line in the script, rather than the subtext, "I got that you were saying this . . ." and here she states the subtext. "But I think the character is thinking this . . ." and here she states the new subtext. This approach can lead to further discussion if the actor needs clarification, but generally the actor will take that information in and Mary Lou will say, "Okay, let's try it again," and the rehearsal proceeds.

Now let's say you and your actors are on the same page, but they need some help. You need to direct them. You need to tell them how to shape or shade their performance. How do you tell them what to do? You do not need to get into a big discussion about anything. In every actor's vocabulary, there are some code words that will help you achieve what you're looking for. The fewer the words, the better. Think of them as pearls of wisdom . . . concise, pithy pearls.

So back to the words—the actor's vocabulary. You have pulled the actor aside, and you are going to give him the magic words that will improve his performance. And we're telling you, it really is like that. It's like a key that turns a lock in the actor's brain. You say the right words, the lock opens, and the magic comes out.

We've already discussed a few of these words, (point of view, subtext, intention, and obstacle), but there is also the lead-in to the magic words. Bethany often uses the phrase, "I'd like you to try [her idea]." She used to say, "Can you do [her idea]?" An older feisty actress with whom she worked liked to reply, "I *can* do anything. What do you *want* me to do, Miss Director?" The actress was putting her finger on a very salient point. When you request that an actor try [your idea], you are claiming your position as director while acknowledging that it's a creative enterprise fraught with judgment. So "I'd like you to try [my idea]" is not threatening. It is saying, "I have a direction for you to go here; let's see how it works, and don't worry—we're just trying it, so there's no heavy judgment."

When you ask an actor to try something, be specific about what you're looking for: "I'd like you to try to play the intention more strongly." Or, "I'd like you to try to play the obstacle more strongly." But because that sentence is still open to interpretation, it helps to use the verb of that particular intention. So you might say: "I'd like you to try to play the intention of rejecting him more strongly." Or "I'd like you to try to play the obstacle of still loving him more strongly." By giving the actor direction and using a verb, you are giving him something specific to do. Take, give. Honor, hurt. Protect, flee.

When you give the actor a job to do, it's a clean and clear direction. You won't have to explain yourself, except to talk about degrees of commitment to the action. That can be as simple as the 1–10 scale: "That was great. But that was about a five. I'd like to see you take it to a ten."

Ask for what you need as the director and the storyteller: "I'd like you to try to do this." If it makes you uncomfortable to speak so forthrightly, you can use the more inclusive "we." You might say, "We need more conflict in this scene." And then, perhaps, you lead your actors where you want them to go by continuing with, "How could we do that?" When your actors come up with the answers themselves, they may be more likely to commit strongly. But whether you use the autocratic "I" or the inclusive "we," the point is to steer your actors toward focusing on achieving their intentions.

Director David Nutter, who has an astonishing record of directing pilots that go to series (19 of 21), which attests to his excellence at the craft, concurs on this point of supporting the actors in their choices. He was interviewed for the DGA Visual History program, and said this:

Actors want to know that what they're doing, the choices they're making, are the right ones. So the most important thing I can bring to it is to let them know I'm really there watching them. I have my monitors, but I'm close enough to be there to watch. I'm focused on what they're doing. No matter what I do as a director, unless you have the actors to bring it together, you've got nothing. I often feel that I'm an artist with no hands or eyes, because the actors are really what it's all about. It's simply about treating them with respect.

DGA.org[2]

Ridley Scott, who has directed visually compelling films like *Gladiator*, *Black Hawk Down*, and *The Martian*, discussed the primary importance of the actors in filmmaking in *DGA Quarterly*: "I don't want to upstage what I'll be doing by having a tracking camera and cranes and shit because I've

got two great actors talking to each other across the table. Leave it. Let it be."[4] You will focus on your actors' performances and help them to make it great. And that means you won't let them get away with less than their

When you give the actor a job to do, it's a clean and clear direction. You won't have to explain yourself, except to talk about degrees of commitment to the action.

personal best—you will call them on it when their work can be better. And if they're really trying hard but not getting it, you will find the right words to help them get there.

As we discussed in Chapter 2, almost any scene will be better with a heightened sense of conflict. It's a matter of energy, of focus, of sparks flying as two characters with opposing needs meet in a power struggle. It's the difference between a tepid scene and a vibrant one. However, it isn't enough to just say, "We need more conflict." You must determine what those opposing needs are and what each character's intention is, and you must ask your actors to play that intention more strongly.

However, one thing to look out for is an actor who is playing the achievement of the intention at the beginning of the scene. In that case, you might say something like, "I feel like you're playing the end of the scene at the beginning. It might be better to **give yourself somewhere to go**, maybe play the obstacle (of whatever it is) more strongly." When you say, "You're **playing the end at the beginning**, give yourself somewhere to go," that's all you have to say. Your actor will totally get it, nod, and on the next take, make the adjustment.

But whenever you approach an actor, say something positive first. We have a shorthand for this in a catchy phrase: We suggest you should "Stroke then poke." Say to your actor, "You are really on the right track. You really touched me. And I think it will be even better if you play the intention—[or the obstacle—with specific verb] more strongly." Tell them they did well.

Then tell them how they can do it better. And when they've accomplished what you asked for, you say, "Print it. Let's move on." There are no sweeter words to the actor's ear. That means they did it. They nailed it. And when you have shown them you are worthy of their respect—because you are a great director—they want nothing more than for you to approve. And print it.

Remember in Chapter 2 when we talked about labels as a shorthand term for a type of character? A label is an adjective that describes a type of overall personality or feeling. That's a positive thing, when you, the director, are thinking of the characters as an archetype. But using labels is a negative thing when you're asking an actor to play a mood, which is giving direction by using an adjective. If you use a label with an actor, like "Play sadder," you'll get a general sad response. If you remind an actor of some specific sad thing that happened, you will get a specific response. The same goes for an ailment. Reminding an actor "You have a headache" isn't as helpful as "You feel like someone is poking a needle into your left eye." Also beware of an actor who figuratively wears a banner or label like "bad boy" or "perky girl." This choice will lead to a caricature who makes clichéd choices rather than a full-blown character who has specific needs. Suggesting an intention to the actor with a verb should steer the actor away from the general character label. Perhaps the character is a "bad boy" because he's an out-

> Tell them they did well. Then tell them how they can do it better. And when they've accomplished what you asked for, you say, "Print it. Let's move on." There are no sweeter words to the actor's ear. That means they did it. They nailed it.

sider, and all he wants now is to fit in with the group of characters in the scene. Now the actor has something specific to do—a goal to reach in the scene—and he can focus on achieving that.

CODE WORDS OR PHRASES THAT TRIGGER PERFORMANCE

What are some other code words from the actor's vocabulary? We've covered four: point of view, subtext, intention, and obstacle. Here are some more:

- **Raise the stakes.**
- **Find peaks and valleys/Find more colors.**
- **Who has the power?/Who's winning?**
- **What's the new information?/What do you find out?**
- **What if your character has this secret . . .?**
- **Did you make the event of the scene happen?**

The first one, "Raise the stakes," also means, "Commit to your intention more strongly." Make the scene more important. Care more. Make a bigger deal out of it. Sometimes an actor's energy is just a little down. All you have to say is, "Raise the stakes" and they get it. You don't need to give them a lecture on where the character has been in the previous scene or the emotional point of view. Just say, "Raise the stakes" and they'll say "Oh, okay," and the scene will be exactly what you needed. If they don't understand how much you're asking them to raise the stakes, you can give it to them in numbers: "I'd say that was a five, and I'd like it to be an eight or nine." Though that may sound nebulous, it's a way for an actor to understand to

You've hired wonderful actors who are excellent at what they do. Let them do it. Don't dictate to them every little nuance. Tell them what you're looking for, but not how to do it. Tell them the shape of what you're looking for and guide them and steer them if necessary, but please respect their craft.

what degree you want them to adjust his performance. On the next take, you may say, "Okay, you moved it up to a six. But I still think you can go stronger. I'd like to see it be an eight or nine." And now they know what you want. And if the actor fears that you're steering him to go overboard and look stupid because he'll be over-acting, you can reassure him that if he takes it to a nine and it's too far, you will bring him back. You're keeping a watchful eye and he can trust you.

The second phrase, "Find the peaks and valleys" or sometimes "Find more colors," is used when the scene is sounding all the same. Vocal inflection is flat. Don't ever, ever give an actor a line reading. Don't tell them where you want the emphasis. Just tell them, "Find more peaks and valleys" or "Find more colors," and they'll do it and probably surprise you with stuff you hadn't even foreseen. After all, you've hired wonderful actors who are excellent at what they do. Let them do it. Don't dictate to them every little nuance. Tell them *what* you're looking for, but not *how* to do it. Tell them the shape of what you're looking for and guide them and steer them if necessary, but please respect their craft.

The third code phrase, "Who has the power?" or "Who's winning?", challenges the actor to not only play his intention more strongly but make sure that the character gets results. This phrase will often make actors pay closer attention to their scene partners and then notice a shift in the scene when their character gains or loses the power. You can even use the analogy of boxing. Ask the actor to notice who is getting in the jabs and who is winning the round.

Next, the phrases "What is the new information?" or "What do you find out?" remind actors that their character makes a **discovery** in the scene. And you don't want to tell him what that discovery is. You do want him to listen and be **in the moment** (freshly aware) when that new information is told to him and see how it affects the scene. When the actor notices the shift and reacts accordingly, it makes the scene more dynamic.

Next, "What if your character has this secret . . .?" is a way for you to add some color to an actor's performance. Of course, you have to suggest something that fits with the character you already know. It shouldn't be a story point because the secret will never influence the outcome of the story, but it will shade the scene in an interesting way.

Finally, "Did you make the event of the scene happen?" is a way for you to suggest to the actor that he, as the character, must evaluate if the character did or did not get what he wanted in the scene. Regardless of the outcome of the scene, this evaluation will color whatever action the character takes next. And the added benefit is that asking that question reminds the actor that his actions or intentions are played to get results and if these results are not reached, then a new, different intention should be tried so that the character is always moving toward his objective.

All of these suggestions to actors are ways of asking them to give you more. You want them to be more specific and more invested in the character's needs. But there is one direction that is asking to give less: you want a less overt demonstration of their emotional point of view. This is called **covering**. An actor can cover, or hide, what their true intention is. It is a way of disguising intense feelings because they may not be appropriate at that moment in a scene. In the thriller *Gone Girl*, Ben Affleck, as Nick, lures Amy back (Rosamund Pike) in order to exact his revenge. He covers his true feelings in order to trick her. In a thriller or suspense story, this covering is easy to spot because the audience is often privy to the double cross or deception. The difficult thing about covering for an actor is that it isn't effective unless a moment of truth is present. Otherwise, it may seem like basically he's just a bad actor. All the audience needs in order to realize that a seemingly non-responsive character really has more going on underneath is just a brief change of expression in the eyes, a momentary flash of passion or anger, or some other escalated emotion, and then the actor's mask of covering is replaced and the scene continues.

Your actors may be exactly on target with the intent of a scene, but they may be lacking **pace**. Although you want the performances to be fully expressed, sometimes actors get a little self-indulgent as they wait for the feelings to rise in them. And in the actors' defense, they should *not* be monitoring themselves. But the director is aware that in looking at the entire scene, more pace is required to tell the story well and keep the audience's attention. Essentially, faster is better. If a two-page scene plays in four minutes, that's too long. You have two choices here. You can ask the actors for a faster pace, or you can create it in the editing room by snipping out their pauses, as we talk about in Chapter 14. It is more organic to create pace in the performance, so if you can nudge your actors along, that's better. One way to do that is to stress the urgency of the actor's intention. But if that doesn't work, Bethany has found that sometimes it's best just to say it straight. Ask your script supervisor how long the scene is playing. Then say to the actors, "That two-page scene took four minutes. We need to trim at least 45 seconds." Most of the time, the actors will accept the competitive challenge, and after the next take, will call out to the script supervisor, "How long was that?" Basically, you're asking your actors to think *and* talk, not think *then* talk. And they can do it, if you point it out to them.

Each of these phrases can be a catalyst. You want to unlock the creativity inside the actors. You might be looking for a result, but you want the actors to find the way there. Guide them so that they make the discovery. They are your collaborators; you can trust their finely honed instincts, their training and their passion for the craft.

That being said, sometimes an actor gets lost or just isn't getting where you want him to go. As a last resort, say the subtext of the line in the way you'd like the line said. Nine times out of ten, the actor will say the line with the same intonation and rhythm you just used. An example from one of Bethany's directing experiences was a scene in which a character said, "Don't you recognize the school quarterback?" Bethany gave the actor an adjustment, the change she was looking for, by saying that he should make the line more personal. But he didn't understand what she meant. So she said, "It's like, 'I hate that f——-ing guy.'" The actor nodded and delivered the line specifically and perfectly, with the same intent and intonation she had used.

> You want to unlock the creativity inside the actors. You might be looking for a result, but you want the actors to find the way there. Guide them so that they make the discovery.

One more thing about line readings. We strongly caution against using them because they are just a bandage that doesn't necessarily fix the problem: the actor may be able to repeat the line with the same intonation and rhythm you used, but may not connect to why he is saying it which causes a superficial performance rather than one rooted in authenticity. That being said, some actors actually like line readings, because it is the fastest way for them to discover the meaning of the line. If actors ask for one, shoot it to them!

HINTS FOR HONING COMEDY

When Mary Lou directs comedy, she often finds that actors employ the wrong **operative word**, or word to be stressed, to give the sentence the correct meaning in a line of dialogue. This problem can **kill the funny**, and it happens most often when an actor stresses information that the audience already knows, rather than the new information that will surprise the audience. The simple way to fix this is to simply tell the actor the word he is stressing incorrectly and which word it should be. If pointing out the word doesn't correct the problem, she demonstrates with this tried-and-true example. She asks the actor, "What kind of ice cream do you like? And please use the word 'ice cream' in your answer." He will reply, "I like vanilla ice cream," or "I like chocolate ice cream," or "I like rocky road ice cream." No matter what the answer is, she points out that "The flavor is the operative word, not the word 'ice cream' because we already know we're talking about ice cream from the question. The flavor is your new information."

She also points out that in any **runs**, or jokes that have three elements, the third element is always the funny part, and should be **punched** or stressed ever so lightly. If the actor is not aware that this is a joke, you can simply— but never condescendingly—point out the three-part structure. Be sensitive to whether your actor wants to know this kind of structural information or whether you need to suggest a method of getting your end result by putting your direction in terms of the character. We'll illustrate the two different approaches with the discussion of the next joke: the **mislead/turn** or a joke that deliberately sets up one expectation but then delivers another. The secret to the perfect delivery of this kind of joke is to disguise that there is a punch line coming. If the actor changes the rhythm or cadence from the mislead part of the joke (usually the **feed** or setup) to the turn part of the joke (usually the **payoff** or punch line), it will also make the humor crisper. So how do you get an actor to do this? The simple way is to point out the two parts of the joke. Tell the actor to "lay out" the feed and "**throw away**" or underplay the payoff. If, on the other hand, your actor is not interested in the structure of jokes, you can discuss with the actor whether the character is purposely misleading the other character. You can suggest the character "disguise his motives."

Another quick fix when you can't seem to get through to an actor is praising her for doing what you want her to do even though she didn't do it quite yet. And then say, "Let's go again" while that idea is fresh in the actor's mind. The actor will feel acknowledged and confident that it went well, but you've subliminally planted the idea of how you want it to go on the next take.

Mary Lou suggests actors **pack a suitcase** full of details about their character. These may be the character's backstory, secret, or secondary intentions and obstacles. Some details may be "worn" at will in the character's thought process. Others may never leave the suitcase. If an actor is not **thinking in character,** i.e. between the lines, it is probably because that suitcase is empty.

> Your ultimate litmus test to believing an actor's work is: Ask yourself, "When this character is not talking, is the actor still thinking 'in character'?"

Your ultimate litmus test to believing an actor's work is as follows. Ask yourself, "When this character is not talking, is the actor still thinking 'in character'?" If not, you can liken a scene to a game of catch. Most of the time, the actor is thrown a ball when the other actor delivers a line or **throws a cue**. The actor's job is to catch it and throw it back when saying the next line. But balls don't always accompany words. Sometimes balls are thrown with nonverbal signals, thoughts, or subtext. It's your job to help the actor to catch appropriately. Because you know from our discussion in Chapter 8 (and more to come in Chapter 14) that you will be editing this scene together in your head as it is being shot, you'll be very aware that listening (or **reaction**) shots are just as important as dialogue/verbal shots. Sometimes the best direction you can give an actor is just to "listen more."

PROTECTING THE ACTOR'S PROCESS

Now that you know what to say to an actor, let's talk more about how to say it. How do you do that? First, do it quietly. Take the actor aside. Do not shout at actors from the monitor. (Hopefully you will be standing on set and not be at the monitor at all . . .) You may even want to disguise your move here by publicly asking the crew for some improvement in the shot, which they can work on while you talk to the actor. Why do we advise this? Because the paramount thing to realize about working with actors is: *They are vulnerable*. Why are they vulnerable? Because what they are doing, in giving a performance, is leaving themselves open to judgment—everyone's judgment, not just the director's. The actor knows that even the dolly grip is thinking, "Hmm, that was great." Or "Hmm, that stunk." And ultimately, it is the audience who is judging his performance. You, the director, must protect your vulnerable actors. You must make actors feel safe from judgment so that they will give you their best work. How do they feel safe? When they know you will not let them look stupid. You will lead them to a truly felt and executed performance. You will not be intimidated by them, even if they are well-respected or famous. You will not let considerations of time and budget supersede what is most important: their performance. Simply, you will respect their talent, courage, and process. And they will respect your understanding of the material, your empathy for their work, and your brilliant ideas that elevate both the material and their performance. It is a vital partnership between a director and her actors, one that dictates the on-set vibe and impacts the tone of the final piece immeasurably.

Some actors may require more rehearsal than others. This can be a tricky thing to navigate. On one hand you do not want to over-rehearse the actor who is ready to film, but on the other hand, you want to give the actor who wants or needs more attention whatever will help him to do his best work. Actors are aware of their process, and it behooves the recently hired director to have a conversation with his actors before they begin shooting. "Do you like to go first (in shooting coverage) or last?" If you have actors with opposing needs, it will make your day easier. If they both like to go first, the director should defer to the most important, particularly if that person is **#1**. (The highest-billed, most important actor is generally listed as #1 on the callsheet. Each actor has a number and is often referred to that way: "#4 is late, let's get #15 **into the works** and we can shoot the third scene before the second.") If you have an actor during rehearsal demonstrate unease with the scene, we find that one-on-one time with that actor is the best idea. It might be a simple conversation that could lead to an offer to run the lines of the scene with that actor. The best time to do this is while the DP is lighting the scene. If the actor needs to do hair or wardrobe finishing touches during this time, just make sure your AD knows that you want that actor (only) brought back to set as soon as he is ready. And be sure to make that actor feel special, not penalized, for this extra attention.

> You must make actors feel safe from judgment so that they will give you their best work.

Another tool that Mary Lou has used quite successfully on set in order to get an actor to be in the moment and stop worrying about past takes, flubbed lines, or what the actor "planned to do" was to explain to the actor that we are *not* making a movie here on set . . . that will be done in editing. The mistakes will be cut out, and only the gold will be used. She explains that what we *are* doing is filming what Tony Bill in his charming and useful book *Movie Speak*[3] calls "wonderful accidents." This explanation serves as permission to the actor to not worry about what will be left on the editing floor and be free to create what will end up on the screen . . . but we highly recommend reading director Bill's book that tells, among many other things, the great story of how he came to this "how to talk to a difficult young actress" epiphany.

Talking to any actor can be difficult, especially in rehearsal. This is the time when the director and actors are tentatively feeling their way into their collaboration, and the vocabulary is different. You can't ask the actor to "raise the stakes" yet, because you're just beginning to figure out the scene together and the stakes haven't been established. The director, having done his preparation, believes he knows how the scene will play, and just exactly where and when the actors move. The actors, on the other hand, want to feel free to interpret the script in the moment and start fresh. So the motives can be diametrically opposed. Then the director can push too hard, the actor can resist. The whole rehearsal can rapidly fall apart.

What seems to work best is for the director call for a quick read-through while standing on set, then give his actors a starting point: "Okay, Lisa, why don't you enter here, and Mark, how about if you begin by folding the laundry here at the counter." Then the director stands where he plans for the camera to (eventually) be. The director says "Action," and the actors start. When the actors reach a point that the director wants something different to happen, the director might say something like "Let's stop here for a second. Lisa, I love what you're doing, how about if that move to Mark just gets interrupted by the intention of that line and you stop a little short, would that work for you?" If she doesn't say yes right away, you discuss it. Then: "Mark, I can see your character is resistant here. Maybe you could actually turn your back on her as part of what you're doing." They assent, or they offer their point of view, and you have a discussion. (This is why we recommend a closed rehearsal, because this process can take some time and you don't want crewmembers watching, judging, and getting impatient.) You say, "Let's try it," and then, "Action." And it proceeds like that, in a stop-and-go manner, the director nudging the actors toward his planned version of the scene. Unless, that is, an actor has a better idea, and then you build on that, working it into your plan if you can or otherwise adapt and think on your feet to create a new plan and shot list.

Often an actor doesn't articulate exactly why something is bothering him. Actors tend to feel instinctively and not examine the reason for the resistance. But you can deduce the reason, or simply respond with an idea that addresses the actor's issue, and pick up the rehearsal again. The basic idea is to nudge, nudge, nudge the actors in tiny incremental steps to achieve the shape of the scene as you originally visualized it, or as it has evolved while incorporating others' ideas, either the actors' or the DP's. But you never want the actors to feel like they are pawns on your chessboard; rather, it's a mutually creative experience under the supervision and yes, direction of the director. The better you become at gently nudging the actors where you want them to go, the more the finished scene will resemble what you planned.

What you cannot do, however, is be disrespectful to these creative geniuses called actors. During rehearsal, do not act the scene out for them. Do not physically touch, push, or manhandle them. Do not disregard their opinions. Get your ego out of the way and lead with gentle command.

During shooting, do not shout at them from the monitors—if you feel that you must be at video village, call "Cut," and get up, walk on set, and deliver your direction calmly and quietly. Yes, it's important to use the camera well to visually tell the story (which is why so many directors get tethered to the monitors), but it is the director's place and responsibility to be on set with those wonderful people who embody those characters and bring the script to life. And besides, the cameras have onboard monitors and additional small ones can be placed on set for the director. You won't miss the shot—but you certainly shouldn't miss witnessing the actors' performance from nearby where you can literally see into their eyes, the windows to their soul. Just do it in a respectful manner, out of their eyeline. Bethany normally tucks herself next to camera and slightly behind the first assistant cameraperson or dolly grip, where she can watch the scene unfold in front of her while occasionally glancing at the camera on-board monitor.

On a practical level, this saves a lot of time during the production day. When the director is present on set and aware of any difficulties, be they crew or cast oriented, the director can address the problem quickly. Additionally, when the director stays at the monitor, a type of phone-tag system gets set up, whereby the director tells the 2nd AD what he wants to do next, which is relayed over the walkie-talkie to the 1st AD on set, which is then communicated to the on-set cast and crew. This takes time and leads to misinterpretation. If you save five minutes on each setup just by being on set, you are probably saving over an hour each day.

Time is always ticking away on set, and the director is responsible for getting the work done in the 12-hour production day. One of the worst feelings you can have is when you've just watched a take and think, "That was crap. What do I do? The crew is looking at me, the actors are standing there waiting. What should I say? How should I fix this? And OMG, I've got to wrap in a half hour." Maybe Table 10.1 will help: it's a cheat sheet of quick fixes to put the scene back on track.

Please remember to give the stroke before the poke. All of the "right words" above could be construed as criticism or at least, correction. Our sensitive actors need to hear the positive feedback first. So the "stroke" is a mention of what they did well. You will make them feel good, make them feel like they're achieving success. Then you gently give them the "poke," the suggestion that will make their work even better. And if you're blanking on how to fix a scene, remember that nine out of ten times, asking the actors to focus on achieving their intention and raising the stakes will turn the scene from tepid to dynamic. And truthfully, you can never go wrong giving this direction. If the actors get too big in responding to this direction, you can still praise them for the effort and for finding whatever new discoveries that were generated by your direction, but now you can gently say, "That was terrific, but let's just bring it down a little bit. Let's back off from a 10 to an 8. You're totally on the right track. Now, let's go again."

TABLE 10.1 Working with actors

PROBLEM	SOLUTION	VOCABULARY
The scene seems unfocused/lacks meaning	Intention/subtext	"I'd like you to commit to your intention of (verb) more strongly."
It's slow/boring	pace	"Let's trim some time off this scene."
Big acting	Covering	"I'd like you to cover more."
Wooden acting	Activity/props	"Let's get busy, we need something to do in this scene."
No complexity	Obstacle	"I'd like you to play the obstacle (of _____)".
All sounds the same	Layers/colors	"I'd like you to find more colors."
Not listening	Mix it up	"Surprise your scene partner."
No arc	Discovery	"You're playing the end at the beginning—what is your 'ah-hah' moment here?"
No pivot point	Power exchange	"At what point do you win/lose the power?"
Low energy	Importance	"Raise the stakes."
Disconnected from text	Continuity	"Where was your character right before this?"
Disconnected from emotion	Sense memory	"How can you make that moment more specific?"

Shaping the Scene

Take the exercises from Chapter 2 where you identified the characters' needs and obstacles. Use the same scene to work on performance as you stage the scene. Break into groups of three. Two people perform and one person directs. Actors, don't make it easy on your directors. But if they communicate something that makes sense to you and that helps you interpret the script, do it. The goal here is not to stand in your director's way but to give him practice at shaping a performance. Each person should get the chance to stage his scene and direct.

Use your intuition to gauge how much or how little help an actor needs. Sometimes the mark of a great director is one who knows to just be quiet and leave well enough alone. Director Woody Allen is one of those. He said, in talking about his technique in directing actors, "I try never to talk to them. There's no point. You have Anthony Hopkins, what am I going to say to him? I hire them to get out of their way. They made great movies before me, they'll make great movies after me, and I just don't want to mess them up."[5] Tantamount to your decision should be your assessment if the actor wants or needs guidance. Some actors just want to do it and not talk about it. The great Spencer Tracy, in his very modest way, described the job of an actor this way: "Know your lines and don't bump into any furniture." If an actor has the craft of a Spencer Tracy, our advice might be: "If it ain't broke, don't fix it." But if it is "broke," use the actor's vocabulary to help her find her way to that wonderful performance. Be aware that you can't do this—you can't make a film or a TV show—without actors and that they are to be respected and cherished. They are your generous and collaborative partners, bringing their creativity to help you tell the story.

From the Experts

Excerpt from Basil Hoffman, *Cold Reading and How to Be Good at It*.[6]

Authors' note: Hoffman wrote this book for actors, but his advice to them is helpful for directors to know, especially because we believe that directors should study acting.

What Do Directors Mean When They Say, "Bring It Down," or "It's Over the Top?"
When you are asked to bring it down or pull it in, you are probably being asked tactfully to make it more real.

If you are asked to make your reading smaller, your first thought should be about the truthfulness of your work. If you are in the life of the person you are playing, the work will, of necessity, be lifelike. Life is what it is. But if you are faking the work, doing less won't help. You can't improve a big, empty performance by making it smaller. You will only wind up with a tiny, empty performance.

If I am Directed to Do the Scene Faster or Slower or Bigger or Smaller or Louder or Quieter, How Can I Make that Quick Adjustment without Being Artificial?
Regardless of how mechanical the direction seems, your adjustment must always be organic. The only way to achieve that is to make it the character's problem and not the actor's problem.

When you make character choices, as all of your acting choices should be, the options are virtually infinite. Here are a few examples:

1. "Make it faster."
   You are excited about something.

You have an urgent need to impart information.
You have an important appointment in fifteen minutes.
2. "Make it slower."
You need to make sure that they understand every point.
You don't feel comfortable about saying it.
You are not feeling well.
3. "Make it bigger."
You are losing your patience.
You are overjoyed.
The other characters are very young.
4. "Make it smaller."
The situation is intimate.
The information is confidential.
The room is small.
5. "Make it louder."
There is a lot of background noise.
What you have to say is very important.
The other characters aren't paying attention.
6. "Make it quieter."
You are ashamed of what you are saying.
You don't want to attract attention.
You are dying.

If you have studied the material, your character's options will be clear. You will be able to respond quickly to direction, and the results will be truthful and surprising. *We'd like to point out that Basil's brilliant character choices are actually directions that a director could give, and most of them incorporate verbs, i.e. you are giving the actor something to do which achieves the tone you want. So instead of saying, "Make it faster," the director could say, "You have an urgent need to tell everybody the information." It's the difference between a general, adjective-laden direction, and a specific, verb-oriented one.*

Insider Info

How Does Your Being an Actor and Director Inform Your Directing?

Well, I believe my having acted on stage fairly extensively provides me with certain advantages. I believe a large part of the job of a director is to be the surrogate audience. That applies to both the shaping of the story and how it's told, but also to providing some kind of feedback to the actor, as an audience in the theatre would. It can be very demoralizing to an actor to feel he is performing in a void. If, by your responses, you can give the actor a sense that you're really watching and getting what they're doing, it can both add to their sense of satisfaction and spur them to greater performance. That doesn't mean you have to literally report back to them every moment you saw them play after every take (god forbid!), but if, through your comments, your performance notes, your jokes, even, you make clear that you're seeing them, I believe it can make a tremendous difference in what they bring. (It also makes it harder for them to merely nod their head and then ignore your direction!)

What Do You Want Other Directors to Know about Acting?
It can look deceptively simple; acting well can be an exceptionally challenging and vulnerable thing to do. I do NOT condone coddling actors, but treating them with genuine respect and compassion is not only the right thing to do, it is most likely to set the conditions for them to do their best work in your project. People work well in creative endeavors when they feel safe to fail; it is part of your job to set those conditions.

What Is Your Advice to Young Directors?
Read everything you can. Study every aspect of the film making process. Know that it is a never-ending learning process. Particularly, take at least a year of acting classes with the best teacher who will have you. Have some sense what you are asking people to do for you, and how to speak to them. Make it your ongoing responsibility to learn THEIR language—every department—so that you can best communicate what you're asking for. Also, don't pretend to know what you don't know; ask for help. Accept that you will continually make mistakes; that's part of it. Ultimately, our job is to be decisive. Sometimes that means making what you know to be a bad decision when you can't come up with a good one. I personally believe that there is a limit to how much I can make the company I'm working with pay for my not having been able to come up with something that feels brilliant or good or adequate or even tolerable. Sometimes you have to take your lumps, accept your limits and failures, quickly make what you know to be a bad decision, and move on.

Paul McCrane
Actor, Director
ER, Harry's Law, Major Crimes, Scandal, Nashville, Glee, Empire (Director)
ER, 24, Harry's Law, Major Crimes (Actor)

Insider Info

How Do You Interact with the Director?
I have been working in the industry for years as an actress, a producer, a coach, and now a professor. I now have the honor of being on faculty at the California Institute of the Arts, teaching acting in the graduate Film Directing Program.

My responsibility to directors who are studying acting with me is to teach them not only the vocabulary necessary to work optimally with actors but also how effective the application of that language is on actors of any level or background. Knowing when and how to use that language to move actors towards deeper, richer performances is also key. The experience of walking a mile in an actor's shoes, even for a short period of time, brings both awareness and compassion to bear on the creative collaboration between actor and director.

What Do You Want Directors to Know About Acting?

I want directors to recognize that acting is one of the most important components of their storytelling. And the degree to which they understand the process of acting and what actors need in order to deliver their best performances will make the director's job easier, not harder.

Exposure to the acting process also allows directors to become great diagnosticians about what might be blocking an actor or hindering a better performance. And if a director can make a quick and accurate diagnosis, he can save himself time and money. Directors should also know that actors are so willing to give directors what they want; please know that they *want* to do the best job possible. They love to work, they love collaboration, and they want to feel as if they will not be bullied or humiliated into a better performance.

What Advice Would You Give Young Directors?

The best advice I could give young directors is to recognize the merit of the acting process. Granted, I am a bit biased, but there will be others on the set who can do certain tasks that require your supervision but not necessarily your expertise—the art director, the DP, the costumer, and so on—but nobody else on the set can deal with the actor. No one but the director. See to it that you know what that process is, so that when you are dealing with an actor who appears to be difficult or stuck or desperate, you can provide them with constructive and specific information in order to get the desired results. And if you're dealing with a seasoned star, you have the means by which you can eliminate your own fear and insecurity in order to get the desired results. Just as a conductor cannot lead an orchestra without some basic idea of how the flute fits into a particular composition, neither should the director attempt to helm a production without knowing the same about the actor.

Suanne Spoke
Acting Teacher Professor, California Institute of the Arts

Vocabulary

#1
closed rehearsal
covering
Did you make the
    event of the scene
    happen?
discovery
feed
find more colors
find peaks and valleys
give yourself
    somewhere to go

in the moment
into the works
kill the funny
line reading
mislead/turn
operative word
pace
pack a suitcase
payoff
playing the end at
    the beginning
point of view
    (for actor)
punched

raise the stakes
reaction
runs
subtext
thinking in character
throw a cue
throw away
What do you find out?
What if your character
    has this secret . . .?
What's the new
    information?
Who has the power?
Who is winning?

NOTES

1   "Meryl Streep Quotes," *Brainy Quotes*, retrieved February 11, 2011, from www.brainyquote.com/quotes/authors/m/meryl_streep.html.
2   "Johnny Depp Quotes," *Brainy Quotes*, retrieved March 8, 2016, from www.brainyquote.com/quotes/keywords/slap.html.
3   David Nutter, DGA Visual History (DGA.org).
4   Kenneth Turan, "Man of Vision," *DGA Quarterly*, Fall 2010, pp. 30–37.
5   Tony Bill, *Movie Speak, How to Talk Like You Belong on a Film Set*. New York: Workman Publishing Company, Inc., 2008.
6   Mark Olsen, "Woody Allen is Already Thinking Beyond 'You Will Meet a Tall Dark Stranger.'" *Los Angeles Times*, September 21, 2010, Sec D.
7   Basil Hoffman, *Cold Reading and How To Be Good At It*. Rancho Mirage: Dramaline Publications, 1999, pp. 45–48.

Chapter 11

Below the Line

The classification of "below the line" refers to the staff, crew, and equipment suppliers who are literally below a line on a production budget. The people who are above the line are the writer, producers, director, and actors. The "above the line" costs are—once negotiated—set in stone. The below-the-line costs are malleable (although there are union minimum salaries established) both in preproduction and production, and therefore the producer and unit production manager (UPM) will do their best to maintain cost control.

Yet those people are no less valuable. They are the ones with whom the director works on a daily basis. They are your crew—the ones who make your vision become a physical reality. They light the set, they carry in the dolly track, they hold microphones above the actors' heads, they download your footage. They work very hard, over very long hours, and we couldn't make any wide-distribution media product without them (except for you making a YouTube video at home with your mom running the camera).

YOUR BACKUP TRIO

The three crew people who "have your back" the most are your 1st AD, the DP, and the script supervisor. In postproduction, the editor is your partner in the editing process, and we will talk more about that in Chapter 14. Each of these people fulfills very specific functions under your direction with the goal of helping you achieve the best possible outcome. We talked about the 1st AD in Chapter 6, recounting how a good 1st AD is your logistics assistant in prep, and the lieutenant to your captain on set. The AD position is not generally perceived to be a "creative" one, but rather, a nuts-and-bolts one. However, there certainly are creative individuals who take on this task and can offer you suggestions as to how to shoot something more efficiently or even just . . . better. Those ADs have a director's sensibility. Be forewarned though, that if you are an AD hoping to move into the director's chair, the industry bias is against ADs: many believe that they can't be leaders and don't have the creative vision component because they're below the line and they've spent their careers dealing with logistics without final authority.

The script supervisor's job is to keep track of the correlation between the script and what is shot. She describes each shot, either on paper or on a laptop, and indicates which takes are preferred after consulting with you. The "scriptie" also makes note of the lens size, the camera roll number, and the sound roll number, so if a shot gets "lost" on its journey from production to postproduction, it will be easier to locate. But the most important facet of the script supervisor's role, as it relates to the director, is as a "second eye," another person watching the shot. She is usually someone who has been on a multitude of sets, has observed much filmmaking, and knows when something is good or not. In terms of quality, she will not express an opinion unless you ask for it. But if you need to talk something through, the script supervisor is an informed and helpful resource.

The DP is really your creative partner on set, helping you bring to life what was previously just in your head. He may use a **viewfinder** (a lens on a stick or grip) to set up a shot prior to bringing the camera to set or may use an application, like Artemis, for the same purpose. But you will discuss what the shot is exactly, based on your vision. You do not have to tell the DP which lens to use. Just describe how you "see" it. You might say something like, "I see this as starting with an empty frame, then when Character A enters, dolly back with her to pick up Character B in foreground, becoming an over. Long lens, kind of moody." Your DP may have questions or suggestions. But at that point, you step out of the way to allow the DP to get the grip, electric, and camera crews working on setting up the shot. Once you see that cameras are in place, go back on set to watch the shot and refine it with the camera operator. After the lighting is complete, you'll do a "second team and background" rehearsal, so the camera crew practices the shot, the DP can check lighting, and you can make sure that when the actors are called to set, all the physical elements are in place and ready.

Prior to working together on set, you will have interacted with the DP in prep. As you begin to block and shot list, you can talk to the DP about what you've planned and solicit an opinion. You should consult with your DP about your planned camera placement and whether you need to order special equipment to achieve the shots. The DP will also, hopefully, have the time (if not currently shooting the previous episode) to survey locations with you, in order to talk about logistics and staging the scene in backlight. This means the actors are facing away from the sun, and the DP can light their faces in individual and subtle ways—for the sun is definitely not a subtle front light. It flattens the planes of faces and makes the actors squint. Not a pretty sight. But when the sun is behind the actor, it gives a "hair light," or glow on the shoulders and top of the head, which is attractive and separates the actor from the background in this two-dimensional presentation. The DP and the gaffer will either work with an old-fashioned compass on the technical scout, or use some smartphone applications, like Helios, which gives you precise information when you're asking a specific question, such as, "This scene shoots next Thursday, third scene up. We anticipate arriving at this location at 2:00 p.m. Where will the sun be then?" Once you have that information, you may want to adjust your planned blocking so that the actors are in the best light, and the shoot goes more quickly and easily because it is staged in backlight.

The main thing is to foster a creative partnership with your DP, who will be the one lighting the set and helping you achieve your desired look. The DP will take your idea and "make it happen," using knowledge and experience to light the set appropriately, communicating with the lighting and grip crews to place lamps and then flag them off to be extremely specific about each light. Because here—just as in every other aspect of filmmaking— more specificity means better work.

The DP is responsible for the "picture" part of "motion picture," which is where this visual medium started. The DP creates mood by lighting and oversees the framing of the shots. If you are not strong in using the camera well, the DP can be an invaluable asset. Most DPs advance to their position after having previously been a camera operator, so they are extremely familiar with the equipment and what it can do, plus they are artistic in nature themselves. If, on the other hand, you feel confident in this area, it may work out that the DP is simply suggesting refinements and backing you up in the case of a mistake in crossing the line or forgetting a shot. The DP also supervises the camera operator's framing and the 1st assistant cameraperson's focus ability. If you are the type of director who is on set with the actors, not sitting at the video monitors (which we hope is true), the DP will watch the monitor and let you know if there are any technical difficulties, like soft focus. The DP continues to oversee the picture quality in postproduction, when he supervises the color correction of the digital final product to make sure that the show is finished in the intended way.

If the AD is your lieutenant, the DP is a sergeant, because many of the crewmembers report to directly to the DP. The electric, grip, and camera departments are under his supervision. No one in those departments is hired without the DP's consent and all consider him to be their boss. So in order for you to command the set, it is necessary to have a good working relationship with the DP and share creative sensibilities.

> Call everyone by their name. Smile at them and interact in a personal and interested way. Ask their opinion when you have a question pertaining to their area of expertise. Gather them in; enlist their support in achieving your vision. Convince them to have the same enthusiasm for this wonderful adventure that you do.

Everyone on the crew and staff is listed on the daily call sheet. We discussed the front of the call sheet in Chapter 6 when we talked about how the 2nd AD lists actors' call times and daily script requirements such as props and wardrobe. The back of the call sheet lists every position needed for that day, and the name of the person who will be doing the job (Figure 11.1).

For a standard TV show or feature film, the staff and crew listed there total about 120, including some of the writing and postproduction staff. It is to your advantage to learn everyone's names and positions in order to communicate clearly and inspire everyone to feel like a vital part of the organization—which they are. Bethany always conceives of this concept as a long line of interconnected cogs. The director is the one at the front, pulling everyone along and leading the way. But the director is the same size cog as everyone else, because if any one cog falls out of the line, it can go nowhere. So everyone is of the same importance. When that is your philosophy, it will be demonstrated by your actions: you will call everyone by their name. Smile at them and interact in a personal and interested way. Ask their opinion when you have a question pertaining to their area of expertise. Gather them in; enlist their support in achieving your vision. Convince them to have the same enthusiasm for this wonderful adventure that you do.

YOUR CREW AND WHAT THEY DO

So let's talk about these "cogs" and what they do. We have already discussed ADs, the DP, and the script supervisor. Here are the rest of those positions, listed by call sheet order.

Camera Department

Camera Operator: Composes and executes the shot using the picture-recording device, whether the medium is film, tape, or digital (Figure 11.2).

SINGLE-CAMERA FILM **CALL SHEET**   DATE:

TITLE:	DIRECTOR:			GENERAL COMPANY CALL:	

#	PRODUCTION	IN	#	MAKE-UP/HAIR	IN	#	TRANSPORTATION	IN
	UPM			Dept. Head Make-Up			Trans. Coord./Coord. Vehicle	
	UPM			Asst. Dept. Head			Trans. Captain/Yukon	
	Production Assoc.			Make-up Artist			Trans. Co-Captain/3 Axel Tr	
				Make-up Artist			Twin Plants/Elec Trailer	
	1st AD			Make-up Artist			Single Plant/Ward Trailer	
	Key 2nd AD			Dept. Head Hair			Stakebed #2/5-Rm Tr.	
	2nd AD			Asst. Dept. Head			Prop Truck/Craft Srv Tr.	
	Add'l 2nd AD			Hair Stylist			9 Axle Tractor Grip Tr.	
				Hair Stylist			Fueler/Makeup Tr.	
	Key Set PA			Hair Stylists			Stake #1/3 Car Tr.	
	Set PA			WARDROBE			Stakebed #2/5-Rm Tr.	
	Set PA			Costume Designer			Stake #3/2 Rm Tr. #1	
				Costume Supervisor			Stake #4/2 Rm Tr. #2	
	Script Supervisor			Shopper			Maxi Van #1	
				Shopper			Maxi Van #2	
	CAMERA			Set Costumer			5 Ton Set Dec #1	
	Dir. of Photog.			Set Costumer			5 Ton Set Dec #2	
	Dir. of Photog.			Set Costumer			Construction Stake #1	
	A-Cam Operator			Costumer/Swing			Electric Trailer	
	A-Cam 1st AC			Tailor/Fitter			Wardrobe Trailer	
	A-Cam 2nd AC			Wardrobe P.A.				
	B-Cam Operator			ART DEPT.			Forklift	
	B-Cam 1st AC			Prod. Designer	O/C		Electric Rigging 10 Ton	
	B-Cam 2nd AC			Art Director	O/C			
	Loader			Set Designer	O/C			
				Art Dept Coord.	O/C			
				Art Dept P.A.	O/C			
	GRIP			SET DRESSING				
	Key Grip			Set Decorator	O/C			
	Best Boy Grip			Leadman	O/C			
	A-Cam Dolly Grip			Buyer/Shopper	O/C			
	B-Cam Dolly Grip			Buyer/Shopper	O/C			
	Company Grip			On Set Dresser				
	Company Grip			Set Dresser	O/C			
	Company Grip			Set Dresser	O/C			
	Add'l Co. Grip			Set Dresser	O/C			
	Add'l Co. Grip			Set Dresser	O/C			
				Set Dresser	O/C			
	Key Rigging Grip	O/C		Set Dec. PA	O/C			
	Rigging Best Boy Grip	O/C		CONSTRUCTION				
	Rigging Grip	O/C		Construction Coord.				
	Rigging Grip	O/C		General Foreman				
				Labor Foreman				
	ELECTRIC			Location Foreman				
	Chief Lighting Tech.			Toolman Gang Boss				
	Ass't CLT/Best Boy			Paint Foreman				
	Set Lighting Tech.			Plaster Foreman				
	Set Lighting Tech.			GREENS			EQUIPMENT	
	Set Lighting Tech.			Greensperson	O/C			
	Set Lighting Tech.			Greensperson	O/C			
	Add'l Set Lighting Tech.			VIDEO				
	Dimmer Op./Add'l SLT			Video Computer Super.	O/C			
				Video Operator			CATERING	
	Rigging Gaffer	O/C		WRITING			Caterer	
	Rigging Best Boy	O/C		Executive Story Editor	O/C		Breakfast	Ready @
	Rigging Elec.	O/C		Executive Story Editor	O/C		Lunch	Ready @
	Rigging Elec.	O/C		Staff Writer	O/C		Craft Service	
	PROPERTY			Staff Writer	O/C		Craft Service	
	Property Master	O/C		Staff Writer/ABC Fellow	O/C		Craft Service	
	Ass't Prop. Master			Script Coordinator	O/C		Layout Board Tech	
	Property Ass't			Writers' Assistant	O/C			
	Property Ass't			Writers' Assistant	O/C		ASSISTANTS	
	Property Ass't			Writers' P.A.	O/C			
	Property Ass't			CASTING				
	Shopper	O/C		Casting Director	O/C			
	SOUND			Casting Director	O/C			
	Sound Mixer			Casting Assistant	O/C			
	Boom Operator			B.G. Casting	--			
	Utility Sound Tech				O/C			
114	Walkie-Talkies				O/C			
	ACCOUNTING			POST-PRODUCTION			OFFICE STAFF	
	Prod. Accountant	O/C		Co-Producer	O/C		Production Supervisor	
	1st Ass't Acc't	O/C		Associate Producer	O/C		Prod. Coordinator	
	2nd Ass't Acc't	O/C		Editor	O/C		Ass't Prod. Coord.	
	Payroll Accountant	O/C		Editor	O/C		Office P.A.	
	2nd 2nd Acc't Analise McNeil	O/C		Editor	O/C		Office P.A.	
	LOCATIONS			Ass't Editor	O/C		Office P.A.	
	Location Manager	O/C		Ass't Editor	O/C		STUDIO SET OP'S	
	Key Ass't Loc. Mgr.	O/C		Ass't Editor	O/C		Open Stage	
	Key Ass't Loc. Mgr.	O/C		Post Coordinator	O/C		A.C. /Heat on Stage	
				Post P.A.	O/C		Power on Stage	
				OTHER CREW			Dressing Rooms	
	HOSPITAL:						Radio Channels:	

FIGURE 11.1 The back of a call sheet listing all the crewmembers.

FIGURE 11.2 Bethany discusses the composition of a shot with A-Cam operator Ben Spek. *Brothers & Sisters* trademarks and copyrighted material are used with the permission of ABC Studios

1st Assistant Camera: Focuses the camera lens during the shot; supervises the physical operation of the camera.

2nd Assistant Camera: Keeps the camera log, noting duration of each shot and the physical statistics (type of lens, focal length), does the **slate** (you know, the board that is slapped shut to identify and signal the beginning of the take), organizes and protects the equipment.

Loader: Makes sure there is film (or whatever) in the camera, also known as "stuffing the turkey"; makes sure the recorded medium gets to the transportation department at the end of the shooting day so that it may begin to be processed.

Digital Technician: Watches monitors to make sure the picture quality is acceptable, adjusts gain and balance on the hard drive as necessary; this is an optional position if the DP wants to handle this himself.

Trainee: Someone who wants to learn!

Electrical Department

Gaffer: Oversees the electrical crew and sets lights; the DP's second-in-command.

Best Boy: Executes gaffer's instructions; may scout locations on behalf of the electrical crew and prepares accordingly, ordering equipment and manpower; next in command to the gaffer.

Lamp Operator: Moves lights into position; may be four or more on crew.

Genny (Generator) Operator: Supervises the power source.

Rigging Crew: Lays cable and prepares sets and locations electrically ahead of time; hangs and pre-rigs lights in the pattern dictated by the DP; consists of a gaffer, best boy, and lamp ops.

Grip Department

Key Grip: Supervises the "workmen" of the crew; building and facilitating camera and electric crew requirements (for example, flag lamps and lay dolly track for the camera); is the go-to guy for set problem solving.

Best Boy: Second in command, may scout and prepare locations, ordering equipment and manpower.

Dolly Grip: Physically pushes, pulls, and otherwise manipulates the dolly to achieve the shot.

Grips: Do any physical labor on set, can be known as "hammers," may be four or more on crew. The grips store and use devices unique to the film industry, like **C-stands** and **apple boxes.** A C-stand (Fig. 11.3) is a portable metal pole with attached adjustable clamps that allow the grips to hang or rig elements like **duvetyne** or flags to control the light. An apple box is a small wooden box (that reminds one of antique apple crates) that has multiple uses, including as a seat for the director next to the camera! It is also handy for raising actors to a different height than God gave them. They come in four sizes: full, half, quarter, and pancake (or eighth).

FIGURE 11.3 An adjustable C-stand is used to mount a camera to the front bumper of a car. Photo by Paul Snider, *NCIS*

Rigging Crew: Prepares locations and sets ahead of time, often by "hanging blacks" to block out windows.

Sound Department

Mixer: Operates the recorder to capture the dialogue separately from the video or picture, supervises the sound crew.

Boom Operator: Physically holds a pole (**boom**) with a microphone attached over the actors' heads. Sound is carried via cable to the recorder; can apply and adjust wireless microphones ("mics") to the actors if that is the method chosen by the mixer.

Cable Operator: Facilitates the cabling necessary to connect the various sound equipment pieces.

Playback Operator: Plays whatever music or video is required for the scene.

Stunt Department

Coordinator: Choreographs scripted stunt action in consultation with the director; hires the stunt performers, supervises for safety and effectiveness during the shoot.

Casting

Director(s): Consults with director/producers on casting concepts, sends out casting breakdown, listing which parts are available and their physical requirements, initiates contact with talent agents and sets up auditions, culls the best choices, supervises producer session, point person for network/studio approvals, negotiates actors' deals.

Assistants: Research actors' availability, run camera during sessions, answer inquiries, and file submissions.

Background Casting

Coordinator: Casts **extras**, or background artists who populate the scenes with the actors.

Wrangler: Supervises the extras cast during the shooting day.

Choreography

Choreographer: Designs dance sequences and teaches them to the actors/dancers.

Associate: Illustrates the moves for the dancers and supervises their physical welfare during the shoot.

Special Effects

Supervisor: Designs and creates unique physical happenings of the script; often uses water, fire, smoke, blood, explosives; generally a team of multiple **SPFX** (special effects) artists are needed. (Known as the "wizards" of filmmaking, the SPFX team works in and with production and their contributions are on set, not in postproduction.)

Visual Effects

Producer/Supervisor: Designs and creates **VFX** (visual effects) of which just one element is in production and the other half of the equation will be created in postproduction; often uses "green screen" or "blue screen" in production, which in post becomes an artistic rendering of whatever background or environment is needed, which is joined to the production footage. (Depending on the project, the VFX team could be three people or three hundred. There are many subspecialties of skills on the team, depending on the methods used. For example, if your VFX uses miniatures, your team could be composed of modelers who sculpt or build the tiny set piece. If you're making a product like *Lord of the Rings* or *Avatar*, your specialty crewmembers would include computer artists and animators.)

Makeup and Hair

Artist: Designs appropriate look and style in consultation with actors and director to augment character presentation; generally, there is a head of each department and assistants reporting to the head; besides being skilled artisans, makeup and hair crewmembers must be ad hoc psychologists who interact with the egos and vulnerabilities presented to them by the actors every morning in the makeup trailer. This group of people (along with costumes) is sometimes referred to as the **vanities**, because they enter the set en masse to inspect the actors between every take to make sure they still look as perfect as when they left the trailer. There are also makeup artists (Figure 11.4) who specialize in special effects makeup, like a burned body.

FIGURE 11.4 A makeup artist touches up a "burned" leg.
Photo by Paul Snider, *NCIS*

Costumes/Wardrobe

Designer: Creates the clothing "look" for each character; head of the department, will shop or originate designs.

Supervisor: Oversees logistics, including most communications with production.

Costumers: Dress the actors; often assigned to individuals, so a large cast requires many costumers; some specialize in prep and being "on the truck," that is, keeping track of inventory and cleaning, others are "on set."

Seamstress/Tailor: Performs repairs and fitting adjustments to the costumes.

Art Department

Production Designer: Designs the sets and coordinates the overall "look" and color scheme of a production.

Art Director: Oversees communication to and from the art department; may coordinate research.

Set Designer: Creates the blueprints and double-checks dimensions and other set requirements.

Coordinator: Facilitates communication.

Graphic Designer: Designs any logos, specialized identification needs, video displays, and prop paperwork.

Set Decoration

Decorator: Chooses all furniture and decorative objects in a set in consultation with the director and production designer.

Set Dec Buyer: Shopper.

Leadman: Responsible for the logistics and physically getting the set ready.

Dressers: Move furniture and place set dressing; prepare sets which have been previously shot so everything matches.

On Set Dresser: Works in production to move furniture and objects to make way for the camera or equipment and then reset to match.

Properties

Prop Master: Procures or has made any object that an actor/character physically touches; consults with director for choices.

Assistants: Handle props and reset them after takes; often called upon to creatively rig or find props when it's a last-minute request; can be two or more on set.

Buyer: Shopper.

Paint

Coordinator: Works with the production designer to obtain and furnish sets with required paint.

Leadman: Oversees crew that paints the sets.

Scenic: Specializes in designs (murals, etc.).

Greens

Head: Supplies and oversees care of plants, flowers, trees, and grass, whether natural or synthetic; places greens on sets.

Locations

Manager: Seeks and finds practical locations that visually tell the story and fit within the producer's budget, negotiates all contracts and supervises any preparation.

Assistants: Troubleshoot on set during production; handle logistics in prep.

Crafts Service

Head: Provides food and drink to cast and crew; cleans up any spill or mess on set; may provide first aid service if medic is not specifically assigned.

First Aid

Medic: Provides first line of defense in case of injuries.

Production Office/Accounting

Coordinator: Oversees staff and logistics.

Assistant: Helps the coordinator.

Production Assistants (PAs): Do diverse tasks from getting coffee to copying scripts to answering phones.

Accountant: Supervises all expenses and income; writes the budget.

Payroll Accountant: Cuts and delivers checks—the one the whole crew likes to see on Thursdays!

Clerks and Assistants: Do office work; bigger budget shows need more manpower.

Producer Assistants: Answer directly to individual producers and assist them in any way necessary.

Transportation

Coordinator: Procures "picture cars" which will be seen on film, oversees the department, making sure the trucks that carry a production's equipment are where they're supposed to be on time; choreographs pickups of others who may need transportation, especially actors, directors, and producers when on a distant location.

Captain: Coordinates schedules and equipment; immediate boss of all the drivers.

Drivers: Drive assigned trucks, also ferry actors and crew from place to place; can be a crew of ten (minimum) to thirty.

Catering

Chef: Cooks and supplies whatever meals are needed; typically both breakfast and lunch.

Assistants: Prepare and serve under the chef's direction.

Construction

Coordinator: Oversees the building of sets; works closely with production designer.

Foreman: Responsible for workers' safety and daily output.

Carpenters: Build the sets; usually at least four on crew.

Additional Labor

Teachers and Social Workers (if child actors are working) and Animal Wranglers (to supply and train animal actors); could also be specialized labor such as a Crane Driver.

Whose Job Is It Anyway?

Choose a partner. Make flashcards from the duties column in the previous list of jobs. Put them in a hat. Play a game to see whether you or your partner can name the right job title to go with the job description. To play a more advanced version of this game, describe scenarios of things going wrong on the set. Your partner has to figure out which person or persons will be needed to resolve these problems.

Often, crewmembers are identified literally and figuratively by their job description. First, they often own the equipment and rent it to the production company as a means of augmenting their income and controlling the viability of the product. So the transportation coordinator may own the trucks, and the Steadicam operator may own his own rig. (If a crewmember does not own the equipment a production wants to use, it can be rented from a company that specifically provides material to the production industry.) Second, most crewmembers are known by their first name, and their new last name is their position. So you may find yourself on set calling out for "Frank Greens" or "Joe Props." People take pride in what they do. No disrespect is intended by referring to them this way; it's just a shorthand communication method used on set.

Most crewmembers are known by their first name, and their new last name is their position. So you may find yourself on set calling out for "Frank Greens" or "Joe Props."

As you can see, it takes many cogs in our lineup of crewmembers working together to turn out the finished product that serves your vision. You—the director—cannot do it alone. You need the help of all of these departments —all of these people. They are all experts in their specialized fields; once they have been enlisted to service your vision, they will work very hard to make it a reality. And when you appreciate their efforts, you truly are a team.

From the Experts

From *Cinematography Theory and Practice* by Blain Brown.
Authors' note. This book is amazing! So well written and chock full of useful info for directors.
    The incredible variety of lighting styles and techniques is what makes it a lifelong learning experience. First some basic principles:

- Avoid flat front lighting. Light that comes from the sides and back is usually the way to accomplish this. Any time a light is right beside or behind the camera, that is a warning sign of possible flat, featureless lighting.
- Use techniques such as backlight, kickers, and background /set lights to separate the actors from the backgrounds, accentuate the actor's features, and create a three-dimensional image.
- Be aware of the shadows and use them to create chiaroscuro, depth, shape the scene, and mood. Don't be afraid of shadows; some cinematographers say that "the lights you don't turn on as are important as the ones you do turn on."
- Use lighting and exposure to have a full range of tones in the scene—this must take into account both the reflectances of the scene and the intensity of the lighting you put on them.
- Whenever possible, light people from the upstage side.
- When appropriate, add texture to your lights with gobos, cookies, and other methods[1]

Insider Info

How Do You Interact with the Director?
As the Department Head Hairstylist, I ask the director if she has any thoughts or ideas on certain characters' hair, for certain scenes. Sometimes, a character may not be written with any specific look, but the director may see the character disheveled, or with a tidy French twist, braids, a mohawk, or any number of styles.

I like to get all of the director's desires during prep, but there are times when the actor comes to set, and the director may come to me and ask me to add more sweat to the "Runner," take away height in the "Housewife's" crown, smooth out the curls on the "News Anchor," or make the "Homeless Girl's" hair even messier, maybe add some dreads at her nape. I have to make sure that myself and my team are always ready for any surprises or last minute wishes.

What Do You Wish Directors Knew About Your Job?
Sometimes, I think directors forget that hairstylists work with human beings (actors), not C-stands.

And, we are constantly battling the elements and outside forces: *Humidity and Rain*—frizz city!

Gravity—if the actress with the long hair is asked to lean over a desk, her hair will fall toward the ground and cover her face. That is never good. Give us a minute to establish it tucked behind her ears, or perhaps put it up, if this style hasn't already been established.

Hormonal Shifts—hair texture can change from day to day.

Product Hell—"I tried a new clarifying shampoo this morning, and I think my hair is stripped of all natural oils." Yes. Yes it is. Sigh.

Bad News—if an Actor is having a bad day, crying, needs to take a phone call, has a cold, taking medication, these will all affect our job as well.

There are circumstances when we may need a little extra time to get the actors ready for the day. That will definitely save time later. We are not taking extra time on purpose.

What Advice Would You Give a Director Who is Starting Out?

Hairstylists (and Makeup Artists, Costumers, Props) are constantly touching the actors, and when they are on set, ready to shoot, the last thing the actors want, is to be poked and prodded between every single take. If there is something specific you want from the hairstylist, be sure to talk to the person in charge of the hair department during prep and give him or her your notes. Directors have so much to deal with during prep, and many times will ask the 1st or 2nd AD to pass along those notes. I have found that not everyone speaks "hair" and it will serve the production better for the director to talk to Hair personally. This will always save time and will keep from having costly holdups on set, and keep the actors from being utterly annoyed, which will also be better for the director!

I strive to get all decisions made and taken care of during prep, so when the actors are on the set shooting, they are left alone to do their jobs, and the only reason I need to bother them is when gravity strikes, or a flyaway needs my speedy attention.

Many times I've heard about a hair need 10 minutes before we are supposed to shoot a scene, i.e.: "Oh, the director wants her hair to be a direct match to the next scene, even though it's a different script day." If I've already established THIS script day, this is a problem: a problem that could have been preempted during prep. If in any meetings, the word "hair" comes up in conversation, make sure someone, hopefully the director, has a conversation with the hairstylist. That definitely falls within the AD's realm, but directors should be all over that as well. Again, it will make for a smoother shoot.

And that is always my goal.

Stacey K. Black
Department Head Hairstylist/Director/Writer/Filmmaker/ Singer/Songwriter
The Closer, Major Crimes, Glee

Insider Info

How Do You Interact with the Director?

I can't tell you how happy it makes me that Bethany and Mary Lou are introducing you to the role of the script supervisor. Many film courses don't teach what the script supervisor does, so as a new director, when you first arrive on set, you may find yourself wondering, "Who is this person and why are they still talking to me?" I am the person who sits next to you. I am your extra set of eyes and ears: the recorder and the reporter!

As a script supervisor, it is my intention to make the director's life easier. It is my duty to ensure that we maintain the continuity and integrity of the script, keeping clear and concise logs, as well as noting your preferences and comments after each take or setup.

Before I meet you on set, I will have been given the script in order to do a breakdown, which will be distributed to all key departments—wardrobe, hair, makeup, props—so that we are literally "all on the same page."

I track the specific days in which the story takes place (Day 1, Night 1, Day 2, Night 2, etc.) as well as the time of day. This tracking keeps us in agreement and is critical for maintaining the continuity. For example, if the script says, "The clock strikes midnight," it's my responsibility and that of the prop department to make sure that the clock reads midnight!

Once on set, I note dialogue changes, screen direction, and camera angles, as well as wardrobe, hair, makeup, and prop details for matching. Some matching notes, for example, would be: "Hair style changes—in front of the ear, behind the ear? Costume changes or alterations—buttons up, buttons down? Specific props—gun in the right hand, gun in the left hand?" Or say there's an accident. At this point in the storyline, would the bandages be on, or would the bandages be off? If the director turns to me, I have the answer.

The director's work method and temperament dictate the general tone on set. A lot of my interaction becomes intuitive as I get to know the director better. My general rule for working with a director for the first time is to ask, "How do you like to work with the script supervisor?" More often than not, most directors don't have too many specifics, except for, "Make sure we're covered before we move on." Equally as important is the question of the handling of the dialogue. If an actor speaks a line incorrectly, I let the director know. I always ask the director, "Do you prefer to give the actor the note or should I?"

Besides the script breakdown, on-set matching and continuity, script marking, and various logs, I am also responsible for reporting to the Production and Postproduction departments an account of the day's work, what has been completed, and what we owe.

What Do You Wish Directors Knew About Your Job?

Again, it's my job to ask questions. I'd rather *feel* stupid asking a question than *be* stupid by not asking! More often than not, the thing I'm questioning is a legitimate concern.

As the director, you'll be bombarded with multiple questions at one time. You may look to your script supervisor for an answer. As we furiously refer to our notes, may I kindly remind you that generally we only get a few days to prep. Be patient with us. The script supervisor's job is far more complicated than you may have imagined.

What Advice Would You Give a Director Who is Starting Out?
When you're first developing your craft as a director, it's safe to assume you'll be directing low-budget/no-budget "labor of love" projects. When you are told you don't have the money to hire a script supervisor, I implore you to emphatically respond, "Find the money." Trust me, you'll save money in postproduction, and if you're saying to yourself, "I am post," again, trust me on this one.

Also, as we move further and further from film into digital, there are no "circles" or "print takes" per se. You'll want to see everything—and that is the beauty of digital. Here's where the script supervisor can be of great service to you. Give specific notes of what worked, what didn't, and what your favorite "starred (best) take" was, before you move on to the next setup.

And my biggest piece of advice is to recognize and appreciate your cast and crew. I can't tell you how much a simple "Thank you, and good job!" inspires us to work harder for you.

Nila Neukum
Script Supervisor
Better Call Saul, Neighbors

Vocabulary

apple box
boom
C-stand

duvetyne
extras
slate
SPFX

vanities
viewfinder
VFX

NOTE

1 Blain Brown, *Cinematography Theory and Practice*. New York: Focal Press, 2012, p. 116.

Chapter 12

All the Other Stuff

It would seem the simplest kind of scene to direct is with two people, sitting quietly in a room, talking about some personal issue. But even two-person scenes can have hiccups that cause them to be difficult to shoot: the actors don't like the script; they don't trust you as their director; the camera operator is out sick and his replacement isn't up to par; the backing outside the window is too close, forcing you to block the scene somewhere you hadn't planned; and so on. The point is that directing even a simple scene can be tricky. And then you get the really tricky ones: those that include animals, children, intimacy, special effects, visual effects, cars, choreography, or stunts. These types of scenes require additional knowledge of how to accommodate the special needs of those with whom you are working.

WORKING WITH ANIMALS AND KIDS

Animals can't tell you what their special needs are, but their trainer can. The trainer is the person who is the conduit for your direction to the animal. Let's say it's something fairly routine, like the dog crosses the room, picks up a toy in its mouth, and crosses back to the "mom." First, you will have to cast the dog. Your prop department will contact the various animal actor companies with the breakdown. ("Needed: one medium to large dog, with happy personality, will interact with regular cast and do some simple action.") The companies will provide you with pictures of their animals that meet the requirements. Then you will have a "casting session," where you can meet the contestants and assess them for your needs. The trainer will put them through some simple exercises (sit, lay down, shake, roll over, etc.) and you will pick one. Be sure to tell the trainer everything that is going on in the scene, even if it doesn't involve the dog.

Mary Lou auditioned a dog that could do every trick perfectly at the audition, but she failed to mention to the trainer that even though this was an interior scene, there was a simulated hurricane happening outside. The actors would be wearing wet raincoats and have wet shoes. This dog *hated* walking on any wet surface. Oops!

After the dog has been duly complimented and handed treats, you will sit down with the trainer and the script and talk about what the dog needs to learn in the next week or two during prep. The trainer will be candid about what the dog may or may not be able to achieve. This is your opportunity to ask how you and the production might be best served in shooting the dog's work. Animals are unpredictable, so your camera operator will need to be flexible and ready to go with whatever the animal does. Generally, the dog will have been trained at home for a particular **gag**, or specific action, using food or treats as his reward. On set, the trainer will show the dog the new environment and walk the dog through the basic concept, and then you and your actors are ready to shoot. Usually there are two trainers, one to start the animal and one where the animal finishes, who stand just off-camera and send commands to the dog via hand signals and small noises. The basic thing to know is that an animal will get quickly bored with repeating the same action, so your best takes will be the first ones. You never rehearse with an animal for that reason. Your prop department will supply some facsimile of the "animal actor," usually a stuffed version in roughly the same size, for the DP to light and for the cameras to rehearse with.

Some animals are more trainable than others. Dogs and horses are the best, but cats are not good candidates, because they are not as eager for approval or treats. Others (snakes and hamsters for example) just do what they do, and you work them into your script. In cases like that, you just try to keep the set quiet (so as not to spook them), work around them while setting up, and then start shooting. Mary Lou worked with a bear that necessitated having *no* food anywhere on set—including craft service. Bethany had a bison in a bank lobby, which worked out fine, except for the craft services person, who had to bring an extra-large pooper-scooper that day!

The basic thing to know is that an animal will get quickly bored with repeating the same action, so your best takes will be the first ones. Never rehearse with an animal, for that reason.

Children wear diapers (thankfully), but otherwise, working with them can sometimes feel like working with animals. But instead of a trainer, you have a parent. Make friends with the parents. Assure them that you will be kind to their child. Many of the same shooting rules apply: keep the set quiet, don't rehearse with the child present, shoot the master and the child's coverage at the same time. Basically, you want to steer the child toward doing what comes naturally and hope your actors in the scene are patient and good with children.

If you want the child to laugh, make funny faces. If you want the child to cry, give him a new toy, roll camera, then take the toy away. (You can allow the child to take the toy when his day's shooting is complete.) Be patient and kind, and use the element of surprise or new things to elicit the reactions you need. You cannot command a young child to give the performance you're looking for; you have to set it up so that the youngster's actions are organically motivated (i.e. keep pulling a toy on a string to encourage the child to walk toward the camera), all the while being upbeat and encouraging. Stern voices and negative energy are not conducive to good on-camera work with children. (Actually, that is true for everyone, including adult actors, since their inner child is very much present in this kind of vulnerable endeavor.) Mary Lou's second book, *Acting for Young Actors* (Back Stage Books), will give you more insight into working with young talent. For an older child, it's much the same, except that you can communicate more clearly and directly. When you give direction to a child or children, be at their eye level and engage them. Mary Lou will give a direction and then ask the child to repeat back the direction. If you're looking for a specific line reading, try to say the subtext using the vocal inflection you want, or equate the situation to something in her own life or age range that she can understand. ("When you're asking for more broccoli in this scene, pretend it's just like the new doll you want, okay?") Be very enthusiastic and give positive feedback when she does what you want. If it's going well, keep the camera rolling and do it again, giving her ongoing direction and encouragement. ("That's great! Now say the line again, and give your 'mom' a big hug this time!") But don't overwork the scene, because a child's performance can get worse with repetition. If you still don't have what you need, change it up. Do something different. Surprise her and keep her interest piqued.

> Don't overwork the scene, because a child's performance can get worse with repetition. If you still don't have what you need, change it up. Do something different. Surprise her and keep her interest piqued.

There is extra pressure in working with children because of their limited working hours. This is for their protection so that they don't get taken advantage of and are not overworked or used at inappropriate hours. A newborn (older than 14 days) can be under the lights (camera rolling) for a total of twenty minutes out of two total hours with the production company. The approved hours increase with older children, but there are restrictions in place until they're 18. That is why on high school-oriented shows the actors are all over 18 but look younger (or lawfully **emancipated**, that is, legally an adult). With school-age children, it is the production's responsibility to make sure they are schooled while at work and that a **studio teacher** is hired. With a nine-year-old, for example, the total allotment is nine and a half hours to be on set. A half hour for lunch, three hours for schooling, one hour for breaks. That leaves you with only four and a half hours to work with a child actor. If he is in a big scene, you may have to **shoot out** the child—that is, do the master and his coverage first, and when you turn around on the other actors, they will be interacting with a stand-in rather than the child actor, who has already gone home.

With animals and children, the director's work is all about spontaneity and being prepared. You need to be aware that there's a limited time frame to capture the magic, so everyone on the crew (and your grown-up cast) needs to be ready. The shot has been rehearsed; the final touches for makeup and hair are done; the actors stand on set and wait for the actor or the animal to be brought in. (You will have made sure your actors have visited with their little scene partner off-set, gotten to know them, created a little bit of a relationship.) So you roll camera first, then ask the trainer, the parent—or sometimes, if it's an infant, the social worker/nurse—to step on set with the child actor. You don't shout out, "Action!" but rather, quietly integrate the child or animal with the waiting actors and let the scene start without any fuss. Unless you need to make some physical adjustment, just keep rolling, reset, and get another take without cutting.

TWO KINDS OF NAKEDNESS

When working with animals and children, your main job is to protect them physically and emotionally because they are fragile. You need to protect your adult actors, too, whenever they are similarly fragile: when doing emotional work or when they have to be physically exposed.

If your script calls for a performance of rage or grief, it will require your actor to open up emotionally, putting him in a vulnerable state. You can honor that and streamline the process by making sure the set is well prepared for his arrival. You have rehearsed meticulously with the second team, then done a **"check the marks"** rehearsal with the actors so there will be no retakes because of camera mistakes. You will require quiet on set, because chatter from cast and crew is the norm, but it is distracting. Limit the crew to the absolute minimum. And you will do the coverage on the actor who is bearing the weight of the scene first. As with children's performances, which are based in a kind of naturalism, the more an actor has to cry or otherwise be emotional, the more difficult it will be to dredge up a performance based in a seemingly spontaneous reality if asked to repeat it too much.

This kind of psychic nakedness demands respect from the director. That means you shouldn't ask for extraneous takes unless you feel the story isn't being told. Tune in to the vibe, the emotional point of view the actor is registering, and communicate quietly and clearly. After you roll camera, wait silently for the actor to indicate (usually with a nod) that he is ready before quietly saying, "Action." It is part of actors' arsenal to go to this deep internal place, another tool in their bag of tricks, but it does ask more of them than usual. So don't baby them, but respect them.

A different kind of nakedness is occasionally scripted for a lovemaking scene. This scene, too, requires finesse from the director and the crew. A **courtesy screen** or drape can be put up by the grip department, which will ensure that only the core crew is there. Your actors will be strategically covered by the wardrobe department in the necessary places with flesh-colored adhesive **moleskin** and will come to set wearing robes. Talk with your actors about what the intent of the scene is, what you intend to depict, and how you can expand their comfort level.

Tell them what the parameters of each shot are, discussing it calmly and precisely. This kind of scene is essentially one of choreography, and you need to be very specific and give them direction while cameras are rolling ("Annie, bring your arm down just slightly, good, now Ben, just a gentle nibble on the earlobe, good, now let's have a strong kiss then pull back a little and look in each other's eyes"). It's up to the director to set the tone for the actors, so approach the work with specific ideas and an aura of calm problem solving. A sense of humor helps, too!

If your actors are standing or sitting, rather than lying down, be aware that kissing is best photographed in a 50/50 shot because if you're in overs (OS), the air or space normally between the two faces gets closed as the actors move in to kiss, and basically all you now have is a shot of the back of someone's head. You will probably have to ask the actors to position themselves during the kiss to the upstage or downstage side, depending on whose story you are interested in telling. A simple, "Your nose to the right," kind of direction generally does it.

> It's up to the director to set the tone for the actors, so approach the work with specific ideas and an aura of calm problem solving. A sense of humor helps, too!

WORKING WITH SPECIAL EFFECTS

Whereas a quiet type of spontaneity is a director's tool when working with the fragile and the natural (children, animals, and intimacy), your best tool with special effects (SPFX) is the opposite. This process is extremely rehearsed, so when you roll cameras, the gag or event will happen just as everyone is prepared for it to be. SPFX crews do the unusual gags in production: anything from a "pipe" breaking and water shooting everywhere to blood pooling under a "dead" body or fire raging through a building. The gag will have been discussed in prep, and multiple demonstrations (often recorded on a smart phone to facilitate feedback) of the process (called a **pre-viz**, or pre-visual demonstration) done to ensure that it will be as big or as small or as colorful as you want it. You will have committed to your camera positions ahead of time, so that when the gag is presented for camera, the operators and assistants are protected, and the crewmembers who are manipulating the equipment are safely off-camera.

Special effects guys (it's a male-dominated bastion) are well represented by the two SPFX men on Discovery Channel's *Mythbusters*. They are curious thrill-seekers who want to blow stuff up, but they're engineers and scientists too who solve the demands of the script in ingenious ways. They can usually figure out a way to do anything you can imagine, as long as there is enough prep time to work it through, rehearse, and **rig** it. They will do a lot of **dry runs**, which are rehearsals up to but not including the gag and then refine their preparation. **On the day**, SPFX guys generally pull off their gag in one take. ("On the day" means "when we do this for real." It could be ten minutes or ten days from now.)

> *You will have committed to your camera positions ahead of time, so that when the gag is presented for camera, the operators and assistants are protected and the crewmembers who are manipulating the equipment are safely off-camera.*

STUNTS

The same concept is true for stunts. These are discussed, choreographed, rigged, rehearsed, rerigged, rehearsed, discussed, rechoreographed, rerigged, pre-vized, and finally shot.

Most of this work occurs in prep, after you have imagined the scene and have begun shot listing. Your script might say, "And suddenly, Joe throws a punch at Bill. The entire place erupts in a bar fight. Joe gets the worse of it." So how are you going to depict that? You know you have three storytelling elements: (1) first punch, (2) fight among the crowd, and (3) Joe and Bill's interaction.

You will have a meeting with the stunt coordinator and your 1st AD. You'll talk about the tone of the fight: is it down and dirty? Or more stylized? Is the first punch a roundhouse or a jab? (Be sure to find out if your actor throwing the punch is right- or left-handed.) What is your next cut/shot? How does that one punch initiate the fight? Then what? How do you bring Joe into it? What does "worse" mean? Communicate your thoughts and discuss them with the coordinator.

Your next meeting will hopefully be on set, or something approximating it. (You need to know what is physically in the space; if someone is to fall over a table, you need to know where the table is and whether any furniture needs to be rigged to be **breakaway**, which means primed to break exactly as designed.) The coordinator will probably bring in two stunt people to demonstrate the planned moves, doing it at **half-speed** so that each step is clear. You will advance your opinion ("That's too John Wayne, what else can we do?") and there's a give-and-take exchange of ideas and choreography. Together, you and the coordinator will work through each move and the camera position for it.

Your next rehearsal will probably take place the day of shooting and incorporates the actors who will be **doubled**, or replaced, for the stunts. The coordinator will have hired stunt performers who approximate your actors' physicality, and the costume department will have doubled the wardrobe, allowing for the extra room in the garment for elbow, knee, and/or back pads if needed. The stunt double will be supplied with a wig by the hair department if necessary to ensure that he looks as similar to the actor as possible. You will rehearse the scene and determine where the "in" to the stunt happens, so the audience sees the actor's face.

For example, let's say the actor playing Joe is saying his lines; then he throws a "punch" toward Bill, missing him by a mile. Now you put the stunt performers in, and the fight commences, punch by punch, shot by shot, overlapping "Joe's" move in the beginning. Each move and reaction will be specifically choreographed and specifically shot. This is one instance in which we recommend that you observe from the monitors with the stunt coordinator to make sure the punches look as if they **land**. Just as you overlapped the beginning of the fight, you'll overlap the end, too, and put your actor in for the final reaction, now with blood on him from the makeup department. When it's cut together, you will have achieved what the script intended. But remember: better safe than sorry. You can't shoot with your actor, or **principal**, if he's got a split lip and a broken rib.

You will rehearse the scene and determine where the "in" to the stunt happens, so the audience sees the actor's face.

This same principle of doubling your principals is also used when shooting anything physical—not just fights. So if your script calls for skiing, or gymnastics, or jumping out of an airplane—anything that might cause your actor to be injured—you should plan to double her. That means extra expense for many departments (actor doubles, stunt doubles, hair and makeup, costume), but it is well worth it. You need to keep your actors safe and healthy (Figure 12.1). Each department will want to know how many takes you anticipate shooting in order to be prepared. So sometimes it's really not doubling, but tripling, quadrupling, and so on.

At the DGA "Action! Calling the Shots" seminar, directors Tawnia McKiernan and Jeff Wadlow along with 1st AD/UPM Stacey Beneville and 2nd Unit Director and Stunt Coordinator Jim Vickers talked about the importance of communication and safety when prepping and doing stunts. Tawnia reminded us that in a fight sequence the tighter the shot, the more exciting it will be, but that all the pieces must tell the story. Jeff, who also stressed the importance of storytelling, talked about doing various passes for various purposes. For example, he said he would start with a "Sports Pass" using multiple cameras, doing the whole sequence front to back (he may use only stunt doubles in this pass). Next he likes to do his "Impact Pass" which might feature the hero actor who is featured in an OS but may be fighting with the stunt double. He follows this pass with his "Specials Pass" which will sell the specially selected moments of the fight. With this amount of coverage necessary, Jim spoke to the trick of "backing into time" or helping

FIGURE 12.1 A stunt person takes a fall to the bag.
Photo by Paul Snider, *NCIS*

a director design a fight to fit the TV shooting schedule. Stacey talked about the efficiency of doing fights a "section at a time." Tawnia shared that you could also "infer," not show, things happening: For example, allowing an actor to leave a frame in one shot, and show the consequences in the next—the actor laid out on the floor.[1]

CAR AND WATER WORK

Writers seem to love writing scenes between characters who are in a car. A moving car. And that is difficult to shoot. It takes way more time and effort than if, for example, the scene took place as the characters are walking *to* the car. But if you can't convince the writer of the value of that scenario, then prepare for a driving scene.

First, you scout the route, taking into account that you'll need extra space at your start and turnaround spots to stage your setup. There are many vehicles involved: the **picture car**, the **process trailer** or **insert car**, and the **follow vans**. Plus there will be police officers on motorcycles who lead and follow the entourage, enabling the lineup of vehicles to travel safely through traffic lights and all other potential obstacles, like railroad tracks or crazy drivers.

The picture car is "driven" by an actor—but not really. The picture car is hooked up to a process trailer, which is a platform on wheels that has space all around the car, enabling camera movement on dollies around the perimeter of the car. Or the picture car is hooked up to an insert car, which has no platform, so the lights and cameras are mounted to the picture car itself and/or to the insert car and the cameras shoot backward from the leading insert car toward the front/windshield of the following picture car. The director, AD, script supervisor, and DP sit on the back of the insert car facing the picture car, watching monitors of the shots, and the director communicates by walkie-talkie to the actors, who are miked. The sound mixer sits in the passenger seat of the insert car. The follow vans are there for support personnel—hair, makeup, and wardrobe crewmembers—to disembark to check the actors whenever the procession has stopped.

It takes a fair amount of time for the grips and electrics to rig a driving shot, and every time you change angles it must be re-rigged. It takes skill to get light into the actors' eyes despite the fact that they're sitting under the car's roof, which shades them. If it's a sunny day or the car is a convertible, the challenge is to control the light. If it's a night shoot, the main challenge is a good exposure, seeing the actors' eyes while balancing that with the ambient lights and believable night aura.

A night scene may be done in a short-cut way called **poor man's process** (Figure 12.2). The car is not on a street, but on stage and it doesn't move at

FIGURE 12.2 The crew surrounds a vehicle to shoot poor man's process.
Photo by Paul Snider, *NCIS*

all. Instead, with a combination of moving lights (as if the car is passing under streetlights, for example), jostling the car slightly, and shooting the scene in tight close-ups against a dark background, the audience believes that they're watching a moving car. If it's a day scene, you may also achieve a poor man's process version of a traveling scene with video projection background of the scenery going by.

There are also free-driving camera cars equipped with small cranes, which lead or move alongside a picture car that the actor is actually driving. This allows for traveling shots with dramatic camera movement. The major challenge there is for the first assistant cameraperson to maintain focus, for the distance between the lens and the actor can be mutable unlike on an insert car or process trailer where the mounting of the car provides a set distance for focus.

A similar problem exists when a scene calls for water work (Figure 12.3), since a lake or ocean is mutable by its very nature. When the camera is on a boat or barge shooting toward actors on the picture boat, wide lenses are a plus since they have a larger depth of field. The director can use longer lenses when shooting on the picture boat itself, usually in hand-held mode.

In shooting poor man's process, insert car, and water work, in order to make the scene clear in its storytelling the director will probably need a **drive-by**. That is an objective shot showing the car or boat moving in its environment. If it's a chase scene, there will be numerous drive-by shots to

FIGURE 12.3 Actors Mark Harmon and Joe Spano are filmed from a platform barge for a water scene on *NCIS*.
Photo by Paul Snider, *NCIS*

depict the route, the obstacles, the danger, and the distance between the racing vehicles, intercut with close-ups to show the actors' reactions and dialogue. So a scene will be the sum of drive-by shots and insert car work.

SHOOTING A BIG GAG

Now let's say your script reads something like, "The tanks roll through the dusty and deserted Middle East town. A roadside bomb goes off, decimating the lead tank. Bodies fly through the air. Joe lands in some weeds, choking and crying, with half his leg gone." It took the writer a minute to write that, and it may play on screen in about the same time, but a lot of planning and work will go into it, making sure that the story is told.

You'll have meetings that pull together the relevant departments: stunts, transportation, props, production design, special effects, visual effects, makeup. It all starts with what you want to see, and they will try to achieve your vision. The more specific you are, the better they can make it happen. If you say, "I need two full blocks of the town, let's make it a commercial district, small storefronts, all in shades of desert brown," the production designer can get started on that. If you say, "We'll make the explosion **CGI** (computer-generated imagery) but I want to see at least 30 chunks of 'metal' flying, doubled in rubber, ranging from two feet in diameter to six inches across, and the bodies can be weighted dummies," the visual effects, special effects, and prop departments can begin their planning. If you say, "We'll CGI the convoy, but I'll need four real tanks for foreground, I'll do a drive-by at four locations and insert car work too," the transportation coordinator can start obtaining the appropriate vehicles while locations can procure permits and the AD can begin to schedule the day. If you say, "I'll need a total of 200 extras, 25 U.S. Army and 125 townspeople, make sure there are at least 15 children," then your AD, costume, and the extras casting people will begin their calls. If you say, "I'll need to double Joe for the landing on the ground," then stunts and costumes can get prepared. If you say, "We'll CGI the leg wound but I want him covered with blood, oil, and dirt," the makeup department knows what to do. And after the first meeting, you'll have numerous individual department meetings to assess how they're progressing with their assignments. And that's for just one moment from your script—something that takes under a minute of screen time!

Working with any prop that is a firearm, whether practical or fake, requires special safety meetings and handling of the prop before and after that gun is handed to an actor. The actor being "shot at" is also part of this meeting so that he is assured that the weapon being pointed at him will not discharge a real bullet. The stunt coordinator and prop master work in conjunction on this task. Safety is paramount and you can never cut corners or the amount of time needed to assure gun set protocol, which is under the supervision of the specially licensed prop master and the 1st AD.

VISUAL EFFECTS

Though visual effects (VFX) are done in postproduction, you have to shoot the production elements properly in order to create the total effect you want. The visual effects supervisor will be on set during production to advise you. Very often, you are shooting the **plate**, or starting image, that will be manipulated in post. For example, let's say you're shooting an urban scene on the back lot of Universal Studios with the actors in foreground, and you want to show the skyline of Boston or New York or wherever in the background. You'll need to shoot a plate that holds enough room in the top of the frame for the visual effects artists to add the skyline later.

Another simple visual effect is when you have a character talking to her twin, as in the movie *Parent Trap*, or in an episode of *Drop Dead Diva* that Bethany directed, or an episode of *Wizards of Waverly Place* that Mary Lou directed. You will shoot the plate for the master with a **locked-down** camera, meaning that there is no movement. Then you shoot the first actor doing the scene, with the camera still in its locked-down position. (The actor will interact with a **stand-in**, someone who will be replaced visually later.) The VFX supervisor may have to physically take some measurements in the set if the actor being duplicated moves a lot. Be prepared to start and stop the scene and be specific with the coordinator when you want to see both actors simultaneously and when you expect to be in tighter coverage. After completing one side, the actor moves to the other side of the frame in the set, and does the other half of the dialogue. Those three takes, all with a locked-down camera, will be married together, or **composited**, to create the scene. For the OS shots, you'll use a double with wardrobe and wig. *The Patty Duke Show* in the 1960s used the same process—sometimes the old and simple ways are the best. You can also use this process whenever you are portraying something in the frame "disappearing": film the background plate with a locked-down camera, film it with the object in the frame, and then—while still rolling—remove it. The VFX team will composite the three images, creating simple film "magic"!

CGI AND BLUE SCREEN

There are also newer ways to do visual and special effects: these are the ones used by Peter Jackson to portray Gollum in the *Lord of the Rings* trilogy, by James Cameron to portray his Na'vi characters in *Avatar*, and by any director making a superhero movie. **Motion-capture** involves having an actor in a Lycra suit play the scene against a **blue screen** (Figure 12.4) with digital

FIGURE 12.4 A boom operator stands behind the actors who face a blue screen. Photo by Paul Snider, *NCIS*

electrodes attached all over his body, which allows a computer to duplicate the body language when the character has morphed into its other-than-human shape. The blue screen is replaced with whatever environment has been designed. (The color of the screen is dictated by other colors needed within the scene. If there's already lots of blue, then you'll use a green screen, and vice versa.) In planning a scene using blue screen, you'll want to design shots (probably the coverage) that do not use blue screen, just to keep your costs down. In other words, the actors in close-up can be filmed against an existing background, but the wide shots will probably use a combination of set and blue screen. The artists and other staff required to create these fantasies can total in the hundreds, but the process for the director of describing the vision and then communicating about it through the process from idea to finished product is basically the same as when shooting any other scene, that is, you tell them what you want to see, but not how to achieve it. They show you their first draft, you make suggestions for revisions, and that process continues.

As technology evolves, visual effects acquire more subtlety and can blend unobtrusively with the production footage. Think, for example, of the miniature gorilla in the original *King Kong*. That was a VFX ahead of its time, but now we think it's primitive. Today's evolution in VFX is called **digital doubling**, and it entails doing a full-body 3-D scan of an actor's body, in order to computer-animate a version of the actor in a scene which would otherwise require wire-and-harness work, blue screen, and stunt doubling. So the digi-double in a fantasy action movie would leap into the air and stop the plane from crashing with his bare hands, and as he gently sets the plane down, the director would cut to a close-up of the actual actor overlapping the last bit of physical action, and then cut to the pilot (actor) through the windshield of the mock-up plane reacting, and the story is told. The digital artists become the collaborative storytellers in realizing the director's vision through their significant talents.

There are many people who work together with the director to make a scene become fully realized. Your stunt coordinator, your VFX supervisor, or anyone contributing to the evolution of the concept may propose a method to which you respond. You may say, "Hey, that's a great idea! How can we incorporate that into what we're doing?" There will be many a discussion around the conference table. One good idea will lead to another.

You will be the one who assesses whether the new idea fits or derails what you're going for and whose enthusiasm will fire everyone up so that they want to help create something cool, new, or big. Everybody in this business got into it because they love making movies: telling a story visually. They then specialize in various areas of contribution to the finished product, offering their expertise in service of your vision. The continuing evolution of an idea may also happen because the first way you tried to achieve it didn't work, and you have to think of something better, which is why you rehearse multiple times during prep and refine the gag until it's ready to shoot.

CHOREOGRAPHY

Another specialized area of filmmaking that requires a lot of rehearsal is choreography. Choreography used to be a fairly rare occurrence in TV, until *Glee* came along. (Every genre rises and falls in popularity with the years; *Bonanza* and *Gunsmoke* and *The Big Valley* were all over TV in the 1960s, but there's nary a Western to be seen now.) When your script calls for music and dance, you will undergo a similar process in prep as with any other specialized aspect: you will discuss your vision, hire someone (a choreographer) to help you, and rehearse and refine until shooting. It helps a great deal to have some personal background in the arena so you know the vocabulary and can express your vision more clearly. (It's easier to say, "Let's see if an arabesque will work here," than "Can you do that thing where your back leg sticks out and one hand is in the air and you're on your tippy-toes?") You will attend rehearsals after the choreographer has sketched out the basic concept and communicate your responses and suggestions, in addition to determining what your camera positions will be, based on what you've observed. If you have a music background, be specific referring to the precise moment to which you are referring. ("Can he enter two measures or bars later?" or "I need a gesture to punctuate the trumpet sting.")

Also be aware that choreographers work by counting sequentially usually in units of eight ("One, two, three, four, five six, seven eight; Two, two, three, four, five six, seven eight; Three, two, three, four, five six, seven eight" and so on). If you don't have any background in this area, just make sure that you talk about the feeling and the energy you're looking for. If you are working to a song, refer to the lyric. If you can find some other excerpt from another film that can be used as a reference point, that's very helpful. As we talked about in Chapter 4, just as one man's red is different from another's, so is one man's "jazzy" style from another's. The music element will follow the same process (discuss, rehearse, refine), although it must be chosen before the cast and dancers assemble to rehearse to it. In that arena, you'll have a composer and a music supervisor to assist you.

Telling a Story to Music

Choose a piece of music. Working from either the music or the lyrics, summarize your story in a paragraph. Mark shots measure by measure (music) or line by line (lyric) that complement your music. Make sure that your story has a beginning, middle, and end. (If you are stumped for a plot, use "Boy meets girl, boy loses girl, boy finds girl again." Or use a country and western song that tells a story.) When you are finished, you'll have the annotated song, the story, and the shot list.

When you watch a movie or TV show, you watch the story as it unfolds and emotionally go along for the ride. And then you remember that nothing is there by chance. Every single thing in the frame is a choice. It's an awesome responsibility for the director to have. We are fortunate to have such experienced and accomplished crews to back us up, to make suggestions, to work so hard to make our dreams become a reality. If you don't know much about stunts, or special effects, or any other part of the filmmaking world, you will have people to help you. They'll be happy to teach you and walk you through it. It's best to confess your naïveté and solicit their assistance. They will still look to you for the inspiration and the imagination; you're the one who has the vision. You are still the final arbiter, the voice that says in the beginning, "This is how I imagine it will look," and who says after it's shot, "That was wonderful, exactly what I was hoping for. Thank you."

Insider Info

How Do You Interact with the Director?
The Director has the big picture of the puzzle. My job is to deliver a piece of that puzzle that fits that picture. Understanding how a director works—their knowledge, talents, weaknesses, and preferences are the keys to great communication. With directors that I have established working relationships there is a level of trust just as in any relationship. The trust built upon these established working relationships enables me to design and deliver whatever piece of the puzzle is required from my department, packaged just for that particular director. As a director, communicate to me your vision and if you have any specialized knowledge, skill, talent or experience to enable achieving it so we can create your vision together.

What Do You Wish Directors Knew about Your Job?
Ask the Stunt Coordinator for input EARLY in the process. Asking early may solve or even prevent most problems. Decisions made by well meaning production people that think they know how stunts work can kill . . . literally. At the least, these

decisions often create creative limitations and potential safety consequences. To save money, production likes to wait to call the Stunt Coordinator. When production calls us in at the last minute, crucial decisions have already been made. As a result, Stunts have not coordinated with other departments. Wardrobe has already established costumes that endanger or limit performers. The great-looking car chosen by Transportation and the Production Designer is inappropriate for the car chase. Skilled talent books early and won't be available for you. Don't have your director's vision suffer when all you had to do was ask early.

What Advice Would You Give to a Director Starting Out?

Depend on each department's expertise! Directors please don't stage fights or stunts that you don't know anything about it. Share your vision, image or film footage that you would like to build upon. Tell me on a scale of 1–10 how violent or comedic, what speed or how long, what point of view or if you want to focus on one actor, if you want it intimate and close up, or confusing, and what story beats are most important to you. Let the stunt coordinator put the technical pieces together and see if the results fit, or even enhance your vision and then together adjust from that point until it is right.

Mary Albee
Stunt Coordinator
Ally McBeal, Crossing Jordan, Murder in the First

Insider Info

How Do You Interact with the Director?

When working with directors, I feel it's best to discuss visual effects using some type of visual aid, such as storyboards, concept art, movie references, photos, or anything that visually can be a starting point to talk about ideas. Not all directors have the same amount of experience or comfort with visual effects, so the visual aids help refine ideas and explain limitations that might exist due to budget or schedule. I try to never tell a director that something is impossible, and if time and money were no object then that would be true, but even in a movie like *Avatar* there are compromises due to release dates and resources.

On set, my goal is always to make the VFX process efficient and painless. I believe that the visual effects should never get in the way of actors' performances or the director's storytelling. In fact, I perceive my trade as just another tool for the director to tell a good story.

What Do You Want Directors to Know About VFX?

The camera move always affects visual effects in complexity and cost. If shooting the same shot three different ways, as a lock-off, nodal move (pan or tilt), or free move (dolly, Steadicam, or crane), the lock-off will generally be the least expensive and least complex option, a nodal camera the middle option, and a free move the most complex choice. With that said, often a more complicated camera move can also be accomplished economically. For example, if shooting a VFX shot on a dolly, sometimes the beginning of the shot can be a nodal pan or tilt, then once the camera is off the section that is visual effects, it's possible to do a push-in on the practical portion of the set.

What is Your Advice to Young Directors?

My advice when working with visual effects is to always plan ahead as far in advance as possible and to stick with that plan on the day of shooting. Last-minute changes to visual effects shooting plans can sometimes become costly in postproduction or not give you the desired look that you want. That does not mean that VFX can't be flexible on set, but always discuss any changes with your on-set VFX supervisor.

My second piece of advice is to express your opinions, constructively, on how you feel a shot could look better. Even if you think that your suggestion might be prohibitive due to time or money, bring it up anyway because another solution might be available to accomplish the same result. Any suggestion is worth listening to, especially if it results in a better-looking VFX shot.

Tony Pirzadeh
Producer, VFX
Stargate Studios

Vocabulary

blue/green screen
breakaway
CGI
check the marks
composited
courtesy screen
digital double
doubled
drive-by

dry runs
emancipated
follow van
gag
half-speed
insert car
land
locked-down
moleskin
motion-capture
on the day

picture car
plate
poor man's process
pre-viz
principal
process trailer
rig
shoot out
stand-in
studio teacher

NOTE

1 Stacey Beneville, Tawnia McKiernan, Jim Vickers, and Jeff Wadlow. "DGA Special Projects Committee presents Directing for Professionals Action! Calling the Shots." DGA Boardroom, June 13, 2015.

Chapter 13

Running the Set

We all know that directors say, "Action!" and "Cut!" We've heard that in cartoons, in movies about movies, and in just the everyday vernacular of American lives. But there are also many other things that directors say as part of the logistics of running the set. Someone has to say the things that indicate to both cast and crew, "What are we all doing now?" Just as there is a vocabulary for actors, there is a vocabulary for directors. And the purpose of it is to keep things on the set running smoothly.

After Bethany's first directing job, an episode of the 1980s NBC show *St. Elsewhere*, her boss called her into his office. His name was Bruce Paltrow (Gwyneth's father) and he had created the show and was the executive producer. He closed the door and proceeded to pace as he angrily dressed her down. He told her she'd done a bad job, and that just because he told her that she was the captain of the ship, it wasn't so until she actually steered the boat around.

Though she was devastated by his criticism, she understood later, when the sting had diminished and he had assigned her another episode to direct, that he had two underlying purposes for this reaction to her initial directing efforts. The first one was, in effect, to say, "Hey, this is a tough business. If you're going to stay in it, you'd better get tough too." (More on this in Section Four, when we talk about stress and mental health!) The other reason was to emphasize this concept of not just saying you're a director, but being one—doing all it takes to inhabit the job. You have to actually steer that ship and make the cast and crew go where you want them to go. And the director's vocabulary provides a shorthand that everyone understands.

So let's go back to **action** and **cut**. "Action" means begin and "cut" means stop. It's what directors say to actors to start and end a shot (or take). Simple. And yet . . . not. The director should be sensitive to the actors' emotional point of view when beginning the scene and fit the starting command to suit that mood. In other words, don't shout "ACTION!" when the actors are in a fragile place, and don't whisper it when they're about to do some action sequence. Ideally, you, the director, are standing right behind the camera, in the same space as the actors, and therefore the command to begin is appropriate to the physical space and the scene timbre.

Though the word "action" is nigh onto Pavlovian for actors in the sense that hearing the word definitely shoots them out of the starting gate, there are other options—especially when rehearsing. As Clint Eastwood does, you could just say, "Go ahead."

HOW DO YOU START?

Before you can say "action" to begin shooting a shot, you and the actors have to figure out what that action is by rehearsing. Holding **sides**, which are the script pages for only that day in hand, you ask the actors to just **read through** the scene, then you **get it on its feet** by physically moving around the set, and then you continue until you and the actors think the physical blocking is correct. It often helps for you, the director, to stand where the camera is planned to be because the actors will naturally orient themselves toward you. It also helps to put obstacles (like furniture) in their path or put props where you want them to be, in order to facilitate your planned blocking. That way, you don't have to discuss or validate your prepped blocking as much—a lot of the physicality is done for you without using any words. (The set dresser and the prop assistants will put things where you want them before the actors are invited to set for rehearsal.) The crew (except for the DP, your AD, and the script supervisor) has been taking a coffee break nearby but away from the set, so you can conduct this time with your actors in a **private** (or closed) **rehearsal**.

When you confirm with your actors that they are comfortable with the blocking (and you are too) you say, "Let's mark it," and your 1st AD calls it out over the walkie-talkie. He will say, "Marking rehearsal!" and the crew gathers. You and the actors run through the scene again, and the 2nd assistant cameraperson puts color-coded tape marks on the floor at each stopping place for each actor. When that is over, you say, "Thank you, second team please." The actors are the first team and their stand-ins are the second team. The actors scatter back to their dressing rooms to finish wardrobe, hair, and.

makeup, and the stand-ins take their places on the marks that have been set. Now is your opportunity to confer with your DP and talk about the overall approach to the scene. You discuss lighting (as a general topic, like whether it's a bright morning or a moonless night) and you agree on the angle, movement, and lenses of the first shot. (You'll use the terminology we discussed in Chapter 9.) The DP may have conferred with you during prep, especially if you've predetermined that you wanted to use a special piece of equipment or if the scene requires extraordinary lighting (Figure 13.1). But now is the time to nail down the particulars. You've probably seen footage in DVD extra features of directors, walking backwards, holding their index and middle finger in a "V" shape. That is the director describing the movement of the dolly and what the camera will "see." Another option is to hold your hands in such a way that indicates the "wedge" of what will ultimately be in the shot.

Then, while the crew works, you have a little free time—you can go over your script, take care of details and decisions for upcoming scenes, or simply take a coffee break yourself!

> It often helps for you, the director, to stand where the camera is planned to be because the actors will naturally orient themselves toward you.

During the lighting process, the set or location is manipulated to create the frame you want. Very often, this is a **cheat**, meaning an adaptation of the reality. Your **on-set dresser** may move a chair a foot from where it started. Your key grip may **gimbal** a mirror in

FIGURE 13.1 Bethany communicates to DP Billy Webb on the set of *NCIS*.
Photo by Paul Snider, *NCIS*

order to not see an unwanted reflection. (Most mirrors on set are created to move slightly up-and-down and side-to-side to facilitate this. If not, you wad up a ball of tape and stick it between the back of the mirror and the wall to achieve the same effect.) These cheats happen regularly and go unnoticed by the audience; they make it possible to design a great shot!

After the lighting is complete, the camera crews will rehearse the shot with the stand-ins. This is your opportunity to watch the monitor to make sure that the shot will be executed as you had planned. Now you can make adjustments to the shot, freeing you up to be next to the camera during shooting. You will probably be checking the shots of two cameras, rather than one, as that is the norm now in order to facilitate the amount of coverage that is required in a day.

After a few of these rehearsals, the DP will indicate to the AD that the crew is prepared to begin shooting. The actors come to set and you will conduct what is called a **stop-and-go rehearsal**. You stop when some issue needs addressing, whether it's a question from an actor or from the dolly grip, the camera operator, or the boom man. Everyone works out the kinks of the execution of the scene and then you're ready to shoot. You say, "**Picture up!**" Upon hearing that from you, your AD will call out, "**Last looks!**" which means the actors will get their **final touches**. The hair, makeup, and wardrobe assistants will step onto the set to make sure the actors look perfect. When the beauty team departs the set, the AD will say, "Let's go on a bell." A **bell** is really a buzzer controlled by the sound mixer, and it echoes throughout the stage, and everyone quiets. The AD says, "Roll it, please," and the sound mixer will turn on his recorder. When the recorder has reached the appropriate speed, the boom operator will announce it by saying "**Speeding**," and then the 1st assistant camera operator turns on the camera and says, "**Rolling**." At that point, the 2nd assistant camera operator steps in front of the camera and hits the slate. Everyone has seen one—the film business has been using them since the first talkie movie was made. The slate is filmed at the top of each take, giving the editor the pertinent information: scene number, take number, director's name, and DP's name. When the slate is "hit," a sound is made, and the film element and the separately recorded sound element can be **synced**, or put together. If you are shooting digital, rather than film, the process is the same—there is still a slate, and the sound is still recorded separately. The assistant returns to behind the camera, the operator's eye is on the eyepiece, the microphone is held overhead by the boom operator. The actors are on their starting marks. The camera operator says, "Set." And everyone waits, in silent anticipation, for you to say, "Action."

THE PSYCHOLOGICAL UNDERPINNING

The main point here is that it is only the director—no one else—who says when it's time to begin. And therefore, ipso facto, you are in control. It's a pretty great feeling when you say that one little word and everyone jumps to do his job. But don't let it swell your head: just as the actors are being judged while they perform, so is the director. After you say "Cut," will you then say "**Print it**"? Or will you ask for "One more, please"? You are not the only one observing the take and deciding whether it's worthy. Though it is up to the director to decide when the intent of the scene and the shot has been achieved, everyone around you will also have an opinion. The writer, the producers, the cast, and the crew will be judging you on your judgment. Do you know when to say, "Cut. Print it. And **check the gate**," or do you keep filming and do a lot of unnecessary takes that may inflict an emotional toll on your actors? Or do you say, "Check the gate," and everyone around you thinks you didn't pull the best out of your actors or your crew? (When a film camera is used, each frame of film is exposed separately as it is held in the camera gate. You "check the gate," because sometimes a sliver of film is shaved off, creating a **hair in the gate**. Checking the gate used to be a way of making sure what you just shot is acceptable.) Now there's no literal gate, it's just a way of saying, "We're finished with this shot." A current (and somewhat tongue-in-cheek) alternative is "check the chip."

A large part of the director's job is the judgment required to know when to check that gate. As you watch the scene, you are simultaneously tallying mentally whether the actors are achieving the intent of the scene and whether the shot is both visually telling the story and being executed perfectly by the crew. And you are expected to render that judgment right after you say "cut," all the while knowing that everyone else around you also has an opinion.

Directors with huge egos may not recognize or care that they are being judged as well. And perhaps it's not relevant, in the sense that the director's word is law and the set will fit itself to the director's instructions. However, it does become relevant when the faction supplying the money questions the director's judgment. Even if the studio head (or financier, or network executive) isn't physically present on the set, he will hear about it.

> As you watch the scene, you are simultaneously tallying mentally whether the actors are achieving the intent of the scene and whether the shot is both visually telling the story and being executed perfectly by the crew. And you are expected to render that judgment right after you say "cut," all the while knowing that everyone else around you also has an opinion.

Every set is its own little world, with factions and politics and tempers and alliances. Because it is a large group effort, that is natural, human interaction. And the buyer, whoever it is, will hear of and/or observe the director's ability. We've all heard of directors being fired. It happens. The director is not the final authority unless she is supplying the money as well.

> *Every set is its own little world, with factions and politics and tempers and alliances.*

But it is a trap for a director to take the opinions of others into consideration. How many times have you discussed a movie with friends and you all have a different opinion? The same thing happens when you are watching a scene unfold in front of you. Everyone has an opinion, but it is you, as the director, who says "Cut, print, check the gate." And the only way for you to do that is to follow your own creative vision—20 people (either on the set or viewing the finished product) will have 20 different opinions. And the fundamental reason that you were hired as the director is for your creative vision with the integrity to see it through. That means you have to listen to your own intuition, your own "gut feeling." If you start thinking, "Oh, the producer won't like that," or "The network executive said they want the show to be edgy/soft/action/character-driven, so I better do this a different way," you are lost. You are lost as the artist you were hired to be.

> *The fundamental reason that you were hired as the director is for your creative vision with the integrity to see it through.*

HARNESSING THE MAGIC

Let's say that you are following your instinct and you don't want to say "Cut . . . print" on one take. What you want to do instead—because you've noticed that your actor is just warming up at the end of a take—is go through the whole scene twice (or more) without cutting. You want to capture the magic that the actor is bringing to the material by allowing the actor to maintain his emotional point of view. (When you say "Cut," it's like the guillotine coming down. Suddenly, it's not about the actor's emotional state, but about the 1st assistant cameraperson's worry that the shot wasn't in focus, or the wardrobe assistant dashing onto set to fix an errant collar.) Your main job is to tell the story through the perfection of performance.

A big part of your job is to get a great shot. But if you're shooting a middling performance with a great shot, you still have only middling film. So you want to keep rolling and allow your actors to stay focused on their point of view. What do you do? You instruct the 1st assistant cameraperson to make sure that he has a **full mag**, that is, as much film as possible in the magazine, which is generally 1,000 feet. (Or, if you're shooting digital, you ask, "Do we have enough (memory) for two?") You tell the actors you're going to keep rolling. And when they've finished the scene for the first time, you say quietly to all, **"Still rolling . . . reset."** And when everyone on both cast and crew sort of "rewind" back to their original positions, you repeat, "Action" and start again, without having cut between takes. This is a terrific tactic when you're trying to build performance because you've sensed that the actors are just getting into the right emotional place just as you're about to call "cut" on a take. That is smart directing. But continuing to roll through multiple takes (more than two) without cutting is problematic for several reasons: (1) It causes the director to shout acting adjustments to the actors, which we know is detrimental; (2) It prohibits other department heads from getting on set and correcting things, like the vanities, prop master, or script supervisor; and (3) It is non-communicative, causing everyone to think, "Why are we going again? What does the director want?" It is part of the director's job to be clear about what he is looking for that necessitates an additional take. If you're not seeking any improvement, you should check the gate and move on.

A big part of your job is to get a great shot. But if you're shooting a middling performance with a great shot, you still have only middling film.

Take 1 is generally to get the kinks out of the scene; by take 2, all aspects of the scene should be accomplished beautifully. Your actors are in the groove, and the shot is playing exactly as you designed it. So print it. Give the actors some feedback by approaching them in person (not shouting from the monitor) and having a short and intimate conversation, using the vocabulary we discussed in Chapter 10 to give them an adjustment. Then go one more time (or two) for editing choices and move on. You have a limited amount of time in which to shoot a lot of material, and you need to know what you're looking for and be decisive when you see it. To review: in current episodic drama, a script is generally around 52 pages, and you have 7, 8, or 9 days to shoot it, depending on the budget. Most shows do about 25 to 30 setups a day, that is, separate shots. The call time, or beginning of the day, is usually 7:00 a.m. If the production takes an hour lunch, you are expected to wrap (finish) in 12 hours, or by 8:00 p.m. If the production caters lunch and the break is for half an hour, you're expected to wrap by 7:30 p.m.

At the halfway mark of the day, at six hours, it is required by law and union agreements to give the cast and crew a meal break. If you are in the middle of a shot at that time, and you think you just need a little more time, the 1st AD can announce, "We're going into grace," and you continue to shoot. However, the **grace period** is only 12 minutes, and you cannot change anything about the shot once you've rolled into grace. If you need a little more time than that, and it will save time later, the production manager may authorize a **meal penalty**. This is a half hour of additional time, but the cast and crew are paid extra for it. An example of saving time later would be if, by going into meal penalty, you completed one direction of a scene, and would be planning to turnaround after lunch. If instead, without a meal penalty, you still had one shot remaining in the original direction to be shot after lunch, you would probably be an hour behind by the end of the day. And every minute counts. If you go past 13 hours, the crew and cast need to be fed again. It's called **second meal**; generally the crew chooses to eat and keep working without actually breaking.

These are long days, and they get longer if the director is indecisive or overly ambitious. The job of the director is to tell the story brilliantly but remain on time and on budget. That bears repeating: the job of the director is to tell the story brilliantly but remain on time and on budget! That means knowing where to spend the time and where to compromise because you were hired to make the day. You have a certain number of scenes to shoot within 12 hours. If a particular shot (or performance) is crucial to your storytelling, take whatever time is necessary. That's important, and it's following your creative vision. But if you know your most important scene is one you're scheduled to be filming in the afternoon (it's listed that way on the call sheet), don't get bogged down in a less important scene in the morning. Prioritize. Know where to spend extra time.

Everyone who works for you, both cast and crew, looks to you to not only create beautiful film but to do it efficiently as well. And the producers would add, "Don't forget to do it on budget, too!"

Remember that every single element in the frame is your choice and requires your approval. So right before you roll, take a moment to really look at what is in the frame (because, boy, you are sure going to be looking at it endlessly in editing). See if your actress's hair is perfect. If not, ask the hairdresser back to pat down those **flyaways**. Look to see whether some background object, like a lamp, appears to be protruding out of the actor's ear. If so, ask the on-set dresser to move the object around until the framing is better. Pay attention to the set dressing: is it all logical, does it make sense and help you tell the story? Double-check: is the wardrobe for each of your characters in differing color palettes, and is it appropriate? Does the wardrobe need to be **aged**, rather than looking like it was purchased yesterday and has never been worn? You can do this last-second review while the 1st AC is **running the tape** (ascertaining that the shot will be in focus) and everyone else is making their final preparations. You don't have to make a big deal out of it, but you do have to do it. It's part of "the buck stops here" mentality, and even though there are departments that supervise each of those elements, approval ultimately rests with you.

> Everyone who works for you, both cast and crew, looks to you to not only create beautiful film but to do it efficiently as well. And the producers would add, "Don't forget to do it on budget, too!"

Also check (during the second team and background rehearsal) the human elements of your frame aside from the actors: that is, the extras. Though the 2nd AD sets background, you should make adjustments to suit your vision. So you may have people crossing close to lens, called a **foreground (fg) wipe**, which helps make the audience feel like the camera is intimate and subjective and in the midst of the scene with the actors. If you have a wide shot holding multiple actors without foreground crosses, it will feel like **proscenium** staging, as in a theatre, where the action is happening in front of a removed audience. Observe the background artists: Are they helping you tell the story? Do they have the right attitude and point of view? Is someone overacting, or worse, walking around like a zombie? (Obviously, that's okay if you're shooting *The Walking Dead*.)

So you have the perfect frame, you do a couple of takes, and you're pretty happy. But there's one thing you want to fix, either in front of or behind the camera, so you may ask for a **pickup**, rather than going **from the top**, or the beginning. A pickup starts the scene somewhere in the middle to achieve the element you believe is missing, whether it's a performance note or something that could be done better on camera. You'll say, "Print that, please, one pickup." Your AD will say, "From where?" And you will tell everyone the **cue**, or script line, that will begin the pickup. Sometimes when you make this announcement, the actor may ask for an extra take from the beginning, because they feel they can't just jump into the performance in that spot. That's okay too, especially if the scene requires emotional depth. But there are some actors who are never satisfied and always want another take. It is up to you to navigate the subtext of what they are requesting. It's important to honor your actors' creative vision as well, but remember that you are the person running the set. If you decide to begin at the top of the scene, you say **"Back to one,"** (everyone's first position) the AD will repeat it for all to hear, and everyone will rewind a little more to get another complete take.

Sometimes you think that although the scene is good, it could stand a little extra energy and some further editing choices. At that point, tell the actors "I've got it," meaning the scene is complete, but "Let's do **one more for fun**." (Some directors prefer to say "for shits and giggles." Bethany's preferred expression is **"Bonus round!"**) Generally, this take gives the actors a sense of freedom and they lighten up (from the huge responsibility of getting the scene right) and are able to discover new things in their performance and literally have fun. Or, occasionally, you think the shot is complete, but when the gate is checked, there actually is a hair there, or there's some other obstruction (like a minimal actor/prop mismatch) that forces you to go for one more take. In our experience, this is a gift. This unpredicted last take somehow captures even more of the magic. Never regret it, but embrace it. It's always worth it.

Once you have finished shooting one angle of the scene—you've printed three takes, you know you have the performance and the shot exactly as you wanted it—you proceed to the next shot in which the camera is looking the same general direction in order to conserve lighting changes. The DP will be instrumental in helping you determine which shots should be done in which order. After you've completed every shot in one direction, you'll call out, "**turning around**," which your AD will repeat on the radio. This signals to everyone that the next setup will require more work. The set dresser will probably need to move furniture, the grips may do "**wall in, wall out**" to reconfigure the set by moving the **wild** (movable) walls while giving more room to the camera, and the electricians will get instructions from the DP and gaffer about relighting in the opposite direction.

Another "in/out" situation on set is caused when you decide to switch elements within a single take without the switch being seen by camera. This is called a "**Hollywood in**" or "**Hollywood out**." For example, an actor is sitting in a chair, and in the midst of the scene gets up and walks across the set. You design a shot that calls for following that character across the room, but the chair is in the way. So you will confer with the DP, and plan to **boom** (raise) the camera as the actor stands, and now the on-set dresser can sneak in under the frame to pull the chair out of the way, and the camera may push through (Hollywood out). Or you may have a shot in which you want to substitute an actor with a stunt double, and you pan off the actor to something else (like an approaching bad guy) and meanwhile the actor steps off set and the double steps in (Hollywood in).

There is one other situation you may be asked about during a shooting day: your AD approaches, and asks if you want to shoot a scene **MOS**. That means, the camera will record picture, but the sound will not be recorded. This generally happens when there is neither dialogue nor significant background sound to record, like an insert or a "surveillance camera" shot. The origin of this appellation may be apocryphal, but most crew people believe that an unknown Germanic sound recordist of the 1930s would ask a director, "Mit-out-sound?" and now we just call it MOS.

ONE DOWN, FOUR TO GO

So let's say you've shot your first scene of the day. You have checked the gate on all of the shots that were designed in prep, prepared in rehearsal, and executed by cast and crew during the shooting. Hooray for you! Now you say, "**Moving on**," or "New deal," or "That completes this scene." Your AD will announce that via the radio, and everyone will mark the first scene off on the call sheet. One down! Now you probably only have four more scenes for the day! And the process repeats itself. By following this pattern, you eventually find yourself near to the end of the day. At that point, your AD may announce that the next shot is the **Abby Singer**, or the **Abby**.

The Abby Singer shot is named for a wonderful gentleman who was an assistant director at the beginning of television in the 1950s. He was known for his high energy and eagerness to complete the work, and would often announce to his crew that it was "this shot and one more." So the second-to-last shot is called the Abby Singer, and crews all over the world know that when the AD makes that announcement, they are almost finished with their day. Both Mary Lou and Bethany worked with Abby in his production manager capacity. He was on *Major Dad*, which was Mary Lou's second directing job, and Abby was also on *St. Elsewhere*, which was Bethany's first. Abby seemed to know everything there was to know about production, and he cared deeply about the finished product. His was a great example of the passion that film people bring to their work.

Passion fuels a set. The actors are passionate about what they do, or else they wouldn't do it. There's too much rejection and too little remuneration for the vast majority of them. But your crew is passionate about what they do, too. You have to know all the technical stuff we went over in previous chapters, but your DP and your crew will know it way better than you. It is not necessary to tell them exactly *how* to accomplish a shot. Instead, you communicate *what* it is you are looking for. What do you want to see? What is your creative vision? Paint a picture for them with words and let the crewmembers contribute their expertise and help make your vision come alive.

That is why they are there. They are also creative people, and they want to be useful. They want to make the film special, too. They want to add their talents to yours; together, you'll create something that you could not do on your own. Filmmaking is not a solo act. It is collaborative, in all the best ways. And at the end of day, you can celebrate that collaboration with

> *Paint a picture for them with words and let the crewmembers contribute their expertise and help make your vision come alive.*

the feeling of satisfaction that abounds when your AD announces, "This is the **martini shot**"—the last shot of the day—right before you **wrap** (end the day).

Sequencing the Commands

 Write all the things a director (or the 1st AD) says that we mentioned in this chapter on index cards with one phrase per card. (You can also do this for the code words to say to actors in Chapter 10.) Now place the cards in the correct order, sequencing them so that you use all of them. Make duplicate cards for the phrases you will say many times a day ("Action," "Cut," "Turning Around," etc.). Do you see why knowing the director's vocabulary is essential to keep things running smoothly on the set?

Your job is to provide not only the creative vision but also the environment in which everyone can do their best work. Your actors feel safe because they know you will not let them look stupid, so they give their best. Your DP is inspired by your ideas, and adds or subtracts light to create a visual tone. Your camera operator and crew, the sound crew, all the departments— they want to follow you, the leader, and give their utmost in service to making this script come alive in the most profound way. So you will pull them in and welcome their talents and contributions.

But the main responsibility of the director is to focus on performance, because the director is the *only* one doing that. All the other aspects of filmmaking have someone to look after them. The DP will watch the light; the camera operator will make sure that the shot is perfect. The prop assistant will make sure that each hand prop is in place. The wardrobe assistant will not allow lint on a jacket; the hairdresser will make sure that not a hair is out of place. You, the director, are the only one judging whether the performance by the actors is telling your story. And you are the only one who is nurturing them, loving them, making them feel secure. You are the only one leading them where you want them to go.

> *You, the director, are the only one judging whether the performance by the actors is telling your story. And you are the only one who is nurturing them, loving them, making them feel secure.*
>
> *You are the only one leading them where you want them to go.*

PERSONALITY IN THE PROCESS

The process will work best if you exhibit the good old-fashioned values of respect, manners, and positive thinking. Remember that everyone on the set is looking to you for signs of how the day is going and how they should feel. If you're grumpy, they will be too. If you're rude, you give them permission to be the same. But if you say please and thank you, if you praise and encourage your actors and your crew, and most importantly, as we talked about in Section One, if you come to set well-prepared, then the magic can happen. You can have a plan, follow it, and release yourself and everyone else from the stress of figuring things out on the fly. And you can be free to deviate from your preparation and allow the inspiration (most especially from your actors) of the moment to elevate what was previously an intellectual exercise. Although you have pictured the scene in your head, the reality will undoubtedly be different.

This work is what makes the job of the director so exciting. You get to see your vision become a reality. But there are so many variables that the end product becomes unpredictable ahead of time. Is your lead actress in a good mood or bad mood? Did the piece of equipment you ordered come in? Was there a late rewrite that affected your preparation? Are there internal feuds, or perhaps love affairs? Are the producers at war with the studio, and both at war with the network, leaving you unsure to whom you're answering? For every scene, there are as many variables as the people involved at every level. And it is your job as director to navigate all

> *Remember that everyone on the set is looking to you for signs of how the day is going and how they should feel. If you're grumpy, they will be too. If you're rude, you give them permission to be the same. But if you say please and thank you, if you praise and encourage your actors and your crew, and most importantly, as we talked about in Section One, if you come to set well-prepared, then the magic can happen.*

that with grace, diplomacy, and the determination that it is your creative vision to which all must adhere. It's challenging, and it's fun. There is no greater creative high than being the director, if you have the temperament and multitasking skills to achieve consummate filmmaking.

We'll give you the insight on how to be that kind of person in Section Four—right after we talk about postproduction and taking storytelling to a new level.

Insider Info

Being on a set is time-sensitive. It is that way for everyone. Everything is about time, so don't spend YOUR time as a director freaking out or annoyed at the advice or "criticism" you hear. The way you receive input may help dictate your possible re-hire. Yes, things stop. Yes, your face gets hot. Yes, it's up to you. Be responsible without killing yourself or anyone else.

It's grace you are looking for and you can't give it or get it if you can't manage your own feelings of insecurity, which we all have. Know that you know what you are doing even if your insides are going a little wacky. It's just physiological. It will go away.

You have three choices. 1. You can be a jerk, disagree and need to be right to avoid the embarrassment of being wrong, which takes time. 2. You can take a crazy amount of time because you are a people pleaser and terrified of not being liked. 3. You can be open, listen and figure it out without second guessing yourself, which takes about 10 to 15 seconds when you are actually present.

In one moment, just one moment you can choose to listen to your gut, which takes no time at all.

Barbara Deutsch
Personal Champion
Author, Open Up or Shut Up

Insider Info

How Do You Interact with the Director?
Each director and each show is unique. I try to get the directors to let me know how they like to work. Some like to prep by themselves at the beginning and give out info as prep goes on. Others like to share all of their thoughts from day 1. From an assistant director's standpoint, it is preferable to have a bit of a medium. I prefer it when a director has thought out the script, then we can get together and discuss the episode. From this point on, I welcome as much information as I can get. No detail is too small.

At the beginning of prep, I like to walk the sets with the director to give him a basic overview of the show and let him know which walls are wild and any other logistical consideration we have on the show. We discuss the cast. We go over how each cast member likes to rehearse and shoot.

We also discuss the dos and don'ts of the show.

After the usual preproduction meetings with various departments, it is good to revisit the sets with a general idea of how to shoot each scene. Some more experienced directors may want to go over larger or more complicated scenes and skip over simpler two-person scenes. We will go over the directions we hope to shoot. This is when the director should share which scenes have specialty shots and/or equipment needs.

What Would You Like Directors to Know About the 1st AD Position and its Responsibilities?

I would like directors in television to remember that we are there for them. We want the director to be able to deliver their vision, yet we have an obligation to the producers of the show to accomplish this task in a timely manner.

The best directors understand that we can help them only if we are aware of all their special requirements as soon as possible. We might not be able to get them what they want for a shot but might have an alternative solution to their request.

What is Your Advice for Young Directors?

Know the script forward and backward. Make sure that you know where each character was in their previous scene and where the characters are going in their next scene. This knowledge will help answer some of the cast questions. Be aware of what you *want* to make a scene and know what you *need* to make a scene. And know the difference!

Remember that on any given set, the crew has years and years of experience that they are willing to share with their director. Do not be afraid to ask for help. If the director is successful, so are we.

Last but not least, be polite. We work long, hard hours and the crew is much more willing to give an extra effort to a nice director than a tyrant.

Jim Goldthwait
1st Assistant Director
Shameless, Awkward, Code Black

Vocabulary

Abby Singer or the Abby
action
aged
back to one
bell
boom
bonus round
cheat
check the gate
cue
cut
final touches
flyaways
foreground (fg) wipe
from the top
full mag
get it on its feet
gimbal
grace period
hair in the gate
Hollywood in/out
last looks
martini shot
meal penalty
MOS
moving on
on-set dresser
one more for fun
pickup
picture up
print it
private rehearsal
proscenium
read through
rolling
running the tape
second meal
sides
speeding
still rolling . . .
reset
stop-and-go
rehearsal
synced
turning around
wall in, wall out
wild
wrap

Shoot

The week or ten days when you actually are in production and doing the principal photography is the *shoot*. During this time, you run the set, shape the actors' performances, and oversee all aspects of telling the story with the camera and sound recording equipment on the sets or on location. You do all this in an orderly and efficient way to stay on time and within budget while expressing your creative vision as you interpret the script.

You use your knowledge of the how the actors prepare and work so that you can speak to them in their language. You provide a closed set so that they can do that work in a protected and safe environment. You have the bigger picture in mind so that you are mindful of pacing and tone, and you pay special attention to their rhythm and timing if you are doing a comedy.

During the shoot, you work closely with your key trio on the set: your AD, the DP, and the script supervisor. These three are there for every rehearsal. The AD is your lieutenant who sees that all your instructions are communicated. The DP is your captain who oversees the crew and the actual execution of how you tell the story with the camera and sound recording equipment. Your script supervisor oversees continuity and can be your backup person to make sure you haven't missed any critical coverage.

When you shoot with animals and kids, quiet spontaneity is your friend; when you shoot special effects, stunts, CGI, blue screen, and choreography, careful planning is key to efficient and safe shooting.

The shoot is the time when all the troops rally together to create the director's vision. It is the time you show how well you lead and how well you capture the elements you need to tell a story.

Post

Overview

What is "post"? "Post" is the time following production when a film is assembled and readied for delivery so that it can be shown or broadcast. It is the director's final chance to reinterpret the script. It is also known as the postproduction phase.

What does a director do during post? The director works closely with the editor to make sure that the film is cut together so that it clearly and artfully tells the story. Together, they add temporary music and sound effects so that the director's cut clearly shows the director's vision. The director may continue to oversee his vision during the other postproduction processes such as color correcting, working with the composer, and dubbing, or simply hand over his cut to the producers, having delivered everything within his power to fulfill.

Chapter 14

Working with the Editor

During postproduction, you get to reinterpret the script when you work with the editor. This is an opportunity to tell your story in a new, fresh, and possibly better way than you originally conceived it. The important thing to remember is that the editor is trying to make you look good by putting together the best episode possible from the footage you have shot. He has no preconceived notions but is simply dealing with putting the pieces of the story together. The editor, aided by his assistants, has done a lot of work before you ever see his initial cut, which is called the **editor's assembly**.

BEFORE YOUR CUT: THE EDITOR'S ASSEMBLY

Although technology changes the medium on which the picture is recorded (tape, film, digital tape, digital hard drive), the editor still usually receives either a master tape or copy of the master tape. If the footage was shot on film or memory **card**, it has been transferred to a **hard drive**.

The editor gets a copy of the footage along with the camera report, sound report, and **script supervisor's notes** for what you have shot. The script supervisor's notes are a blueprint for finding and retrieving the information about all the footage shot and especially about the footage the director printed. It is all organized by **nonlinear editing methods** (**NLEs**) in consecutive **bins**, or giant files, on the editor's computer that follow the order of the script. (In the old days, prior to 1990, when dramas and features were shot and edited on film, the individual strips of film hung from hooks in a literal canvas bin.) Each scene has a separate bin. If all the footage for that

237

scene is shot, a bin is said to be **complete**, but if an insert or special effects shot is missing, that bin is still **incomplete**. Once the assistant editor gets the final shooting script, the appropriate words of the script also go into the bin. Certain editing programs have the capacity for the editor to lay the cursor over a certain line of dialogue and automatically see the various footage that has been shot containing the line in that selection.

You get a copy of the unassembled footage when you are handed a DVD containing dailies or printed daily footage. Unassembled footage is so named because the producers and the director used to have a daily screening of the film that was shot the day before. Now that we're primarily digital, you have already seen the shots on the video monitors, either the onboard camera ones or at video village on set. You don't need to look at every minute of what you shot. You can look at dailies to make sure that you got the specific shots or performances that are critical to your story, however, Bethany does not, because she feels it kills the fresh eye she needs when screening the editor's cut. The editor takes the dailies and cuts them together scene by scene (not necessarily in order), using his fresh eyes to either take an educated guess as to how you saw your footage fitting together or assembling the footage to tell the story so it makes sense to him. If you have specific ins and outs and it is clear where you anticipated cutting out of the master, it will be apparent to the editor how you intended your episode to be cut together. It's like a jigsaw puzzle and you both are looking at the same picture on the box lid.

But sometimes what you intended might not be apparent to the editor. Steve Welke, coproducer on *Eureka*, suggests that the editor really *wants* to know the director's plan or vision. He reports editors saying, "I have all this footage. I wish I knew what the director was thinking when he shot it. It would help me put it together if I knew how he wants to see it." So touch base with your editor prior to you coming in for your cut to see *if* the editor wants some guidance from you before working his magic.

You can avoid the editor's picture being radically different if you know the look of the show and have shot your footage appropriately to mesh with that established look. During prep, you will have discussed in your tone meeting with the showrunner what the style preferences are (see Chapter 7).

If you have specific ins and outs and it is clear where you anticipated cutting out of the master, it will be apparent to the editor how you intended your episode to be cut together. It's like a jigsaw puzzle and you both are looking at the same picture on the box lid.

As a freelance director, it is your job to give the producer and the network exactly what they're looking for while expressing your individual creativity within those parameters. The exception, of course, would be a pilot, for which you create the look of the show.

Recognizing the Edits

Record an episode of any one-hour TV show—preferably one that has a lot of action and that is not shot in handheld style. Play it back without the sound, starting and stopping so you can write every time there is an edit. Describe the shots using the list we gave you in Chapter 8: establishing shot, master, mini-master, 50/50, two-shot, insert, OS, CU. With CU, note whether it is cowboy, waist, two-t, choker, or extreme. When you are done with the list, go back with a highlighter and note any patterns that you see within scenes and within acts. Record another episode of a different show and describe the shots. Compare and contrast the styles of the shows.

KNOWING THE CLASSIC PRINCIPLES OF EDITING

The look of the show dictates how the show gets put together. Although some shows deliberately break the classic rules of editing, it is always important to know a rule—and why it exists— before you break it. Here are the traditional rules that editors begin with:

- Change size or change angles between shots that will be cut together.
- Cut back and forth between complementary shots.
- Cut into a tighter shot when the information gets more important or the mood more intimate.
- Cut wider to show movement or geography.
- Match for continuity.
- Don't cross the line.
- Cut on movement.
- Pace (time between edits) is part of the storytelling.

Nearly all these rules exist so that the edit seems seamless; that is, it doesn't draw attention to itself when the picture is changing. You want your audience to be enthralled by your story, not noticing how a scene was shot or how it was edited. If they're noticing those things, they're looking at your technique, which should be invisible. Having said that, there are times when a director wants to break the rules for effect: to startle or otherwise alert the audience to storytelling points. When you feel the need to break these rules, we encourage you to do it artfully.

As you'll recall from Chapter 9, the director plans not only how to shoot the scene, but also how those shots will be edited together. The director specifically shoots an opening visual and an ending visual, and although that visual should be clear to the editor when looking at the footage, you can also instruct the script supervisor to include that information in her notes.

The director also has in mind where the first cut is from the master or opening shot because that begins to dictate the **cutting pattern** and **rhythm** of the scene.

Every scene is like a piece of music that is carefully constructed to be structurally sound and tell the story. The pattern and rhythm is a part of that. Is the scene legato, or is it staccato? The editor brings a "fresh eye" to the footage and may discover things you never anticipated. But ideally, the editor is assembling the film according to your vision while following the accepted rules.

> *Every scene is like a piece of music that is carefully constructed to be structurally sound and tell the story. The pattern and rhythm is a part of that.*

The first rule—"Change size or change angles between shots that will be cut together"—assures that there will not be a **jump cut**, which is two shots in a row *of the same subject* from nearly the same camera position. If edited sequentially, these subjects appear to jump, hence the name. Changing angles prevents this problem; the suggestion is to change that angle by at least 30 degrees. Some editors also believe that it helps to avoid a jump cut if you change the size of the shot.

Following the next rule—"Cut back and forth between **complementary shots**"—also makes the edit seamless. Imagine an intimate moment between the Soldier and his Wife standing at the door facing each other. Complementary shots would be their matching OS or CUs (whether they are cowboys, waists, two-ts, or chokers). What makes them match or complement each other is that their faces are the same size when you cut back and forth. Ideally, they should also be shot with the same lens and at the same depth of field to ensure not just that the faces fill the same amount of space in the frame, but also that the background behind the faces is equally sharp or blurred. This approach ensures that the complementary shots have the same feel. Bethany experienced this on *Ally McBeal*, on which the camera department didn't even carry a lens wider than 75mm. They wanted a "filmic" look, but it was challenging to shoot masters on that kind of long lens. Nevertheless, by not even offering another option, the show's producers ensured that all of the episodes had a similar look. Conversely, a director can exploit the difference between a shot and its reverse for emphasis and point of view.

The next two classic editing practices are "Cut into a tighter shot (i.e. from a two-shot to a close-up or from a cowboy to a two-t) when the information gets more important or the mood more intimate" and "Cut wider to show movement or geography." Often (but not always) a scene will begin with the master to show the geography of the space and where people are physically in that space. As the scene progresses, the editor will sequence shots to tell the story, generally in descending order from the wider shots to closer as the scene reaches its climax. The most basic information is where the characters are in relation to each other and when they choose to move. The viewer must be aware of this basic movement. Subtler, though, is when the eyeline becomes closer (as we discussed in Chapter 9) from the objective viewpoint to the subjective. The editor will cut to a tighter eyeline to place the viewer "inside" the story or to say "pay close attention now." An interesting example of this is in *The Social Network*, when director David Fincher and his editors, Kirk Baxter and Angus Wall, would often cut to an extreme close-up with a very tight eyeline when there was a pivotal piece of dialogue.

> *For good storytelling and flow, it's important to not cross the line, and the editor will do his best to keep the screen direction clear and consistent.*

The next classic rule is "match for continuity." There are so many ways that this guideline is used. If a character is sipping wine throughout a scene, the editor must make sure that the same hand is used for drinking, that the glass ends up on the table on the same lines of dialogue and in the same place if it is visible, and finally, that the amount of wine in the glass progressively lessens as the scene progresses. The script supervisor will watch most of these things carefully during shooting, but if objects or actions don't match, the footage will be awkward, no matter how good the actor's performance.

We looked at the next rule—"Don't cross the line"—in Chapter 9. You know that it disorients the viewer. The editor will always avoid doing this, unless that is part of the look of the show. Both *NYPD Blue* and *Homicide* were TV shows in the 1990s that played with crossing the line as a means of keeping their viewers on edge. It worked. But those kinds of shows are the exception to the rule. For good storytelling and flow, it's important to not cross the line, and the editor will do his best to keep the screen direction clear and consistent.

The primary rule for seamless editing is next: "cut on movement." The less attention the viewer pays to an edit, the better the edit is. It's hiding or disguising when the picture changes. A simple example of this is the turn of a head. Let's take our two characters Alice and Bob. If the editor wants to bring our attention to the fact that Bob walks into the room, he might cut to the door when Alice turns her head to see who has just come in. Notice that this edit specifically helps tell the story. Another example here would be if there is a camera **angle** (shot) outside the door too. As Bob steps away from camera, over the threshold, the editor could cut back to the angle from inside the room, and the audience would be barely aware that there was an edit there. They would just accept the two versions (angles) of Bob entering.

This editing rule is why directors instruct actors to **rock into coverage** during shooting: if you shoot a walk 'n' talk and plan to cover the last part of the scene when the two actors stop walking, you would begin shooting those close-ups by having the actor take a step onto that final mark. You wouldn't have them already there, flat-footed. By having them step onto the mark, you can make the edit seamlessly from the master to the close-up shot in the middle of the last step, so that there is movement on both sides of the cut. It fools the viewer's eye and leaves the audience focused on the story, rather than how it was shot and edited.

Just as a character's movement facilitates the cut, so does sound. As you're planning your transitions—the way you go from one cut to another—take into account that it may not be visual movement that helps the cut but auditory movement instead. For example, someone is exiting a scene, and you add an extra "door opening" sound as that happens, but continue the sound **over the cut**, as someone enters in the next scene. Or perhaps it's something of a background **fill** (an ambient sound) in which a "car-by" sound starts on the **A side** of the cut and the sound continues onto the **B side** of the cut. That sound going over the cut just smooths it out and makes the audience less aware of the edit. (We talk more about sound editing in Chapter 15, because it's an important component of completing your story.)

In conversation with your editor, it's helpful to use an editor's vocabulary, just as with actors.

When talking about a particular edit, or cut, you will talk about how you want to see the A side and B side, generally using the terms **add to** or **trim**.

So if you want an edit to happen sooner, you might say, "Let's trim the A side of the cut." If you want to **massage the cut**—that is, find the absolute best place for it—you might say, "Let's trim the A side and add to the B side of the cut," or the other way around, "Let's add to the A side and trim the B side." Other terms referring to the same thing are **head** and **tail**, as in, "Let's trim the tail" or "Let's trim the head," referring to the end and beginning of the shot.

> In conversation with your editor, it's helpful to use an editor's vocabulary, just as with actors.

Much of that kind of discussion regards the final rule: "Pace (time between edits) is part of the storytelling." A faster pace (quicker cuts) is good for comedy and action. A more leisurely pace is good for drama, particularly when the actors are filling those long moments with their performance. But in TV drama today, a faster pace is encouraged, no matter what the material is. We are all conditioned to expect a faster pace, when much of what we see in feature films (like *The Avengers*, or any action movie) is extremely quick editing. If you find in editing your shooting pace was too slow, you can trim the time by **prelapping** incoming dialogue (the audience hears Bob start talking over the picture of Alice) and then cutting away from Alice to Bob as he is already in midsentence, thereby losing the **air** or the pause between the two characters talking. This is also known as **pulling up**, meaning that the editor is pulling up the dialogue so there is less space between the character's dialogue than there was while shooting. Good editors have lots of tricks like that to help you adjust the pace of your finished product.

BREAKING THE RULES

Now that you know the rules, you should also know that these rules are made to be broken. The only thing that really matters is telling the story. Some shows or films deliberately break the rules; they want to bring attention to the style or look of the film in order to tell the story. For example, let's say you are introducing your antagonist villain, who has been sighted by your protagonist hero across a crowded city plaza, similar to the scene we discussed in Chapter 9. The first shot might be the hero's POV shot in which he sees the villain among business-attired people hurrying to work. The next shot might **punch** into a waist-size shot of the villain and then immediately punch in again to a two-t of the same guy. This is a deliberate jump cut to reveal the identity of the villain to the audience. (A punch is a **straight cut in**, from a wider shot to a tighter one, of the same subject in the same angle, without first going to, or editing in, a reverse shot.) Edited rhythmically, it has an impact and gets across a story point. On a show such as USA Networks's *Burn Notice*, this series of shots might accompany the protagonist Michael Westen's narration, as he says this villain is an "arms dealer with a grudge"; then the words "Arms Dealer with a Grudge" appear on the screen under the villain's face. Then, to continue the show's characteristic tongue-in-cheek humor, the **chyron**, or printed words, changes to "Michael's New Boss." This jump-cutting is breaking the rules for a reason and with great style and effect.

CREATING THE DIRECTOR'S CUT

The editor has been working the whole time you have been shooting. So when do you first see your story assembled? And how soon should you deliver your cut? It differs from show to show, but there are mandates from the DGA that set the standards. You should not only know your creative rights and responsibilities, but also should observe and respect them. They include:

- You should see the editor's assembly of your show no later than 6 days after the close of principal photography.
- Only the editor will see an assembly of the episode you directed before you do.
- You may ask that no other person view this cut for 24 hours after you view it.
- You must begin your cut within 24 hours of receiving it.
- You have 4 days to complete your cut on an episode (more on a made-for-television movie).
- Your contract states that your cut should be no longer than 1 minute over the length of the broadcast time.

In practice, this final rule is often ignored because the showrunner will generally want to see the show complete as written. The protocol on this differs from show to show, and it's something for you to discuss with the showrunner and your editor.

Most shows will give the director a copy of the editor's assembly to preview before the first editing session with the director. It is your choice whether to look at it before the session. Mary Lou does, and she comes to the edit session with notes she has made to herself about things she wants to change, review, or consider. Bethany, on the other hand, likes to start the edit session with "fresh eyes" and to watch the editor's assembly for the first time sitting next to the editor. The important thing, either way, is to be open to what the editor has done. Don't ever dismiss something just because it is different from what you intended until you decide whether it is better than what you intended. It will eventually add up to the same puzzle, so just ask yourself whether this is a superior, clearer, or less predictable version of this puzzle. The goal for both you and the editor is—first, last, and always—to tell the story.

Don't ever dismiss something just because it is different from what you intended until you decide whether it is better than what you intended.

CUTTING FOR STORY

Regardless of whether you've previewed the assembly, we suggest watching the entire episode all the way through without interruption with the editor when you begin your first session with him. See if anything **bumps** you. We know that doesn't sound like a technical term, but every good director instinctually has that gut reaction to a screen moment that doesn't ring true or seems wrong. Some directors say "it made me blink," or others "it made my neck or shoulders twitch," still others "felt it in my gut." It truly is that visceral. You just know you want to fix it. But you don't need to write anything down this first time through. Just notice when you are completely wrapped up in the show or if it loses your interest.

If you haven't already, thank the editor and his assistants for their hard work and artistry. Then jump in and get to work. Rewatch each scene, stop, and discuss the changes you want to make, then sit back *patiently* and let the editor do his job. His bins should be organized in an easily accessible fashion so that you can look at another take or another angle readily. Know that you can experiment or play with an idea without the danger of destroying the work the editor already did because it is easily retrievable in the event that you end up preferring the editor's version to yours.

> *This is your one and only chance to assemble your cut. Use your time with the editor efficiently and respectfully. If you were clear and efficient in your shooting, a good editor will almost always deliver a cut to you that is structurally correct; that is, the opening visual, the ending visual, and the first cut out of the opening shot are exactly as you intended.*

This is your one and only chance to assemble your cut. Use your time with the editor efficiently and respectfully. If you were clear and efficient in your shooting, a good editor will almost always deliver a cut to you that is structurally correct; that is, the opening visual, the ending visual, and the first cut out of the opening shot are exactly as you intended. A director's work with the editor afterwards is generally subtle and accomplished in tiny ways, whether that's changing takes for performance, cutting to an insert to make sure the point is made, or pulling up the pace.

From the Experts

We have both worked with Brandi Bradburn. She is an experienced editor and teacher, and she applies her experience as both to her more recent directing career. She shared these insights with us.

Editing is often incorrectly boiled down to matching continuity with the notion that an editor simply fits "tab a" into "slot b." This is the mechanical side of editorial and an extremely small part of the process. Once an editor assembles the footage, then the real cutting begins. And just to clarify, an editor does not turn over an assembly. An editor turns over a complete first cut of the show or film that truly "plays." Typically, a vast majority of this first cut remains intact throughout the process of editing toward and including the final cut.

The word cut is a bit of a misnomer because what we editors are actually doing is joining images together, and that is where the true power of editing comes into play. The juxtaposition of two moving images can convey a concept or an emotion that simply does not exist if those two images stand alone. Taking it further, as an editor sculpts the rhythm and pace of the story, she can create tension or shock or emotion where none existed. In the cutting room, in order to achieve the best work in a show or film, an editor must constantly be thinking as a director, as a cinematographer, as an actor, as a writer, as a storyteller.

Beyond educating yourself in the art of editing, my best piece of advice to directors is to work at articulating your notes in a way that your editor can go after them. Often a suggestion or "fix" is given without explanation. To employ your editor to your full advantage, tell her what you would like to happen, and allow her to use her expertise to artistically solve the problem. There are so many moving parts to a cut, and your editor is keenly aware of and intimate with all of them. She is also well-versed in the copious ways a problem can be addressed editorially. For example, if you ask your editor to cut to a character at a certain moment in the scene she can do that easily enough. However, without a reason why, it may or may not solve the issue you have with the scene. A more useful note might be, "I am not feeling this character enough," or "the tone feels too light here," or "the scene is lacking in emotion or tension." Then you can discuss the heart of the problem with your editor and give her the information she needs to address the note in a meaningful way. The solution may indeed be a cut to the character at that moment, or it could be a need for line lifts for rhythm and pace, or the addition of a sound effect or a new piece of music. Let your editor know what you want and they will find a way to achieve it.

Above all, a director should enjoy a highly collaborative relationship with her editor, and ideally the cutting room should be a safe haven where the director can explore, discover and accomplish her vision and story.

CUTTING FOR TIME

After you have made sure the story is clear, your next task is to be aware of the **running time**. Episodes of television must be delivered at a precise length, measured to the *hundredth of the second*. You will make trims to tighten the show and deliver the best cut possible. But the showrunner has final cut and will make sure the show is at precisely the right length for airing after consultation with the network regarding omitting scenes. For most shows, a director's cut that runs about four minutes over running time seems to be an ideal paradigm, allowing the showrunner to cut out dialogue and/or scenes that aren't needed. But sometimes your cut will be much longer, just because it was a longer script.

If your episode is really long, begin by looking for entire scenes or parts of scenes that might be **lifted** or removed. Never cut out something that moves the plot forward. Then tighten what is already there. (We'll talk about this more in a moment.) And build some separate planned edits to show how you would propose trimming to the running time. Because editing is now done in a digital format, it is easy to construct an alternative version of a scene so that the producers, network, or studio can actually see how you envision your cuts for time working. Those **alts**, or alternative versions, and lifted scenes can be available for viewing at the end of the show. And showing is always better than describing.

To tighten what is already there is more tedious. It means trimming everywhere. Editors call it "getting the air out." In some cases, it might be seconds or even just frames of film. Either way, they add up. The good news is that usually, it makes for a better pace, better story, and a better show.

With humorous moments, a quick pace will improve the show because one of the comedy precepts is "faster is funnier." That being said, it can't just be fast; it must also observe comedy rhythms.

With humorous moments, a quick pace will improve the show because one of the comedy precepts is "faster is funnier." That being said, it can't just be fast; it must also observe comedy rhythms. A comedy editor whom Mary Lou worked with on two different series, Mark West, does multiple passes pulling out tenths of seconds at a time to perfect the comic timing and **tighten** the pacing, which used to be called **getting the scissors in** there. Editors used to literally cut and paste pieces of film together; today, they press buttons and click and drag. But the concept is the same. In the hands of a talented editor, this skill of creating a rhythm for a scene can ensure that the viewing audience laughs precisely on cue. With drama, less is often more. As the director, you should know that when the person on the screen is indulging in a huge moment of some deep feeling, it is sometimes wiser to show less. The audience may feel it more deeply if the actor is not shown lingering in the moment because people tend to shy away from overt emotionalism. It often works out that if you want the audience to cry, you should ask the actor to refrain from doing so.

ADDING MUSIC AND SFX

After you have cut for time and cut for story, you should add music and sound effects in order to complete your cut. Your music will probably be **temp tracks**, or temporary, place-holding music. If the show has been airing for more than a season, your editor will reuse the composer's **cues** (short pieces of underscoring) from previous episodes that supply the same emotional tone. If the music is a song, it doesn't matter whether this temp music is **cleared** (bought for broadcast use, wherein the artists who composed and performed it get paid). This music is laid in just to get a feel for where you see music in the show. Again, it should always enhance the storytelling. That is why it is important that the first time your cut is viewed, your music choices are included. (Later, after the show has been locked, the legal department will get clearances on the final choices for songs.) Sometimes a song has already been cleared even before you start shooting.

This clearance almost always happens when there is an artist who actually performs a song in the show. *Glee* did this multiple times in every episode. The songs are prerecorded and mixed and the performers **lip-sync**, or mouth the words, to their own voices during filming of the scene. If this is the case, the editor cuts your footage to the same tracks to which the singers lip-synced. Everything will match except for that occasional mouth that stays open too long. Editors cut around this and make sure the singers *appear* to be singing live. There are occasions when the song is not prerecorded, but performed live on set, usually when it's a personal issue for the singer who feels more authentic doing it that way. In that case, it's important to have multiple cameras (usually four or more) so that the sequence is cuttable. But for a director, the prerecorded method gives you more options in the cutting room. The other time an editor will cut to already cleared music is when the a specific song is so integral to the story that the song is cleared in prep to be used as the underscoring for a scene or montage that moves the story forward. *Dawson's Creek* was a trendsetter when it featured multiple songs in this way from popular artists in every episode.

Adding sound effects (**SFX**) is the final component to completing your cut. Every editor has a library (legal or not) from which they draw the SFX for every episode. Ideally, these sounds will be replaced with cleared sounds that the studio has paid to use. Make sure that your editor finds the best and most appropriate effects at his disposal. For example, the sound of the perfect gunshot can make a huge difference to the impact of your story. The sharpness, volume, reverberation, and echoing that follow the shot make a difference. You want the shock, fear, and veracity to be felt when someone watches your cut, and the soundtrack is an integral part of your storytelling. You also want to make sure that **room tone** (the background sounds of a practical location, recorded during production) and temporary **walla** (the murmur of the background crowd) is laid into restaurant or any crowd scenes. These temporary sounds will be replaced later by **loop groups** of actors who create specific background voices for each scene. (We talk about all of the final postproduction processes in the next chapter.)

Even though your DGA creative rights contract offers you the opportunity to be notified of the date, time, and place of every postproduction operation, and in good faith allowed to be present and consulted, the next time you see your episode after delivering your cut will most likely be on the air. You will probably be on to your next episode and this episode will be completed and delivered under the competent hands of the postproduction supervisor. Feel free to take advantage of your creative rights, but know that directors—

unless they are also producers on the show—don't usually participate in the next steps of postproduction, so your presence and/or participation might be a surprise.

Some people say shows are "made in the cutting room." It is true that the editing of a film has a huge impact on its ultimate presentation and audience response. An editor can make good film great. But the editor can't make bad film good. (One exception, historically, is Elmo Williams's cut of 1952's *High Noon*. Producer Stanley Kramer and director Fred Zinnemann authorized Williams to make an experimental version, cutting the film to echo real time. That experimental cut became the final cut of a classic film.) It is the director's responsibility to deliver the film that tells the story, and a good editor will be your partner in turning your raw footage into the polished jewel that is its full potential. When you hire an editor, look for someone who shares your sensibilities—a person who understands your vision and will bring his prodigious talents to the editing room to turn what you envisioned into something even better than you anticipated. As director Peter Weir said:

The fine line is getting from them [the editors] what you haven't thought of yourself, and at the same time needing them to accept that you will make the decision in the end. You don't want a rubber stamp at all. In casting these parts, as it were, you want somebody who can say, OK, let's dig deeper into what your point of view is, see if we can go further with this. When that sort of collaboration emerges, it's wonderful.[1]

AN OPPORTUNITY WORTH TAKING

We want to end this chapter with a piece of advice. We think there is an enormous amount you can learn by watching an editor work. When you watch pieces of film (or another medium) put together, you begin to understand the building blocks of visual storytelling. You should take advantage of this viewing. It doesn't have to be a show you directed. In fact, we recommend otherwise. What would be helpful is if you got a chance to watch something being edited that you also watched being shot so that you know the footage the editor received. Either way, you can see how he assembles what he eventually shows the director. Notice the choices he makes and the things he tries. This kind of experience is invaluable. If you do get the opportunity to watch an editor, be respectful and don't talk during the process; just watch. Make a list of questions you might like to ask and make your inquiries at lunch. There is a formula that says editing time expands by one hour for every individual who is in the room. Don't be the person who makes the editor's job longer. Rather, be the director who will be a better director for having taken advantage of an editor's generosity and be considerate enough to value the gift you've been given.

From the Experts

Excerpt from *Cutting Rhythms* by Karen Pearlman

When cutting a dance scene or a fight scene, [. . .] ask yourself or the director: Where are we now in the movement's "story"? Where have we come from? The answers guide the direction of the editing. If the fight starts between equally matched opponents, you may start by looking for shots in which their movement energy in the frame is equally strong. If one fighter then gets the advantage, it is important to know where in the movement story that happens, on this punch or that fall, or this jab or that stumble; otherwise you risk emphasizing the wrong energy for telling the physical story. It is possible to shape the movement of time and energy in physical rhythm to tell innumerable different physical stories, and it is often the case that the editor changes the story or how it unfolds, because particular shots have more impact, beauty, or energy and so the physical story she cuts unfolds different from that which may originally have been intended. This is an excellent way of working, and very common, but not the only way. It can also be creatively stimulating to get the director to make a narrative translation of the physical movement, which may otherwise be quite abstract—to tell you the movement's story. Either knowing the director's version of the story in movement quality/energy terms or building a version of the physical story based on what the material is asking for informs decisions about how long to stay with things, how quickly to build or to establish them, and where their development is leading.[2]

Insider Info

What is the Editor's Creative Role in Helping the Director to Create a Finished Product?

When I approach a scene, I look at all the dailies scene by scene or page by page and mark takes and reaction shots. Then I have a better idea about how to approach the scene. Some scenes need to be edited in a way to help the outcome or set up a blow. Looking at the dailies before editing saves precious time as editors are usually under a time constraint. Adding roomtone, sfx, music, and stock to a scene helps give the director a better feel for the scene and it means less work later. When the director comes into my edit bay I need to be ready with answers to why I cut it the way I did. Look at all the alts so you can give your opinion on them. If the director shot several alts or different elements, edit them together in a subclip to show them. They will appreciate this.

Before a person jumps into the directing chair I like to invite them into my edit bay. This also goes for Script Supervisors, Technical Coordinators, even cameramen stop by occasionally.

The slowness of the edit bay as opposed to being on the floor with a meal penalty looming is very comforting. I show them the matching, continuity, blocking and technical problems that I deal with every day. Sometimes they see things that never occurred to them on the floor.

What Advice Would You Give a Director?

My two pieces of advice to directors is please don't stop the actors in their tracks because of a small flub or minor technical problem unless the scene is going nowhere. Let the scene play out.

If you must restart, go back a couple lines to get all the reactions. Then give a note and shoot a pickup or another take. Actors appreciate this as it keeps the words in their head rather than stopping and starting over.

Brian Schnuckel, MPEG
Editor
Lucky Louis, Baby Daddy, The Game, Chris Rock: Bring the Pain

Insider Info

What is the Editor's Creative Role in Helping the Director to Create a Finished Product?

The editor's job is to collaboratively strengthen, enhance, and hone the director's vision in order to bring the most effective version of the story to screen. Creatively speaking, this is done in a variety of ways—that in turn change throughout the duration of the project. Often, it can become a love/hate relationship because we fluctuate between being your best friend and the stern cold voice of objectivity.

Although many would say creativity is the most important aspect of any job in the industry, for editing, creativity is tied with objectivity. Both are vital. Think of us as the friend who tells you, "Yes, you look fat in those jeans." We love you but if need be will protect you . . . from yourself.

During preproduction, the editor talks with the director often to "try to get into the director's head" as much as possible. The more an editor understands the director's vision and intent, the closer that editor's cut will be to that vision. However, during the editor cut process, the editor also has an obligation to explore alternate, accidental, and previously unthought-of possibilities the footage may present.

As the production process continues and (in the case of television and when the studio has final cut) the director moves on, the editor often becomes the last defender and champion of the director's original vision. Mainstream network television is not terribly interested in making art—they're playing a numbers game: the more people they can get to watch, the more ads they can sell. This reality can result in horrible lowest-common-denominator story decisions (such as "Let's put in more voiceover so people who are just tuning in will know who everyone is," and "Does it have to be so sad? I know she dies, but can you make it happier? We don't want people sad").

At the end of the day, it is the editor and the executive producers who must try to bridge this gap, and when push comes to shove, it is usually only the editor left trying to salvage as much "art" as possible while making the bean counters happy. Many who don't understand the process blame editors for "cutting everything out" without ever understanding how hard we fight to just to keep *what's left in.*

What Makes a "Good" Director in the Room and a "Bad" Director in the Room?

Trust: we're both on the same team. Don't treat me like the enemy. I'm not trying to destroy your movie and maybe—just maybe—I know what the hell I'm talking about, too.

Patience: some things take time. You standing at my shoulder watching me work will not get it done any faster.

Collaboration/open mind: just because it wasn't your idea doesn't mean it's a bad idea. Take a chance and watch where new things lead—you might be pleasantly surprised. If not, we can always put it back.

NEVER, EVER SNAP YOUR FINGERS! We're not dogs.

If you're a writer/director, don't bring the script into the cutting room. That time has passed, and holding it in your lap while reviewing the cut will only make you see your preconceptions rather than your movie's reality. Remember that the audience will *not* have a script. They will not know that we lifted two lines and swapped the order of an argument. They will only know if it "feels right" and if your words get in the way of that "feeling," let 'em go or no one will stick around to hear anything else you have to say. Contrary to what you may think, people do not follow dialogue, they follow *story, drama,* and *emotion.* Learn the difference.

Let me be clear, though: a well-written script *is* the cornerstone of any good movie. And 99 percent of movie problems are script problems that are never solved. But in the end, a movie is as much the script as we are our DNA. Our genetic codes dictate who we will be, but not *who we will really be.* They create our bones, hair color, and eye color, but not our loves, how we laugh, and the pauses between our sentences. To constantly compare a person's life to their DNA is to lament a concert pianist for only being 5'2" when they should've been 6' tall—not only have you missed the whole damn point, but quite honestly, if you had never pointed it out, no one ever would have known. Don't do this to your movie.

What Do You Wish More Directors Understood About Editing?

The term "fix it in post" is a lie. Things are never fixed in post—they're just made to suck less. You want something fixed—fix it *during production* or better yet *on the page.* Again, 99.999999 percent of a show's problems (aside from budget issues) are script problems. Your two young lovers will not be *fixed* into an Oscar-winning heart-breaking duo if they still have to say crap lines and work through poorly plotted arcs.

Akin to "fixing" in post—"figuring it out" in post is also a no-no. Have a plan. Make sure your vision is as precise and well laid out as it can be. Know how you're getting in, when you're close, here's a cutaway, the end is a pullback, and how you transition out *before you shoot.* See the cut movie in your head. Remember that my job is to collaboratively bring *your* vision to screen—if you don't have a vision, it's not my job to give you one. Your vision should be so apparent that when I open a bin, I shouldn't even need the script—I should just be able to follow the angles and the takes and cut the movie you see in your mind's eye. So when I open a bin and see three hours of footage for six lines of dialogue shot from every conceivable angle, my respect for you as a storyteller goes right out the window.

Editing is the nexus of creativity for any movie or show—the place where all the pieces come together and the story comes to life. And although the process can be arduous and insanely repetitive, the result is worth it. To hone an actor's performance. To carve a storyline. To piece together moments from here and from there—that look, with this response; juxtapose that shot, with this music—to weave all those moments together and create a reality that makes an audience member lean forward and gasp or cry or laugh. To make an audience believe: it's a wonderful rush.

Tirsa Hackshaw
Editor
A.K.A. Jessica Jones, Agent X, House of Lies

Vocabulary

A side	editor's assembly	pulling up
alts	fill	punch
angle	getting the scissors in	(visual)
B side	hard drive	rhythm
bins	head	rock into coverage
bumps	incomplete	room tone
card	jump cut	running time
chyron	lifted	script supervisor's notes
cleared	lip-sync	SFX
complementary shots	loop groups	straight cut in
complete	massage the cut	tail
cues (music)	nonlinear editing	temp tracks
cutting pattern	methods (NLEs)	tighten
	over the cut	trim
	prelapping	walla

NOTES

1 Terrence Rafferty, "Uncommon Man," *DGA Quarterly*, Summer 2010, pp. 30–37.
2 Karen Pearlman, *Cutting Rhythms, Intuitive Film Editing*. New York and London: Focal Press, 2015.

Chapter 15

Working with the Post Supervisor

There is a tremendous amount of work that continues after you hand in your director's cut and before the final version gets delivered to the network for airing. Knowing what happens may not make you a significantly better director, but we think you should have a working knowledge of the sequence and respect for the skilled people who do it. We mentioned in the previous chapter that you have creative rights. But practically speaking, you will see that television postproduction is really the producer's domain and most producers exercise their control over all of it.

It is said that theatre is the medium in which actors have the most control, film is the medium in which directors have the most control, and television is the medium in which writers have the most control. To elaborate: After opening night, a play is in the hands of the actors who do a fresh performance every night. The director's job is done and the bulk of the producing job is also finished once the show is mounted (except running the show, which is left in the hands of the production and company managers). With a film, the director stays involved with the decisions (with the exception of distribution and marketing) until the picture is locked and it premieres. Writers supervise a television show from beginning to end. Why? A writer creates a show, pitches it to a network, and proves that his idea has legs to last many seasons. He hires multiple directors to direct the many episodes. The network that is spending the money is not just buying a one-time

> The network that is spending the money is not just buying a one-time product; it is buying a sustainable product that will hopefully last many years on the air.

product; it is buying a sustainable product that will hopefully last many years on the air.

The viability of the continued success of that product depends on a series of new stories every season. A writer is responsible for generating that product; therefore, he garners the title Executive Producer and will certainly always be known as the creator of the show. That is usually only the beginning of his responsibilities. If that writer is also the showrunner, which is often the case, he is responsible for every aspect of the show, beginning with finding writers to write, actors to act, directors to direct, and a line producer to be in charge of production.

That showrunner also delegates. The person who reports to the showrunner for postproduction is the post supervisor or postproduction supervisor. The title is an apt one. There are a lot of different people involved in completing an episode. Lots of things happen simultaneously; others occur in a strict sequential order. The postproduction supervisor coordinates and supervises it all, much as the director does during production. This supervisor contributes similarly by making choices and applying her creative vision to the various processes of post, as well as leading each postproduction department on a journey toward one goal. The postproduction supervisor may have earned a more advanced title (associate producer or coproducer) based on her years of experience, but for our purposes here, she will just be referred to as the postproduction supervisor. Or you could call her the lifesaver, because production deficiencies are often obscured by brilliant work in postproduction.

OFFLINE VIDEO

Post is divided into two categories for video editing: offline and online. All of the cuts (editor's assembly, director's cut, producer's cut, studio cut, and network cut) are part of the offline process until the picture is locked. These cuts have been made from "copies," not the original master you shot. The online part of editing is actually quite fast. It involves taking the computerized list of all the final editing instructions, called an **EDL** (edit decision list) and using your original footage to create a **VAM** (video assembled master). So the offline process can take weeks to accomplish, and is really the preparation for the online process, which is the creation of the master of the episode that has made it through prep, shoot, and postproduction.

The online part of editing is actually quite fast. It involves taking the computerized list of all the final editing instructions, called an EDL (edit decision list) and using your original footage to create a VAM (video assembled master).

Once the VAM is created, copies of it go to the following departments and individuals: visual effects, the composer, the music editor, the sound editor, closed captioning, and the network promotion department. This VAM has a rough audio component that serves as a template for all the final sounds that will be mixed into the show. At this point, the postproduction supervisor may make changes to the temp audio track.

The VFX still have to be created. If you discussed them during pre-production, the preliminary work was begun then. Remember that SPFX are done during production, but VFX are created artificially and added in post. An example of a VFX is CGI, which uses three-dimensional computer graphics to create images such as a crowd in an arena. CGI animation at its most sophisticated can create a three-dimensional world where the Na'vi of *Avatar* live. It costs less than hiring and costuming thousands of extras and has possibilities that are continually being explored. However, the old-fashioned way of building miniatures to create large or different environments still works, and works well, especially in the sense of making the scene look "real" and not like something out of a video game. Director Christopher Nolan (*Interstellar*, *The Dark Knight Rises*) explained his strong feelings about this topic:

We try to enhance our stunt work and floor effects with extraordinary CGI tools like wire and rig removals. If you put a lot of time and effort into matching your original film elements, the kind of enhancements you can put into the frames can really trick the eye, offering results far beyond what was possible 20 years ago. The problem for me is if you don't first shoot something with the camera on which to base the shot, the visual effect is going to stick out if the film you're making has a realistic style or patina. I prefer films that feel more like real life, so any CGI has to be very carefully handled to fit into that.[1]

After the VFX are added, the VAM needs to be **color corrected**. Even though many cameras have color correction filters and the DPs have carefully lit every scene, the light is never exactly the same; therefore, the image recorded from take to take never matches exactly. A computer artist (sometimes referred to as a **colorist**) with a great eye for matching color (sometimes with the DP present) makes sure that the red wine in the glass is always the same red or—even more noticeable—that the color of an actor's skin is always consistent. He may also enhance color balances for creative reasons. Once color corrected, it is called a **CTM** (color timed master). Suzanne Welke, the postproduction supervisor on *Girlfriends*, defined it like this: "A CTM is the same as the VAM, only pretty."[2]

Now the episode is ready for **titles** or credits: the text that is placed on top of the picture or a black screen and includes those important words

"Directed by." The people who create the text must do their job perfectly. People hate when their name is spelled incorrectly or their title mislabeled. It's why every newspaper in the country prints corrections. It is why people who work in television and motion picture have contracts that spell out what text will appear on the screen, how big it will be, in what order, and sometimes for what duration of time. It is also negotiated whether your name appears alone (single card) or simultaneously as someone else (shared card) on the same screen. Directors always get a single card, and it is nearly always listed last in the up-front credits (the ones at the beginning of a show). If,

Directors always get a single card and it is nearly always listed last in the up-front credits (the ones at the beginning of a show).

for example, your story begins with a visual montage, you may want to shoot extra footage to allow for credits to finish before the dialogue begins.

From the Experts

There is some preplanning that a director can do in regard to titles and credits. Suzanne Welke told us:

In regards to planning your shots for the part of the show that is titled: the post supervisor will know the specifications for duration and placement (and also for the "bug" or network logo that often appears in the corner, and the ratings bug). Knowing this comes in handy when you have a lot of close-ups, as you won't want credits covering up half of your actor's face, or if you have a lot of quick cuts (a credit will never go "across the cut" or span over two shots), as you don't want to still be running credits halfway into the show.[3]

You should first review the titles and credits for a previous episode of the show and then consult your postproduction supervisor if you have any questions.

OFFLINE SOUND

Meanwhile the postproduction supervisor is also concerned with sound editing. During your shoot, sound is recorded on different tracks and monitored by the mixer we talked about in Chapter 11. The master of that track is called the **O track**, for original track, and is always the preferred track when assembling sound because the quality of the sound decreases the further generation you go from the original. In digital recording, in which there is no degradation of quality, the O track is preferred simply because it is the single origination of material. As soon as the EDL is completed, it goes over to the sound house or company so they can start to assemble a time-coded master audiotape or locked digital audio file. But that step is not possible until all the sounds are ready for the final mix. The sound categories are the dialogue, the sound effects, and the music. Those sounds are edited and assembled by the sound editorial team, and each member will specialize in one of those specific types of sound. So each episode will have a sound effects (SFX) editor, a dialogue editor, and a music editor.[4]

The bulk of your dialogue will come from the scenes that were recorded and mixed live during the shoot. But some of that dialogue may need to be **looped** or replaced, which is done at a looping or **ADR** session. Looping was a process used in filmmaking until the 1970s in which an actor would listen to a physical loop of audiotape repeated over and over (without the picture) and would mimic the line reading, which was then recorded and inserted into the soundtrack of the final product. ADR stands for automated or automatic dialogue replacement. It is done on a looping stage at the sound house where actors watch the VAM while they listen to themselves do the dialogue. They then try to repeat their dialogue to fit their lip movements. Actors must contractually do these sessions. They are asked to either replace dialogue that can't be heard well or add new dialogue. If there is a sizable amount of dialogue that needs to be looped, it is a good idea for you to show up at this session so that you can direct your actors.

Mary Lou did this on a series she directed when one of the guest stars gave a great acting performance, but her accent was so thick that it was unintelligible. During the ADR session, Mary Lou had three responsibilities: to listen with fresh ears to dialogue to make sure that it was understandable, to see that the lip-syncing looked credible, and to see that the actress maintained her hysterically funny performance without getting frustrated by the many attempts it took to get it.

> If there is a sizable amount of dialogue that needs to be looped, it is a good idea for you to show up at this session so that you can direct your actors.

The principal actors' dialogue is not the only spoken word. There is improvised dialogue for textured background atmosphere provided by a loop group or **walla group**. ("Walla" is a made-up name referring to the wall of sound a large crowd creates.) These are union actors who specialize in this craft. A loop group is necessary because your background artists during production were pantomiming, not speaking aloud, so that the principal actors' dialogue could be recorded **clean**, or without any extraneous sound. The walla group does many layers of sound to fill in what is missing. They can do an array of things. They can provide the voices for the people chatting next to your hero table in a restaurant or the moans of soldiers dying in pain on a battlefield. Mary Lou's friend, Randall Montgomery, is an actor who both does walla and re-voices actors. He was hired to replace Patrick Stewart's voice in the first X-Men movie. It was a temp dub, but when Stewart came to do the final voice he asked whether the director could just use Randy's voice as he thought he sounded more like him than he did. He also was hired to do Bill Clinton's voice on a film called *Silence of the Hams* and ended up re-voicing both Clinton and George HW Bush arguing with each other. And it can also get a little bizarre: Mary Lou's husband, Charles Dougherty, provided extra slobbering sounds for the Saint Bernard in the movie *The Sandlot*! Loop group actors are a talented lot who are called upon to do many unusual things, including kissing. To augment a kiss sound, a loop group actor will kiss his own hand, making sure that the lip smack provides the appropriate texture: is it quick and light? Or prolonged and wet-sounding?

The sound effects part of the audio digital file will come from many sources. Some will be sounds recorded on the set or on location while you were filming the scene. Others will be **wild sounds** recorded after the shoot; that is, the sound is unrelated to a specific picture. Some sounds will come from industry libraries. Still others will be manufactured, either electronically or in a studio.

The ones manufactured in a studio are often ordinary, everyday sounds such as feet walking. These sounds are called **foley**, named after Jack Foley, the Universal Studios sound effects pioneer. Foley artists duplicate or augment production sounds to make them more specific and audible. A foley stage is an amazing place, with different kinds of flooring, a bin of shoes with different types of soles, a huge array of props, and pits filled with water and sand.

Within that one space, the artist can create the sounds of a horse running, an arrow leaving a bow, or the ping of a table knife against a glass as the actor calls for attention in the scene playing on a screen at the front of the stage. The foley artist watches the picture and attempts to sync his motions to it. If adjustment is needed, the sound editor will physically manipulate (edit) the sound element to put it in its rightful place. In addition to foley, there may be bigger sounds to edit or add to the soundtrack, like explosions and crashes or smaller constant sounds like room tone or a crackling fire.

A foley stage is an amazing place, with different kinds of flooring, a bin of shoes with different types of soles, a huge array of props, and pits filled with water and sand.

No matter where the sound effects come from, they must be organized according to time code to be ready for the **mix**, or **dub**, which is the process of putting all the sounds together.

Meanwhile, the music requirements for the episode are being addressed. As soon as the composer received the EDL, he began writing all the music cues for the episode after screening the show with the post supervisor and/or possibly the showrunner. The composer writes **underscore**, which is music played along with a scene to lend emotional impact. Cues can be as short as three seconds (known as a **sting**, this is usually for an act-out) or cover an entire scene. Almost all act-ins and act-outs will be scored. The job of the composer is an integral one to the success of the final product because the music almost functions as one of the characters, communicating to the audience how they should feel. After the composer writes the music, it will be performed by hired musicians on a **soundstage** with natural instruments, or it may be a synthesized track created with a digital keyboard played by the composer himself, or it may be a combination of the two. Some music in the show may be a song that has been cleared for use in the episode as we talked about in the last chapter. Wherever the music comes from, each cue has a **start and stop**, or a point when the music begins and ends that is matched to the picture. The starts and stops are precisely coordinated with the time code of the picture by the music editor.

ASSEMBLING THE DUB

After all three of the sound components are ready, they get assembled together in what is called the mix or dub, which is when the postproduction sound mixer assembles all the sounds in relation to each other. It is when you determine at what levels your music, dialogue, and sound effects will be heard. The mixer also can **sweeten** any and all of the sounds. Sweetening might include using noise filters that can reduce certain sounds and enhance others. It might be boosting low- or high-end sounds or adding an echo or reverb to others. The goal is to make it sound the best it can and make our ears happy. The postproduction supervisor is present for the dub to supervise the process of adding, subtracting, balancing, and refining all the audio elements. The showrunner may listen to a preview of the mix to give final approval. Just like the video online product, the sound dub should be seamless so that the audience views it and hears it and is aware only of following the story, rather than noticing the techniques that were used to create the episode.

Once the tracks have been mixed down, the sound mixer will take care of Dolby, surround sound, and stereo components of the mix. When all of these aspects are complete, the audio portion of the episode is added to visual part: the **layback**.

Scoring the Scene

 Record a scene and mute the existing sound. Find a piece of music that you think would fit the mood and dynamic of the scene. Play them simultaneously.

AFTER THE LAYBACK

Once the layback is done, you have a **final air master**. It needs to be **closed-captioned**. If you don't personally use this option when watching television, you may not know that it exists. But it is there. And it is required by law so that people with hearing disabilities have equal access to public information, which is why the people who do this in post have access to the script and the VAM, and then also check to make sure that they have the dialogue correct after ADR. They even add descriptions of other sounds when applicable.

Once the closed-captioning is done, copies must be made or **dubbed** for distribution. Where do they go to get broadcast? They go to the network, which has a license and is federally regulated. Each network might have different specifications and limitations. It is the post supervisor's job to know what these are.

From the Experts

Suzanne Welke shared some specific examples:
The SyFy channel requires that the running times for each act must be at least six minutes. So if, in your director's cut, you want to change where an act break is, postproduction may tell you that you cannot do that, as it will make the act too short. The overall length may be different for the syndicated version versus network/broadcast version. So when you see the show in syndication, know that the production company does not always control this trimming; it is sometimes handled by the studio and their own set of editors. Another example in this area is zooming in on a shot or **"blowing it up."** In the director's cut, you may want to get in closer by blowing up a shot. You might be told that you cannot go in as much as you'd like because it will get bounced back by international. The post supervisor would know that once the "international" master is made, that particular shot would not be technically accepted.[5]

Welke also cautions directors to not "fall in love" with songs used as temporary tracks. Music is just not clearable for any number of reasons: it may not be available, or permission may not be granted, or it may be too expensive to license.

Once the networks receive their copies, they send them out to their stations and affiliates, who broadcast it in the specified times. Just to give you an idea of the scope of a network: the ABC television network is an American television network made up of 10 owned and operated stations and nearly 200 affiliates. The broadcast networks (ABC, CBS, NBC, FOX, and CW) can be seen by nearly 100 percent of the population, delivered for free over the airwaves. The cable networks (such as USA, TNT, Lifetime, and Spike) could reach nearly that many, but their services must be picked up by distributors. Pay cable channels (HBO, Showtime) require viewers to pay for their service. Once you have directed a show, it requires distribution of some kind to an audience. Those opportunities are growing. The Internet is the new media, delivering previously unthinkable paradigms for audience viewership with downloading and live streaming, and allowing audiences to **binge watch** an entire season of a show in only a few viewings. The Internet and its hunger for additional content also creates opportunities specifically for **cross platforming**, or having online content that supports and hopefully increases a show's viewership. This additional content has a much smaller budget than broadcast TV and may be a great place for a new director to break in, especially if the number of Internet **hits** is tracked and that number is sizable enough to add to a new director's credibility.

Broadcast television shows get a second life in many forms of **syndication** or reruns. These often occur on smaller networks or cable stations that purchase a package of many episodes—usually a minimum of four seasons (88–100 episodes) and pay for the right to air them multiple times. Successful shows in syndication can cover production costs and make a profit, even if the first run of the show was not profitable. Directors, writers, and actors in TV particularly like when a show they have worked on gets syndicated because they receive compensation in the form of residuals each subsequent time an episode airs.

In addition to the copies that go to the network, the postproduction supervisor also sees that you get a copy of the show, usually on DVD, which is guaranteed by your DGA contract. You will usually get it the day after the show airs for the first time. And when you watch it, you should notice all that went into completing it after you finished your cut. Postproduction is not an afterthought, just because it comes at the end. It is the part of the process that polishes the jewel.

From the Experts

Excerpt from *Music Editing for Film and Television* by Steven Saltzman, MPSE.[6]

The director or filmmaker may begin thinking about music early in the process of writing the story, considering songs or even a style of score. Songs are sometimes intrinsic to a film, with an actor or a particular artist performing a song on-camera in order to create or reinforce emotional impact or contribute to the story. The director should be very careful of tying a specific song into the story, particularly early in the scriptwriting process, since licensing it may constrain the film's budget, and it may be too expensive altogether. [. . .] At the demo stage, [. . .] when there may be extensive exchange of ideas, revisions, and more ideas—the music editor can often help the composer and director to reach a common understanding, their communication skills being used to support the sometimes emotional creative process. [. . .] They often have experience of a director's likes and dislikes, and intimate knowledge of their responses to the temp score and to the composer's work. This insight can often be relayed to the composer to help guide their creativity, for example helping to shape the demos or mock-ups the composer presents.

There are many possible issues, some quite subtle, which mean a cue may not be compatible with the director's vision or taste—perhaps the instrumentation, the shape of the melody in relation to the dialogue, or the emotional impact is not quite right; or perhaps the director feels the tempo or shape of the music isn't providing the right pacing. [. . .]

In a situation like this, the music editor can help prevent a whole piece of music being thrown out by suggesting a solution. Some simple techniques—editing, or speeding up or slowing down the piece—might resolve the issue. As a further example, if a director feels that the tone of a score cue demo is too "positive," too "optimistic," this might indicate that the piece sounds too "major." The music editor might suggest to the composer a simple shift of the chord structure from major to minor, or perhaps adding a dissonant-sounding pad or instruments to create a "darker," more conflicted feel.

The music editor's goal here is to help the composition of the score to proceed quickly and in a positive creative direction. Sitting between the director and composer, they can act as a bridge between film language and musical language. The complexities of music can be difficult to communicate—this is one of the reasons why it is important for a music editor to study compositional techniques for film scoring.[7]

Insider Info

How Do You Interact with the Director?
Because time in post is so short for episodic television, I usually limit my discussions with directors to their post schedule. We discuss the editing timeline: when the editor's assembly will be ready for the director to work on, how long they have with the episode, and when the director's cut needs to be scheduled for the producers to screen.

What Would You Like Directors to Know About Postproduction?
I think directors might be interested in what happens to the show once they deliver their cut. Briefly, each episode goes through the editing process with the showrunner and writer/producer. It is sent to the studio and network for their notes then locked and onlined.

It is spotted for music, dialogue, and sound effects. It goes through color correction, visual effects, titling, and dirt fixes. At the same time, we are doing our sound effects and dialogue editing as well as ADR. We then spend two days on the dub stage mixing the episode, then playback for producers and do final fixes. We layback the mix to final picture, go through another QC [quality control check], caption it, and make our dubs, then deliver it to the network and elsewhere.

What is Your Advice for New Directors?
We can jump back and forth between drama, mystery, and comedy all within a single scene, and that can be a minefield for a new director. The director needs to get inside the writer's head and understand his intentions as much as possible.

I think it is important for a new director to understand that in television, it is usually the writer's vision that has to be considered first and foremost. Although one might want to shoot an episode of television that is visually engaging and uniquely imaginative, it is essential to keep in mind not only the words but also the intentions of the writers as they are channeled through the characters.

I would suggest that if you want to direct episodic television, always know who is calling the shots. It is usually the writer/producer/showrunner with whom you need to be in collaboration.

Stephanie Hagen
Producer, Desperate Housewives

Vocabulary

ADR	dub	soundstage
binge watch	dubbed	start and stop
blowing it up	EDL	sting
clean	final air master	sweeten
closed-captioning	foley	syndication
color corrected	hits	titles
colorist	layback	underscore
cross platforming	looped	VAM
CTM	mix	walla group
	O track	wild sounds

NOTES

1 Ressner, Jeffrey, "The Traditionalist," DGA Quarterly: Spring 2012, pp. 26–33, 76.
2 Suzanne Welke. Via email, November 18, 2010.
3 Ibid.
4 Richard Campbell, Christopher R. Martin, and Bettina Fabos, "Sounds and Images," *Media and Culture: An Introduction to Mass Communication*. Boston: Bedford/St. Martin's, 2000, p. 113.
5 Welke. Ibid.
6 Steven Saltzman, *Music Editing For Film and Television*. New York: Focal Press, 2015.
7 "Syndication," retrieved from https://en.wikipedia.org/wiki/Broadcast_syndication, last modified July 3, 2015.

Post

During post, the director gets a final chance to reinterpret the script by creating the director's cut. During the postproduction period, you work closely with the editor to refine his assembly, and then the rest of the tasks are taken over by the postproduction supervisor, who sees that the final version of the episode is readied for delivery so that it can be shown or broadcast.

While you have been shooting, the editor has been working on his assembly. It is helpful that you know the editor's vocabulary and process in order to best use your time together. It is important to be open to what the editor has done. Together, you will cut for story, cut for time, and then add temp music and sound effects. This cut will be viewed by the executive producer, who may do another pass at editing it down closer to time, often removing entire scenes or chunks of scenes to shorten the episode. The network will approve a final cut before the episode goes through the final stages of post.

Further postproduction processes include offline and online editing. Video processes such as creating a VAM and color correcting and audio processes such as ADR (where you may want to supervise), foley, adding the music cues, and doing the mix are done separately and then assembled back together in what is called the layback.

Finally, the postproduction supervisor sees to the closed captioning, dubbing, and delivery. If you are shooting anything other than episodic

TV, you will stay with your project to completion. If you're an episodic director, you will probably depart the show after delivery of your cut. If you are director breaking into TV, the Internet might be a great place to start your work.

Being a Director

Overview

What does it mean to be a director? To be a director, you need a passion for storytelling and an ability to be a leader. You need to have a rich aesthetic sense so that you can judge what is good from what is bad. It means having good taste.

To be a director, you need to able to handle the rigorous demands of the job both mentally and physically.

Finally, and most fundamentally, you need someone to give you a job: to hire you to direct!

Chapter 16

Being a Director

Bethany tells this story about the first Hollywood director with whom she worked: "His name was Jackie Cooper. He had been a child movie star in the 1930s and a TV star in the 1960s, and by the time I met him, in 1978, he was a grizzled cowboy, wearing boots, rodeo-type silver belt buckle through the loops of his jeans, smoking a Cuban stogie. He was loud and brash and totally sure of himself. He was the director of the first show I worked on, called *The White Shadow*, which was about a white basketball coach teaching at an inner-city high school. Jackie was a fantastic director, especially for the young men who were the actors on the show; he gave them a lot of tough love, using cuss words and confrontation to get what he needed from them. He made a huge impression on me. I thought every director was or should be like Jackie. So that was kind of a problem for me when I started directing. A soft-spoken 28-year-old woman is no Jackie Cooper."

Directors come in all shapes and sizes, all ethnicities, all educational backgrounds, and both genders. There is nothing to physically or mentally link this group of people. In television and features, the theatrical world and the commercial, in reality shows and low-budget indies, there is an infinite variety of people who choose to direct. What links them are two qualities: a passion for storytelling and an ability to be a leader. But what is that? What is involved in "a passion for storytelling?" And what does it take "to be a leader?"

NEEDING TO TELL A STORY

Wanting to be a storyteller is something you're born with—it is not something that can be taught. It is the innate need to make sense of the world and to entertain oneself and an audience by framing real-life experiences and eternal questions (such as "why are we here?") in a fictional way that illustrates what it is to be human. It's one of those things that is part of your DNA. Either you like to read or you don't. You prefer savory to sweet. You're more right-brained or left-brained. You want to be swept away in a story or you'd rather face the world in a more prosaic fashion. You are a storyteller or you're not.

> Wanting to be a storyteller is something you're born with—it is not something that can be taught. It is the innate need to make sense of the world and to entertain oneself and an audience by framing real-life experiences and eternal questions (such as "why are we here?") in a fictional way that illustrates what it is to be human.

If you are, then there are things you can learn that will help you do a better job of it. We've been talking about those things through this entire book, but the basic recap is this:

Job Requirements for Being a Storyteller

- Interpret the script.
- Shape the actors' performance.
- Choose every element within the frame.
- Use the medium (film/tape/digital) well in production and post-production.

A DIRECTOR'S INNER SENSE

All of those things are learnable, up to a point. But there must be a pre-existing condition that is a psychological factor, an inner sense that again is inherent in your makeup. That innate sense tells you which shot is better, which color is better, and which communication method will work best with each actor. It is basically a sense of good taste that is instinctive rather than logical.

But that inner sense doesn't arrive full-blown in your psyche the day you decide to pick up a camera. It needs to be tested and honed, challenged and refined, with every decision you make. Can you enhance that inner sense? We think you can do so by exposing yourself to everything. Directors are lifelong learners. The world is your university. Politics, popular culture, the arts, the sciences, cuisine, psychology, sports. And don't just stay in your comfort zone: venture out! No knowledge will be wasted. You can start at the public library. Or online. Read every day.

Observe life around you.

You should also watch TV shows and movies. Contrast and compare. Know what you like and why you like

There must be a preexisting condition that is a psychological factor, an inner sense. That innate sense tells you which shot is better, which color is better, and which communication method will work best with each actor. It is basically a sense of good taste that is instinctive rather than logical.

it. In the same way, determine what you don't like and why. Study each episode or film by turning the sound off and just watching the screen; we are, after all, a visual medium. Discover whether you can follow the story without hearing the dialogue. In a well-made piece, you should be able to get the gist of it without hearing a word.

Tell a Story

Choose any movie you've seen recently. Describe it in the following ways:

- Figure out the one-liner (for example, "Boy meets girl, boy loses girl, boy gets girl back").
- Describe the movie in more detail. What is the setup, the conflict, the climax, and the ending?
- Describe the main characters, including three physical characteristics.
- Describe three "moments" or sequences in which the director employed camerawork that helped tell the story well.
- If you were making a poster for this movie, what would be the iconic image from the film?

It is highly unlikely that your first film or TV episode will be brilliant. It may have flashes of brilliance, but there's so much that can be learned only on the job. It stands to reason that with more experience, you will become a better director. With more life experience, you will as well. Mary Lou, who studied to be an actor at Penn State, took one required directing class. She admits frankly that she wasn't very good. Although she had a lot of leadership skills, she simply didn't have a lot of life experience. She had a limited point of view. What she did have was an insatiable desire to grow and learn everyday.

Let's say you are a born storyteller and you have studied how to be a good one. And you've shot some film, tape, or digital media and cut it together. You've practiced your craft. That's what you've done on your own—perhaps even with people who claim to be actors. But now you want to really direct. You want to lead a cast and crew toward achieving your creative vision.

You want to interact with studio executives and financiers. You want to navigate the politics necessary to ensure that your product—your film, your episode—is seen by many people, hopefully millions of them. How do you do that?

Try Something New

 This is a long-term exercise. Every week, give yourself the gift of opening your horizons and experiencing something new. This new thing should be experiential, rather than just reading about something. Put yourself in a position to see, hear, taste, smell, or touch something that was previously unknown to you. Do something you haven't done before. Go somewhere new. Try something outside your comfort zone. Get a different viewpoint, look at other cultures, and expand your previous boundaries. Keep a journal about what you've learned.

BEING A LEADER

You become a leader. It's a little different than when you were in first grade, and your teacher picked you to be the leader in the lunch line. It's a very sophisticated concept that has to do with, well, something that a president of the United States said: "To grasp and hold a vision, that is the very essence of successful leadership—not only on the movie set where I learned it, but everywhere." That was Ronald Reagan speaking. What we're saying here is that the "grasping" of the vision is an innate quality you either have or you don't. The "holding" of the vision is the leadership part. How do you hold on to your vision?

LEADERSHIP QUALITIES OF A DIRECTOR

Determination—Often, you win just by not giving up. You will have many people against you, just because they're not with you. They have other opinions. They think something else might work better. They don't understand what's in your head.

Communication—If you are able to clearly describe your vision, you can get everybody on board. First, you have to clarify your own thoughts, which is why it's so helpful to block and shot list, as doing those things makes you organize everything into individual pieces, or shots. After you've done the work and know exactly how you want each scene to look and feel, you can describe it to others.

Enthusiasm—When you describe your vision, it is your enthusiasm that will carry the day. You are essentially saying, "C'mon, people, come along with me! We're going to make something wonderful and magical and I know you really want to be a part of it!"

Gentle command—Once everyone is committed to your vision, keep them following you by projecting an aura of decisiveness and kindness—a sense that you know where you're going and everyone is going to enjoy the ride. In that way, you will earn your cast and crew's loyalty and desire to work hard to help you follow your vision.

When you commit to directing, you commit to taking on a leadership role. But there are other places and ways in your everyday life to use these skills in preparation for stepping into directing. Any small group needs a leader, whether it's a committee or a classroom. You need not wait until you have a script in hand to begin employing these four leadership tips. Especially if these extroverted qualities do not come naturally to you, it is extremely helpful to employ them as often as possible so they begin to become an organic way of being—a part of who you are.

Mary Lou honed her abilities running her household when her mother reentered the workplace when Mary Lou was 12. Mary Lou, the fourth of five children, cooked, cleaned, and did the laundry for her family of eight people. She delegated work so that she could have a normal teen life. She first practiced her leadership qualities bossing her siblings around! Once in college, she loved not only being on stage, but stage-managing plays she wasn't in. She also did administrative work for the dance company she performed with. It's important to see directing as an outgrowth of your previous life experiences and predilections.

THE BUSINESS OF THE BUSINESS

Directors need a team of support personnel for the many demanding aspects of being a director. There will naturally be the personal ones, like family. But there are also professional support staff, two of whom are required if you are directing anything for distribution: an agent, and the Directors Guild of America (DGA). According to its website:

The Directors Guild of America is a labor organization that represents the creative and economic rights of directors and members of the directorial team working in film, television, commercials, documentaries, news, sports and new media. Founded in 1936

when a small group of the best-known directors of the time joined together to protect
the economic and creative rights of directors in motion pictures, the DGA is the world's
preeminent organization representing directors and members of the directorial team,
including Directors, Assistant Directors, Unit Production Managers, Associate
Directors, Stage Managers and Production Associates—16,000 strong worldwide.

dga.org[1]

The DGA faces negotiations every four years with the AMPTP (Alliance of Motion Picture and Television Producers—the business side of the "business") and fights for our creative rights, our work conditions, our salaries, and our health and welfare contributions. And it does incredibly well, because each member—if they qualify by the amount of money they earn—is entitled to extremely good benefits.

One of those benefits is the minimum salary cap. Currently, a director of a one-hour, single-camera network show earns $41,457 for a 15-day contract, which excludes postproduction time, and the director of a half-hour, single-camera primetime network show makes $24,413 (a seven-day contract). A director of a one-hour basic cable show earns $26,607. The rate for a two-hour basic cable movie is $69,096. If you direct features, the rate is based on the budget and is negotiable. Pilot directors may negotiate their salary and royalty (payments that are made as long as the series runs, in recognition of the creative input to the long-term interests of the show).

Though the director salaries are quite respectable, they can disappear quickly when you have a large support team. Every director who works for the networks—whether broadcast or cable—must have an agent as legal protection on both sides. The networks will not do business with an individual who is unrepresented. There are numerous agencies that represent acting talent and literary (writing and directing) talent in New York and Los Angeles. The agent is the go-between who imparts information and mediates between the hiring party (buyers) and the client and is licensed to do business by the state in which they operate. Your agent will seek out work for you, set up meetings, be your biggest fan and cheerleader, negotiate deals, plan an overall career strategy and execute it to the best of her ability, and be the bearer of bad tidings (that you didn't get the job, or you didn't perform well on a job you did get) if necessary. The agent is the buffer in good times and bad. For doing all that, your agent will take a ten percent commission from the money you make. You may also have a manager who is part of your support team. A manager is not licensed by the state and may expand his role beyond advice and intercession with media buyers to become a producer on your projects. Managers generally commission 10–15 percent.

You may also have an attorney to negotiate contracts. Additionally, you may have a business manager since most successful directors are paid through their personal service corporation, which requires specialized tax knowledge. Therefore, you could be paying commissions totaling 20–40 percent of your salary, as well as paying DGA dues. The obligations can be stressful, especially when the work is slow. The bad times happen because it's a subjective and cyclical business. Mary Lou and Bethany, being female directors, have occasionally experienced bad times, in part because they are in a distinct minority. The Directors Guild of America reported that women held just 16 percent of the directing jobs on primetime programs across broadcast, basic cable, premium cable, and high-budget original content series made for the Internet in the 2014–2015 season. Why are there so few women directors? (There is also a dearth of minority directors, as the DGA study reported that minority males directed just 18 percent of the available episodes.) There is only our experience to go by because there are no studies or statistics to report on the amorphous underlying cause. Because directors are leaders and because the time and budget constraints of television are so pressurized, there seems to be an inherent ingrained attitude from the production companies and the networks that they are best served in this job category by white men. (The recent appellation for this phenomenon is "unconscious bias.") But Bethany's experience over 30 years of directing is that once on set, neither the cast nor crew care about her gender—just her abilities. Will she shoot the day's work efficiently and well, allowing all to return home to their families in less than 13 hours? Cast and crew only care about "good." They don't care about gender.

There is much you can do to prepare by studying, learning, and practicing on a theoretical level. But ultimately, it is a job that you learn by doing, by making innumerable mistakes, and by being grateful for each failure that teaches you how to direct.

There's a t-shirt sold in Hollywood that references the inside joke of the business: On the front it says, "I am an actor." On the back it says, "But what I really want to do is direct." Everyone wants to direct—because you're the boss, you make a lot of money, your name is on the screen. But directing is not really about the external trappings of the job. It is about immersing yourself in this all-encompassing passionate need to tell a story in a visual way. It is a multi-leveled job that utilizes numerous skill sets. If you are a born storyteller, you have to learn to work with script, actors, camera, and editing. And then you need to hone your ability to lead others in service to the story, potentially working with hundreds of people, navigating their personalities, and sculpting their contributions to fit your vision. There is much you can do to prepare by studying, learning, and practicing on a theoretical level. But ultimately, it is a job that you learn by doing, by making innumerable mistakes, and by being grateful for each failure that teaches you how to direct.

Go into this knowing that it takes a while and that you'll have to practice these multiple skills over and over again to become proficient. It's an exciting journey to take, full of discovery, growth, and *fun*!

NOTE

1   DGA website, www.dga.org

Chapter 17

The Demands of the Job

When you are the director of a project, people are going to judge you. The buyers ask the producers, "Is the director staying on time and on budget?" By that, they mean, are you someone who knows the craft and will return their investment? The producers ask the DP, "How's the director doing?" By that, they mean, do you know how to make the day? The makeup artist asks the actor, "How is he?" By that, the makeup artist means, do you know about character and performance and how to get it? The dolly grip asks the camera operator, "What d'ya think?" By that, the dolly grip means, do you know how to use the camera well? The writer asks the script supervisor, "Is she sticking to the script?" By that, the writer means, are you a good storyteller? And all of those questions are asked within the first hour of your appearance on set. Everyone is waiting to judge because everyone has a lot riding on your competence, and everyone wants to know if you're any good. Everyone wants to get home to their families at night (or some other aspect of their personal lives), but they want to do work they can be proud of, too. So they're going to judge you: Are you fast? Are you on budget? Are you good?

You can be all three of these things; you don't have to "pick two of the above," as the industry saying goes. When you are prepared, when you know your craft, and when you are passionate about storytelling and have that inner sense of good taste we talked about in the previous chapter, you can be all three. But you have to have done your homework, and you have to be a leader. And you have to understand storytelling. It requires hard work, intuition, and creativity. Because it's such a complex job, not many

Are you fast? Are you on budget? Are you good? You can be all three of these things; you don't have to "pick two of the above," as the industry saying goes. Because it's such a complex job, not many people are really, really good at it.

people are really, really good at it. So everyone judges. They want to know whether you can be trusted to make this project happen.

That kind of intense scrutiny can be stressful, especially when it happens every day. You're only as good as your last dailies. Every day, the questions are asked. Every day, you must pass the tests and get good marks from every single person associated with the production, down to the production assistants, who carry the gossip on their rounds from set to office to postproduction to studio or network suits. By stepping up to the job, you are stepping up to never-ending judgment.

Sounds brutal, doesn't it? But it doesn't have to be.

SUGGESTIONS FOR DEALING WITH STRESS

Your level of stress depends on your attitude. Mary Lou and Bethany are both known for their positive attitudes, and over their 50 years' combined experience in dealing with this kind of fishbowl existence, they have come up with the following ways of dealing with stress.

- **Focus on what you have to give, not what you want to get.** What we all want to *get* is approval, that figurative pat on the back that says, "You did a good job." But putting your attention on something you can't control (someone else's opinion) is a sure way to undermine your confidence. The thing that you can control is what you have to *give*: creative vision, and the ability to execute your vision by leading cast and crew in a decisive and enthusiastic manner. Keeping your focus on what you have to give pushes you to keep your eyes on the road, do your job to the best of your ability, and not get distracted by outside forces.
- **Do the work in prep.** Although it may seem tedious next to the excitement of shooting, being consistent about prep work provides the foundation for your success as a director. When you know how you plan to shoot something, you are able to be confident when you step onto the set. You know what the story is, you know who the characters are, and you know how you've blocked it. You can be decisive and clear.
- **Enlist the support of your team.** The crew is your team on set, pulling together to create one project. If any one element of that team falls out, everyone is affected. So everyone is of equal importance. Ask the key grip how to achieve the crane shot you want in the best way; in doing

so, you reap the benefit of the key grip's experience plus make him feel needed and appreciated. Ask the script supervisor if there's any shot you've missed. Ask the costume designer for her opinion on colors and style. Make everyone want to give their best effort to help you succeed.

- **Be in good health.** Eat well, sleep well. Stay off of anything that fogs your mind or clogs your system. Exercise, even if it's only a short brisk walk after a meal or a stretch while you're waiting for the crew to finish lighting. Wear sturdy shoes and sunscreen.
- **Believe in yourself.** This one is easier said than done, of course. The longer you direct, the more confident you'll be, given the breadth of your experience. But if you're just starting out, you really have to take a leap of faith. How do you do that? We suggest the following:
  - *Assess your passion.* Is it absolutely necessary that you direct? If you can honestly say yes, you're probably in the right place.
  - *Face your fear and do it anyway.* (Remember this old Nike slogan?) You're never, ever, going to start directing something and not be afraid. You just have to know that and do it anyway.
  - *Do your best.* That's all you can do. You cannot control outcome, just as (from a Zen point of view) you cannot really control anything at all. Just be prepared, and do your best.
  - *Break it down into its smallest pieces.* When you look at the enormity of the whole project, it's intimidating. Don't look at that. Look at the first step. On the first day of shooting, that will be the first rehearsal of the first scene. You can do that. Now what's the next step?
  - *Surrender.* You cannot carry tension, or fear, or your own self-judgment into a creative enterprise and have it work out for the best. Let it go. Know that whatever happens, you're going to be fine. And if you can't do that, act "as if" until it becomes second nature to you.
  - *Embrace the joy.* Yes, it's scary. Yes, it's intimidating. But it's also pure joy, pure adrenaline rush. Remember that you got into this because you love telling a story with a camera. Have fun!

Bethany and Mary Lou both have stories that illustrate this excitement/fear dynamic.

Bethany was sick to her stomach every single morning of her first job directing (*St. Elsewhere*, 1985) but describes the experience still as "the best seven consecutive days of my life." When Mary Lou was hired to direct her first single-camera film hour (after 20 years of directing multiple-camera shows), she was told by two executive producers—both of whom were experienced directors—to expect a night of sleeplessness prior to the first day of shooting, as that's what they themselves were accustomed to. Despite being exhilarated and exhausted, we all reach the end of the first day of shooting, or the eighth (if you're shooting a network drama), or the 88th (if you're doing a big-budget miniseries). We get through it, dealing with stress all the way. It won't be the sweat-inducing fear or sleepless night that you have before you begin shooting; it will be the ongoing kind that requires stamina, the kind that wears you down if you're not prepared for it.

Let's say you're on the third day of shooting. The initial rush has worn off, and you're trying to keep your energy, creativity, and enthusiasm up. After all, you're the leader on set. Bumps in the road are showing up everywhere: the actor doesn't like the script, the producer doesn't like your blocking, the DP complains that the cloudy day is messing with his lighting, and so on.

Everyone turns to you for solutions. Ideally, you are able to solve problems in an inspired way that will not only make the best film, but also soothe wounded egos and encourage everyone—both cast and crew—to keep their own energy and commitment levels up.

Everyone turns to you for solutions. Ideally, you are able to solve problems in an inspired way that will not only make the best film, but also soothe wounded egos and encourage everyone—both cast and crew—to keep their own energy and commitment levels up.

PROBLEM SOLVING

It is this problem-solving ability that is at the heart of the director's job. If you are not a good problem solver, your stress level will skyrocket simply because in each day of shooting, the director is asked to solve a myriad of problems. All roads lead to you. You've already experienced this in prep, when questions like the following were asked: If the location manager can't get a permit, should he attempt to get one for your second-choice location? If the prop master can't find the hero baseball bat in silver and orange, should he have the art department make one, or would you be willing to go with the one that's silver and red? If the casting director can't make a deal with the actor you want, should more money be found in the budget, or should he arrange another session for you to read more actors? When you're shooting, the questions are more immediate: Should you print

Because the job of a director is inherently one of problem solving, it stands to reason that the way you cope with this dimension of the job is a bellwether of your overall performance. If problem solving does not come naturally to you, there are skills you can learn.

takes 3 and 4 and move on? Or do you think you can get a better performance from the actor? Should a particular shot be Steadicam or dolly? It's
a half-hour before lunch, and you have two shots left; after lunch, you're
scheduled to shoot three more scenes. Can you get the work done in half
an hour?

There are numerous procedures out there for problem solving, but Mary
Lou has one she particularly likes. She says, "It informs who I am and how
I operate in the world." Because the job of a director is inherently one of
problem solving, it stands to reason that the way you cope with this dimension
of the job is a bellwether of your overall performance. If problem solving
does not come naturally to you, there are skills you can learn. The following
steps should help.

Six Steps to Problem Solving

1. Identify the problem.
2. Brainstorm solutions.
3. Choose a solution.
4. Act.
5. Evaluate results.
6. Be satisfied with the result or go back to step 3.

These steps provide you with a thought process. They are concrete and
productive to help you answer whatever question is being asked of you. You
might run through the first three steps in just seconds, depending on the
situation. Or you may take longer to consider, especially if the problem is
slow to develop, like this common one: You're on an exterior location and
one look at the sky tells you it's probably going to rain. The UPM and 1st
AD ask you what you want to do. Do you want to pull the plug, quit
shooting, and move the company indoors or to another location? Do you
want to keep shooting and hope for the best? If it starts raining, can you
make it work for the scene, or is it a complete mismatch, and therefore a
disaster? The choice, as with everything on the set, is the director's, until
the lightning bolts start zig-zagging across the sky, and then it's out of your
hands, because it's too dangerous around the power source, the generator.
Whether the question is what to do in case it rains, or what to do when your
lead actress refuses to deviate from her personal hairstyle even though it's
a period movie (this happened to Bethany on a Danielle Steel movie
adaptation; she solved it by putting the actress in a hat), the problem-solving
steps provide a structure in which to think through the challenge.

A director has to have a certain amount of tunnel vision in order to get his goal accomplished. Phil Alden Robinson, who wrote and directed *Field of Dreams*, said, "The actor may not want to do it your way, or the cameraman may say, 'We can't get that shot, the sun will go behind a cloud.' The sound-man will say, 'I can't use this take because the airport is so close.' The art department may say, 'We don't have enough money to do this.' . . . Part of the job of directing is being able to think fast on your feet, improvise, and come up with some other idea that does what you wanted to do in the first place."[1]

In the same article, Jason Reitman (director of *Up in the Air*, *Juno*, and *Thank You for Smoking*) elaborates why this decision-making ability is important:

A director makes a thousand binary decisions a day. Now, let's say I get one of those questions wrong. It wouldn't be a big deal. Even if I got 5 percent wrong, it'll probably fly. But let's say I got half of it wrong. What if this was a really intimate scene and it didn't feel intimate because the location seemed too modern? Or the background actors brought too much attention upon themselves? All of a sudden, enough questions come up that, for whatever reason, you've stopped believing in the reality of this movie . . . and all of a sudden, the movie is poorly directed.[2]

Problem Solving

As a group, talk about examples of "problems." For example, you have an appointment five miles away, scheduled for ten minutes from now, and when you get out the door, you realize your car has a flat tire and/or the bus is broken down a block away. Each scenario should consist of a goal and an obstacle. Another example might be you're on the international space station with two other astronauts, your oxygen system will fail in five hours, but it will take six hours for the rescue craft to reach you. Each person writes three problem scenarios on separate slips of paper and puts them in a "hat." Each person pulls a slip of paper from the hat and has a minute to think of a solution. Take turns describing your scenario and your solution. Someone else in the group challenges the solution maker with an alternate solution. The group votes to decide which is better. Be creative. Have fun. Whether your solution is practical or far-fetched, the question is: would it work?

You want your show to be well directed, and that means making good decisions quickly. If making quick decisions flusters you, directing will be difficult. It's important to remain the calm leader, because as Rudyard Kipling said, "If you can keep your wits about you while all others are losing theirs . . . the world will be yours"[3] (and maybe the Oscar or Emmy, too!). And although it can be a very intuitive skill, there are some additional tools that can assist you in being a better problem-solving, decision-making director. Using these tools will help you keep your stress level down, which is always beneficial to the creative process!

TOOLS FOR SUCCESS

- **Never lose your temper.** At least, not in front of anyone. When you scream and shout, it means you have given in to your frustration and lost control of the situation. That is not something your followers need to see. If you're in danger of blowing your stack, take five minutes, walk away from the situation, and breathe. Repeat silently to yourself: It's all good. It's all good. It's all good. Breathe. A solution will occur to you when you are calmer. Then you can return to the set and solve the problem.
- **Don't rush to judgment.** A good decision is an informed decision. Ask questions. There are two sides to every story. Do not respond to an "emergency" until you have all the facts. Then you can assess what needs to be done.
- **Listen before you talk.** Just as there is subtext in a script—the meaning under the words—so there is often subtext in interpersonal communications. Try to discern what is *really* being said. That way, you respond to the *real* problem.
- **Get your ego out of the way.** Inherent in the role of leader is the danger of succumbing to the allure of being the big shot. When you think you're more important than everyone else, you lose the perspective that we are all human and imperfect. Yes, people come to you to solve problems. That does not mean you need to impress them, pontificate on your views, or denigrate them for having the problem in the first place. Nor do you need to think of yourself as hot stuff. As the expression goes, you put your pants on one leg at a time, just like everyone else.
- **Be kind.** You get more flies with honey than vinegar. Your grandmother may have said that, and it's true. People respond much better to kindness than cruelty. You need people to do things for you, unless you're going to hang lights or push a dolly yourself. So speak softly and smile. If you can't do it out of the goodness of your heart, do it because it's a practical approach.

> *People respond much better to kindness than cruelty. You need people to do things for you, unless you're going to hang lights or push a dolly yourself. So speak softly and smile. If you can't do it out of the goodness of your heart, do it because it's a practical approach.*

- **Trust your instincts.** Your instinct is your "gut feeling." It is not a rational, thought-out decision. It is a sure knowingness of what is right and what is not. Yes, the construct of your vision is in your thoughts, but adherence to it comes from the center of your being.

Do not second-guess your decisions by wondering if someone else (the producer, the network, the studio) will approve. As soon as you start trying to think "like them," you will lose your own internal rudder that tells you what is right and what is good, because it is impossible to be in someone else's mind. Cling to your own perspective, your own vision.

> *As soon as you start trying to think "like them," you will lose your own internal rudder that tells you what is right and what is good, because it is impossible to be in someone else's mind. Cling to your own perspective, your own vision.*

Did you ever hear the expression, "Too many cooks in the kitchen spoil the broth"? Just as multiple cooks might say, "You need more of this, you need less of this," you might imagine that kind of reaction to your film. If you get more than one voice in your head, the voice of doubt, the voice of insecurity, saying "They might not like it, I better do something different/ safer/acceptable," you are doomed. That's a big word, but it's true. You were hired for your vision—for being the one and only voice that says, "This is how I interpret the script. This is how this set should look. This is how these characters should act. This is how the story will be told."

COMPROMISING WISELY

What if the voices are not inside your head, but outside? What if you literally have others (producer/network/studio) telling you, "More of this, less of that"? Do you listen? Do you accede to their wishes? Do you deviate from your vision? They are, after all, the ones writing out the paychecks, and just as they hired you, they can fire you. So what do you do?

This is the crux of the matter behind the scenes when you read that a director is no longer on a movie or an episodic director is not asked back because of "creative differences." When the hiring faction agrees with a director's vision, everything usually goes well and it's a happy set (which, more often than not, leads to a successful product: good energy begets good energy). But if there is disagreement, you have three ways to go: do what they want, refuse to do what they want, or try to maintain your vision while addressing their notes. The latter requires diplomacy, which is a skill that not all passionate directors of vision have, and it may lead to a muddled mess. Or it may work out. The point is that as with everything else in the director's job, it's all subjective. The suits, or people holding the purse strings, are not necessarily wrong. They may have some good points. And just maybe your vision is sometimes imperfect, despite the fact that you've thought it through carefully. Sometimes an outside perspective is needed. If you find yourself in this kind of quagmire, you will handle it in the way that suits your personality and the situation. Bethany experienced this situation recently, when an executive producer told her that her blocking of one scene was flat and her shot selection was ill-conceived. Her choice was either to bristle at the criticism and reject it, or ask herself if there was truth in his statement. After her ego recovered, she acknowledged to herself that although the scene was good, perhaps it hadn't been her finest hour. And she resolved to do better. This realization doesn't make her weak; it makes her continue to learn, evolve, and work.

You have to make all kinds of choices in the job, and some of them are for your own survival. If you want to work as an episodic director, that means maintaining a solid reputation, which would be sullied if you were fired or word spread through the community that you were "difficult." The way you handle creative differences is a moral judgment call that only you can make. If you are directing a film, and it's more important to you to be right than to be finished, then you can stand on your principles and lose your financing. Or if it's more important to get your film out into the marketplace, you may find that you are willing to make compromises.

"Compromise" is often perceived to be a dirty word in the entertainment business—the same as "giving up" or "selling out." You will find that compromise is often a necessary thing, up to a line in the sand at which you say, "I won't go beyond this point." You know what your bottom line is: the place where you will stand on your principles, no matter what the cost. Until then, however, many decisions are, by their very nature, compromises. In his *Wake Me When It's Funny: How to Break Into Show Business and Stay* (Newmarket Press), director Garry Marshall says, "One of the best characteristics a director can have is the ability to compromise wisely."[4] Very cleverly, he explains how he lets the "studio win lots of little battles" so that he can "win the war." He also advises, "The trick is not to compromise when you're exhausted or running behind schedule. Compromise when you are clear-headed and full of ideas."

Because it's a group endeavor to make a movie or a TV show, there are multiple opinions, and it is a process of soliciting, acknowledging, then accepting/rejecting the input from many sources to get to the finish line. But your job is to lead all those people with their opinions toward the promised land of a project that fulfills *your* vision. Try to get along, to give respect, to honor a different point of view while being aware that you're trying to

You know what your bottom line is: the place where you will stand on your principles, no matter what the cost. Until then, however, many decisions are, by their very nature, compromises.

keep everyone on the same path. It's an overused expression, but the project can be a "win-win" for everyone if you have that attitude.

The major element that separates a television director from a feature director is this ability to navigate the culture and to interact successfully with multiple cast, crews, producers, studios, and networks. A good freelance director will direct eight episodes a year, on probably at least four different productions. So in addition to being a good shooter, or knowing how to use the camera well, you have to be a good psychologist, acting coach, story editor, and diplomat. You can do all that by having your priorities in order. Be a well-rounded person first and a filmmaker second. You will have a DP and an entire crew behind you to support your knowledge of filmmaking. You have to bring everything else to the table. So learn. Travel. Study. Practice.

Understand what it means to be a leader and commit to doing it well. You can do it.

Insider Info

How Do You Interact with the Director?
Directing episodic television is one of the most quixotic jobs in the industry because it requires serving two opposing instincts. The first instinct is to be ARTISTIC; to film innovative images and discover emotionally unexpected (but honest) moments. The second instinct is to be PRACTICAL; to make the show live totally and completely in the world of the series, while staying on time and on budget. Shorter . . . the job is equal parts being TOTALLY DIFFERENT and COMPLETELY THE SAME. Because of all this, I try as hard as possible to be open and honest with directors . . . give them all the actor's quirks . . . inform them of how "we" make our show . . . imbue them with everything we've learned up to the point of their episode . . . and then I get the hell out of the way. Once an episode has started, I try to step back, answer questions and (if necessary) put out fires.

What Should Directors Know about the Job of the EP?
We Executive Producers are overwhelmed . . . always. Yes, we're invested in the prep of your episode, but at the same time we're editing an episode (or two), writing an episode (or two), working on an outline and a story document . . . all while trying to figure out how to cut $20,000 out of some budget. We're not purposely ignoring you, so much as trying to figure out when your problem rises to the level of NOW. Also, directors should also be acutely aware that Executive Producers are often caught at the crossroads of what the network wants, what the studio wants, and what the actors want . . . which never seem to completely line up. If we're saying

no to you, it's most likely our way of saving you from someone's (or multiple people's) wrath.

What Advice Would You Give to Directors Just Starting Out?
Your greatest commodity is TRUST. Can the actors trust you to hear their needs and protect their performance? Can the Executive Producer trust you to shoot efficiently, so the crew isn't exhausted and the budget blown? Also, remember that you're a link in the chain. YES, this is your episode and you should make it the best you possibly can, but still . . . there's another episode in front of you and one coming up. If you get lost in a scene . . . take 6 hours to shoot what should be done in 2 . . . consequences of that can reverberate for days or even weeks. So: Art, YES. Imagination, YES. But also COMPROMISE, because no single shot or scene or image should ever risk throwing a production into chaos.

Jeffrey Lieber
Executive Producer
NCIS New Orleans, Necessary Roughness

Insider Info

Relaxation Ritual
Recognizing your body's messages that send out a type of red flare, signaling there's tension within, is where this ritual begins.

A clenched jaw, a sharp tone of voice, toes curled up tightly in shoes, picking at a hangnail until it bleeds, biting fingernails or a lower lip, a bellyache, a headache, or inability to sleep are some of the physical symptoms that alert us that we're experiencing stress.

A relaxation ritual is something chosen while calm, while there's time to consider an action that can be taken once realizing that one's tension level is rising.

Mike, a film student, places his St. Christopher medallion around his neck every morning before going off to direct one of his projects. Once only worn to protect him when surfing, he uses it now as a source to remind him of the peace he feels when paddling out as the sun rises. As soon as he starts biting the inside of his cheeks when working with his production team, he holds his St. Christopher medallion, remembering the sensation of being in the ocean, which relaxes both his mind and body.

Martha packs a backpack of ritual objects before heading off to her first day of production. A box of her favorite tea, a small picture frame that holds a photo of her twins, and a Nintendo Wii game that will be made available for the entire cast and crew. When she starts to feel mentally overwhelmed, she sips a cup of her tea, gets some fresh air, thinks about the issues at hand, says the Serenity Prayer, finishes her tea, and faces the challenges at hand.

Mark uploads his favorite podcasts the night before a shoot, and when he can't get the shot that's in his head to match what's coming out on film, he heads for the bathroom, closes the door, and listens to his favorite sports program, giving himself a mental break and allowing room for a new perspective when he returns to the set.

Kerry emails her mentor when she's fallen behind schedule and is facing an anxiety attack. Simply writing out her difficulty uncensored and letting it go brings with it a type of comfort that she's not alone, and this in and of itself assists in rebuilding her confidence.

The key here is to select rituals that fit who you are. They are a gift to yourself and—when practiced—bring a calm that restores confidence and faith in your unique talent.

Robin Bernstein
Marriage and Family Therapist (MFT)

NOTES

1 Anne Hornaday, "A Director's Work is Never Done," *Los Angeles Times*, December 25, 2009, Sec. D, p. 2.

2 Ibid.

3 "Rudyard Kipling Quotes," Brainy Quotes, retrieved May 7, 2011 from www. brainyquote.com/quotes/authors/r/rudyardkip401624.html.

4 Gary Marshall, *Wake Me When It's Funny: How to Break into Show Business and Stay.* New York: Newmarket Press, 1995.

Chapter 18

Getting Started

Every director has a different story about getting a first job. That's because there is no stepladder to success—no approved way to follow. Everybody "gets in" in his own way. Even if you go to film school, there is no guarantee of a job when you graduate. You have to find your way in and work your way up. In this chapter, we are going to tell you our stories and also let our colleagues tell you theirs. We'll wrap it up with some advice on getting started.

Directing an episode of television is a big responsibility. The producer, who gives you a job, must know that you will deliver both artistically and fiscally. How can producers be certain if you've never delivered before? They can't; so every time a new director gets a shot, it is a leap of faith on the part of the producer. Your job is to earn the trust and respect of that producer (and studio and network who will also "approve you") so that he wants to take that leap.

> Everybody "gets in" in his own way. Even if you go to film school, there is no guarantee of a job when you graduate. You have to find your way in and work your way up.

BETHANY'S STORY

Bruce Paltrow took that first leap with me. He was the executive producer of a CBS show called *The White Shadow*, and I was his assistant. (I had gotten an interview for the job through a connection from my college.) When Paltrow co-created *St. Elsewhere* in 1981, he promoted me to associate producer, which meant that I supervised all of the postproduction. After a couple of years at that, I began to ask him (all right, to beg and plead) to direct. He kept saying, "You're not ready." I would answer back, "What do you mean, I'm not ready? I supervise picture editing, and so I know how to visually tell a story. I've taken an acting class for five years, so I know how to talk to actors. And I spend every minute I can on the set. What do you mean, I'm not ready?" What he meant was that I was young and stupid. It takes a strong leader—a person of gravitas—to command a set. And I wasn't ready. But in the fourth season of *St. Elsewhere*, when I was 28, Paltrow gave me the shot.

Paltrow was known for giving untried directors the opportunity of a lifetime. He was a generous mentor who liked to provide that hand up. But, as I found out, it often seems harder to get the second job. That's because the second person to hire you is hiring someone with extremely limited experience, while the first person gets the pride of saying, "I spotted her talent first. I went out on a limb for her, I got her started on her career." The second person to hire me was Jay Tarses, the showrunner of *The Slap Maxwell Show*, in 1987. I was a good fit there, and directed eight of the half-hour, single-camera episodes that season. I got a lot of practice, struggled, made mistakes, and learned tremendously—all displayed in front of a national audience. I have always said, "Whenever I win an award of any kind, I have to thank Bruce and Jay first."

We'd like to point out that Bethany mentions, "I was a good fit there." That's a crucial word. You can be a good director but not a good fit with either the style of the show or the personalities involved. If you have a bad experience on a show and you're not asked back, it probably does not mean you're a bad director, but that perhaps it was a bad fit.

MARY LOU'S STORY

"I began my show business career as an actress. My first job in network television was as an understudy for a teenager on a sitcom that lasted only ten episodes. I got this job because of my height (4'11") and stage experience. At the time, the position was a weekly Screen Actors Guild contract; that position no longer exists. The director of the show, Will Mackenzie, wanted the adult actors to be able to really rehearse when the younger actors were in school; because of child labor laws that require minors to be schooled on set, this was a good portion of the day. I acted with Martin Mull and Judith-Marie Bergan on a show called *Domestic Life* while teenager Megan Follows, known for her PBS role of *Anne of Green Gables* and now Queen Catherine on *Reign*, was learning algebra.

I transitioned from being an understudy to a coach for young actors and finally to being a director. I did this on the second series where I worked with young talent. It was called *Charles in Charge* and starred Scott Baio. I was already entrusted by the producer, Al Burton, as well as the director, Phil Ramuno, with delivering a good performance from teenager Nicole Eggert.

When I wasn't performing Eggert's part (when Eggert was in school) or coaching her (when Eggert was on stage), I was observing what the director was doing. I stayed with director Ramuno when he marked shots every week until I felt comfortable designing my own shots for the show and comparing them with Ramuno's. I made sure that the producer Al Burton knew I was doing my homework to learn about cameras. Simultaneously, I was directing and producing theatre. Every time I got a good review, I made sure that Burton was aware of the good press I was receiving as a stage director. I called it my "paper assault" because I literally photocopied each and every review I got, highlighted the good things said about me, and handed them out to anybody who might help me get a directing job. Four years into *Charles In Charge*, I was given the opportunity to direct by Al Burton. I was invited to direct another episode the next season.

Years later, after directing more than 100 episodes of sitcoms, I wanted to expand my directing opportunities. And my fairly recent entry into the single-camera world was mentored by many generous directors who allowed me to observe them, but especially by my coauthor and now dear friend, Bethany. The genesis of this book came from our realization that she talked about directing so clearly and so passionately that it was enough to fill a book—and how much fun it would be to write it together!"

We'd like to point out that Mary Lou had to be patient. She worked hard at *Charles in* Charge for four years until she was given the opportunity to direct. It often happens that way. Producers are wary of just handing over a precious episode of their cash cow to someone who is an unknown in terms of their ability to deliver. And who can blame them? Very often, you just have to stick it out, do your best in the job you are currently doing, remind them often you'd like to direct, and be patient.

HOW I GOT MY FIRST DIRECTING JOB

Here are some of our colleagues' first job stories.

Michelle MacLaren

Game of Thrones, Breaking Bad, The Walking Dead

I started in the TV/Film business as a Production Assistant, worked my way through locations, assistant directing, production managing, line producing, eventually developing and producing TV movies, one of which I co-wrote.

During this time I knew I ultimately wanted to direct so for years I took directing classes on the side, at night, on weekends, through the DGA and privately. I made shorts with friends, I studied acting for three years so I could better understand what performers go through and hopefully learn some communication skills for directing, and I watched every director I worked with. I joined *The X-Files* in season 7 as a Co-Executive Producer and worked with inspiring directors such as Kim Manners. At the end of season 8 I asked the producers if I could direct in the coming season and they said yes. I was absolutely terrified but beyond excited. During our summer hiatus, I went to a film school in Rockport Maine and took a week intensive class taught by Alan Myerson. I was very fortunate that the first episode I directed was written by the brilliant Vince Gilligan. My first day of directing I had that AH-HAH moment—I am doing something I love.

Pamela Fryman

How I Met Your Mother, Two and a Half Men, Just Shoot Me, Frasier

I started out as a production assistant in game shows—and didn't realize at the time that that experience would be critical to my getting my first directing job. A writer I met on a game show told me that he thought I'd make a good comedy director—I promise that what he saw in me I did not see in myself. Cut to years later, when this writer was running a sitcom at Warner Brothers called *Café Americain* and put my name on the schedule. At the time I was directing daytime dramas (soap operas), having worked my way up—but knew nothing about directing comedies—on film, with dolly cameras, etc. I was wildly intimidated. I was lucky enough to observe Jimmy Burrows for a week—and stepped up and directed my first sitcom. I should mention that hours before I was scheduled to camera block, the Northridge earthquake happened. My shooting week was pushed a couple of weeks. As if that wasn't enough, when we finally did shoot, in between our dress rehearsal and filming, the show was cancelled. It's incredible that I didn't switch careers.

Zetna Fuentes

Pretty Little Liars, Grey's Anatomy, Jane the Virgin

I got my first directing job in episodic television on *Pretty Little Liars* for ABC Family. I was in the Disney/ABC Directing Program and I marathoned the first season of PLL and I was hooked—it was really well done and in my wheelhouse so I asked if there was anyway I could shadow. ABC Family wasn't part of the program at the time but the Program set up a meeting with the executive who covered the show. She was incredibly supportive and got me a meeting with Lisa Cochran-Neilan, who produces PLL. Lisa championed me to the showrunners, Marlene King and Oliver Goldstick, and set me up to shadow the talented Chris Grismer and to then shadow a second episode, with the incomparable Lesli Linka Glatter. Amazingly, Marlene told me she wanted to give me an episode and called her agent on my behalf to get me representation. From that point on, it was everyone going to bat for me to convince Alloy, the studio, that I could do it—the Directing Program, ABC Family, Lesli, Odetta Watkins from Warner Bros, called and put in a good word. And in the final hour when it looked like it wasn't going to happen, Marlene, Lisa and Oliver did not give up and asked me to fly to LA so we could all sit down with the studio to convince them to give me the episode. I got it! Ever grateful.

Norman Buckley

Gossip Girl, Pretty Little Liars, Rizzoli and Isles, The Fosters

I began my career in 1981, working in postproduction on many theatrical films and TV movies. In the year 2000 I started editing various pilots for Warner Brothers Television, and every pilot that I worked on was picked up to series. After editing the pilot of *Fastlane*, I stayed with the series and found that television editing was a tough, thankless job—essentially the equivalent of cutting half a feature film every three weeks. But the work taught me efficiency in thinking and I edited for many different directors, from whom I learned a lot. When I was offered the editing job on the pilot and series of *The OC*, I agreed to do it on the condition they would let me direct. I'm grateful that the producers and Warner Brothers agreed to do so, and by the fourth season I was able to quit editing and begin directing full-time. I am grateful to all of the directors who encouraged me along the way and shared with me their process. I was taught by masters.

Millicent Shelton

30 Rock, American Crime, The Flash

In 2002, I was an ex-music video director who was blackballed in movieland because I had directed a mini-major film that didn't make a lot of money. I turned to television because a friend thought I would be good at it. I couldn't continue in the meaningless though fancy visuals of the music video world anyway. I craved storytelling.

Paris Barclay, a fellow former music video director, was mentoring me and allowed me to shadow him from Preproduction through Postproduction on a pilot he was directing, *The Chang Family Saves the World*. I was like a fly on the wall watching everything, absorbing what transpired during every meeting, listening to every director's note, and staying seated in video village when it felt like my presence would be out of place in the flow of work. That is when John Ridley, the show's writer/creator, began talking to me. He was also seated in video village working on one of his numerous books at his laptop computer. We didn't have deep meaningful conversations. He asked me about my work as a music video director. I told him about my film fiasco and that was all. Little did I know that meeting this man, would 3 years later change my career forever.

I stayed in touch with him through his assistant. When another of his pilots went to series, I flew myself out to Toronto to observe. John wanted me to direct an episode but the Network rejected me because I had no prior TV directing experience. They then hired a male ex-music video director who had the exact same level of experience as me to direct the episode.

After that, I was really motivated to get a job in Television. I applied for the ABC interstitial program and was selected. I directed a short film that played in (3) 1-minute acts during the Comedy night commercial breaks. Even though it wasn't an episode, it was a start in the television world.

John Ridley contacted me again in 2005. He was the show runner for the television adaptation of *Barbershop*. He offered me an episode. This time the network, Showtime, agreed because they watched the interstitial. I got the job! Plus they made Paris Barclay promise to mentor me through the episode and agree to step in if I completely started screwing up. Paris told me not to "F" it up.

I'll never forget how nervous I was. I practically storyboarded the entire episode because I was scared I'd forget how to direct on set. Thank God I didn't freeze up when I was actually tested. I had this big scene with almost the entire cast and a lot of dialogue. I had blocked it in my head but on set that blocking was not working. I remember sweating and wanting to cry. I looked around for help but all eyes were on me with expectant looks. So I hid my fear and went with my gut. I moved actors around, freed up the cameras, and it worked!

Michael Zinberg

The Bob Newhart Show, The Practice, The Good Wife

Lou Grant was my first single camera assignment, and although I had directed many multi-camera half hours and several main titles, this was a BIG DEAL. It was a very hot new show with a wonderful list of directors and a great cast, not to mention being an MTM Series and that Grant Tinker had been my boss and mentor for many years by this point in my young career. Alan Burns, whom I knew well, and Gene Reynolds, who I admired for his work on *MASH*, were the Executive Producers and the wonderful cast was headed by Ed Asner, a good friend from my days as Associate Producer and writer on the *Mary Tyler Moore Show* . . . but I had never directed him. Ed was an imposing man, a really strong actor and really smart. I had seen him work with the directors on Mary's show and also now on his own set, he could be . . . imposing. Still, I was thrilled to get the assignment and did all the homework I could, watching every episode, hanging on the set and talking to everyone I could corner.

So I get my script (a very good one) and my schedule and see that my first day opens with a four and a half page scene in the newsroom, a gigantic set where all of the newspaper's staff sat and hung out. It set the whole story in motion and Lou Grant (Ed) prowled the terrain like the king of the realm he was, going desk to desk getting needed information to drive the narrative and giving out instructions. A really great scene. I'm excited to start with it. So I go to my office and prep, prep, prep . . . notes, notes, notes. Plans, plans, more plans. Walked the set a thousand times, it seemed, I knew every word, every beat, every move. To paraphrase the old saying . . . Slowly I turned, step by step, inch by inch.

And at call that first day I entered the stage filled with confidence and enthusiasm. I grabbed a mandatory cup of coffee and a donut and got to work. We read the scene, as I heard the words I saw every move, every nuance. Now comes time to stage it and I move to Ed, start with him. I go through it, walking the place as he would, stopping when he would and indicating when he would turn, talk and motion, and who to. It worked, it was impressive, I knew it was good. I wait for a response . . . Crickets (silence). I turned to Ed, he had listened intently and everyone was waiting for his ideas, his thoughts, and I was sure, his approval. Beat . . . beat . . . beat . . .

"That's goooooood," he said slowly. I almost breathed, till ". . . BUT . . . I think I (dramatic pause) should really start here, by my desk . . ." And he proceeded to lay out an entirely different scenario, different moves, different places at different times. I thought my hair would catch on fire. TOTALLY different! But what about MY plan, rattled around in my head, mercifully NOT coming out of my mouth. I watched, listened and Ed finished. "What do you think?" Big Ed asked me, smile on his face. Fortunately I heard my voice say "Very cool, let's do that," having no idea how to shoot it. Please, I silently thought, DO NOT let anyone see the PANIC in my heart.

"Let's mark it!" the First AD hollered and that process began with all the actors falling right in to Asner's plan. I watched closely . . . Holy Crap! How am I going to figure all this out, let alone get a fucking camera on it?

The DP was a fabulous guy named Bobby Carimico and the A-camera operator was another wonderful gentleman named Bobby Liu, both of whom I knew from around the lot, and they were professionals I looked up to. Carimico was a big guy, I felt his hand rest on my shoulder . . . "Don't worry, kid," he said, "We got you covered." I looked at he and Bobby Liu and they, I am sure, saw the relief in my face. And, yes, they carried me through that first morning till I could get back on my feet and figure out the scene. We got it done by lunch, on schedule, and I fled to my trailer to re-prep the balance of the day.

Multi-Camera was easier, I had thought, because you got to stage the scene for the audience, like a play. Then watch it and then put the cameras on it days later. Here, you had to stage and shoot immediately, and 360 degrees in addition. And clearly, you needed more than ONE PLAN! I had done it backwards, I let the plan drive the scene instead of letting the scene drive the plan.

In dailies the next day (Yes, that was what we did then, went to see the rushes in a screening room, all of us watching and talking and learning . . . God, I miss that . . .) Gene Reynolds complimented me on most of how that scene was staged and shot. I quietly said thank you and in front of everyone said that it was mostly Mr. Asner's idea and that the two Bobby's figured out how to shoot it and that I was more of a student than a participant. Carimico jumped right in, "Bullshit . . . we all did it," he stated. Reynolds then said that it was as it should be, a team . . . and we should get back to it. But a student I was, and in that eight days I learned enough to fill volumes, things I use to this day. Carimico and Liu and I did many shows after that, many series . . . and always had a good laugh about that first morning. And I was always grateful for their help and kindness . . . also to this day.

I don't worry about how to shoot anything much any more, I let the staging and the actors tell me where the camera should be. And I come in with several ideas of how to stage scene, ready to accommodate any actor's idea, or anyone else's for that matter, if it makes the scene better, or more comfortable, or more interesting. Staging is always the most fun, and working it through to bring the scene to life. And, for sure, I've never once since stepped out a scene for an actor . . . ever again. Asner and I have worked together many times over the years and he is still among the smartest and most interesting and, yes, imposing actors I have ever worked with. He's a pleasure, and it's my pleasure to let him do what he wants.

David Paymer

The Fosters, The Mentalist, Grey's Anatomy, Hart of Dixie

My first directing job was very much related to my career as an actor. After over 25 years of acting in film and television, I was eager to get behind the camera as well. I knew that I needed to at least make a short film to use as a "calling card." At that time, Showtime was producing a series of shorts called "Quickflicks." They were specifically looking for actors to direct their fellow actors. Michael McKean starred in my comic short called *Candor City Hospital*. This six-minute film was well received but I still didn't have a directing job.

I showed the film to my dear friend Treat Williams who was then starring in the series *Everwood*. Treat wanted to work with directors who "spoke the same acting language" as he did. Although my short had no resemblance to *Everwood* in tone or content, Treat brought it to his producers, Greg Berlanti and Mickey Liddel. They knew my work as an actor and kindly offered me an episode to direct. The show turned out well and I went on to direct more episodes of *Everwood*. These became another calling card (someone said yes!) and my agent successfully brought me more opportunities and offers.

When I'm directing now, I feel a special affinity with the actors I work with. They know that I've stood in their shoes and I like to joke that we share the actors' secret handshake. In this case it helped me launch my directing career.

Karen Gaviola

Sons of Anarchy, The Blacklist, Lost

I had been working for 5 years as a first assistant director on many television shows and had worked with many directors.

One Saturday, a friend of mine asked if I wanted to tag along with her as she ran errands in Santa Monica—a city I never go to. I was bored, so I agreed. We stopped for lunch at the Broadway Deli. As we ordered, I noticed a man at the counter staring at me. I mentioned to my girlfriend that I thought this strange man was trying to hit on me!

Next thing I know, the man is standing at our table and says, "What's the matter, Gaviola, don't you recognize me?" He had a distinctive voice, and only then did I recognize the man to be Mark Tinker, a director with whom I had worked on several series (and yes, he looked different!). After exchanging pleasantries, he said, "I'm producing a show and we need a first AD. Are you working?" I said, "What's the show?" He said *"NYPD Blue"*— at that time, the hottest series on the air. I lied and said, "No! I'm not working!"

I got the job and did good work. At the end of each season, for the next three years, I asked Mark for a directing shot. He granted me one the fourth year.

So: the moral of this story is, eat out a lot and be nice to strangers! Opportunity knocks in the strangest ways!

Tom Verica

Scandal, Harry's Law, The Mentalist

I got my first directing job on the NBC show *American Dreams*. I was an actor on the series, however, I always had the desire to direct. I immersed myself in a film course to learn the technical aspects of visual storytelling because I was dedicated to learn as much as I could about the craft. In an effort to convince the producers of my passion, I directed a 30-minute short film which I screened for the cast and producers of *Dreams*. Luckily, it was a huge success and they felt confident enough to let me helm an episode. My experience went very well. That opened the door for me to go on to direct many other shows and, fortunately, gave me a career in directing.

Jerry Levine

Hawaii 5-0, Elementary, Life Unexpected, Scorpion, Monk, It's Always Sunny in Philadelphia

My first film directing assignment came as a result of a one-act play I directed for the stage. The play was a success onstage and had a unique quality to it. It was character-driven and required us to pay great attention to the performances. The play was *Big Al* by Bryan Goluboff.

When we realized that we had a unique project on our hands, we decided to invite the Showtime Network to see it, with the hope that they would support us in filming it as a short film. It worked. They saw the potential and produced the film version of the play. A project of this nature requires one to call in every favor you can in order to get the final product completed. We did just that, and God bless all of our friends who supported us in this adventure. *Big Al* premiered on Showtime and went on to win prizes at Film Festivals and a Cable Ace Award in the Best Actor category for David Packer.

The result for me was a unique piece of film that I could use as a calling card to demonstrate whatever skill I was beginning to develop as a film director. Eventually, the film found its way into the hands of Michael Pressman, who was directing and producing the TV series *Chicago Hope*. Michael gave me an opportunity to direct that series. Later, when I realized how much I didn't know, I asked Michael what he was thinking when he hired me. Why would he give someone with so little film directing experience an opportunity like that? His response was that based on what he saw in the performances in *Big Al*, he was convinced that I could direct actors and tell a story. Not exactly blind faith, because there was a piece of film he could watch—a film that demonstrated that I was beginning to develop a point of view and a voice as a director.

It is also important to mention the incredible relationships we build up through the years and to acknowledge in this article all the help we received from friends, agents, managers, and relatives, who made phone calls, made introductions, shared contacts, and offered support.

However, at the end of the day, it was tenacity and the play that was the thing. Without our ability to self-generate and use all of our resources to push it through and shoot the film, there would have been nothing to show to anyone. So my advice is to get out there with a camera and start shooting.

Paul Holahan

Castle, Unforgettable, White Collar, The Last Ship, Burn Notice

After directing commercials for a few years, I was desperate to direct something with actual lines of dialogue. But there was no clear path for how to get into dramatic television. It seemed like a closed community. The one TV director I knew didn't take shadows. I knocked on a fair amount of doors, read the trades, wrote ideas, and spent a lot of time not directing.

Then one day I realized that a guy, a friend I had DPd for (worked as a cameraman for), was now a producer of a comic book-inspired live-action cable television series. What luck! I showed him my commercial reel and he was very impressed, saying, "You'd be perfect for our show. Love to have you. But it's never going to happen." He explained that there was no way the studio was going to let him hire a director who hadn't directed an episode of episodic television. Television's ultimate catch-22 was revealed to me: in order to direct an episode of TV you need to have first directed an episode of TV. And all I had were a bunch of commercials, so I wasn't getting on the list. Another brick wall.

Two months later, on sunny day in Los Angeles, my friend calls from out of the blue and asks, "You got anything going on tomorrow?" I was available. Turns out that his show had shut down suddenly when their star was hospital-ized. The directors' schedules were thrown into confusion. Miraculously, there was an open director slot that had to be filled quickly, and he was going to book me. The studio was busy worrying about their star. And I slipped in unnoticed. But they liked the show and wanted me to do another. And another . . .

Lesli Linka Glatter

Homeland, Mad Men, Masters of Sex, Ray Donovan, West Wing, Walking Dead

My first job in Hollywood was directing *Amazing Stories* for Steven Spielberg. How in the world did that happen? I was a modern dance choreographer with a story I was passionate about telling, so I made a short film through the American Film Institute's Directing Workshop for Women.

Early one morning, the phone rang, and it was Spielberg calling me to tell me how much he liked my short film. I thought it was a prank call and hung up on him. Thank goodness, he called back!

I met with Spielberg several days later and he offered me the extraordinary opportunity to direct an episode of his new anthology series. He also gave two other new directors, Todd Holland and Phil Joanou, their first opportunity to direct. As I was so new to directing, I asked Steven if I could apprentice with him on his episode before I directed my own. Lucky for me, he said yes. Watching Steven work was the best film school anyone could ever have. In addition, I prepped my episode for a month—storyboarding it over and over, doing anything I could to be prepared.

My first day on my first episode (I ended up directed three *Amazing Stories*), I had a hundred guys storming a beach in World War II, stunts, explosions, seven cameras, and two eyemo's. [Author's note: a type of remote-controlled camera used when it's too dangerous to have a camera operator in the location.] It was trial by fire, exhilarating and terrifying, and I never looked back. And every day since then, I have felt incredibly grateful to be able to be a storyteller.

Arlene Sanford

Nashville, Bones, Desperate Housewives, Ally McBeal

After working in daytime soaps for a minute, I wrote, produced, and directed a short film. Because I had a friend who was friends with Jamie Lee Curtis, I was able to call Jamie and ask if she would kindly pretty please agree to play the lead in my thirty-ish-minute film called *Welcome Home*. I needed only five days of her life and although I could not offer her any payment, I promised it would be fun—at least for her. I was scared to death.

She said "yes"—a small miracle. When it was finished, because she was in it (along with Richard Masur, Bonnie Bartlett, and William Windom), a number of people were interested in watching it. A friend of a friend (these are valuable people) had begun coproducing a new show called *The Days and Nights of Molly Dodd*, which was created by Jay Tarses (father of prolific producer and one-time network executive Jamie Tarses). This friend, Roz Doyle, gave Jay my film, and he asked to meet me. I sat down in his office and he asked me if I wanted to direct his show—just like that, did I want to direct his show. (This was years ago, before the director needed to be approved by a slew of studio and network people. The job would not have happened if that were the case, as I knew none of those people.)

And then I called my agent who I had just met through, you guessed it, a friend of . . . a distant cousin. She was very proud that she had been able to get me my first primetime directing job.

Scott Ellis

Undatable, Dr. Ken, Weeds, 30 Rock, The Closer

My first job came from David Lee, who created *Frasier*. He was a fan; we came from the same agency, and he knew my work in theatre. [Author's note: Prior to this, Mr. Ellis had received multiple Tony nominations and had won a Drama Desk Award. Mr. Lee had probably seen Ellis's New York productions of *She Loves Me*, *Steel Pier*, *Picnic*, *1776*, and *Company*.] He asked to meet with me because, he said, "We're always looking for people who really know how to work well with actors on our show." We had lunch. He said, "Is this something you're interested in?" I hadn't really thought about it that much; I had thought about it, but getting your first shot was always tough. I said, "Sure." And he said, "Why don't you come out [from New York to Los Angeles]. You'll be here for a week." So I did. At the end of that week I said, "I think I can do this." He was a great teacher. He gave me a shot. At the end he said, "Okay, I can give you the first one, but you'll have to get the second one yourself." He meant: if you don't do a good job, they aren't going to ask you back; you do, they probably will ask you back.

Henry Chan

The Neighbors, Zoe Ever After, Fresh Off the Boat, Scrubs, 10 Things I Hate About You

I was an editor on *The Cosby Show*. I won an Emmy and the producers, Carsey/Warner, really liked my work. There was going to be a spinoff called *A Different World* and I was invited to edit the new show. I accepted and told the producers I wanted to direct. I kept on badgering them until finally they said, "Okay, okay! Give him an episode." I ended up directing five episodes.

Elodie Keene

The Wire, Glee, Jane the Virgin

Way back in 1975, the fact that I had a master's degree in film production and had an award-winning film in the festival circuit meant very little to anyone—except possibly me—with regard to my potential as a film or television director. I had, however, developed the ability to edit film, so even though my announcement that I was a "director" met with resounding, echoing silence, if not outright hostility, the announcement that I was an editor got me jobs. For fifteen years, that is what I did.

By a very circuitous route, I made my way to the doorstep of a new show called, *L.A. Law*. During the second year of that show, which was an enormous hit, I won an Emmy for editing. The next year I was nominated for another Emmy for a TV movie I had cut called *Roe vs. Wade*. The commonly held conviction among editors was that this recognition would catapult my editing career into some new sphere of editing, possibly into bigger movies, made for television, or a feature. I kept cutting *L.A. Law* and waited for the phone to ring.

In the meantime I had married, had a beautiful daughter, bought a house, and was trying to "om" myself into being content with where I was in my life. Things could have been a lot worse, or so I told myself. If I never got to direct, so what? Everything else was pretty darned good, so let go, be happy!

Right around then, while shooting the breeze over lunch with Rick Wallace, the executive producer of *L.A. Law*, he asked me why, out of all the many people who were in his office every day, I had never asked to direct an episode. So stunned by the unexpected turn in the conversation I was that I barely stammered out all my lame reasons, all of which amounted to being afraid of rejection. He then said I needed to think hard about whether I had the courage to take the leap, because he would be willing to take the risk of hiring me as a first-time director. After getting over the shock of the whole thing, I said I would very much like the opportunity.

In subsequent conversations, Rick asked me if I would help him produce the show, so in 1990, I became one of the producers of *L.A. Law* and I shot one episode toward the end of the season. By the time that show came to the end of its eight-year run, I was the co-executive producer and I had directed twenty episodes. That was the beginning of my pretty much nonstop, twenty-year directing career. I owe it all to Rick.

Joe Pennella

The Neighbors, Life Goes On, Monk, Everwood

I was shooting a series in the late 1980s called *Life Goes On*; it went for four years and I went to the executive producer, Michael Braverman, in the third year and told him that I'd like to direct one. I had worked as a director/cameraman prior to that doing commercials, so it wasn't going to be such a big jump; narrative filmmaking is like prose and commercials are like poetry. He said fine, and I got to direct the next-to-the-last-episode. It was a real challenge because it was a story that was told backward. And I went to Michael and said, "I think I can do this, but I'm overwhelmed." He said, "Joe, this is it. If you want it, this is the one you have to do." I did. And for that episode, Kellie Martin was nominated for an Emmy and Tony Graphia won the Writer's Guild Award.

David Breckman

Monk, Pulled Over, Pic Six

As the frequent writer-on-set on the USA Network series *Monk* from 2002–2009, I had the privilege of watching a lot of outstanding directors in action. And "action" is the operative word because TV is low-budget filmmaking. You are required to shoot what amounts to half a feature in eight —occasionally even seven—days, so there's no time to indulge in navel-gazing. It's all go-go-go and you'd better have your kit packed when you arrive on set or you're screwed.

For me, a longtime movie buff, it was a tremendous experience—like being paid to go to film school—and I very quickly caught the directing bug. In my downtime, I tried to apply what I'd learned on set by shooting a five-minute short called *Pulled Over* in 2005, and then another, a 17-minute magnum opus called *Pic Six* the following year.

I was proud of *Pic Six*. It nabbed some festival awards and made a good enough impression on our supervising director (the wonderful Randy Zisk) that he allowed me to direct my first *Monk*, "Mr. Monk and the Three Julies," in 2007—which is all you can expect from a short film.

What I think I brought to the *Monk* party was an instinct for comedy: knowing what funny looks like and finding ways of enhancing it on the spot, as the occasion demands, and knowing when to hang back and do nothing—which can be just as valuable.

Two more *Monk* episodes followed, each one (I hope) better than the last, before Monk solved his final case in 2009.

Paris Barclay

In Treatment, Glee, Sons of Anarchy, The Bastard Executioner

After 12 years working as an advertising copywriter and eventually a creative supervisor, I was content to make money making ads. But after directing a few small spots, an opportunity arose to become a partner in a music video company. Masochistically missing my impoverished life as a struggling artist, I took it.

It was the dawn of the 1990s, and I directed music videos for the then-waning New Kids on the Block, the rising Harry Connick, Jr., the iconic Bob Dylan, and was celebrated largely for eight videos I made for LL Cool J, including "Mama Said Knock You Out" and "Jinglin' Baby," which were acknowledged with awards from MTV and Billboard. Fortunately, almost every video I did told some sort of narrative story, indicating that I might have promise in longer forms of film. My manager got a reel of my videos to John Wells, then a relatively new writer-producer, and he hired me to come to Chicago to direct a short-lived show he had created called *Angel Street* starring Robin Givens and Pam Gidley as homicide detectives.

The show was cancelled after six episodes were shot (I directed two of them), but I suddenly was a DGA member and had an advocate. And, as luck would have it, John's next show was a juggernaut called *ER*, and he called me back up from the minors to direct.

Ricardo Mendez Matta

Hart of Dixie, Thieves and Liars, Nash Bridges, Touched by an Angel

There are basically only six ways to become a director:

1. Hire yourself: either you personally raise the money to make a film, or you're a producer or studio chief, but either way, you appoint yourself director.
2. Writing: write a script that someone wants to make very badly, and insist on directing it.
3. Acting: you're a coveted star and in order to appear in their movie, you insist on directing it.
4. Nepotism: get a powerful relative to hire you.
5. Film school: direct a hot short film as part of a class.
6. Below the line: work your way up as DP, AD, script supervisor, or editor.

Number 6 worked for me. I was a 1st AD on the TV series *Weird Science* when the director I was prepping with, Max Tash, was suddenly called to do an MOW (movie-of-the-week.). He begged the producers—Tom Spezialy, Alan Cross, and Robert Lloyd Lewis—to let him go, and when they asked who would take over, he said, "Let him do it, he prepped it all with me and is totally ready to do it." They agreed, partly because they had little other choice, but also partly because we had been working together for several years and I had earned their trust. I directed nine episodes of that series, but that was only the first step (getting a friend to hire you). The second step— getting a stranger to hire you on a new show—was harder, but at a DGA mixer, I was lucky enough to meet Carlton Cuse, who hired me on *Nash Bridges*. Talent and hard work are required, but the bottom line is without a lot of luck, none of it would have happened. They say you need to be at the right place at the right time. Well, no one knows when the right time is going to be, but you can figure out where the right place is, and stay there patiently until the right time comes.

Rob Bailey

CSI: NY, CSI Cyber, Grimm, Grey's Anatomy, Gotham, Criminal Minds, The Wire

My big break came when—after bombarding a producer to give me a shot on a show for about a year—he finally got a job somewhere else and agreed to hire me because he wouldn't be around to deal with the consequences of his decision.

I had been fortunate to get into the National Film and Television School in England, which was a fantastic environment that encouraged students to have confidence in their own creativity and also to go out and watch other directors working in the professional world. So I graduated thinking the world lay at my feet. Two years later, I was back working in the construction business where I had been the day I first got into film school.

It was a frustrating time waiting for that first job, but I had other colleagues from film school who were in the same boat and some who had just started getting work, and I felt that sooner or later I would get a chance. I also knew how reluctant most producers were to take a shot on directors who had yet to prove themselves.

I was naïve enough to think that their main worry was that the director wouldn't know how to tell the story. The truth came home to me at lunch on the first day; [we were] hours behind and did I have a plan to get us out by 7:00 p.m. and "make the day"? So I got to learn the most valuable lesson of all on day 1: come to the set prepared but also flexible.

Randall Zisk

Monk, Scandal, Blacklist, Madam Secretary, House, Weeds

I was in postproduction working my way up the ladder on an NBC show, *Midnight Caller*. The executive producer, Bob Singer, knew I wanted to direct because I mentioned it to him every day for about a year. One of my jobs was to shoot the inserts for each episode, usually something simple and easy that didn't require actors. Finally, Bob Butler—one of the most respected pilot directors of all time—had an additional scene to shoot for his episode. The show filmed in San Francisco and our offices were in L.A. He couldn't make the trip, nor could Bob Singer, so I got the chance. Bob Butler took out a piece of paper and drew a rudimentary storyboard for me and wrote out a quick shot list. He asked me if it made sense and I just looked at it, confused, and answered, "yes." I studied that piece of paper for the next 24 hours, and the following day, with the help of the DP, directed the scene. I don't remember it being particularly well done, but Bob Butler's work on the episode was so special that it fit in without too much scrutiny.

The next season, I shadowed Bob Singer every opportunity I got, and when a director fell out of the lineup, I was called into his office. He told me to pack my bags: I was getting my shot to direct *Midnight Caller*. Bob was an amazing mentor and—along with Bob Butler and Les Moonves—he gave me an opportunity I'll never forget.

Over the next five years, I directed eighteen episodes for Bob Singer on his various shows and just recently had the rare fortune of bringing him in to direct an episode of *Monk*.

Terrence O'Hara

NCIS, Grimm, Rosewood, NCIS: LA, Lie to Me

The year was 1991, and my first network show was *Silk Stalkings*, starring Rob Estes and Mitzi Kapture. It was advertised on CBS as "crime time after prime time." The producers were Stu Segall and Stephen J. Cannell. Up to that point in my career, I had done a few low-budget features and some commercial work after I had graduated from the two-year masters program at AFI. I received a call one day out of the blue that went something like this, "Hi, Stu Segall here, I just saw a tape of yours. I don't remember what was on it, but I liked it!" That said, he asked if I would be interested in coming down to San Diego to do the show. Of course I said yes. I had a ball; I loved the idea of shooting a one-hour show in six days. I loved working with Stu and ended up doing both *Silk* and *Renegade*, another six-day show with lots of action, starring Lorenzo Lamas. It was like going back to film school—

a wonderful camaraderie with both cast and crew. Because of my work on these, I was asked to do *Dr. Quinn* for CBS. The rest, as they say, is history. I've been working in television since and I absolutely love it.

David Rodriguez

Once Upon a Time in Queens, NCIS: Los Angeles, Scandal

Growing up in the Bronx with a blue-collar family was a tough place to foster creativity but I loved music, photography and writing for as long as I could remember. After a variety of jobs including being a police officer, I left myself no choice but to go for it. I sold my house, paid off all of my bills and took myself, five thousand dollars and a 3 minute sizzle of the film I wanted to make to New York City. There I pounded the pavement until I found financing and 10 weeks later I was on set directing my first independent feature film, *Push*.

Antonio Negret

Arrow, The 100, Forever

I was 10 years out of film school, and had directed 3 feature films and some commercials. I was surviving as a director, but on a constant roller coaster of emotions. When it was good—it was really good. When it was bad—it was really bad. For years, I had tried to transition into TV, but was always told the same things—*it's a different world, it's impossible to break into, it's a closed club, etc . . .*

I was licking my wounds from yet another independent film that was "fully financed" yet somehow fell apart, when my agent called and told me he'd set up a meeting with Chris Mack over at Warner Brothers. I met Chris, and we hit it off right away. It was there that I learned about the Warner Brothers Workshop, and instantly knew I had to apply.

Long story short, I got into the inaugural class of the WBTV Director's Workshop, taught by the fabulous Bethany Rooney (with special contributions by Mary Lou Belli). And yes, it was based on this amazing book. I felt invigorated and hopeful. These two incredible directors taught me so much. And I got to meet several showrunners along the way, as well as shadow multiple directors. I soaked up everything I could, both in the Workshop and on the sets, and yes, I ate a lot of craft service as I watched and learned!

Ultimately, it was Jason Rothenberg who gave me my first shot at TV directing, by hiring me on *The 100*. And he freed me when he said he *liked* that I hadn't directed TV before. It was then that I realized I had to somehow embrace the unique demands of television, while emotionally treating every episode like a feature. And that has stayed with me to this day. I directed *The 100*, which got me an episode of *Forever*, which got me an episode of *Arrow*. In less than a year after doing the Workshop, I had gotten my feet wet in television. And I've never been more excited, or grateful.

Arthur Allan Seidelman

Six Dance Lessons in Six Weeks, A Christmas Carol—The Musical, The Sisters

When I think of my first film or television job I actually think of two, both of which, in my mind, were first.

The first came as a result of a revival of Clifford Odets' *Awake and Sing* which I directed off-Broadway. One of the producers had a day job as a UPM. His name is Willard Goodman and he came to me one day and said he had just been assigned a spoof of the then popular Steve Reeves *Hercules* movies, which was to star the reigning Mr. Universe. He wanted to know if I would be interested in directing. He offered me $1,000 a week for nine weeks. I said yes before he came to the end of the question. The film was *Hercules in New York*. The star was Arnold Schwarzenegger. His first. My first.

My second first also was born in a theater. I directed a play at the American Place Theater called *Ceremony of Innocence* by Ronald Ribman. It was well received and PBS wanted to make a film of it for their American Playhouse series. Ron, bless his heart, insisted I direct the film. I did. It starred Richard Kiley, Larry Gates, James Broderick and Jessie Royce Landis. It too was well received and my career in TV was set in motion; slow motion at first, but still motion.

Angela Barnes Gomes

Let's Stay Together, Eve, Gillian in Love

I had been working as an Assistant Director for about 10 years when I got a job as the 1st AD for a multi-camera sitcom called *Eve*. Meg DeLoatch was the show's creator, and she and Dave Duclon were the showrunners. It was a great set—we had a lot of fun, and the cast and crew really did feel like family. I was there for all three seasons, and both Meg and Dave knew about my desire to direct, as I was pretty open about it, although not very pushy. At the beginning of season three, they called me in for a meeting shortly before I was due to start prep, saying they had some concerns about a certain episode. They handed me the episode breakdown, and the first thing

I did was look to see who was directing, and there was my name! Up until that point the only directing credits I had were a few music videos, so I was a little surprised, although it made sense as to why they chose to give me a shot. I had made myself valuable as the 1st AD, so they knew I understood the production side of things. I'd been there from the beginning, so I knew the show's rhythm both tonally and logistically. They had always been cool about me pitching jokes when we were shooting, and liked my sense of humor. When it was my turn to direct, I was incredibly supported by the producers, cast and crew, who again, felt like family. The episode turned out great, but unfortunately the show was cancelled shortly after my episode. My next couple episodic directing opportunities were also on shows that I worked as the 1st AD for a season or two.

Paul McCrane

Scandal, Nashville, Empire, Major Crimes, Glee

I had worked for Steven Bochco and Greg Hoblit as an actor on *Cop Rock* (insert jokes here), and they then allowed me to shadow directors during the first season of *NYPD Blue*. I picked the brains of as many directors as I could, either on set or through lunch invitations, etc. I took a workshop on directing for film. I read everything I could find, but all the technical aspects of film-making felt utterly foreign and incomprehensible to me, until Sidney Lumet's book *Making Movies* illuminated for me that, ideally, all the elements of production were meant to be in service to the telling of the story. Decisions about the lens, angle, shot composition, lighting, set and costume design, etc., could be evaluated in terms of their contribution toward the objectives of the story and the writer—the intended effect on the audience—just as decisions about character were in a play. This gave me a foothold into this foreign world.

My first TV directing job came on *ER*. I had been acting on the show for years, and started formally observing directors with some regularity. I requested meetings with John Wells, Jonathan Kaplan, Chris Chulack and other producers, to ask them what I could do to get them to consider giving me a shot. I was never given any specific requirements, but was often told of their need to be sure I was serious, etc. This went on for a little more than a year. Eventually, I wrote a short, and made plans to direct it over the summer. Just before we went on hiatus, the good folks at *ER* told me I would get an episode to direct the following season. I still made my short, for several reasons: (1) I didn't want my first time in the chair to be on what was still one of the most successful and challenging shows on TV; (2) Out of a sense of responsibility, and to bolster my confidence, I wanted to make some mistakes on my own dime (which I certainly did!); and (3) My long-term interests were—and are—in developing my own projects anyway, so I saw this as my first opportunity to do so. So I made my short. The following fall, I directed my first episode of *ER*.

Peter Tolan

Rescue Me, The Job, The Larry Sanders Show, Style and Substance

How did I get my first job directing TV? I hired myself on my own show. It's easier that way.

GETTING YOUR FOOT IN THE DOOR

The similar parts of our stories are that we all wanted something and went after it. So the first thing we advise you to do is to show up. Prove that you are worthy of the job. That might require you directing a short film or observing on a series for as long it takes to make the producer comfortable with entrusting you with directing an episode. It might mean finding a generous director who is willing to mentor you by allowing you to shadow, or follow, him.

Make a Networking List

This is an ongoing project. Create a database of the people you know in the business.

Note how you met them, subsequent meeting(s) or contact, and personal data about them (name of spouse, do they have a kid(s), any pet charity). Choose three who you think are most generous or in a position of power. Google them. Write a personal note *not asking for anything* but rather acknowledging something they've done.

> If you don't see an opportunity, create one for yourself. Once you have the opportunity, don't squander it.

If you don't see an opportunity, create one for yourself. Once you have the opportunity, don't squander it. Mary Lou and Bethany are often approached by directors who want to observe. The individuals who show up at crew call, at the beginning of the day, and stay until wrap (the conclusion of a day's filming), get our attention. If those same individuals design shot lists to compare their work with what we are doing, we really start taking them seriously. Finally, we like to see individuals who know when to ask questions and when to be a fly on the wall. This final trait is the one that reflects someone who sees the big picture.

You probably won't be able to get an agent until you have a film or television episode to showcase your talents. Again, be methodical with your approach. See if the producer who gave you a job or a director whom you trailed will give you an introduction to her agent. Use any personal contact you may have, even if it seems far-fetched. Sending a DVD of your short film to an agency cold—or without an introduction—will result in it being returned to you with a standard letter saying that they don't accept "unsolicited submissions." But if your landlady gives it to her niece, who works in the mailroom at an agency, and she gives it to a VIP agent's assistant, who likes your short film and slips it to his boss at the perfect moment, it could work.

Writing is another way in. So is producing. Because television is a writer-dominated medium, if you create a show, you can hire yourself to direct it! Or, more likely, if you start your career as a writer's assistant, then work your way up the ladder (research assistant, staff writer, story editor, co-producer, producer, executive producer), you will at some point find the perfect moment to suggest that you might be the best director for your script. (But we hope you will have taken acting classes and studied the craft of directing first!) If your skills lie in producing, you can prove yourself in that field and have access to the people making the director-hiring decisions. Regardless of how you do it, the secret to working your way up the ladder to becoming a director is to be good at whatever you do, even if you're in an entry-level position. Put in extra time, remember that the boss likes two pumps of sweetener in her coffee, read everything that goes in and out of that office, stay on good terms with everyone.

If you do your job well, and always go the extra mile, people will notice. The important thing is not to get stuck there. Always have the goal in mind and clearly let people know you are happy to be doing what you are doing, but also that you are steadily working towards that bigger goal.

If you do your job well, and always go the extra mile, people will notice. The important thing is not to get stuck there. Always have the goal in mind and clearly let people know you are happy to be doing what you are doing, but also that you are steadily working towards that bigger goal.

There are no set rules for getting your first job. Think out of the box. Do it your way because that is what will make you stand out. As you've learned from the stories in this chapter, 28 directors had 28 different ways to get in.

And you will have yours. Get ready, learn, and be prepared to take advantage of the moment when someone gives you that hand up, because that's something we all have in common. Someone had to reach down and lift us up. So be in that right place at the right time, with your skills sharp and ready to go. Good luck!

Being a Director

Directors come in all shapes and sizes, all ethnicities, all educational backgrounds, and both genders. What they have all in common is a passion for storytelling and the ability to be a leader.

If you are a director, you are born with the need to tell stories. You want to make sense of the world and to entertain yourself and an audience by framing real-life experiences and eternal questions.

You need perspective and a point of view. You need to judge what is good from what is bad.

It boils down to having good taste.

It a huge job to interpret the script, shape the actors' performance, choose every element within the frame, and then use the medium knowledgably and efficiently. You need great leadership qualities such as determination, enthusiasm, and the abilities to communicate and command gently.

Even with talent and great leadership qualities, the job is by its nature stressful because of the immensity of the position and the intense scrutiny that happens every day. We have found four ways of coping with that stress: do the work in prep; enlist the support of your team; be in good health; and believe in yourself.

Directing an episode of television is a big responsibility. The producer, who gives you a job, must know that you will deliver a great show and put the money up on the screen.

There are no set rules for getting your first job. Some people have found success shadowing a director, or finding a mentor. You must think out of the box and do it your way. Once you've completed that first episode, an agent might be willing to represent you. It's just another problem waiting to be solved.

We want to end our book by reviewing some simple rules for success. They're good advice not just for being a director, but for life in general:

- Never lose your temper.
- Don't rush to judgment.
- Listen before you talk.
- Get your ego out of the way.
- Be kind.
- Trust your instincts!
- And we'll add one more: Go after your dream!

Mary Lou can be reached through her website: www.maryloubelli.com. Bethany can be reached through her website: www.bethanyrooney.com.

Original Scenes

1 MAN/1 WOMAN SCENE

INT. SOLDIER'S LIVING ROOM—DAY

The Soldier and his Wife stand in an embrace in the doorway. Then she pulls away.

>   WIFE
> Come in, come in, let's not stand
> here, let me get your—
>   (she reaches for his
>   duffel bag)

>   SOLDIER
> No, it's fine, just leave it on the
> porch.

They walk into the room, and stand there a moment, awkwardly.

>   WIFE
> It's just, so good, so . . . why
> didn't you call? I would have picked
> you up—

>   SOLDIER
> I just wanted to get home.

>   WIFE
> And you did. And here you are.
>   (suddenly, starting for
>   the kitchen)
> Can I get you something? You must
> be—

                          SOLDIER
          I'm fine.

                           WIFE
          Some water? A beer?

                          SOLDIER
          No, I'm fine. Thank you.

He wanders around the room a bit, touching things.
She watches him.

                           WIFE
          It's so good to see you.
                    (he nods, continues to
                    wander)
          Are you okay?

                          SOLDIER
          I'm okay, yes.

                           WIFE
          Really?

                          SOLDIER
          You mean like, am I okay, like not
          hurt? I'm okay. Do you mean like, am
          I mental? No. Do you mean like, am I
          me? No. I'm not.

                           WIFE
          Well, that's to be expected, of
          course I didn't think that you
          would be, I mean, it's just, that'd be
          silly, do you want to sit down?

                          SOLDIER
               (beat)
          Sure.

He sits in a leather chair, across from the TV, it's
probably where he used to sit all the time. Before.
Another long beat.

                    SOLDIER (CONT'D)
          How's everybody?

                         WIFE
          Everybody? Everybody's good.

                              SOLDIER
               Where's Blue?

                         WIFE
                    (beat)
          You remember, I wrote. Remember?

                              SOLDIER
               Remind me.

                         WIFE
          He . . . it was in his liver, Dan, I
          had to—

                              SOLDIER
               You put him down?

          She looks at him, then lunges for a lumpy clay
          ashtray, with garish paint swirls on it.

                         WIFE
               Jake made this. For you.
                    (he takes it)
               For Father's Day. At preschool.
                    (his fingers caress it)
               I told him we'd celebrate with you.
               When you got home. Whenever that
               was. And here you are.

                              SOLDIER
               And here I am.

                         WIFE
                    (pretend clapping)
               Yay! Daddy's home!

          He just looks at her. She stops her silly little
          clapping.

> SOLDIER
> Where is he?

> WIFE
> He'll be home at three, he has a
> play date with Justin on Tuesdays,
> you remember.

> SOLDIER
> (he clearly doesn't)
> A play date.

> WIFE
> You'll be so proud of him, Dan. He
> insists on being the one to put up
> the flag every day at school —

The Wife kneels next to him, strokes his arm.

> WIFE (CONT'D)
> I love you, Dan, I'm so glad you're
> home -

She stops as he lurches out of the chair, escaping her
touch. She watches him as he stands there, breathing a
little ragged.

> WIFE (CONT'D)
> You know what? I'm gonna run up,
> comb my hair, put on a little
> lipstick, for cryin' out loud, my
> husband came home and I, well, I
> could look better.
>   (beat)
> And then I'm gonna make you some
> lemonade, you're probably thirsty,
> I'm just gonna give you a minute to,
> you know, settle in.

Smiling at him through tear-glassy eyes, she turns and
runs out of the room.

He stands there a moment, then goes to the front door,
and exits. There's a beat—did he leave? But no, he
carries his duffel bag back in and sets it on the floor.

And then he sits on it, just sits there, rubbing his
face, blinking back the tears.

2 MEN/1 WOMAN SCENE (1)

INT. OFFICE—DAY

JIM bursts through the door, in a rage. He's followed
by SANFORD, who shuts the door behind him so the whole
rest of the office won't overhear. There are two desks
in here, Jim and Sanford share an office.

                    JIM
          You can't keep pulling that crap
          with me, Sanford, it makes me look
          bad.

                    SANFORD
          That wasn't my intent, Jim—

                    JIM
          It's never your intent, you're just
          a douchebag.

                    SANFORD
          Hey now—

                    JIM
          Don't hey now me, I hear that ten
          times a day.

                    SANFORD
          Well you wouldn't if I didn't always
          have to save you from yourself.

                    JIM
          What the hell does that mean?

                    SANFORD
          Open mouth, insert foot.

                    JIM
          Screw you.

                    SANFORD
          Back at 'ya.

As Sanford goes to reopen the door, it suddenly is
pushed open by CYNTHIA, their boss.

                    CYNTHIA
          I can hear you two quarreling like
          sisters down the hall.

                      JIM
          We're not, we're just—

                    CYNTHIA
          I don't care, I don't have time for
          it.
                    (she throws a folder on
                    Jim's desk)
          They've rejected the proposal.

                      JIM
          What?

                    SANFORD
          Who?

                    CYNTHIA
          The board of trustees. They said it
          lacked forethought and fiscal
          responsibility.

                      JIM
          That blows.

                    CYNTHIA
          We've got to have a new plan in
          place by Monday. Emergency meeting at
          noon.
                    (turning back toward door)
          I'm going to grab my laptop, be
          right back.

She exits.

                      JIM
                    (turning to Sanford, who
                    is starting to say something)
          Don't even.

                    SANFORD
What?

                      JIM
Get out. Go home. I'll do this.

                    SANFORD
No way.

                      JIM
I said I got this.

                    SANFORD
I'm not leaving you alone with her.

                      JIM
Get your mind out of the gutter.
I wasn't thinking about —

                    SANFORD
That's all you think about.

                      JIM
        (beat)
So what? You got morals, now?

                    SANFORD
No, but I want to keep my job. And
help you keep yours.

                      JIM
        (a new tack)
Hey, dude, this could be the best
thing that ever happened to me.
A weekend locked in battle— hot,
debating, thirst-quenching, raunchy
battle—with the Virgin Queen. And
what's good for me is good for you.

                    SANFORD
You think a lot of yourself, don't you?

                      JIM
I am, I say modestly, undefeated.
I came, I saw, I conquered. And came
again.

                    CYNTHIA
                        (entering)
                Going somewhere?

                                JIM
                Um. No.

                                    CYNTHIA
                                (putting her laptop down
                                on Jim's desk)
                Well, now you can. Have a nice
                weekend.

                                JIM
                You mean—

                                    CYNTHIA
                Yes. I do.

                                    JIM
                No, you can't. I mean, no, this is
                our project, together, you can't—

                                    CYNTHIA
                But I can. You blew it. Butt out.
                        (he stands there)
                    'Bye.

        After a long moment, as Jim looks to Sanford and back
        to Cynthia, and then he grabs his cell phone and car
        keys from the desk and backs out the door. Cynthia
        closes the door after him. She turns back to Sanford.

                            CYNTHIA (CONT'D)
                I hope you didn't have plans for
                this weekend.

                                SANFORD
                Nope.
                                    CYNTHIA
                Good.

        She crosses to him, grabs him by the tie around his
        neck, and pulls him to her for an intense kiss.

2 MEN/1 WOMAN SCENE (2)

INT. KITCHEN—EVENING

JOHN and STEVE stare at a broken dinner plate on the table that is romantically set for two. A baseball sits next to the broken plate.

                    JOHN
          She's gonna kill me.

                    STEVE
          Not if she doesn't find it.

          Steve moves across the room to the
          wall cabinet. He opens its doors
          looking for something.

                    STEVE (CONT'D)
          Perfect.

He removes a stack of matching dinner plates and carries them back to the table.

                    JOHN
          What are you doing?

                    STEVE
          Watch and learn.

          Steve takes the broken plate and
          places the pieces between two other
          plates in the stack. He moves back
          to the breakfront, puts the stack
          away, then returns with an unbroken
          plate he has removed from the top of
          the stack.

                    JOHN
          The plate is still broken.

                    STEVE
          Yeah, but now she'll never suspect
          it was you who broke it.

                         JOHN
          Me? You're the one who missed the
          ball.

                         STEVE
          Irrelevant at this point.

                         JOHN
          Look, Leila and her roommate are
          barely speaking to each other. If
          she blames her for this, it could go
          nuclear.

                         STEVE
          Then, things get tense with the
          roomate and she'll wanna spend more
          time at your place . . . seems like a
          win-win to me.

                         JOHN
          I'm not ready for that yet.

                         STEVE
          Clearly, she is! Dude, she's setting
          the table for dinner. She's ready to
          play house . . . maybe even hide the
          sausage.

                         JOHN
          Stop!

A key is heard in the door. Leila comes in carrying a
bundle of flowers.

                         LEILA
          Oh, hey, Steve.

Leila moves to the sink with the flowers while John
picks up the baseball and tosses it to Steve.

                         STEVE
          Well, I'll leave you two to your
          romantic dinner. What's on the menu?

                              LEILA
              Whatever John ordered.
                    (Looking at John)
              Let me guess, Thai?

                              JOHN
              Your favorite.

                              LEILA
              Maybe I should get out bowls if you
              ordered the curry.

Leila takes the plates from the table and carries them
over to the cabinet.

                              STEVE
              Enjoy!

Steve smiles at John as he exits.

                              LEILA
              Remind me why you like that guy?

                              JOHN
              I'm not sure I do.

He fills up a vase with water, and places the flowers in
it, and puts it on the table.

2 MEN SCENE

INT. DARRYL'S ROOM—NIGHT

Darryl, at his laptop, listens to his iPod while he
works. Reggie, his older brother, enters and stands at
his desk. Darryl's earbuds and homework renders Reggie
invisible. Reggie waves his hand in front of Darryl's
face, startling him.

                    DARRYL
          What the . . .????

He takes out his earbuds.

                    DARRYL (CONT'D)
          How'd you get in here?

                    REGGIE
               (looking at the door)
          Duh.

                    DARRYL
          Well, duh, you can leave the same
          way.

                    REGGIE
          Is that any way to treat your big
          brother?

                    DARRYL
          I'm not going there. Look, this
          paper is due tomorrow. I'm asking
          you to go.

                    REGGIE
          Sure. But I need to borrow your car.

                    DARRYL
          No.

                    REGGIE
          What do you mean, "No"?

>   DARRYL
>   I mean, get out of my room.
>
>   REGGIE
>   Give me the keys and I will.
>
>   DARRYL
>   Not gonna happen.

Reggie crosses to Darryl's bed, picks up his
sweatshirt and Reggie rifles through the pocket.

>   DARRYL (CONT'D)
>   (jiggling keys)
>   Looking for these.
>
>   REGGIE
>   Stop screwing around. I need the
>   car.
>
>   DARRYL
>   (standing)
>   Then give me a couple twenties, I
>   just filled the tank.
>
>   REGGIE
>   Like that'll happen.
>
>   DARRYL
>   I'm serious.

Reggie grabs for the keys. Darryl dodges his attempt.

>   REGGIE
>   What is your problem?
>
>   DARRYL
>   No problem. Just not letting you get
>   your way again.
>
>   REGGIE
>   What are you talking about?

                          DARRYL
         I'm tired of it.

                          REGGIE
              (seething)
         I need the car.

                          DARRYL
         And I need the cash.

                          REGGIE
         I'll give it to you when I get back.

                          DARRYL
         Right.

                          REGGIE
         You calling me a liar?

                          DARRYL
         Yeah.

                          REGGIE
         Give me the keys.

                          DARRYL
         No.

                          REGGIE
         GIVE ME THE KEYS!

                          DARRYL
         NO!

Reggie grabs Darryl's shirt and yanks him in.

                          REGGIE
         You're pissing me off, kid.

                          DARRYL
         Don't call me that.

                         REGGIE
          That's what you are. A punk ass kid.

                         DARRYL
          Stop it!

                         REGGIE
                   (taunting)
          A punk ass kid who's got the keys to
          Mommie's car.

                         DARRYL
          SHUT UP!

Reggie has hit a nerve. Darryl throws the keys on the
floor. Reggie picks them up.

                         REGGIE
          You're such a girl.

He walks to the door.

                         REGGIE (CONT'D)
          Don't wait up!

Darryl is shaken.

2 WOMEN SCENE

INT. KITCHEN—DAY

Kristin is setting the table for six. Elizabeth enters,
carrying a pink bakery box.

                    ELIZABETH
          Jonathan's here. Says this needs to
          stay cold.

                    KRISTIN
               (without looking up)
          There's room in the fridge.

Kristin crosses to refrigerator.

                    ELIZABETH
          You should see what else he brought.
          Another blond and this one's just
          out of the cradle.

Kristin doesn't comment.

                    ELIZABETH (CONT'D)
          Where's the salt? Joe needs more for
          the next batch of Margaritas.

Kristin bangs down a glass, she still doesn't look at
Elizabeth.

                    KRISTIN
          Above the sink. I better say hi.

Kristin moves to go.

                    ELIZABETH
          I don't get why you're mad at me.

Kristin stops and looks at Elizabeth.

                    KRISTIN
          You've known about this for a week
          and didn't tell me!

> ELIZABETH
> It might have been innocent. He was
> just buying some flowers.

> KRISTIN
> Not for me!

> ELIZABETH
> I didn't know that!

Kristin walks to the refrigerator, Elizabeth blocks her way.

> ELIZABETH (CONT'D)
> Look, I'm not the one you're mad at.

> KRISTIN
> Don't be too sure about that.

Kristin walks around her.

> ELIZABETH
> What's that supposed to mean?

> KRISTIN
> I saw you finish his Margarita just
> now.

> ELIZABETH
> What?

> KRISTIN
> At the bar.

> ELIZABETH
> I squeezed those limes myself, I
> wasn't pouring a drop down the
> drain.

> KRISTIN
> That was pretty clear.

                    ELIZABETH
O.K. Now you're just pissing me off.
What is this about?

                    KRISTIN
You're a flirt.

                    ELIZABETH
What?

                    KRISTIN
How can I expect Joe to keep it in
his pants when even my best friend
is panting for him.

                    ELIZABETH
First, no offense, but I'm not
interested. Second, I don't cheat.
And third, this is about you and
Joe. If you have a problem with him,
talk to him. It was just some flowers
and you don't even know who they
were for.

Beat.

                    ELIZABETH (CONT'D)
It's a big leap from flowers to
affair.

                    KRISTIN
Do you think I'm being paranoid?

                    ELIZABETH
I think you always assume the worst.

                    KRISTIN
I do?

                    ELIZABETH
Yeah.

                              KRISTIN
            But shouldn't I?

Kristin just looks at her.

                         KRISTIN (CONT'D)
            I'm doing it again?

Kristin doesn't answer again.

                         KRISTIN (CONT'D)
            Sorry.

                             ELIZABETH
            Don't be. Do something about it.

                              KRISTIN
            I'll try.

Elizabeth opens her arms. Kristin steps into a hug.
Kristin doesn't see Elizabeth's relief that she and Joe
have dodged another one.

                             ELIZABETH
            Come on. Let's see if Jonathan's
            toddler speaks.

1 MAN AND 1 WOMAN SCENE

INT. KITCHEN — NIGHT

24—year old LAURA sets the table as a sweaty
25—year—old JASON enters behind her. As she hears the
door close —

> LAURA
>
> Put it on the counter.

> JASON
>
> What?

> LAURA
>
> The chicken. I hope you got some
> kind of sauce too —

> JASON
>
> What chicken?

> LAURA
>
> (turning)
> The rotisserie chicken. That you
> said you would get. On your way
> home.

He looks guilty, wipes his sweaty face with a towel.

> JASON
>
> Sorry. The gym was —

> LAURA
>
> Jason —

> JASON
>
> I know, but some a-hole was hogging
> the bench press, so by the time I —

> LAURA
>
> Nice.

                          JASON
          What is the big deal about some
          stupid chicken?

She just looks at him. Then she goes back to setting
the table. There is a long beat.

                       JASON (CONT'D)
          Oh.

                          LAURA
          Yeah.

                          JASON
          When do they get here?

                          LAURA
          In fifeen minutes. You better get in
          the shower.

                          JASON
          Laura —

                          LAURA
          I'll just order in. Ply them with
          wine and pour some cashews in a
          bowl. It'll be fine. Go take your
          shower.

Jason comes toward her, reaching out to her, trying to
diffuse the situation.

                          JASON
          Laura, I'm sorry.

She turns away, heading for her phone on the counter.

                          LAURA
          You want to order from Hiroshi or
          Giannato's?

                          JASON
          I'm really sorry.

                    LAURA
        Just go. At least you'll be
        presentable.

                    JASON
        Honey, you're wrapped so tight . . .

He hugs her from behind, strokes her shoulder.

                JASON (CONT'D)
        In the history of the world, me
        messing up is not —

                    LAURA
        You messing up is what I expect.
        What they expect.

                    JASON
        Hey.
            (he turns her around)
        You're not the same as them at all.
        Don't say that. You know me. They
        don't. And you know that I—

She pulls away, he grabs her back.

                JASON (CONT'D)
        I love you. And that's all we need.

                    LAURA
        Yes but—

                    JASON
        That's all we need.

                    LAURA
        We NEED this to go well. I was
        going to ask Daddy to help with a
        down payment.

                         JASON
            And I, I was going to ask your
            Daddy for his permission. To marry
            you.

This is news — good news — to her.

                         LAURA
            But I thought —

                         JASON
            We're gonna buy a place, I figure
            we should just go all the way.

He kneels in front of her.

                    JASON (CONT'D)
            Laura, would you do me the honor of
            marrying me?

                         LAURA
            Yes! Yes I will!

She stands there, waiting for something.

                    LAURA (CONT'D)
            . . . A ring? . . .

He stands up, kisses her.

                         JASON
            Tomorrow. When I go out to buy
            some chicken.
                    (beat)
            They carry diamonds at Kroger's,
            don't they?

They laugh, they hug — and the doorbell rings.

#1: The first actor listed on the callsheet, generally the highest-paid and highest-billed

50/50: (Fifty-fifty); shot in which the two characters face each other

A

A side: In editing, the part of a shot right before the cut

"A" story: The basic plot of the show

Abby Singer (the Abby): The second-to-last shot of the day

above the line: The producer, writer, director, and actors who are above the dividing line in a budget

act: The formal division of the parts of a play, teleplay, or screenplay; in TV, the segment between commercials

act-in: The beginning of the next segment after a commercial

act-out: The end of the segment before it goes to commercial

action: The command that indicates to the actor when to begin

actor's director: A director who doesn't merely move the camera but also fine-tunes the performances because he understands the actor's process

add to: Adding more time/footage before a cut

adjustment: The change requested in an actor's performance by the director

ADR: Automated or automatic dialogue replacement

AFI: American Film Institute; a national arts organization that trains filmmakers and preserves America's film heritage, and has a library that is open and free to the public

aged: Made to look older or not brand-new

air: Pause between two characters talking

Alliance of Motion Picture and Television Producers (AMPTP): The producers' group that negotiates on behalf of the networks, production companies, and studios

alts: Alternate choices

American Federation of Television and Radio Artists (AFTRA): One of the actors' trade unions, now merged with the Screen Actors Guild

angle: Another name for a shot

antagonist: The rival, bad guy, or enemy; often played by a guest star

apple box: A multi-purpose wooden box used on-set by the grips

archetype: A way of labeling a character that uses clichés of well-known types of people

art director: Person who assists the production designer primarily with creating the blueprints and administering the department

art vs. commerce: The daily internal dilemma of every director (you always want more, in every possible way, to tell your story, yet more of anything will undoubtedly mean it costs more, too)

axis: Directional plane; one way of shooting efficiently is having all the action of the scene on one axis, which allows the director to shoot in two directions instead of four

B

"B" or "C" stories: The subplots of the show, which can echo, replicate, or complement the "A" story

B side: In editing, the part of a shot right after a cut

back to one: An instruction given during shooting that means everyone should return to their starting positions

backlight: Light coming from behind the actors rather than in front of them; especially relevant when working with sunlit scenes

backstory: A character's history

band-aid fixes: Small suggestions given to help the script; often given by director very close to the first day of shooting

base camp: Where the trucks park for a shoot; the location hub

bell: A sound that signals the need for quiet before a shot begins

below the line: Everyone on the production except for the producer, writer, director, and actors, whose costs are maintained by the UPM

billing: On screen credit; a negotiable issue

binge watch: Watching multiple episodes of the same series often because they have been made available for downloading on the same day

bins: Folders or directories of related shots on the editor's computer

block shoot: A method of shooting that condenses lighting setups by shooting all coverage of multiple scenes in one direction before turning around; often used when shooting courtroom scenes

blocking: The first task of the director; how, where, and when the actors will move

blowing it up: Zooming in on an image in editing

blue/green screen: A blue backdrop or cyclorama against which an actor in filmed with the plan to replace everything that is blue (green in also used)

boarding: Chronicling what specifics are needed for each eighth of a page of a script; it used to be done by hand using cardboard strips mounted on a folding board

bones: The basic requirements for a location

bonus round: A take that the director may call for after he feels he has achieved the scene; for the actors, it feels like there is less pressure and more room to play

boom: (camera) To raise up or down

boom: (sound) An arm, often in segments to which a microphone can attach

break frame: Enter the shot

breakaway: A prop rigged to break exactly as designed

breaking stories: Figuring out the plot lines for upcoming episodes of the series

bumps: Makes the director feel as if something doesn't ring true

C

call sheet: Page that lists the start time for the beginning of the day, the scenes to be shot, and the personnel and equipment required; prepared by the 2nd AD and distributed to staff, cast, and crew at the end of the day

call time: Beginning of the day, usually 7:00 a.m.

camera: The device for recording pictures; used to be film cameras but are now often digital

camera angle: Direction in which the camera is pointed

camera left: The left from the camera's point of view

camera right: The right from the camera's point of view

card: Jargon for flash media on a digital camera; a method of recording pictures

casting concept: An idea of how a show should be cast

casting director: The person who checks actor availability, auditions the actor, sets subsequent audition sessions, negotiates deals, and books all roles

CGI: Computer-generated imagery; uses three-dimensional computer graphics to create images such as a crowd in an arena

cheat: To manipulate elements of the set away from its reality in order to achieve the shot

check the gate: Cue from the director that the shot is concluded, checking for a sliver of film, hair, or dust that would show up on the picture

check the marks: A rehearsal in which the actors walk to each mark in turn to check focus but do not say their dialogue

choker shot: A close-up shot in which the bottom of frame is the neck

chyron: Printed words on the screen during a shot

circled takes: Completed shots that are the directors' choices; printed or downloaded for use by editor

clean: No one else in frame except one actor

cleared: Bought for broadcast use

cliffhanger: Ending moment at the end of each act that will compel the audience to come back after the commercial to see how that moment turned out

climax: The big moment to which a story builds

close-up (CU): A tight shot of a character, it has no one else in the frame; also called a "single"

closed-captioning: Displaying text on a television or video screen so that people with hearing disabilities have equal access to public information

closed rehearsal: Rehearsal at which no crewmembers are present apart from the director, script supervisor, DP, and first AD

color corrected: Having had the color of the scene or scenes changed or created

colorist: Computer artist with a great eye for matching color or creating color

company move: When all the trucks, as well as cast and crew, have to move and re-park close to the next location

complementary shots: Shots that match each other because the actors' faces are the same size when you cut back and forth

complete: The status of a bin when all the footage for a scene is shot

complications: The obstacles that arise and keep the attention of the audience

composited: Two images that are put together, such as marrying together a blue-screen image with a plate or background image

concept meeting: Meeting for all the department heads to discuss the script and receive information from the director about the approach

condor: Construction crane used for lights

conflict: When two characters are at cross-purposes; the stronger the conflict, the stronger the story

continuity: The consistency and logic of the show, overseen by the script supervisor

costar: A small role that appears in only one episode; less pay and lower billing than a guest star

costume designer: Works with the production designer to create a wardrobe look for each character that is consistent with the overall look of the production

counter: A type of lateral dolly move in which the camera moves the opposite direction from a walking actor

courtesy screen: A screen or drape placed strategically to give actors privacy while they are performing intimate scenes or scenes where they are scantily clad

coverage: The number of shots it takes to do a good job of telling the story

covering: When an actor hides his true intention

cowboy shot: Bottom frame is where the gun holster would be

crane: Camera is on an arm that allows it to swing up, down, and sideways

crane shot: Shot using a crane; often used at beginning or ending of an act

crew call: Time of day when the work begins, takes into account when the pre-call work in the hair and makeup trailer is finished

crisp: Quality of being in focus

cross camera: When an actor wipes the frame (passes through the camera lens)

cross the lens: Same as "cross camera"

cross the line: A mistake in which shots are on the wrong side of the axis; incorrect screen direction

crossover casting: When a role is a given part for an actor who is doing another show for the same network, often playing the same character; does not require any casting session because actor is offered the part

cross platforming: A distributing company's practice of creating extra content, especially for the web, in order to drive more viewers to the show

C-stand: a metal pole with holders that the grips use to rig light-controlling elements

CTM: In postproduction, the Color-Timed Master is the final version of the production

cue: Script line that leads an actor into his line or begins a pickup

cues (music): Short pieces of underscoring

cut: A stop; direction given by director to end filming

cut together: When film is edited or assembled

cutting pattern: A sequence of shots that follow a pattern or plan

D

dailies: Printed raw, unedited daily footage

dance floor: Floor of plywood or plastic over the existing floor that is used to create a smooth surface; used when the camera movement is not in a straight line to give more flexibility

daybreaks: When shooting changes from one script day to another

day-out-of-days (DOOD): A chart that tells which day of the schedule each actor will work

dénouement: The resolution that completes a story

department heads: Leaders of each division

dialogue: The scripted words that the actors say

Did you make the event of the scene happen?: A question an actor asks himself to determine if he achieved his intention

digital: When information is coded in numbers as in a binary system

digital double: A digital 3-D replica of an actor's body and face

directionally: To shoot everything in one direction, using the same group of lights

director of photography (DP): Person who helps with lighting design and organizes the construction of each shot; crew leader of the camera, electric, and grip departments

Director's Guild of America (DGA): The union that protects the creative and economic rights of members working in feature film, television, documentary, new media and other forms of production

discovery: New information that comes to an actor while playing the character

dolly: The platform or wagon on wheels to which the camera is attached

dolly back: When the camera rolls back from the character

dolly shot: Shot where the camera is mounted on the dolly

dolly track: The track on which the wheels of the dolly roll; looks like a railroad track; it comes in sections and is laid by the grip department

double-check: After shot listing, a process by which a director makes certain that she has all the coverage needed by indicating next to the dialogue/ description of the script page which shot she would anticipate using

doubled: Replacing the hero actor with a stunt person, look-alike (camera double), or duplicating a prop or costume piece with multiples

downstage: The part of the stage closest to the audience from the actor's point of view so named because when stages are raked (angled) this area is lowest

drive-by: An objective and often wide shot that shows a car or boat traveling in its environment

drop a scene: Decide not to shoot a scene that was planned

dry runs: Practice runs that simulate but don't actually do the big gag

dub: The assembled sound components; same as mix

dubbed: Made, duplicated, or created

dutch: Tilting the camera so the frame is askew

duvetyne: A thick, black fabric that the grips use to block light

E

editor's assembly: The initial cut the editor shows the director

EDL: Edit decision list; the computerized list of all the cuts

emancipated: A legal determination that allows actors under the age of 18 to work by many of the rules that govern adult actors

establishing shot: A shot that shows the environment from a wide point of view

exit frame: When the characters leave the shot

exposition: The background info that gives basic information about characters

extender: A device that doubles or quadruples the capability of the lens with a corresponding significant reduction of light/exposure

extras: Background artists who populate the scene in addition to the actors

extreme shot: The frame can hold only a part of the face, also known as an extreme close up

eyeline: The angle at which a character's eyes are looking

F

feed: The setup of a joke

fill: Ambient sound

final air master: The master that is dubbed and sent out for broadcast

final touches: Last bits of fine-tuning by the hair, makeup, and wardrobe assistants to make sure the actors look perfect

find more colors: A direction to give an actor to elicit more highs and lows in the character's needs

find peaks and valleys: Same as "Find more colors"

first assistant director (1st AD): The conduit between the production and the director; makes sure every department head knows what the director requires ahead of time; generates preproduction schedules and runs the set during production

first cut: Edit where the director cuts out of the opening shot

first draft: Initial version of the script

first team: The principal actors, the second team are their stand-ins

fish-eye lens: A lens that distorts what is in front of it; it is at the wide end of the lens continuum

fixed lens: A lens that gives you only one focal length, also known as a prime

floor plan: A blueprint of the walls, doors, windows, stairs of a set as well as the furniture within it

flyaways: Strands of hair that are sticking up from an actor's head

foley: Adding to/augmenting sounds, named after Jack Foley, the Universal Studios sound effects pioneer; includes doorbells, car doors, tire squeals, footsteps, and so on

follow van: A vehicle that ferries support personnel during driving scenes

foreground: Area close to camera

foreground wipe: When a principal or background artist crosses in the foreground of the shot; makes shot feel more subjective

foreshadowing: Deliberate clues that must be created earlier in the show to earn or reach the climax of the show; information that warns ahead of time

frame the joke: To limit extraneous movement, such as having an actor remain still, in order to bring audience attention to the punch line

from the top: Beginning at the first word or camera move of a scene

full figure: Framing from head to toe

full mag: As much film as possible in the magazine, which is generally 1,000 feet

G

gaffe: Arrange anything

gag: Stage bit or business

get it on its feet: Having the actors physically move around the set; blocking scene as opposed to just reading it

getting the scissors in: Making an edit, generally where there isn't much air or space to do it well

gimbal: To manipulate or pivot anything that causes a reflection, i.e. a mirror or window

give yourself somewhere to go: A direction to give an actor who is playing the result of the scene too soon and needs to explore the process the character travels to get there

grace period: The 12 minutes of extra shooting time before a meal is required to facilitate efficient shooting

green room: Waiting room for actors and/or extras

guest star: A large role for an actor who is only contracted for one episode or the amount of episodes it takes to tell his character's story

H

hair in the gate: A sliver of film, dust, or hair in front of the lens; if this occurs, the shot has to be repeated

half-speed: Rehearsing at a slower speed

handheld: A way of shooting when the camera operator simply holds the camera and moves to create the best shot as the actors move

hanging a lamp on it: Being too obvious about the subtext

hard drive: Place for storing digital information

head: In editing, the first part of a shot

hero: Anything that is the main focus of attention; can be a prop, a set, a shot or an actor's movement

high and wide shot: Shot that takes in all the action from above, often a crane shot

high-definition (HD): Better quality of digital recording

high-hat: A flat mounting device that can sit on the floor or be attached to a ladder; camera can be attached it for a high or low angle

hits: Each time a person clicks on a website or advertisement on a website

holding area: A room or trailer where background artists wait until they are needed

Hollywood in/out: Substituting or switching elements within a shot while the camera is framed on something else

honeywagons: Bathrooms in a trailer and small dressing rooms

I

iconic image: The singular image that communicates the essence of the story

imagery: Images that can be seen or imagined

IMDB.com: (Internet Movie Data Base) Website that lists all television and film credits

in the moment: A state in which the actor is completely thinking and reacting in character in present time, with no thought other than what is happening right then

inciting action: The incident that kicks off the story and engages the audience

incomplete: In editing when all the shots needed to assemble a scene are not yet filmed; usually when an insert or special effects shot is missing

insert car: A tow truck that pulls the picture car; lights and cameras are mounted on it

inserts: Tight shots on objects

integrated insert: Inclusion of a close-up of an object within another shot

intention: Another word for a character's need, an important word in an actor's vocabulary

into the works: Having an actor begin the process of being made over by the hair and makeup artists

J

jump cut: Two shots in a row of the same subject from nearly the same position

K

kill the funny: Destroy an attempt at humor

L

land: To make contact (stunt); make the audience laugh (comedy)

last looks: Actors to receive final attention from hair, makeup, and wardrobe departments before shooting

lateral dolly shot: Shot in which the camera moves sideways across the plane in front of the actors

layback: In postproduction, when the audio portion of the episode is added to the visual part

license fee: Amount of money given to the production company by the network

lifted: Removed from the project through editing

line producer: Person who assists the executive producer in getting the most out of the budget; in charge of crew; oversees day-to-day operations

line reading: Saying the exact line in the script for an actor with the intonation and rhythm desired in order that the actor will duplicate the delivery

lip-sync: Mouth the words, done when actors are singing to prerecorded tracks of their own voice

location: A preexisting place chosen for shooting

location manager: Department head whose job it is to find potential locations and, once they are chosen, to negotiate the deal and oversee the interaction between the shooting crew and the site

locked-down: Physically fixed camera, makes it impossible to move the frame

logline: A sentence that summarizes the plot

looks: Refers to the direction, right or left, in which the actor is looking

loop groups: Actors who create specific background voices for scenes

looped: Dialogue replacement or augmentation process

M

make a cross: When an actor as the character moves from one place to another in a scene

make a deal: Agree on dates and/or money; usually pertains to hiring or renting equipment

make the day: Complete the scheduled work on time and on budget

makeup and hair designers: Crew members responsible for hair and makeup; the behind-the-scene psychologists, as they help the actors face the day with confidence

marks: Locations the actors have to stand on in each shot, usually marked in tape

martini shot: The last shot of the day

massage the cut: In editing, finding the absolute best place for the cut

master: A shot that holds all the actors in the frame, it is usually shot first and creates a template for the scene

match: To repeat, usually referring to the actors repeating their movements and actions from the master shot

meal penalty: A payment given to union members for exceeding the negotiated amount of time allowed between meals

meat of the day: Biggest and hardest scene

mini-master: A smaller grouping of actors within the same scene, from the same camera position as the master

mislead/turn: Joke that deliberately sets up one expectation then delivers another

mix: The assembled sound components; same as dub

moleskin: Flesh-colored cloth adhesive used to cover an actor's private areas

montage: A storytelling device of putting non-dialogue shots together, usually accompanied by music scoring

MOS: "mit-out-sound," a silent shot because the sound is not recorded

motion-capture: Tracking and recording movement for a digital model

motivated: Driven by organic character impulse

moving on: Instruction the director calls that a scene is completed

N

new information: Details of the plot that are revealed and must lead logically into the next scene

NLE: Nonlinear editing or editor; software used by the editor to assemble the film or teleplay or the editor himself

notes: The comments given to the showrunner by the network executive or studio

O

O track: Original track

objective: How one describes the shot when it is observing as a non-participant

obstacle: Circumstance that gets in the way of the protagonist fulfilling his intention

offer only: In casting, when an actor is offered a role rather than auditioning for the role

on the day: When the shot is actually accomplished

on the nose: Dialogue that too obviously refers to the subtext of the scene

on-set dresser: The crew person who moves furniture and props to help achieve the shot

one-liner: A short version of the shooting schedule, it lists for each day: the scene numbers, page count, scene description, actors needed, and what script day it is in the continuity of the story

one more for fun: An extra take once the director knows that she has a good take; generally free of performance pressure for actor

one-offs: Episodes that stand alone without further installments

oner: Shooting all the coverage for a scene in one shot

operative word: The word in a sentence that should be stressed

organic: Correct because it feels natural

over the cut: When a sound continues from one shot into the next

over-the-shoulders (OS): A camera shot in which the camera looks over the shoulder of one actor toward the other actor

overlap: To do it again; repeating a movement or dialogue; used to make an edit appear seamless

P

pace: The rate at which an actor speaks or a scene's moments progress

pack a suitcase: To have details of the character in mind

pan: A move of the camera from side to side

pattern budget: The cost of a typical episode

payoff: The punch line of a joke; the turn of the joke in a mislead/turn

permit: A license that allows shooting in a public location

pickup: Starting the scene somewhere in the middle to achieve the element the director believes is missing

picture car: A vehicle that will be seen on camera

picture up: What the director says when ready to shoot

pilot: The first episode of a series

pipe (laying the pipe): An area where the writer has had to share a lot of information

pitch: A potential solution, fix, or suggestion; helpful to have ready if you have a criticism

pivot: The person or thing upon which the scene turns; the new information

plate: Background image that is photographed to be composited with another image that has more foreground information

playing the end at the beginning: A trap that actors fall into when they know more than their character does and play the scene as if they already have the information

point of view (for actor): Way of being within the world created by the script; the character has an opinion about his emotional starting point for the scene

point of view (POV): When the camera sees what a character sees

poor man's process: A method of shooting a car-driving scene without driving the car

practical: The real thing, referring to a location that is not a built set, or a prop that actually works (a lamp that turns on)

pre-call: The time at which a crew or cast member reports for the day which is prior to the general crew call

prelapping: Hearing the dialogue of the next character that speaks before the image of that character appears

preread: Preliminary audition

pre-viz (pre-visualization): A means by which the stunt coordinator or special effects supervisor film a rehearsal of a planned gag in order to show an early version to the director to get notes and/or approval

principal: An actor in a major role

print: To forward a completed shot to the editor

print and move on: Move on to the next scene instead of going for another take

print it: Instruction from the director that the take is useable

private rehearsal: Rehearsal with actors away from most of the crew

procedural: A show with a tried-and-true formula that is the spine of every story, usually in the law or police genre

process trailer: A tow truck with a rear-appended platform upon which the picture car is mounted; equipment may be staged around the car on the platform

producer/director: A staff person who stays on one show for the full season and fulfills both functions, usually directing the first and last episodes

producer session: The audition where producers are present; usually the second or third round of casting

production design: Everything in the frame that is nonhuman; the "look" of a production that is cohesive and artful

production designer: Person who supervises several art departments; a pivotal link between the ideas in the director's head and the realization of them on the finished product; uses architectural and artist skills

production draft: Version of the script the writers feel comfortable sharing with the entire production team; it is the one (with subsequent revisions) that will be shot

production report: An accounting of what took place during the day by the 2nd AD, distributed to accounting, production, studio, and network

production value: Quality of the production, often higher with more money; the value seen on the screen

profile: A shot showing a side view, usually a face in close-up

prop master: Person who provides the things that actors physically touch or use in a scene

proscenium: The archway in theatre that defines the front of the stage, the action usually plays upstage of it; in film, it refers to a shot which is staged away from the camera on a wide lens

protagonist: The hero, the main character of the story who moves the plot forward

pull out: The shot becomes wider as the camera moves away from the actor

pull the plug: To end production suddenly, often due to poor shot planning; a decision made by the producers based on the budget

pulling up: When the editor is lessening the space between the characters' dialogue from the distance it was during shooting

punch (visual): A straight cut in, from a wider shot to a tighter one, of the same subject in the same angle without first going to, or editing in, a reverse shot

punched: Stressed lightly

push in: The shot becomes tighter as the camera goes toward the actor

Q

quote: The amount of money that an actor was last paid

R

raise the stakes: A direction to give an actor to have him play his intention or use his obstacle more strongly

rake: (raker, raking)—A side-angle shot

reaction: The nonverbal or verbal response that an actor has when listening

read through: Having the actors just read the lines, without any movement or commitment to an intention

recur: Appear again, referring to a character that appears in multiple episodes, usually for a specific story arc

reverse: A shot looking in the opposite direction from the previous shot

rhythm: Timing an edit to feel a beat

rig: To prepare or assemble for use

rising action: The part of the story that builds to a climax as complications arise once the audience is engaged

rock into coverage: What an actor does to begin a shot by stepping into his mark rather than already being on his mark

roll the carts: Moving the handcarts that store equipment and can be wheeled short distances

rolling: Signal from the first assistant camera operator that the camera is on

room tone: The ambient sounds that exist in a room when nobody is speaking

running the tape: Measuring the distance between and actor and the lens to ensure the shot is in focus; done by first AC

running time: How long the project or episode is for broadcast

runs: Rhythmic jokes that have three elements.

S

scout: A trip organized to see potential locations

Screen Actors Guild (SAG): One of the actors' trade unions, now joined with AFTRA

screen direction: Whether a character is looking right to left or left to right, whether object entering frame is moving right to left or left to right

script coordinator: Person who types and issues the version of the script for all departments

script day: The day it is in the world of the script, kept track of for continuity purposes

script supervisor's notes: The blueprint for finding and retrieving the information about all the footage shot and especially about the footage that the director printed

second meal: When the crew is fed after shooting has exceeded 13 hours

second team: The stand-ins who stand on the actors' marks while the set is being lit

self-taped auditions: Auditions submitted by actors to casting directors that have been self-generated

serial: A story that plays out over many episodes

series regular: The actors that appear in each episode

set: A room, building, or area designed and created specifically for a shoot

set background: Placing the daily hires of extras that populate the frame to create the human environment of the film, usually supervised by the 2nd AD

set decorator: Person who turns a set from bare walls to a finished room, doing the job of an elite scavenger hunter who finds or selects just the right pieces

set piece: A scene that requires additional manpower or equipment, and is therefore outside the pattern

setups: Individual shots

SFX: Sound effects; added in postproduction

shared card credit: A name on the screen with others

shoot out: To finish coverage on one actor (usually a minor) first

shooter: A director who specializes in using the camera in a visually dynamic way

shooting schedule: A list of the order of shooting; job of the 1st AD after the first concept meeting; it tells everyone involved in the production what is to be shot each day and what elements are necessary

shot list: How the director plans to break down the scene into individual shots

showrunner: The person who is the boss of the show; usually the creator of the show and supervisor of the writing staff

sides: Script pages for the day

single card credit: A name on the screen alone, often given to the top-of-show guest star, placement negotiated depending on their TVQ

single shot: A tight shot of a character, it has no one else in the frame; also called a close-up

slate: The board that is slapped shut to identify and signal the beginning of the take; the slapping sound enables picture to be synced with the separately recorded sound; to identify the scene on the slate either at the beginning or end of the scene

snap-zoom: When the zoom is done quickly for effect

soundstage: A hangar-like building used for shooting motion pictures that hopefully eliminates sound from outside

special needs chart: Section of the shooting schedule which shows what special equipment or personnel need to be ordered for each day that the company does not normally carry

speeding: Signal from the boom operator that the sound recorder has reached the appropriate speed

SPFX: Special effects; done during production to create unusual events like explosions

split looks: When an actor says his dialogue to actors who are on both sides of the camera

stack the frame: Filling the frame with elements in foreground, mid-ground and background

stage directions: The instructions the writer has left in the script that nearly always lead to the truth about the characters, may include references to the set, props, etc.; what the writer "saw" in her head as she wrote

staging area: Place where equipment can be kept while waiting to be used

stakebeds: Smaller trucks that can move small pieces between multiple locations

stand-in: An actor who watches blocking and replaces first team for lighting purposes

standing set: An already existing, previously constructed, and used set; sets that remain standing for use in each episode

start and stop: Point when the music begins and ends

starting point: Where the characters begin in each scene

Steadicam: A handheld device for moving the camera, the operator wears a harness and the camera is attached to a floating head

still rolling . . . reset: Cue from the director that the actors have finished the scene for the first time and that the director wants to do the scene again without cutting

sting: A short music cue, usually at the end of an act

stop-and-go rehearsal: Rehearsal where you stop whenever an issue needs addressing

story point: A plot point

storyboard: Visual depiction of how each shot should look

straight cut in: Direct cut closer

strike: To tear down or remove, generally refers to taking down the sets

studio teacher: A teacher (often also a social worker) who instructs child actors as required by law and is responsible for the child's well-being while at work

stunt casting: Hiring a huge celebrity for a small part on a TV series in hopes the guest appearance will jump-start the fortunes of the show and sometimes the celebrity

subjective: How one describes the shot when it is depicting the feelings of the character

subtext: Meaning under a line of dialogue; the story under the story, what is really going on in a scene and is not revealed in plot or dialogue

sweeten: To clean up and enhance sound

swing set: A set that is designed specifically for the needs of an individual script

swingle: When the camera pans from one character in close-up to the next

synced: When the film element and separately recorded sound element are put together

syndication: A method of selling programming to secondary distributors

T

tag: To pan or tilt the camera to see an integrated insert within one shot

tail: The end of a shot

take: Version of the shot

take a pass: Look over the script, done by the showrunner, who sharpens it up

Teamster: Union driver

technical scout: A trip back to the chosen locations in which other crew members participate to discuss how to make the location ready for the shoot

temp tracks: Temporary placeholding music

theme: The underlying idea of the script, and every scene should help illuminate the concept

thinking in character: An actor remains in character throughout a scene, listening and responding as the character, not as the actor

throw a cue: To deliver a line that directly precedes another actor's line

throw away: To underplay; technique employed by actors in both comedy and drama

tighten: To make the pacing sharper

tilt: A movement of the camera up or down

title card: A screen image with the movie title that hopefully captures the essence of the story

titles: Credits

tone meeting: Meeting with the writer at which he reveals the important elements of story and/or style in episode; opportunity for director to ask questions or make suggestions

top of show: Where the biggest guest stars are listed, as opposed to the end credits; also refers to the basic union salary cap

tracking shot: Shot that moves with the actor

trailers: Portable dressing rooms and offices on location

transitions: How the frame looks from the end of one scene to the beginning of the next

transportation coordinator: Responsible for picture cars (those that appear as part of production design) and transporting the company and its equipment during the process of production

trim: To edit a small section out

turn around: Have the camera look in the opposite direction

turnaround: The amount of time off between completing work on one day and beginning work on the next day (union actors are given at least 12 hours off)

turning around: Cue called by director that the AD repeats on the radio for the shot to be filmed in the opposite direction

TVQ: TV quotient, or how well known an actor is

two-shot: Two people are in the frame

two-t shot: Two tits are at the bottom of the frame

U

under 5s: Roles with five lines or fewer

underscore: Music played along with a scene to lend emotional impact

unit production manager (UPM): The person in charge of the day-to-day operations of the crew, with direct supervision of those below the line

upstage: The part of the stage furthest from the audience from the actor's point of view; so named because when stages are raked (angled) this area is highest

V

VAM: Video assembled master; the original footage from an episode used for postproduction

vanities: A term for the group of technicians who work in the wardrobe, hair, and makeup departments.

VFX: Visual effects; added in postproduction to augment or change the image shot in production

video village: Where the monitors are, directors chairs are grouped there to enable people to view the shot directly from a camera feed

viewfinder: A small handheld lens that the cinematographer looks through to compose the shot; it sees what the camera will see

vision board: A board full of pictures and words that illustrate concepts and provide a reference point for discussion

visual aids: Visual examples of exactly what one is talking about

W

waist shot: Waist is at the bottom of the frame

walk 'n' talk: Scene in which the actors walk while talking

walk the sets: To look at the sets with an eye toward camera blocking

wall in, wall out: Moving the set walls in and out to give more room to the camera

walla: Murmur of the background crowd

walla group: Same as loop group

What do you find out?: A question to ask an actor to remind him that the character makes a discovery in the scene

What if your character has this secret . . .?: A question to ask an actor to help him find some colors in the scene by suggesting information that only the character would be privy to

What's the new information?: A question to ask an actor to remind him that his character makes a discovery in the scene

Who has the power?: A question to ask an actor to help him play his intention more strongly by examining whether he or his scene partner is in charge; makes an actor react more in the moment

Who is winning?: A question to ask an actor to help him be aware if he is getting what he wants; makes an actor react more in the moment

wide lens: A lens that allows the camera to capture a large amount of action; can hold a wide peripheral frame

wild: Moveable pieces of the set

wild sounds: Additional sounds recorded that are extraneous to the picture

wrap: Finish the day

writers' draft: The first version of the script, usually distributed only among the writing staff and withheld from production

writer's room: The room where the showrunner organizes the writers who create the scripts

Z

zoom: When the lens moves in or out without the camera moving

zoom lens: A lens that allows multiple focal lengths

Index